PRAISE FOR *YOU ARE PSYCHIC*

Sherrie Dillard's *You Are Psychic* is one of the best books I've read to naturally develop your intuitive skills. This book offers comprehensive teachings to help you develop your intuition and know yourself, from the basics to in-depth exercises. A must-read to improve success for personal awareness, protection, and the ability to interpret your intuitive realizations. You'll refer to Dillard's book again and again.

—Margaret Ann Lembo, author of *Chakra Awakening: Transform Your Reality Using Crystals, Color, Aromatherapy, & the Power of Positive Thought*

Having worked in the field of energy medicine for over fifteen years, I have run across so many people who wish to open up their psychic awareness but don't know how. Wouldn't it be nice if there was an easy and effective way to open up your intuition?

Well, look no further than *You Are Psychic* by Sherrie Dillard. Sherrie beautifully addresses one of the key secrets of developing your intuition that is rarely addressed: opening up your psychic abilities is not a rational, step-by-step process! Instead, she shows us how we can naturally and spontaneously connect with our innate psychic awareness in a way that is inspiring, empowering, and easy to follow. I highly recommend *You Are Psychic*, whether you are intending to expand your practice or even just enhance your intuitive abilities to improve your everyday life!

—Jennifer Taylor, CEO of Quantum-Touch Inc., www.quantumtouch.com

In Sherrie Dillard's new book *You Are Psychic*, she states up front that "we need psychic awareness." Sherrie shows you exactly why you need it and how you can achieve a more open and loving relationship with the intuitive awareness that lives within you by helping you understand your psychic type. *You Are Psychic* is filled with practical exercises that urge your energy to recognize and embrace your intuition and an abundance of personal and client experiences, which add clarity to your own path of intuitive growth. Sherrie opens your mind to all that you can achieve while pointing out why you may be holding back, which is so very helpful when trying to understand and nurture your psychic abilities. Throughout *You Are Psychic* there is a deep sense of the importance of becoming one with your intuitive energy and psychic type so that you can become the most complete, aware, and evolved spiritual being possible. Sherrie says that we need psychic awareness. I say everyone needs to read this eye-opening and extremely helpful book! Thanks so much for writing it, Sherrie!

—Melissa Alvarez, author of *Believe and Receive*,
Your Psychic Self, Animal Frequency, and
365 Ways to Raise Your Frequency

you are

Psychic

ABOUT THE AUTHOR

Psychic since childhood, Sherrie Dillard has been a professional intuitive, medium, medical intuitive, and teacher for over thirty years. Among her international clientele are spiritual leaders, celebrities, and business executives. Sherrie's love of service combined with her intuitive ability has catapulted her intuitive practice around the globe. She has given over 50,000 readings worldwide.

Sherrie has taught intuition development, how to communicate with the other side, and medical intuitive development classes in such diverse places as Duke University and Miraval Resort, and across the US, Europe, Costa Rica, and Mexico. Her passion for the fusion of intuition, health, spirituality, and conscious self-growth has made her a popular speaker and teacher at retreats and conferences. She has been featured on radio and television for her innovative books and her work as a psychic detective, medical intuitive, and medium.

Sherrie holds a BS in psychology and a MDiv in New Thought pastoral counseling. Originally from Massachusetts, Sherrie has made Durham, North Carolina, her home for the past twenty-five years and can often be found walking along the river with her dogs.

S HERRIE D ILLARD

you are
Psychic

Develop Your
Natural Intuition
Through Your
Psychic Type

Llewellyn Publications
Woodbury, Minnesota

First Edition
Second Printing, 2018

Cover design by Ellen Lawson
Interior chakra image by Mary Ann Zapalac

Llewellyn Publications is a registered trademark of Llewellyn Worldwide Ltd.

Library of Congress Cataloging-in-Publication Data

Names: Dillard, Sherrie, author.
Title: You are psychic : develop your natural intuition through your psychic type / by Sherrie Dillard.
Description: First Edition. | Woodbury : Llewellyn Worldwide, Ltd., 2018. | Includes bibliographical references and index.
Identifiers: LCCN 2018012162 (print) | LCCN 2018003122 (ebook) | ISBN 9780738756028 (ebook) | ISBN 9780738751320 (alk. paper)
Subjects: LCSH: Parapsychology. | Psychic ability. | Intuition—Miscellanea.
Classification: LCC BF1031 (print) | LCC BF1031 .D585 2018 (ebook) | DDC 133.8—dc23
LC record available at https://lccn.loc.gov/2018012162

Llewellyn Publications
A Division of Llewellyn Worldwide Ltd.
2143 Wooddale Drive
Woodbury, MN 55125-2989
www.llewellyn.com

Printed in the United States of America

OTHER BOOKS BY SHERRIE DILLARD

Sacred Signs & Symbols
(Llewellyn, 2017)

Discover Your Authentic Self
(Llewellyn, 2016)

Llewellyn's Complete Book of Mindful Living (contributor)
(Llewellyn, 2016)

Develop Your Medical Intuition
(Llewellyn, 2015)

You Are a Medium
(Llewellyn, 2013)

The Miracle Workers Handbook
(Sixth Books, 2012)

Love and Intuition
(Llewellyn, 2010)

Discover Your Psychic Type
(Llewellyn, 2008)

DEDICATION

To all of my clients and students, thank you for being part of my journey. Your faith and trust in me has blessed me.

Acknowledgments

A special thank you to Angela Wix, who invited me to write this book. It was your persistence that made this happen. Andrea Neff, your positivity and support encouraged and motivated me. Thank you for liking the book so much. Thank you, Vanessa Wright and Kat Sanborn, for being the voice of this book in the world, and Anna Levine and everyone else at Llewellyn for your time, effort, and energy.

CONTENTS

PART I: YOUR INNER PSYCHIC, FRONT ROW AND CENTER

Part 2: The Psychic Characteristics and Potential of Each Psychic Type

PART 4: YOUR PRACTICE: PSYCHIC MEDITATION EXERCISES

Exercises and Meditations

Interpretation Glossary for the Meditation Exercises in Part 4

Chapter 12: Path Meditation Exercise to Intuit Career and Life Path

**Chapter 13: Rose Meditation Exercise to Intuit
Relationship Insights**

Chapter 15: Going Backward Toward a Goal Meditation Exercise to Intuit Steps to Attain a Goal

Introduction

I recently moved out of my home of thirty years to a new town. When people here ask me what kind of work I do, I find myself stumbling over my words. I am surprised by my sensitivity and reluctance to readily identify myself as a psychic and medium. Eyes grow wider and the casual friendly hello is soon met with an open stare once my occupation becomes known.

As with many professions, there are a lot of stereotypes and a lot of assumptions and judgments made about what it means to be psychic. However, unlike many other professions, being psychic is more than a job. It is a kind of declaration that informs others that you live outside the box of convention and linear thought. Put another way, you may be viewed by some as woo-woo, one of *those*, or a bit kooky.

For those who have never gotten their feet wet in the psychic waters and claim never to have had a psychic experience, the topic of psychic phenomena can inspire such things as laughter, doubt, and fear. It might also be met with curiosity, questions, and a desire for proof. However, all of this changes once an individual has had a personal psychic experience of some kind.

Once it stirs the heart, mind, and soul, psychic awareness is no longer a distant and abstract concept to be debated or ignored. It is a force, an energy, and a part of us. Through it we can receive not only guidance and insights but also an unexpected feeling of connectedness to a higher source of wisdom and love. Once you have had a psychic experience, however dramatic or mild it may be, you no longer stand outside the door and curiously and maybe with some apprehension wonder what this being psychic is all about. Instead, a life-changing, thrilling, transformative, and sometimes frustrating relationship has begun. Having piqued your interest and woken your slumbering soul, the misunderstood, persistent, and sometimes fantastical presence of psychic awareness becomes a part of you.

THE TIMELESS INFLUENCE OF PSYCHIC AWARENESS

For all the doubt and scrutiny that psychic awareness is subject to, it is as old as recorded time. Most ancient spiritual traditions and religious and spiritual texts speak of how dreams, visions, angels, and divine beings guide the human realm and reveal the mysteries of life. Throughout time, cultures across the globe have looked to seers, diviners, shamans, and prophets to explain, heal, and intervene and act as intermediaries between the human and nonphysical worlds. Being psychic is more than a fad or an interesting pastime. It is an essential aspect of the fabric of our being. It weaves in and out of our psyche and binds together different cultures with the thread of sacred presence.

We need psychic awareness, not simply to know what is coming our way or to make good decisions and improve our lives, but also to know who we are and what we are capable of and to activate the true potential of our humanness.

Like a match that ignites a fire or a star that lights the dark sky, psychic energy sparks our awareness and perception. It lights a way for us to shift from the mundane and finite to the spiritual and eternal. Approach psychic development with faith, and trust in its possibilities. New awareness, support, guidance, help, love, and goodness flow into your life when its doors swing open. In this life there are few things that wholeheartedly give without restraint and ask for so little in return. Psychic awareness is this kind of blessing.

The Beginnings of My Psychic Ability

As awkward as it has been for me at times to explain my occupation to others, I have always felt comfortable with psychic energy and psychic phenomena. As far back as I can remember, I have been aware of a subtle and comforting spiritual presence that communicates, comforts, and guides. However, I didn't always recognize it as psychic, intuitive, or spiritual or as anything unusual or questionable.

As a child I had a lot of freedom. My parents divorced when I was six and my mother went to work full-time. By the time I got home from school, she was gone and didn't return until late at night. Some weeks the only time I saw my mother was when I went into her bedroom to say goodbye in the morning before school. I didn't have much of a connection with my father either, since he moved to a distant town after the divorce. My siblings and I spent most of our time with babysitters, usually high school girls who lived in the neighborhood. Our longest-running babysitter's idea of watching us was talking to her friends on the phone and shooing us outside to play until dark. We didn't complain and always found something to do.

With a fair amount of alone time, I often found myself in the woods near my home. Burrowing into the green trees and brush, I pretended to spy on others or hide from make-believe predators. I would also just listen. I don't know if this started as a pretend game, but I never felt alone. Huddled in the thick foliage in the summer and in the winter when the frozen snowy hills and valleys were vacant, I sat alone and listened to the inner whispers.

Often accompanied by buzzing and tingling sensations of energy moving up and down my arms and on my scalp, I could feel things that made sense and felt good to know. Sometimes if I closed my eyes, I could see pictures and images. These sensations and images were accompanied by feelings that at times moved through my heart with an intensity that brought me to tears and other times lulled me into a soft feeling of being loved. The feelings and thoughts that I floated into my body, heart, and mind helped me to better understand my mother and father and myself. Although I didn't always understand all that I received and experienced, it didn't matter. There was something warm and comforting close to me, and I held on to it.

Even though I spent a lot of time alone in the woods, no one ever asked me what I was doing there and I felt no obligation to share my experiences with anyone. There really wasn't anyone to tell, and I had no words to explain what was happening anyway. Many of my friends had close grandparents or other family members or a special teacher or neighbor they gravitated toward. I had this presence, and I was not going to let anyone spoil it for me.

As I got older, my curiosity and interest in understanding and knowing why people acted the way they did and why life was the way it was became a driving force. This was likely the result of my chaotic home life, which included an absent father who liked drinking more than being with his kids, an unpredictable mother who could go from one emotional extreme to another with no notice, a second marriage and divorce for my mother, and the failed experiment of a blended family. I listened and clung to an invisible source of comfort and caring. Perhaps this intuitive connection was my way to have some form of control or create a sense of security. Knowing and feeling what was coming before it came and understanding and having insight into another's behavior helped me to feel a sense of order and predictability in what otherwise felt random and out of control. Connecting to this calm presence felt good. Being at church, home, school, or even with my friends couldn't match the electricity and feelings of peace that came over me when I was quiet and listened.

If there was a choice about what to place my faith and trust in, the invisible won hands down and it still does. While I didn't have a name for it when I was young, I now know that my psychic development began in the woods huddled in the trees, simply listening. Psychic awareness is still a source of spiritual connection that provides me with a loving and wise nurturance that I do not want to live without.

GUIDANCE ON THE PSYCHIC JOURNEY

I have been a professional psychic, medium, medical intuitive, and psychic detective for over thirty years, most of my adult life. During this time I have given readings to all kinds of people all over the world. I have worked with celebrities, those who have suffered great losses, business leaders, police detectives, physicians, people who are ill and dying, those seeking more of a spiritual connection, women and men who are perplexed by their relationships, and those who desire to create more abundance and happiness in their lives. Most of the people I work with are seekers who know that there is something more than the five senses can touch, feel, and know, and I am honored to help them along the way.

Along with performing psychic and medium readings, I also teach others to develop their own intuitive, psychic, and medium abilities. Through this process I have discovered that while many people have trust in my ability to receive guidance and insight into their most private and personal issues, their confidence in their own intuitive and psychic capabilities is low and at times nonexistent.

If you are like many others, there may be a divide between your psychic aspirations and your ability to actualize your innate psychic potential. Like a mountain climber, you see the majestic summit of the mountain high in the sky. However, as you travel the path of psychic development, you may encounter obstacles or what feel like impassable crevasses along the way. If this is true for you or if you would just like to know more about psychic awareness, consider me to be a guide here to support your passage.

The Psychic Experience

There are a number of books that explain psychic abilities and how to develop them. Most teach psychic development as a subject to be read about, understood, and then practiced. However, psychic awareness cannot be learned through a purely logical and rational approach. Although well-meaning, this method tends to increase the divide between the reason-oriented mind and the elusive non-logical energy of psychic awareness. This sets up a dynamic of false expectations and allows the thinking mind to judge and control the process.

One of the biggest challenges that I confront in my intuitive and psychic development classes is breaking through what the participants think it should be like to receive psychic impressions and insights and the actual experience of it.

For instance, here is a typical discussion that occurs in every class I teach.

In this conversation I am talking to Karen, who has just completed an intuitive psychic exercise with her partner, Blair.

I ask Karen, "Can you share what you received for your partner in this exercise?"

Karen casts down her eyes, pauses, and then replies, "I didn't really receive anything."

"Can you describe what you did experience, even if it does not make sense or seem important?"

Karen shifts uncomfortably in her chair and says, "I don't think I'm good at this. I thought I was a little intuitive, but it doesn't seem to be working for me."

"Please just give it a shot. Did you see, hear, or feel anything?"

"Well," she begins, "my body started to feel warm and tingly and I felt that something good was going to happen. I think I may have made this all up though, because I saw an envelope. Only it was more like a cartoonish-looking envelope. It was stuffed with money. I had the thought that money was coming. But isn't that what everyone wants to hear? I don't think that it was real."

Karen's partner, the woman whose energy she was intuitively tapping into, smiles and is almost in tears. Confirming what Karen intuitively received, the woman tells her that she has been waiting for a much-needed check in repayment for a loan.

Like many people, Karen disregarded her psychic impressions because they were not what she thought they would be like. She assumed that psychic information would come to her in a way that would be more clear and verifiable. The images she received were not realistic-looking, and she felt that the thoughts, sensations, and feelings she experienced were her own. What she received did not match her expectation, so she disregarded it. Like others, she assumed she was making up her impressions and doubted their validity. However, once she realized the accuracy of the images, feelings, and awareness that she experienced, she began to trust the process and make progress in her development.

The kind of psychic information that Karen intuited is typical for a person who is just beginning to develop psychic abilities. She received energy information through sensations in her body, through her emotions and thoughts, and through images. Not only are these kinds of intuitive impressions common when developing psychic skills, but they occur naturally and spontaneously for everyone in everyday life. We just don't notice them or pay much attention to them. Psychic abilities are not foreign and elusive and something outside of ourselves to strive for; they are already a part of us and they occur naturally and frequently.

The easiest way to develop your psychic abilities is to recognize when you are already intuiting and then build from there. Through observing participants in my psychic development classes, I have discovered that everyone intuits somewhat differently. Some people receive energy information primarily through a sense of knowing, others see images, and some feel unexplained emotions or experience sensations in their body. When I encourage my students to build on these kinds of spontaneous and natural ways of intuiting, they more quickly recognize and embrace their innate intuitive awareness and develop psychic abilities.

What's in This Book

In my first book, *Discover Your Psychic Type*, I describe the four most common ways that we naturally intuit. I call these *psychic types*. Soon after the book was first published, I began to hear from readers who were enthusiastic about this approach. Not only was it easier for them to develop psychic abilities through this system, but they were also better able to understand and make sense of previous intuitive experiences and increase their confidence and self-awareness.

Following the success of this intuitive approach, I went on to write other books that describe how to develop intuition in relationships, medical intuition, and medium abilities through the four psychic types. In this book, *You Are Psychic*, I circle back to the basics of developing psychic abilities. Through continued feedback from readers and students, I have further refined my understanding of psychic types and how to best help others develop their innate psychic abilities.

You Are Psychic begins with a description of the four psychic types and helps you identify your natural intuitive strengths and weaknesses. This insight empowers you to become more aware of when and how your innate intuition operates. As you read through the descriptions of the four psychic types, you will likely recognize aspects of each type that feel familiar and that you can identify with. There may be one or two types that particularly stand out. However, the focus of this book is not to find your intuitive type and stick to it, but to become more aware of and comfortable with the intuitive impressions and hunches of each type and use them as an integrated whole. *Discover Your Psychic Type* explains the varied facets and characteristics of the four psychic types, and this book expands on these aspects and information. It then provides easy-to-follow steps for the development of the psychic abilities associated with each type, such as clairvoyance, clairsentience, clairaudience, claircognizance, telepathy, and psychometry. Along the way, you will learn strategies to deal with and negotiate the doubt, fear, and other obstacles that inevitably crop up.

We also delve into the difference between intuitively tuning in to another and intuiting your own personal issues and questions, what to do when your intuitive impressions are confusing or incorrect, and how to become more adept at interpreting the energy information you receive. The unexpected gifts of psychic awareness and the spiritual inclinations and potential of the different intuitive types are also explored.

Psychic awareness is only as good as your ability to put it to use in your daily life. For this reason I have included exercises to help you apply your psychic awareness to practical and everyday issues and concerns. These step-by-step exercises empower you to use your psychic ability to intuit energy information and guidance in the areas of finance, abundance, relationships, and career and life direction. There are also intuitive exercises to help you reach a goal and receive spiritual guidance. A glossary is included to assist you with interpreting and understanding the intuitive feelings, sensations, impressions, images, and other information that you may receive during the exercises. In the last chapter there is a summary of the psychic development process for future reference.

The information in this book builds from chapter to chapter. For this reason, it is best to read one chapter after another. However, after having read the book, you can refer back to the material and exercises on a continuous basis. Throughout the book I use the words *intuition* and *psychic* interchangeably. They both describe the phenomenon of becoming aware of energy information without relying on an outside source.

TRUST THE PROCESS

Have patience and compassion with yourself throughout the psychic development process. It is also helpful to have a sense of humor and have fun. If you are judgmental and critical of your intuitive attempts, you will lose interest. What fuels this journey, keeps your interest, and helps you to develop and improve your psychic abilities is curiosity, a sense of adventure, and the desire for truth. Take your time and allow your psychic awareness to unfold.

There may be times when you want to give up. You may become frustrated, and the whole business of being psychic may feel like a waste of time. However, feelings of doubt and confusion are not indications that you lack psychic ability. Instead, these are some of the signs that you are about to have a breakthrough. When your mind tells you that being psychic does not make sense, you are on the right path. Psychic awareness is non-logical and can feel irrational to the thinking, conscious self. Let your mind give up; you will be better off. This allows the wise inner psychic you to surface and lead the way.

There will also be moments of enlightened connection and transcendence. Perhaps while you are practicing a psychic exercise, driving in your car, or sitting and looking out the window, psychic awareness will bubble up to the surface. From the inner shadowy depths, its light will shine and illuminate your consciousness. Your body may shiver, your mind may feel like it is expanding, and your heart may want to burst with a lighthearted feeling of joy as it recognizes this illusive yet familiar feeling of psychic connection. Trust these moments. They call to you to continue the journey. As you evolve and move beyond the five senses and the known and predictable, be brave and true to yourself. Invite the electrifying and transformative energy of psychic awareness to have its way with you.

PART I

Your Inner Psychic,
Front Row and Center

CHAPTER 1

The Many Expressions
of Psychic Awareness

Imagine a classroom full of students who have just been asked a question by the teacher. One of the students, a young girl in the back of the room, knows the answer and raises her hand straight up into the air with confidence. You can almost hear her inner plea to the teacher: "Pick me, pick me!" The teacher slowly scans the room of upraised hands. The young girl in the back of the room is now frantically waving her hand in the hope of being picked. Yet the teacher passes her by, almost as if she does not notice her, and asks another student to explain the answer.

This little girl in the back of the room is very much like your psychic awareness. It knows the answer to many of your questions and concerns but seldom gets chosen to offer its guidance. Instead, it is the familiar students up front—the fives senses, logical thinking, past experience, and wishful thinking—that you most likely notice and listen to.

However, despite your reluctance to trust it, psychic awareness is determined. Not content with being invisible and in the back row, it devises clever ways of making itself known. It cozies up to the front-row students and looks for an opening. When it discovers the path of least resistance, it takes the opportunity to express its insights and guidance.

Psychic awareness has likely crept into your consciousness in this kind of way.

For instance, do you ever suddenly know something without knowing how you know it? Does it sometimes feel as if you can feel a family member's or friend's emotions even though they are miles away? Do you ever experience a gut knowing or feel tingles of energy move up your spine, or does the hair on your arms stand up? Even though you may not always know what these kinds of signs and signals mean, do you have a sense that they may be trying to tell you something?

Your psychic awareness is often cleverly camouflaged within your thoughts, emotions, physical body, and energy field. It is through these four avenues that your intuition most often emerges. As you become aware of those times when you naturally receive psychic energy information, you will have more confidence in your intuition and be motivated to further develop the spontaneous intuitive insights into reliable abilities.

Your Psychic Type

Your primary way of intuiting is called your psychic type. Everyone is a combination of one or more types, and some people are more balanced in all four types. Your psychic type not only describes how you receive energy information but also reveals aspects of your personality and preferences and your soul gifts and provides insight into the way you connect to a higher power or divine source.

Mental Intuition

If you are a mental intuitive or have a high degree of mental intuition, you receive energy information primarily through your thoughts and a sense of knowing. You are a creative thinker and may spontaneously intuit new ideas and insights. As a mental intuitive, you possess intuitive intelligence and may unknowingly intuit others' thoughts, perceptions, and knowledge. However, because mental intuitives are inclined to be skeptical, you might dismiss and dispute your intuitive capacity.

The psychic skills associated with mental intuition are telepathy, claircognizance, and clairaudience. Telepathy is the ability to intuit another's thoughts or to mentally communicate with another or a group through thought messages. Claircognizance is the ability to receive energy information through a sense of knowing and mindful awareness. With clairaudience, it is possible to receive thought energy information through psychic inner hearing.

Emotional Intuition

If you intuit primarily through your emotions or have a high degree of emotional intuition, you likely intuitively feel and soak in others' feelings. You may even feel another's emotions from hundreds of miles away. However, you may not always be aware that you are doing this. Instead, you may mistake intuited feelings as your own and become confused and possibly overwhelmed by their intensity and depth.

Emotional clairsentience and clairempathy are associated with emotional intuition. Emotional clairsentience is the psychic ability to intuit through the heart and receive energy information through a sense of feeling. Clairempathy is the psychic skill of feeling another's emotions and the ability to heal the emotional wounds of others outside of the limitations of time and space.

Physical Intuition

Physical intuitives absorb psychic energy into their body. If you are a physical intuitive or have a high degree of physical intuition, you may experience psychic awareness as a gut knowing or as tingles of energy running up your spine or arms. You may also unknowingly experience another's aches and pains in your own body. Because you are unaware that these physical sensations have been intuited, this may cause confusion when physical symptoms disappear as mysteriously as they began.

The psychic abilities associated with physical intuition are physical clairsentience and psychometry. Physical clairsentience is the ability to receive energy information through gut awareness and through other bodily awareness and sensations. Psychometry empowers you to intuit information by holding an object or looking at a photo. Hands-on energy healing is also closely connected to physical intuition.

Spiritual Intuition

If you are a spiritual intuitive or have a high degree of spiritual intuition, you may see energy information as flashes of light, color, or orbs, and you may have intuitive dreams and daydreams. With a natural connection to the spirit realm, you may sense the presence of loved ones on the other side, angels, or spirit guides. As a spiritual intuitive, you tend to be a sensitive creature who may feel overwhelmed in crowds and overstimulated by excessive noise and activity. You may need quiet and alone time to come into balance and feel an inner sense of harmony.

Clairvoyance and mediumship are connected to spiritual intuition. Clairvoyance is the psychic ability to receive energy information visually through symbols or realistic images. Mediumship is the psychic skill of communicating with those on the other side and other spirit beings.

LOGIC VERSUS INTUITION

Everyone is intuitive and can further develop the ability to access their most natural and innate wisdom. Intuition is the bridge between a greater source of power and love and the personality and ego self. In this chaotic and intense world that we live in, our intuition is our connection to a primal and pure source of positive energy and guidance. Discovering our innate psychic abilities leads to increased insights, wise guidance, and new understanding and awareness of our past, present, and future. It adds a new dimension to how we view ourselves, others, and the world, and deepens our connection to joy and authentic living.

Yet for all of the benefits that psychic awareness has to offer, we can be suspicious of it and ignore and discount it. Unfortunately, we are not always able to fully understand and appreciate its unique forms of expression. Because we are accustomed to a more rational and logical approach to receiving information and making conclusions and decisions, we may miss out on its positive benefits.

The personality and ego self approaches reality through finite understanding. It makes use of the thinking brain, the unconscious, emotions, experiences, and the five senses. Although we can at times be quite brilliant, the scope of the personality and ego self is still limited. It cannot scale the walls of time and space like intuition and psychic awareness can. Through the lens of psychic awareness, reality is perceived in its wholeness; the past, present, and future are all accessible. Transcending the boundaries of physical matter, your psychic senses can reveal and provide you with a glimpse of what lies outside of everyday consciousness and the known.

However, for all of its potential and unlimited scope of possibilities, psychic awareness communicates energy information in ways that the conscious personality self does not always understand. Psychic information is often denied, ignored, and skipped over because of the unique ways that it surfaces. We are more accustomed to and accepting of information that streams in through our five senses and our thinking mind, emotions, judgments, and past experiences.

Here is an example. Imagine that you have applied for a position in a company that you have always been interested in, and you get offered the job. Yet as much as you want to take it, you are not sure that it supports your long-term career goals. Although your current position has its drawbacks, you know that in time you will be offered a promotion and increased pay. Confused as to what to do, you begin to search for answers.

Most often the conscious ego self approaches this kind of situation by examining the known information. You may compare the salary and benefits of the job that you have just been offered with the long-term security potential of your current job. You may explore your feelings about leaving your present employer and contemplate your current job satisfaction. If possible, you may talk to others who work in the company where you were offered the job to find out more about what it's like to work there. You might also talk to friends and family and get their input. These are all useful and important strategies to pursue. However, let's imagine that after doing all of these things you are still confused and not sure if you should leave your present job. Something in you feels led to take the leap and leave your job, but you are not sure you trust it.

With this in mind, you decide to do something different and intuitively explore your options. Having had a few unexpected psychic experiences in the past that revealed helpful information, you are open to all possibilities.

Intent on receiving intuitive clarity, you get comfortable, close your eyes, breathe and relax, and ask your psychic awareness for input. At first your mind is racing and you feel a little anxious about this process. You question your intuitive ability and wonder if you are being a little silly for seeking advice this way. However, as you continue to breathe and relax, you begin to feel a heaviness in your heart and a sadness that you don't understand. As you feel the feelings, the spontaneous awareness that you are not expressing your true potential emerges. Although you had not really considered this, you know that this is the truth. As you listen within, you hear a voice telling you that it is time to move on from your current job. You are not sure who or what is telling you this, but you feel as if you can trust this guidance. As you consider this advice, you sense an image of a door with light streaming from it. This door, you realize, is the door to the new job, and you can pass through it. There is a part of you that wants to turn the other way. You can feel the stress building up. In your present job you are safe and there is no risk. You wonder why you would give up this security. As these feelings bubble up, your connection to your psychic awareness begins to weaken. Your mind begins to race and you start to think about what might happen if the new job does not work out.

Recognizing that your thoughts and feelings are taking over, you go back to focusing on your breath and begin once again to slip into a more receptive state. You feel a warmth and comfort surround you, which helps you to relax even more. Using your imagination, you create an image of the door and imagine yourself passing through it. As you do this, positive waves of energy flow through you. You have the sure feeling that the new job is in your highest good. It feels right. You know that it is time to grow and that this job offer is a step in the right direction.

You open your eyes and contemplate all that you have just received. It feels right; you are sure that taking this new job is the right thing to do.

Later that day you get ready to make the call and accept the new job. As you look for the phone number, doubt begins to surface. You begin to question the psychic information that you received and you wonder if you are making it all up. *Maybe this is what I wanted to hear and feel,* you say to yourself.

Within a few minutes, you question the validity of the psychic impressions you received. You no longer feel that the information is significant and that you can trust it. You decide not to make the phone call.

This scenario of receiving psychic energy information only to discount it soon after is all too common. Energy information emerges through thoughts, feelings, sensations, insights, a sense of knowing, and images without the benefit of a thought process and reasoning. Because of this, the ego mind works hard to discredit and deny it. The only way the thinking mind can rationalize psychic awareness is by telling itself that it is all made up. In the finite realm of understanding, no other explanation makes sense.

The straight-talking, convincing voice of the ego and logic cannot grasp the communication style of psychic awareness. Unable to understand the intuitive impressions, feelings, and flashes of insight, the ego self pushes them to the back row, brushes off the inconvenience, and goes on its merry way. Unfortunately, essential psychic insights are ignored.

Although we all too often dismiss psychic energy information because it appears nonsensical and made-up, it is possible to begin to better recognize psychic insights and interpret and understand their meaning and to trust the process.

THE ENERGY BODY: THE SOURCE OF PSYCHIC AWARENESS

At its most minuscule level, everything that we experience through our five senses is vibrating energy. Our physical self is made up of thousands and thousands of tiny cells of energy, and an invisible network of energy surrounds our body. Psychic information and insights emanate from this web of energy within and surrounding us.

Unlike the mind, which collects both internal and external data and then uses reasoning and logical thought processes to come to a conclusion or an understanding, psychic awareness is an open state of energetic receptivity. Even though psychic energy information may come by way of our thoughts or emotions or our physical self, its origin is pure energy. Noticing, receiving, and interpreting this energy is the work of being psychic.

The Energy Field: Intuition's House

Human thinking is limited to the functioning of the mind, whereas psychic information utilizes the mind, body, and spirit. The human energy field, or *aura*, and its system of power and energy information centers known as *chakras* contains an energy imprint of our thoughts, feelings, and the totality of our experiences, along with our beliefs and our past wounds and judgments. This energy field is also imprinted with our life purpose, soul plan, and divine gifts.

The energy field, or aura, is an egg-like web of energy that surrounds the physical body. Our natural sense of intuition and psychic ability emanates from the aura. This is intuition's house. The aura is both a protective shield and an energy transmitter and receiver. It broadcasts our energy vibe and interacts with and tunes in to the energy of others and our environment. The aura also repels negativity and toxic energy. When the aura is weak or if there is a tear in it, we may absorb and be adversely affected by harmful and negative worldly and spiritual influences. A healthy aura absorbs energy influences that are in our highest good and repels what is harmful.

A pulsating and vibrating web of energy, the aura varies in size and color. People with large, colorful auras have the ability to influence others and are highly intuitive and easier to psychically tune in to. People with a tight or small aura may be more difficult to psychically tune in to. Fear and stress can cause an aura to tighten up. Many of the exercises in this book help you expand, strengthen, and repair your aura and activate the psychic energy of your chakras.

The Chakras: Windows of Intuition

If the aura, or energy field, is intuition's house, then the chakras are its windows. Chakras are spirals of energy that contain the energetic imprint of our thoughts, emotions, beliefs, and experiences as well as our future possibilities. We have seven primary chakras, located from our feet to a bit above our head (see illustration). Through these windows, or portals, we send and receive intuitive energy information. Our intuition often prefers and is most comfortable intuiting through one or more particular chakras. Becoming familiar with the energy information and intuitive strengths of the different chakras provides a glimpse into the innate wisdom, information, and psychic abilities that we all have access to.

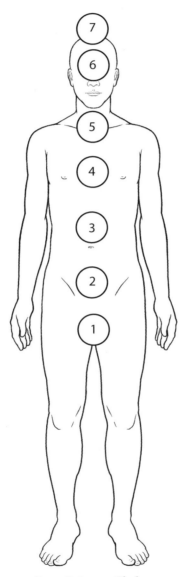

Seven Primary Chakras

First Chakra: Rooted to the Earth

The first chakra is located at the base of the spine and extends down through the lower part of the body. People who intuit primarily through the first chakra tend to be connected to nature and animal and plant spirits. They are often intuitively aware of and enjoy working with earth and elemental energies and may be aligned with and able to communicate with fairies and earth spirits.

Physical intuition tends to feel comfortable and at home in the first chakra. However, spiritual intuition can also set up camp in this chakra. When it does, it brings with it the ability to live and manifest our soul and life purpose.

Psychically tuning in to the first chakra provides energy information that has to do with early childhood influences, a sense of tribe and connection with others, and issues of safety and security. This chakra also provides insight into the obstacles and other issues related to manifesting our soul and life purpose.

Second Chakra: Practical and Prosperous

Located a little below the belly button, the second chakra is a busy chakra. Physical and mental intuition join forces through this chakra, which is energetically connected to many of the practical issues of day-to-day life. People who naturally intuit through the second chakra tend to have an intuitive instinct for how to make money and create positive relationships and fulfilling work and career opportunities.

Energy information from this chakra tends to surface as a hunch or what many consider to be common sense. The intuitive energy of this chakra offers direction and guidance through phenomena such as coincidences, synchronicity, and good or bad luck. It is through the second chakra that we access intuitive energy information that has to do with our own and others' finances, career and work issues, relationships, creativity, and sexuality.

Third Chakra: Personal Power

The intuition of the third chakra is more noticeable and direct than that of the first and second chakras. Those who naturally intuit through the third chakra often receive energy information through a gut feeling or other physical sensations. This chakra is the preferred window for physical and emotional intuition.

Have you ever felt butterflies in your stomach after first meeting someone? When you listen to your gut feelings, do things tend to work out? Do you ever have indigestion or stomach issues when you go along with something that you intuitively know is not right for you? This is your third chakra intuitively speaking to you.

Our sense of personal power, our self-trust, and our psychic awareness are all connected. Trusting ourselves, listening within, and having positive self-esteem are integral to developing psychic ability. This chakra connects our sense of personal power with our intuition and can assist us in following through on intuitive direction and guidance.

Those who naturally intuit through the third chakra may unknowingly absorb the aches, pains, and negativity of others into their body. For instance, I did a reading for a physician who was interested in further developing his medical intuitive abilities. Already comfortable with using his intuition to diagnose illness, he wanted to further refine his innate ability. However, he told me that when he intuitively tuned in to his patients, he became tired and drained, and he wanted to know what he could do to feel less exhausted.

When I intuitively looked at his chakras, I realized that he not only was intuiting energy information about others through his third chakra but was also absorbing their energy. I suggested that he strengthen his mental intuition, and we practiced a few exercises to help shift his primary intuitive receptivity from his third chakra to his higher chakras. (These exercises are outlined in chapter 3.) I assured him that he could expand his psychic awareness and intuit without absorbing others' energy. I heard from him a few months later, and he was happy to report that he was experiencing more intuitive success and less exhaustion.

The third chakra emits energy information that has to do with our self-esteem and personal power, and is an emotional center where past and present memories and experiences are housed.

Fourth Chakra: Love

The fourth chakra is located in the heart and is the window through which emotional intuition sends out its love energy current and receives energy information. The vibration of this chakra is connected to our ability to love ourselves and others, practice empathy and compassion, and heal emotional wounds.

If you have a high degree of emotional intuition and intuit primarily through the fourth chakra, you may feel as if you are on an emotional rollercoaster at times. Seemingly out of nowhere, you may feel waves of love, sadness, happiness, fear, and all of the emotions in between. You may find yourself feeling another's pain as if it were your own and attracting people who are in need of love and healing. Those who intuit through the fourth chakra can have a difficult time saying no and tend to give to others without restraint. They may need to learn how to receive and focus on their own needs.

The fourth chakra psychically reveals past emotional wounds and relationship issues and can provide information and guidance on to how to heal and love yourself and others.

Fifth Chakra: Expression

The fifth chakra is located in the throat area and vibrates with the energy of mental and emotional intuition. Those who naturally intuit through this chakra often unknowingly receive and share psychic insights while conversing with others.

For instance, my friend Sharon has a lot of friends. She loves to talk on the phone, text, and email. Along with being funny and caring, she is naturally psychic. Her abilities surface best when she is talking to others. When engaged in conversation, she may unknowingly or more consciously receive quick insights or psychic information about the person she is talking with. She freely shares what she receives without giving it too much thought. At times, psychic energy flows through her so effortlessly that she does not even recognize the intuitive significance of what she is saying.

People who intuit through the fifth chakra may not always be aware that they are sharing psychic information with others. Because they communicate with such ease and express without restraint, they often do not realize that they may be a natural channel of psychic information.

Psychically tuning in to the fifth chakra reveals energy information that has to do with the ability to be true to ourselves and others and express this truth. Self-will, addictions, and emotional repression and stress are also energetically connected to this chakra.

Sixth Chakra: Higher Mind

The sixth chakra is located in the head, directly behind the eyebrows. It is the primary center for mental and spiritual intuition. Our thoughts, beliefs, judgments, and prejudices are located in this chakra. Connected to consciousness and to the thinking mind and the divine mind, this chakra is a spiritual transition portal where we experience the shift from human knowing and thinking to intuitive and psychic receptivity. Sometimes referred to as the *third eye*, the sixth chakra can be an active psychic center.

Associated with mental intuition, the sixth chakra reveals our predominant thoughts, patterns of thinking, beliefs, and willingness to receive and accept higher divine thoughts. The transformative gateway through which judgmental and limiting beliefs and finite thinking are revealed, this chakra can transform and enlighten.

Seventh Chakra: The Spirit Realm

The seventh chakra, or the *crown* chakra, is located a few inches above the head and is connected primarily to spiritual intuition and, to a lesser degree, physical intuition. Although it may seem to lie at the other end of the chakra spectrum, physical intuition can be highly beneficial in the seventh chakra. As a manifesting and earth-centered form of intuition, physical intuition can help to ground the higher gifts of the seventh chakra. Through the combined forces of physical and spiritual intuition, our higher soul energy is made available in the here and now and can be used in everyday life.

Associated with higher or divine awareness and the soul and spirit, the seventh chakra is the portal to divine presence and offers direct access to the spirit realm. Those who naturally intuit through this chakra tend to be aware of angels, spirit guides, and loved ones on the other side. Although this chakra can be a clear psychic channel, it is important to stay connected to the energy of the other chakras to ground your psychic impressions and intuit useful and practical energy information.

The seventh chakra psychically reveals whether or not we are in the flow of our life purpose and living in integrity and wholeness. Through this chakra it is possible to communicate with loved ones on the other side, spirit guides, and angels.

Because our energy self (our aura and chakras) is not easily known through the limited functioning of our five senses and the thinking mind, we tend not be aware of our psychic potential. You are fully equipped to start developing and using your natural psychic ability. It is not essential or necessary to fully understand how the energy field, the chakras, and intuition all work together. As you move through this book and learn about and practice accessing your natural intuitive and psychic abilities, you will experience for yourself the brilliant psychic energetic network that is yours to use and benefit from.

Chapter 2

Obstacles to Developing Psychic Abilities and the Corresponding Gifts

Becoming aware of your innate psychic abilities and making the decision to further develop them embodies many of the characteristics of the hero's journey. In his book *The Hero with a Thousand Faces*, Joseph Campbell describes the universal archetypal pattern of the hero and how it guides human development and spiritual transformation. Since the beginning of recorded time we have sought the adventure and challenge of exploring the unknown and reaching beyond ourselves. Although each story is unique, with different characters and challenges, the hero's journey is a common theme found in many current books and films.

The archetypal pattern of the hero begins in the safe and comfortable environment of the ordinary world. Within this predictable shell of the known, the hero goes about his or her daily routine with little thought as to what lies beyond. The hero does not necessarily crave adventure or new experiences. However, unexpectedly and seemingly out of nowhere, something comes along and calls the hero out of his or her comfort zone.

The invitation into psychic awareness often initially begins this same way. You may be going about your daily routine and suddenly an uninvited psychic experience comes your way.

Here are a few common ways that psychic awareness may unexpectedly enter our lives:

- You suddenly think of someone whom you have not heard from in a long time. Then later that day you receive a phone call from the person.
- After dreaming of a lost item, you find it in the exact place where you dreamt it would be.
- The gut feeling that a financial investment will not work out goes ignored. Despite the intuitive warning, you go forward with it, only to lose money when it suddenly loses value.

These kinds of psychic insights and feelings often open the door to our curiosity and hint at a reality that goes against the accepted norms.

When an unsought psychic awareness comes our way, the carefully laid inner structure of how we thought the world worked cracks a bit and leaves us wondering *How did I know that? Is this just an odd coincidence? What else is possible?*

Questions begin to flood our mind and we find that we have no answers. The rational, logical conscious self is perplexed and confused. We may even try to rationalize, ignore, and talk ourselves out of believing what we have experienced. However, we may also be curious, energized, and motivated to know and discover more.

It is at this crucial juncture that we confront the next step of the hero's journey. We can either cling to the old beliefs and sense of reality or move forward into unknown territory.

Changes That May Occur While Developing Psychic Awareness

To successfully develop psychic awareness, we need to let go of our assumptions and beliefs about what is possible and allow our curiosity and desire for truth to guide us. It takes courage to answer this call and move forward and further explore the mystery of psychic awareness.

Most of us are initially nervous about our ability to receive and interpret psychic energy. We don't want to fail, appear foolish, or be disappointed by our lack of intuitive potential. While these concerns are understandable, everyone is intuitive and can further develop their innate ability. While some people might catch on faster than others, our intuitive sense has an intelligence that knows what it is doing. Similar to our five senses, our natural intuition is programed and encoded with its function. We don't need to know how to see in order to see or how to smell in order to smell; it is natural and easy. While we do need to learn how to better listen to and access our intuition, psychic development is more of an act of allowing than of making something happen.

In addition to these fears, there are other obstacles that lurk in our mind and heart that can sabotage our intuitive efforts. Although we are not always conscious of these concerns, most of us harbor fears and stress about other changes that may occur as a result of psychic development. We may wonder how being psychic will change us, how others will view us, and if we might become vulnerable to dark forces or unseen dangers.

Chelsea's experience is a good example of the changes that often happen when we embrace our psychic potential. A software salesperson, Chelsea experienced success in her career and personal life and lived with her husband and two children in an affluent part of town. Life was working out the way that Chelsea had always hoped it would.

Chelsea contacted me for a reading at the suggestion of a friend who is a client of mine. Right on time, she nervously made her way into my office and sat timidly at the edge of my couch. After our initial hellos, I began the reading and immediately felt her apprehension. I found this interesting because she seemed to be quite psychic herself. When I told her this, she seemed to become even more nervous. When I gently asked her about her own psychic experiences, she shared a recent psychic experience that she'd had while meditating.

Feeling stressed from high sales goals at work, Chelsea thought that she would give meditation a try. After just one session, she felt better and so continued to meditate before work. After sitting down on her meditation cushion half-asleep one morning, she was surprised by a spontaneous vision that seemed to come out of nowhere. In this vision she saw one of her coworkers, Keith, walk out of the office and then into the office of a competing company. She thought this was odd and didn't give it too much thought.

A week later the office was all abuzz with the news that Keith, a top salesman, had just quit his job to take a position with a rival company. Chelsea was shocked at the news, not so much because Keith was leaving but because she had seen him leave during her meditation. She was uncomfortable and didn't know where the vision had come from and why. We talked a little more about this, and I continued with the session. When our session ended, Chelsea asked me about psychic development classes and seemed determined to further explore her abilities.

The next time I saw Chelsea was in one of my classes. She was a natural, with an open and determined attitude, and her psychic abilities blossomed.

Over the next few years, Chelsea took every class I offered, and her psychic abilities grew and strengthened. However, her family was not always enthusiastic about Chelsea's new interests. When she shared her psychic insights and some of what she was learning, her husband looked at her perplexed and her mother and sister rolled their eyes in mock belief. Although she still attended the Methodist church that she had belonged to for many years, she no longer agreed with all of the accepted beliefs. When she found a spiritualist church where the minister gave medium and psychic messages to the congregants, her family became wary and alarmed. The occult had no business in the church, they told her, and they refused to discuss it further.

Other areas of Chelsea's life were also changing. No longer satisfied with her career, she longed for more meaningful work and wanted to make a difference in the world. Unfortunately her family and friends were not supportive of her psychic exploration and the changes she was considering. They hoped that it was a phase and that she would soon return to the sensible woman they knew her to be.

With a lack of support and understanding from family and friends, Chelsea also wondered if her interest in developing and exploring psychic abilities was just a passing interest. The feeling of being misunderstood by others was uncomfortable, and at times she felt nervous about what other changes might come her way.

THE OBSTACLE OF FEELING DIFFERENT AND ALONE VERSUS THE GIFT OF THE INNER COMFORTER

Like the archetypal hero who chooses to leave the comfortable and ordinary world and embark on the hero's journey, Chelsea left the predictable rhythm of her day-to-day life to explore her psychic awareness. Once the hero begins to explore the unknown, unforeseen tests, challenges, and obstacles crop up. However, when confronted, these obstacles and challenges bring with them unexpected gifts and an increase in power and awareness.

As you move forward and develop and explore your psychic awareness, you too will likely confront obstacles and tests.

For instance, like Chelsea, you may want to share your interest in psychic awareness with others and invite those closest to you into this experience, yet your efforts may be met with resistance. Your new interests may feel threatening to family and friends, and they may fear the unknown. Although psychic awareness has opened your heart and mind to new possibilities and insights, the people in your life may be guarded and approach you with puzzled questioning. You may feel as if you are alone, odd, or no longer as connected to others in the way that you had been. Feeling judged and misunderstood, you may begin to question yourself and the repercussions of your budding interest in the psychic world. But it is difficult to simply walk away.

At some time during the process of developing psychic awareness, many people confront the challenge of feeling at odds with and disconnected from family and friends. When we accept this uncomfortable passage and continue to grow instead of backing away, an unexpected new awareness often comes our way.

Every obstacle and challenge brings with it a transformative gift. Although we may initially feel more detached and distant from family and friends, psychic development brings the gift of presence. Although unseen and intangible, psychic energy often brings with it the awareness of a comforting divine, loving presence that assures us we are not alone. Something in this vast and unknowable universe reaches out and lets us know that we are loved and being guided. When we intuitively open our heart and mind, we encounter the divine presence of the spirit realm. With psychic awareness we become aware that we are never truly alone. There is a kind, unseen gentleness that touches our heart, mind, and soul. Although it is difficult to know and grasp this illusive energy, the gift of this presence invites us into a world of meaning and connectedness where we feel known and cared for.

The Obstacle of Religion versus the Gift of Spirituality

Our past and present religious beliefs and practices may or may not always support our interest in psychic abilities and the new understanding and insights that come our way when we listen to them. Our beliefs about God and our sense of our own spiritual nature may be challenged, and we may feel spiritually lost and vulnerable.

If we were brought up in a religious tradition that believes that psychics and spiritualists are messengers of the dark side or the devil, then accepting our psychic awareness may be especially difficult. Even if our place of worship is more open-minded and nontraditional, developing psychic abilities may still be viewed as nonspiritual nonsense.

The gift of this obstacle is a personal connection with the divine spirit that resides within. While developing and using psychic awareness, many people experience the intuitive realization that God is not outside of ourselves. The awareness that the power and presence of God emanates from within may slowly make its way into our consciousness or suddenly surface, challenging our religious convictions.

Another gift that tends to surface as our personal connection and relationship with the divine begins to strengthen is the awareness of the intrinsic goodness of the unseen. One of the most compelling obstacles to developing psychic abilities is the fear of psychic energy and the spirit realm. The uncertainty of what and who may be lurking and ready to negatively influence and harm us prevents many from developing their intuition.

However, as we open our heart and mind, we begin to feel the warmth of an inner light that is comforting, warm, and all-encompassing. We become aware that beyond the fear-based dogma and restrictive beliefs of many religions, the Most Holy is positive, loving, wise, and always available to guide and help us.

The Obstacle of Rational Intelligence versus the Gift of Intuitive Intelligence

Another common obstacle that many people encounter is the belief that psychic awareness is nonsense, unintellectual, woo-woo, stupid, and a waste of time. This feeling and belief may come from our own inner judgments and from others' judgments.

Along with religious objections, this attitude was particularly strong in my family. When I was young, getting good grades was highly prized. While my brothers and sister were making scholastic gains, I struggled to pay attention and find interest in my studies. However, this did not stop or slow down my intuition, and more than once I relied on it to provide me with the correct answers to tests and to supply me with information when called upon in class.

Many of my clients and students initially approach psychic awareness through intellectual curiosity. They often place an emphasis on definitively proving its existence in a way that makes sense to the rational mind. I appreciate their passion and attempts to wrangle the wild child that psychic awareness can be into a controllable research object. However, the desire to intellectually grasp psychic awareness can keep the experience of it at bay. Your psychic awareness has to be experienced to be known. You cannot place the thinking mind in charge of your intuition. It will repress, deny, and ridicule it as if it were a rebellious insurgent attempting a coup. Psychic awareness is a few steps ahead of your conscious ego-centered thoughts. The psychic playing field has no limitations, and if you try to confine and control it, it will dissipate and become elusive.

Believing that intuition is not a legitimate form of intelligence is an obstacle. Even though intuition does not fit within the parameters of the kind of logic and reasoning that we most promote and trust, it is still a valid form of intelligence. If you have been led to believe that intuition has less to offer than other types of intelligence, let go of your judgments and adopt the beginner's mind.

The gift of this obstacle is the awareness that intuition is our most natural wisdom. Experience this truth for yourself. Don't define your intuition and your interest in psychic abilities according to outer standards and others' beliefs. Listen to it and trust that psychic awareness is worthy of your time and attention. As you do this, you discover the positive and powerful contribution that it can make in your life.

The Obstacle of Doubt versus the Gift of Soul Awareness

Doubt is a common obstacle that many people must confront when developing psychic awareness. We may at times doubt that psychic awareness is natural and real, doubt our capacity to develop it, and doubt the intuitive messages that we receive. Doubt is a product of the ego, and it will regularly surface when developing psychic abilities. How could it not? The ego does not want the surly upstart of psychic awareness to take over the reign of your day-to-day consciousness.

Recognize doubt in its many disguises. It can surface as skepticism and a need to have psychic phenomena meet an unreasonable standard of proof. It is always healthy and a good idea to question psychic information and be mindful of errors in insights and interpretation. However, there is no perfect science to psychic ability. It is an evolving art, and while it is important to notice any mistakes that you may make while working with it, learn from them and keep moving forward. Too often, psychic abilities are held to a higher standard than other skills and talents. For instance, we do not dismiss the medical profession as invalid when an illness has been misdiagnosed, and we are not expelled from school when we do poorly on an exam. It is all part of the process of growth and increased awareness.

Doubt often surfaces in my psychic development classes, and I encourage my students to confront and work through it. Almost everyone experiences doubt, but don't let it control and limit your psychic growth. Recognize the difference between doubt and questioning. Questioning is a positive tool that can help you refine your psychic abilities and become aware of their subtle nuances.

For instance, it may at times be necessary to question the source of your intuitive impressions. It can be helpful to ask yourself if you are receiving psychic energy information or if you are generating insights and impressions based on your own thoughts, beliefs, and desires. You may need to question your interpretation of what you are psychically receiving, and it may be helpful to ask yourself what you may need to do differently to better improve your abilities. Questions can play a crucial role in the process of developing psychic abilities, but this is not the case with doubt. Instead of encouraging your development, doubt stops you in your tracks. It says that you have no psychic aptitude and natural abilities or that psychic phenomena are fake and phony.

Confront doubt and move through it and you will receive the gift of soulful knowing. When you feel truth deep within, you experience a recognizable and sure sense of knowing. This kind of awareness comes from the soul. Doubt may overwhelm you with confusion and produce anxiety, yet your soul always knows when it meets the truth.

When you experience a clear, gut-affirming psychic awareness, hold on to it and feel it. You may not always understand and be able to adequately put what you receive into words and interpret it correctly. This will come in time. It is enough at the beginning to recognize the unique feeling that accompanies a true connection to psychic energy information.

Once you have received energy information and insights, you may begin to doubt your ability to interpret and understand what you have received. In this phase, questioning can also play an important role. If you are not sure if your interpretations are correct, intuitively check for accuracy. Ask yourself if it feels right. What does your gut or heart tell you? These are messages from your soul that will let you know if your interpretations are correct.

There will be other times when doubt surfaces. When it does, remind yourself that your insecurities are coming from your ego. Shift your awareness deeper within, and feel and listen for the voice of your soul. Trust your inner sense of soul awareness when it surfaces and you will be able to rely on it whenever you use your psychic ability.

These are a few of the common obstacles to psychic development. You will likely confront one or more of them, and a few others may crop up. Remember that within every obstacle you confront during psychic development there is a gift. Once you acknowledge and continue to explore and work through the obstacle, resistance gives way and new awareness and deeper levels of insight emerge.

PART 2
The Psychic Characteristics and Potential of Each Psychic Type

CHAPTER 3

Psychic Knowing
(Mental Intuitive Type)

Mental intuition is the ability to receive energy information through thoughts, a sense of knowing, and inner hearing. Intuiting energy information through mental intuition usually feels natural and normal. You may not recognize it as a psychic experience. You simply become aware of or know something without knowing how you know it.

For instance, have you ever suddenly known what someone else was going to say immediately before they said it? Have you ever experienced an unexpected sudden awareness or realization about yourself or another that provided helpful understanding? In a spontaneous aha moment, have you ever received understanding and insight into an issue that has been plaguing you? Do you ever know the outcome of a situation without knowing how you know it?

Mental intuition is the ability to absorb and become aware of energy information through your thoughts, consciousness, and mindful awareness. Mental intuition might be experienced as the ability to know what others are thinking or becoming aware of complexities that you have no logical way of knowing. Many receive personal guidance and insights through spontaneous intuitive knowing. Mental intuition may also emerge as a sudden idea that solves complicated issues or problems or the awareness of how to do something in a new and more efficient way. For instance, new technologies and inventions are often intuited through mental intuition. Some may be so revolutionary that they are not easily understood and their potential is not fully realized.

COMMON CHARACTERISTICS OF A MENTAL INTUITIVE

People with a high degree of mental intuition share some common characteristics. For instance, those with a high degree of mental intuition tend to be creative thinkers who enjoy exploring all possibilities before coming to a conclusion or making a decision. Nonjudgmental and open-minded, a mental intuitive is curious and tends to collect information about a wide range of issues. Nothing is too far-out for them to consider and probe a little bit deeper into. With this natural desire to know and search for the truth, they can be overly objective, ignoring the subjective and emotional. For this reason, a mental intuitive may be viewed as detached and impersonal.

With their love of complexity and ability to generate new ideas and solutions to problems and issues, they can be leaders in their chosen field. Scientific research, engineering, technology, computer science, and advanced studies are often populated by mental intuitives.

Unlike the emotional intuitive who may be overly sensitive or the spiritual intuitive who may be aloof and enjoy hanging out in the ethers, a mental intuitive is tough-minded and likes a problem to solve or a puzzle or mystery to uncover and decipher. No-nonsense people, they may keep probing and following their intuition when others have given up and walked away. At times their reliance on logic and reasoning can hinder their psychic development, as this highly attuned thinking function can get in the way of intuitive receptivity. Those with a high degree of mental intuition may experience an excessive amount of mind chatter, be indecisive, overthink, and think more than feel.

Although psychic awareness is often viewed as a paranormal phenomenon, it naturally and frequently occurs within conventional fields such as science, medical research, engineering, and similar areas. Intuitive people may be stereotyped as free-spirited, creative, and artistic, or perhaps a bit kooky, out of the box, naive, and out of sync with the status quo. Yet intuited energy information often provides useful insights into broad-based issues and practical areas of concern.

Throughout my career as a psychic and medium, I have often been asked if any of my other family members are psychic. Just as musical talent, intelligence, and athletic ability tend to run in families, so does psychic ability. However, in my family there were no free-spirited or gypsy-type psychics. Instead, intuitive and psychic tendencies were more evident in my scientific and engineering-focused family members.

For instance, one of my uncles worked on the Manhattan Project, the enterprise that led to the development of the first atomic bomb in 1946. This uncle also had dozens of electrical and nuclear patents and inventions. Years later his work is still included in scientific textbooks. Another one of my uncles, an aerospace engineer, was the project manager for the main engine of the first space shuttle and worked on many other inventive technologies. Of course, like most mental intuitives, they would argue against the idea that their intuition was aiding their efforts. However, you did not need to be in their company for long before it became evident that they were perceiving energy information that others did not have access to.

For example, years ago I was backing out of my driveway with my uncle Bob, the aerospace engineer, sitting in the passenger seat next to me. Before I made it to the street, he told me that there was a problem with the car's engine. When I did not understand what he was talking about, he wrote down what he believed was the issue and told me to take it to a mechanic. He never looked under the hood or asked me any questions about my car's performance. I didn't think there was anything wrong with my car, but I was curious and took it to a mechanic. When he asked me what the problem was, I felt a little silly handing him the notes that my uncle had written down on the back of a napkin.

I went back to the car repair shop the next day and the mechanic told me that he had hooked the car up to a machine that checks the engine and everything seemed to be in working order. However, just to be safe, he tested some parts himself and found there was a problem. He was surprised, he told me, to discover that this was the issue that was written on the napkin. The machine had not yet been able to detect the problem with the part in question, which was in the beginning stages of decline.

For someone with a high degree of mental intuition, events such as these are often viewed as logical and easily explained. Mental intuitives assume that their access to insights and unknown information is a normal mental function. There is often a fine line between the biological functioning of the brain and the intuitive ability to absorb energy information and translate it into useful material.

For a mental intuitive, reality is malleable, and what may appear to lie out of their cognitive grasp can be as real and concrete as solid matter to them. There is little that a mental intuitive will not explore and consider, as they are generally curious and driven to understand and make sense of all things. Energy information flows into their thoughts with ease, and they accept them without questioning their source.

Yet an interesting dynamic occurs when there is the possibility that the information they have received has been accessed through psychic channels. When it comes to a sixth sense or paranormal phenomena, a mental intuitive may want proof and verifiable evidence in order to accept this possibility. It is not so much that they disbelieve in psychic energy and awareness. Instead, they want to know the definitive truth of what lies beyond the five senses and, if possible, to control and use it for their own purposes. Although they are driven to understand the unknown, they do not want to waste time and energy pursuing empty suspicions and illusions. Their inner drive is to harness the potential and power of any creative force or phenomenon, including psychic energy.

SELF-GENERATED THOUGHTS

Because mental intuition surfaces through the mind, the most difficult obstacle to developing and using it may be the ability to discern the difference between intuitive and self-generated thoughts. Although the two types may initially appear to be similar, self-generated thoughts are created from cognitive awareness, the conscious mind, the personality self, the subconscious, and the ego. They involve reasoning, memory, past experience, recall, and logical thought progression. Self-generated thoughts derive from our unconscious beliefs and biases and judgments.

When we have a problem to solve or need a new idea or understanding, we usually draw from what we believe is possible, past experience, and the known. Self-generated thoughts are consecutive and linear. One thought leads to another thought, which in turn leads to another thought, and on and on, until we arrive at a satisfying conclusion. Most self-generated thoughts are driven by our emotions, feelings, and beliefs. Listening to and acting on these thoughts reinforces what we feel and believe. This cycle then continues to recreate and confirm our reality.

For instance, if we fear and believe that change in our work environment may lead to possible job loss or instability, we will likely become pessimistic and defensive when some form of change inevitably comes into our work life. These negative thoughts will in turn create a negative outcome. Unfortunately, self-generated thoughts tend to stay within the security-driven arena of the known, where there is no room for true insight and awakened thinking.

Psychic Thoughts

The human mind is capable of connecting to a vast source of energy information. It is not paranormal or spooky to use your higher intuitive mind to access energy information. We tend to have an expectation or preconceived idea that a psychic thought is markedly different from an everyday self-generated one. However, psychic thoughts seldom stand out or appear significantly different from self-generated thoughts. Everyone has psychic thoughts, and without knowing it, you likely receive them on a daily basis. To better discern and notice them, especially at the beginning of psychic development, it is important to become aware of the different types of psychic thoughts.

Individual Thoughts

The ability to psychically tune in to the thoughts of family members, lovers, friends, colleagues, or even those we do not know is likely the most common form of mental intuition. Over time we tend to form a mental bond and connection with those we are close to and those we encounter in our day-to-day environment. We begin to think alike and even think the same thoughts. This happens in simple ways that we do not always notice.

For instance, as Carla, a client of mine, passed a barbecue restaurant on her way home from work, the thought came to her to stop and pick up ribs for her husband for dinner. When she arrived home, she was surprised to see his car already in the driveway. She opened the door and called her husband's name a few times, but there was no answer. When she walked to the back of the house, she found him on the patio at the grill, barbecuing ribs.

Although this and other similar types of situations may appear to be just chance encounters or coincidences, we often form a psychic mental bond and psychically communicate with those we are close to.

Collective Thought

Collective thought is a potent collection of similar thoughts and beliefs that are generated by individual thoughts. When we think a thought, especially a habitual one, we release it out into the energy environment. Similar thoughts and beliefs share an energetic vibration and bond to one another. Collective thought energy can be a positive or negative force and can affect individual thoughts and beliefs. Political beliefs, societal norms, and cultural shifts and changes are influenced by our collective thoughts.

As people accept a collective thought, it increasingly affects and influences more and more people. It can become dangerous when the collective thought is negative, judgmental, and prejudicial. Throughout history, political and influential people have used collective beliefs to gain power and control. The rise of many political movements such as the Nazi regime and cultural norms such as slavery were successful in large part because the collective thought of their acceptability influenced weaker-minded individuals. Many of our beauty standards and beliefs about what is sexually desirable are based on the collective thought of attractiveness and sexuality.

Collective thought can also have a positive effect on others and the planet. When we let go of negativity and think positive thoughts, we send this vibe out to the planet. Knowing the goodness within ourselves and perceiving the good in others reinforces others' ability to perceive this within themselves. We never do anything in the solitude of our mind. Our thoughts affect others and contribute to the collective energy that influences others near and far.

The next popular trends in art, music, and fashion and soon-to-be popular political and cultural movements first exist as collective thought energy. Many people unknowingly and some knowingly intuit these trends before they manifest in our collective experience. When it is time for an idea, invention, gadget, technology, or evolutionary step in our mass consciousness to manifest, there are individuals who intuit this information before others. Most of the time these inventors, creative geniuses, financial wizards, politicians, and evolutionary thinkers do not recognize the intuitive nature of their thoughts. They simply know what is needed and what direction we are collectively moving in. Capitalizing on this awareness, they often become wealthy, popular, highly admired, and successful as they usher in and manifest what is already present in our collective thought.

Higher Source Awareness

The source of creative, original, and pure thought energy is higher consciousness and the divine mind. Our higher self, spirit, and divine presence speaks to us through intuitive thoughts and awareness. Quite often these intuited thoughts and messages do not seem extraordinary. Instead, they address everyday conditions and situations and often provide comfort and guidance. Higher source messages are often intuited through a still and quiet inner knowing. Quite often these thoughts are so subtle that we dismiss and disregard them. However, when we notice and listen to them, we are guided to positive outcomes and a deeper truth.

For instance, Emily, a client of mine, lived in the same house for over thirty-five years. She raised her children in this house and continued to live there after her divorce. Since it was a large and older home, the cost to keep it up continued to mount year after year. Emily wanted to move but didn't know where to go. Looking at homes for sale and talking to friends and family about a possible move only created more confusion. In the midst of indecision she began to inwardly hear this message: *Be patient.*

It is not yet time. This message gave her a sense of peace, but she still continued to look at homes for sale and widened her search into neighboring areas. During this time she continued to hear the same inner message: *Be patient. It is not yet time.*

Feeling frustrated by the lack of results after a year of searching, she decided to listen to this voice. She gave up her search and decided to focus on gardening, volunteering, and relaxing with friends. Several months later, during a meeting with her garden club, a friend of hers mentioned that she was planning to move to a distant state to be closer to her grandchildren. Her friend was excited about the move but shared with Emily that it would be difficult to leave her home and garden. For years her friend had devoted time and money to create a home that was an oasis of beauty and peace.

Emily asked if she could take a look at her friend's home before she put it on the market. When she stepped into the home a few weeks later, she knew that this was the home she had been waiting for. Her friend accepted her offer, and she moved in a few months later.

Divine Thoughts

Intuited divine thoughts bypass logic and may be referred to as revelations or enlightened thoughts. One way to identify if a thought is from a higher divine source is by examining the effect it has on you. The ego mind does not argue against a divine thought, while a self-generated thought often provokes an inner argument.

For instance, when you think an affirmative thought, such as *I am connected to a vast source of love and abundance,* a thousand little voices inside your head may disagree and persuade you to disregard this belief. Your mind cannot comprehend how this is possible. It informs you that this is illogical and there is no evidence to back up this assertion. You may want to believe the statement, but your personality and ego self may refuse to accept and embody this truth based on your past experiences and subconscious thoughts.

However, when you intuitively receive and absorb the same truth from the divine mind or higher consciousness, its transformative energy bypasses your thought processes. You know and experience it as an aha moment of clarity and truth. The experience of this truth overrides your subconscious thoughts, past experiences, and limited, finite thinking and replaces it with a new truth to act on and create. This intuited enlightened thought alters your experience. This is one reason why meditation is so important. It gives us the opportunity to receive and absorb intuitive, transformative, and higher truth.

Messages from Angels, Spirit Guides, and Loved Ones on the Other Side

Many of the intuitive messages we receive through mental intuition are sent to us by our angels, spirit guides, and loved ones in spirit. When spirit beings speak to us, most of the time we are not aware of their presence. When we experience a helpful new idea, an aha moment, or a spontaneous insight, we do not give too much thought to its origin. It is not necessary to know where the message is coming from. Overall it is more important to listen to and receive the message than to definitively know who may be sending it. As psychic ability strengthens, it becomes easier to discern who may have sent it.

Angelic messages help us to feel loved and watched over. However, they can also be instructive and informative and warn us of potential danger or conflicts. Mental intuitive messages from your angels may be subtle, like a soft whisper, or more dramatic and feel almost like a command.

For instance, Madeline, a client of mine in her mid-twenties, was in a relationship that was becoming more and more difficult. She knew that Robbie, her boyfriend, had experienced a troubled childhood, and she tried to do all she could to help him feel loved. Still, his insults and angry moods just seemed to get worse. Feeling that love could conquer all, she endured his bad behavior in the belief that one day he would recognize how much he loved her and treat her better.

On her way to pick him up from his job one evening, she heard a soft inner voice telling her that the relationship was not going to get better and that it was time to leave. Although she ignored the voice, it kept coming back, and each time it did, it got louder and louder. Then one night at Robbie's home after she had endured a few stinging insults, the voice in Madeline's head told her it was time to leave—now! The voice was so forceful and startling that she picked up her things and left.

A few weeks later while reflecting on her relationship with Robbie, Madeline suddenly felt a warm wave of energy surround her, and she became intuitively aware that she was being watched over by her guardian angel. Her self-esteem had sunk so low that she knew she wouldn't have had the strength to leave Robbie on her own. Although the relationship was over and she had a lot of healing to do, her heart filled with courage and strength knowing that her angels were guiding her.

Mental intuitive messages from spirit guides often nudge us to take action, move through a limitation, or learn a new skill, and they steer us in the direction of opportunities. They can help us to be in the right place at the right time and guide us to our highest good. Wherever and whenever we are growing, learning, helping, or creating positivity for ourselves and others, spirit guides are present. It is not always easy to tell the difference between an angelic message and a message from a spirit guide. However, messages from spirit guides tend to be more matter-of-fact and often offer insight and guidance, while messages from angels can feel loving and comforting.

Loved ones on the other side often communicate through mental intuition. While we are often not aware of the presence of angels and spirit guides, we tend to better intuitively recognize when a loved one on the other side is communicating with us. We may simply know who is present without knowing how we know. It is common to telepathically converse with loved ones, much more so than we may think is possible. We naturally do this while driving or doing other mundane tasks. If you suddenly wonder what your mother, father, grandparent, or another loved one might think or what their advice might be about a current condition, they likely want to share it with you.

Identifying Psychic Thoughts

Whatever the origin of a psychic thought, you can become more aware of when you are naturally intuiting them by detecting and becoming aware of the subtle differences between psychic thoughts and self-generated ones.

Unlike self-generated thoughts, which are driven by the ego and our emotions and desires, psychic thoughts are free of these influences. Compared to ego thoughts, psychic thoughts may feel flat, unemotional, and not personal, yet there is often a calm awareness that accompanies them. Usually persistent, psychic thoughts tend not to arouse or invoke an emotional response. Even in situations where you would normally have an emotional reaction, psychic thoughts may be persistent, repetitive, and even-toned and not alarming.

For instance, imagine that you are getting ready for work one morning and you have the thought to take a different route to your office. You find the thought interesting but not necessarily important. As you get into your car, the thought returns. It may even sound like an inner voice telling you to *take an alternative route to work today.* You dismiss the thought and head out onto the highway listening to your favorite music. A few miles down the road, the traffic comes to a standstill because of an overturned tractor trailer. However, it is too late to turn around and go another way. You are stuck in traffic and end up arriving late to an important meeting.

Psychic thoughts can feel like a matter-of-fact awareness. Unlike self-generated thoughts, psychic thoughts are not linear. One thought does not lead to another and then another. Instead, they surface spontaneously and are concise, simple, and cohesive. Quite often a psychic thought may be a statement that repeats itself over and over.

For instance, have you ever had an easy choice to make where you know exactly what you want yet you repeatedly receive the thought or message that your choice is not going to turn out the way you expect it to? Still, you dismiss the thought because you have no known evidence or reason to trust it. Later, when the outcome that you had hoped for does not manifest, you remember the thought and wish that you had acted on it.

Psychic thoughts do not try to convince you that they are right and that you should listen and act on them. They simply repeat a statement without making you fearful or anxious or appealing to your ego. Psychic thoughts do not reinforce our illusions, as they are not necessarily what we want to hear. For example, when I was single and dating, I would at times receive the psychic thought that a hoped-for relationship with someone was not going to work out. More often than I would like to admit, I would argue against the little voice that calmly stated, *This is not the right person for you.* I ignored it more than once and, of course, later regretted doing this, as it was always correct.

IDEAS AND INSIGHTS

Psychic thoughts also emerge in the form of ideas and insights. They, too, are matter-of-fact and do not arouse stress or other emotions. However, instead of being a simple, concise statement, some psychic insights and ideas surface in a cohesive whole, with a complete understanding of an area of concern. Providing deeper knowledge or a blueprint-like overall awareness, some psychic ideas and insights are often described as aha moments. They are not always logical and rational, but when you experience one, you recognize it as truth. Like a flower bud that gently unfolds, an intuited idea or insight may have many facets that lead to a complete but unexpected awareness.

Psychic thoughts often inspire new inventions, scientific insights, and genius-like knowledge. Artists, musicians, writers, and others in creative fields, along with engineers, scientists, and inventors, are often led and guided by psychic ideas and insights. In a moment of synergy where the mind receives and absorbs what it may have not been able to fully grasp through linear and self-generated thought, psychic energy arrives with the answer.

Psychic insights can also provide personal guidance and increase self-awareness. They empower us to perceive and understand new aspects of who we are, and inspire us to change and evolve. When the source of psychic thoughts is divine energy, they guide us to our highest good. Some may be experienced as subtle whispers that gently open our heart and mind to new awareness, while others offer a profound awakening that alters our sense of reality and what is possible. One of the telltale signs of a divine thought is the sensation of connectedness to a vast source of all-knowing wisdom. Such thoughts expand consciousness and can be transcendental, uplifting, and transformative.

The Psychic Abilities of Mental Intuition

The three primary psychic abilities of mental intuition are claircognizance, clairaudience, and telepathy. You unknowingly receive these kind of psychic thoughts on a daily basis. However, further developing the psychic abilities of mental intuition enables you to harness the power of the mind to intuitively receive guidance and information when you need it most.

Claircognizance

Claircognizance is the psychic ability to receive energy information through thoughts and a sense of knowing. Energy information received through claircognizance may surface as a spontaneous awareness, a persistent thought or message, or a series of insights. When you receive a claircognizant thought, there is a spontaneous awareness of its truth. Even if others disagree and there is no confirming evidence to back up your intuition, there is little doubt of its validity. Although you may question yourself at a later time, an initial positive and without-a-doubt sense of knowing and insight is the hallmark sign of claircognizance.

For instance, when my son was five years old, he told me, "I am going to go live in New York City. Is that okay with you?"

"When are you planning on moving?" I jokingly asked.

Without a pause he answered, "When I am older, but not too old. I need to live in New York City."

At the time we lived in North Carolina and had visited family on the West Coast a few times, but he had never been to New York. I was surprised that he even knew of the city.

However, his five-year-old claircognizant knowing was right on target. Many years later he received a scholarship to a college in Manhattan and now lives and works as an artist in New York City.

🪷 Exercise: Differentiating Between 🪷 Intuitive Thoughts and Ego Thoughts

To develop claircognizance and receive thought energy information at will, begin to pay attention to your everyday thoughts. As you do this, notice their quality and look for clues as to their origin. Do they fit the description of a psychic thought, or do they embody more of the characteristics of a self-generated ego thought? This simple practice encourages and allows for claircognizant awareness to emerge.

Here is a simple format to guide you through the process of increasing your awareness of psychic thoughts.

To begin, find a quiet place, get comfortable, and begin to breathe cleansing breaths. Inhale a deep and relaxing breath and exhale any stress or tension through the out-breath. As you do this, listen within and continue to breathe. You may want to close your eyes to further relax and focus your attention inward. Imagine a bubble of high-vibration white light completely surrounding you.

Notice each thought that emerges and become aware of signs that indicate whether it is a psychic thought, idea, or insight or a self-generated one.

Psychic thoughts do not invoke emotion, desire, or stress. They are not linear, one thought after another, but are concise, even-toned, and matter-of-fact. Psychic thoughts are often subtle and not as intrusive or attention-getting as self-generated thoughts. They are a quiet, still knowing.

When a thought emerges that you feel may be a psychic thought, write it down. Do not overthink it and try to make sense of it. Just write it down and continue to breathe and remain attentive. If your mind begins to wander, pay attention to your breath.

If you feel as if you are not receiving many psychic thoughts, or if the thoughts you are receiving do not necessarily feel as if they are psychic in nature, continue to breathe and listen. Eventually psychic thought messages will begin to flow in. Be patient and let go of your expectations as to what kind of information you will receive. It will likely not feel earth-shattering. Remember that psychic thoughts tend to be quiet and nonintrusive.

Many psychic thoughts are precognitive and provide information about future events, issues, and concerns. However, they may not feel significant and may make sense only when something occurs that confirms the message.

If you begin to feel overwhelmed with thoughts and energy information, focus on your breath and ask within to slow down the process. When you are attentive and open to receiving psychic energy information, you may be flooded with thoughts and insights.

If this happens, give space for all of your thoughts to surface, one after another, and be patient. As you allow them to surface, they will dissipate. Once the random thoughts begin to slow down, listen and write down the psychic thoughts. Don't try to ignore and push self-generated thoughts down. Just notice them without focusing on them and they will begin to dissipate.

Eventually you will be able to better identify psychic thoughts from random thinking. As you notice, pay attention, and act on the direction of psychic thoughts, they will intensify and increase.

Clairaudience

Clairaudience is the psychic ability to hear energy information. Clairaudient thoughts may sound and feel like your own inner voice. Only rarely do they sound as if they are coming from someone else or an outer source. We all talk to ourselves. Sometimes our self-talk is spoken aloud, but usually we talk to ourselves silently and inwardly. Just as some thoughts are self-generated and some thoughts embody psychic energy information, some of our inner self-talk is ego-based and some of what we inwardly hear contains psychic energy information.

Clairaudient messages are never negative, judgmental, or critical of who we are or of others. They also do not put us on a pedestal and tell us that we are better or more worthy than others. These kinds of thoughts and messages are from the ego and the unconscious. Instead, like claircognizant thoughts, clairaudient messages are subtle, even-toned, and informative. They are positive and affirmative and lead to our highest good. Clairaudient messages may be personal and lovingly guide us through our day-to-day affairs. For instance, they may whisper to us to avoid certain situations or people or inform us of what route to take to a destination or what kinds of food to eat. Looking out for our best interests in every area of our lives, clairaudient thoughts can help us to feel watched over and taken care of.

Clairaudient and claircognizant thoughts are often intertwined and occur simultaneously. It may be difficult at times to differentiate between the two, and it is not necessary or important that you do so, as they complement and reinforce one another.

🌼 Exercise: How to Receive 🌼 Claircognizant and Clairaudient Messages

This exercise empowers you to use claircognizance and clairaudience to gain insight and guidance into a particular issue or area of concern. It also helps you to further understand the difference between psychic thoughts and self-generated ones.

To begin, choose an area of your life that you would like to psychically tune in to. For instance, relationships, career, finances, or spiritual guidance all work well. It is best not to begin with an area that is too philosophical or a question that is too specific. This exercise is focused on helping you strengthen your mental intuition and become more familiar with the process of receiving energy information through claircognizant and clairaudient thoughts.

Once you decide on an issue or area of concern, write it down. Think about this issue and write everything that comes to mind with the following questions:

In relation to your issue or area of concern, what kind of energy information would you like to receive? What are your concerns about this area of your life? What are your desires, hopes, and expectations surrounding your question? Do you have any fears or stress about this issue?

Write down everything that comes to you. This step may not seem essential or worthwhile and you may want to skip it, but please don't. Gaining an awareness of your personal biases, desires, and expectations will help you to be able to discern and receive psychic information, feelings, thoughts, and sensations.

Once you feel that you have written down the thoughts, concerns, feelings, and expectations you have about this area or issue, begin to relax. Breathe long, deep, relaxing breaths and exhale any stress or tension. You may want to close your eyes to further relax. Imagine a bubble of high-vibration white light completely surrounding you. When you are ready, focus your awareness on the area or question of concern. Continue to breathe, relax, and focus inwardly.

Listen within to your thoughts, and identify those that may contain energy information. Pay attention to the still, small inner voice. Clairaudient thoughts will most likely sound like your own inner voice, as if you are talking to yourself. Only rarely do they sound as if they are coming from an outer source. Take your time and listen. The tone of a clairaudient or claircognizant thought will be persistent, even-toned, and repetitive. Intuitive thoughts do not go into a lengthy explanation or try to convince you of something or argue against your desires and hopes. They are concise, simple, and repetitive. You might hear one word or phrase or receive a spontaneous insight through a sense of knowing.

As you listen and discern ego thoughts from psychic ones, be patient. Your mind may flood with thoughts, and you may feel overwhelmed and begin to overanalyze them. Pay attention and be alert to the common signs that indicate claircognizant and clairaudient thoughts. When self-generated thoughts emerge, guide yourself back to the breath, taking long, deep inhales and exhales. When you receive what you believe to be a claircognizant or clairaudient message, write it down. Don't overthink it and try to fully understand what you receive. Then turn your focus inward, breathe, and become receptive.

When you feel that you have received all the psychic thoughts that you can at this time, pause and ask within if there is anything else you need to know. Listen, be patient, and continue to breathe and relax. Write down anything else that you receive.

Take a deep breath, come back to a normal state of consciousness, and review the energy information that you intuited. Did you receive any new insights or unexpected guidance? Did you have an aha moment of insight? Do you feel that you can trust and act on the thoughts that you intuited? Write down your impressions.

Repeat this exercise often. You can use it to intuit useful energy information about personal issues or experiment and tune in to more global issues, such as a political situation or future event. This will help you get a better sense of the differences between tuning in to issues that personally affect you and tuning in to issues where you may have more objectivity.

The more you practice this exercise, the easier it will become to elicit claircognizant and clairaudient psychic information when you need and desire it most.

Telepathy

Telepathy is the transmission of thoughts between two individuals or between an individual and a group. Through telepathy it is also possible to communicate with another's higher mind. We naturally use telepathy in our relationships. It is so common to know what a loved one is thinking and tune in to their thoughts that we tend not to view it as psychic.

Telepathy is also commonly used as a research tool to study the validity of psychic awareness. Those with a high degree of mental intuition innately understand and are comfortable with telepathy, as it involves the transference and receptivity of thought energy between individuals. Many of the scientific studies of psychic abilities are conducted by mental intuitives. They tend to enjoy researching and testing the authenticity of psychic phenomena. For this reason, telepathy has become a standard testing model in scientific circles for proving or disproving psychic abilities.

Zener cards have been used since the early 1930s to develop telepathy and to conduct telepathic research. They were designed by psychologist Karl Zener and were used by parapsychologist J. B. Rhine at Duke University. Similar in size to playing cards, each Zener card has a specific symbol printed on it. Zener cards can be used not only to research and test telepathic and clairvoyant ability but also to help develop it.

In research studies with Zener cards, two people sit opposite each other. One individual picks a card from the deck and forms a mental thought image of the symbol printed on it. This thought message is then sent to the other individual, who receives the thought message.

✿ Exercise: Developing Mental ✿ Telepathy with a Partner

In this exercise you can practice developing mental telepathy through the kind of method often used in research studies.

This exercise requires a willing partner. To send and receive a telepathic message may take a few minutes to fifteen minutes or more. After this amount of time, the ability to clear the mind and focus diminishes. When you begin to develop telepathy with a partner, you may want to have a timer set at ten to fifteen minutes and then end the session at that time.

Designate who will be the conductor and who will be the receiver. Then decide what kind of message you are going to send. Items that are good for mental telepathic development and transmission include such things as a name or short phrase or the name of a state, town, song, or movie. Other possibilities include a specific time, a number, or a calendar date and year. You can also use one card out of a deck of playing cards or a tarot card. If you are the conductor, choose the one item or subject that you will telepathically transmit to your partner before you begin.

You do not have to be physically close to the receiver to practice telepathy. It is possible to send and receive telepathic messages to another at a distance. However, when beginning to develop telepathy, it may be helpful for you and a partner to sit facing each other. If you have a high degree of physical intuition, you can hold hands or touch knees.

Before you begin, talk with your partner and pick a sign that will signal your readiness to send a message and alert the receiver to receive it. For instance, when you are ready to send a telepathic message, you can tap your partner's knee a couple times, or if you are not physically close, you can put one finger in the air. If you are doing this by phone, you can simply say that you are ready.

To send and receive telepathic messages, it is crucial to relax and clear the mind. While you and your partner sit and face each other, take a few minutes to breathe long, deep cleansing breaths and exhale any stress or tension. As you breathe, allow any thoughts or emotions to surface and then release them through the exhale. Continue to breathe cleansing breaths. As you do this, imagine a protective white-light bubble that surrounds both you and your partner. Imagine that within this bubble the vibration of psychic energy intensifies.

If you are the sender, form a mental thought message of the item that you are sending to your partner. You can inwardly speak the name of the item or think it. When you are ready to send the message, signal the receiver. Continue to focus on the mental thought and project this thought to the mind of the receiver. An alternate technique for sending a thought message is to imagine a white-light tube of energy that extends from your mind to the receiver's mind, then imagine sending the thought message through this tube of white-light energy.

If you are the receiver, wait for the signal from your partner. While you are waiting, breathe long, deep breaths and relax. Allow any thoughts and emotions to surface and then release them through the exhale. Once you receive the sign that the sender is ready, signal back with the same sign when your mind is clear and you are ready to receive. Take your time, continue to breathe, and stay in a relaxed and receptive mode. You may receive the message immediately or it may take more time. Become aware of everything that you receive without judging or rejecting anything. Keep in mind the qualities of a psychic thought: even-toned, repetitive, and matter-of-fact.

When you feel that you have received all you can, give your partner the agreed-upon signal that you have completed receiving. Before relaying what you have experienced, write down your impressions. Sometimes when we write down our psychic impressions immediately after receiving them, more psychic energy information surfaces and we gain additional clarity.

Once you have written down what you received, share this with your partner. Try not to judge the experience as being either right or wrong. Instead, review the process and get a sense of your intuitive strengths and weaknesses. At times the receiver will intuit the sender's feelings or thoughts instead of the intended message. Be open to exploring any information other than the intended message.

Higher Mind Telepathic Communication

Telepathy is a common form of communication between people who know each other well. Our thoughts intermingle with others' thoughts on a daily basis, and we rarely notice or pay much attention to it. As you become more aware of telepathic communication, it is possible to focus on an individual and receive their thoughts and further communicate with them. This is possible to do with those you have a close relationship with as well as those you do not know well or at all, as telepathic communication speaks to another's higher mind. The higher mind is connected to our soul and is free of the influences of the personality and ego self. In this free and open state of nonjudgment and acceptance, the higher mind communicates our core truth. Spiritual teachers, guides, and gurus often impart wisdom and knowledge to others through this kind of telepathy.

❀ Exercise: Telepathic Communication ❀ with Another's Higher Mind

To practice higher mind telepathy, find a quiet space and become quiet. Take a few deep breaths and relax. Imagine a bubble of high-vibration protective white light completely surrounding you. When you feel calm, imagine an image of the person you would like to communicate with and say their name. This can be someone in the physical body or someone in the spirit realm. You may not see a clear image of the person, and this is fine—the exercise still works.

Send a thought message to this person asking permission to communicate with their higher mind. Continue to breathe and relax.

Ask this person a question through a thought message. Make it a simple question asking them about their thoughts regarding a specific area, issue, or topic. Think and focus on the message, then imagine sending it to the person's higher mind.

Breathe, be patient, wait, and listen. The intuitive thoughts you receive will most likely feel as if they are your own. Remember, an intuitive thought is an even-toned, matter-of-fact, concise statement. At times they may be subtle and repetitive. However, when another knowingly sends you a telepathic thought, it may be louder, stronger, and more persistent.

Once you have received a telepathic thought, you can continue to ask questions, one at a time. Then be patient and wait for a response. If you have waited patiently for a response and do not receive one, it may be that the person you are tuning in to does not want to communicate. This is through no fault of your own. We all have free will, and some decline to intuitively communicate. If you are not sure what is happening, try communicating with someone else.

It is best to keep these sessions short to reduce confusion and mental exhaustion. To keep the intuitive connection strong and reliable, it is best to receive just a few thought messages and, if needed, continue in another session.

Once you have completed this telepathic conversation, send the person you have been communicating with a white ball of cleansing love energy. Imagine white light filling the person's mind and body. Then imagine a pure ray of white light filling your mind and discharging any thoughts, feelings, and energy that are not in your highest good.

Mental psychic awareness tunes in to day-to-day concerns and issues and empowers us to create and live better lives. Through it we can receive personal guidance and insight into everyday challenges. Mental intuition can inspire cutting-edge and valuable inventions and provide ideas and solutions to long-standing problems. Grounded and pragmatic, mental psychic skills tend to be straightforward and easy to put into practice in every area of our lives.

CHAPTER 4

The Psychic Heart (Emotional Intuitive Type)

Emotional intuition is the natural heart-centered intuitive awareness of emotions, feelings, and emotional energy. One of the most common ways that emotional intuition emerges is through intuitively feeling another's emotions and feelings unknowingly. To varying degrees, most of us do this, especially with those we love and care for.

For instance, have you ever asked someone how they are feeling and their reply of *fine* or *good* does not ring true to you? Despite their protests, you can feel their grief, fear, or stress. Have you ever felt a heaviness in your heart, yet there is no known reason to be feeling this way? Then soon after the onset of these feelings you get a call from a loved one who shares a recent disappointment with you. In a similar way, do you ever feel heart-centered and positive only to discover that someone close to you is in the midst of a joyful experience?

One of the differences between emotional intuition and simply knowing someone well enough to know how they feel involves time and space. With emotional intuition, we do not need to be physically close to another or know of their current situation or circumstances to intuitively feel their emotions and feelings. Even if we have not recently spoken to a friend or family member and they are hundreds of miles away, we may still intuitively feel their feelings.

It is also possible to intuitively feel the emotions of those we do not personally know. During times of national or global tragic events, we may emotionally absorb the grief and fear of another or a group even though they are thousands of miles away. We may also intuitively feel the uplifting and positive emotions of others during celebratory times. The energy of joy and love travels quickly. The universal law of like attract likes applies to intuitive receptivity. Positivity is an intuitive magnet that attracts more positive energy to you, while negativity intuitively attracts negative energy.

COMMON CHARACTERISTICS OF AN EMOTIONAL INTUITIVE

Those with a high degree of emotional intuition often share common characteristics. Most are highly sensitive and empathetic, especially toward those who are in pain or suffering in some way. With a desire to support, help, and be of service to others, they may believe that love can heal all. It is not surprising that those with a high degree of emotional intuition also tend to be emotionally intelligent. Common traits of emotional intelligence include such things as the ability to be aware of, communicate, and express emotions as well as the ability to skillfully help others to process their emotions. Not only can an emotional intuitive feel another's emotions, but they are also able to reduce another's emotional stress and worries through a kind of emotional psychic intervention. They often do this unknowingly by sending pure waves of unconditional healing love energy to those whom they intuit are in need.

Because an emotional intuitive is naturally attuned to others' emotional energy, they may find that they are continually in or getting out of intense emotional relationships. Those with a high degree of emotional intuition may also have a longing to experience perfect love through union with another or through experiencing an inner state of mystical divine love.

The raw openness through which those with a high degree of emotional intuition intuit can leave them feeling vulnerable and overly sensitive. Stressful environments, disagreements, witnessing another's suffering, or being in the midst of angry or unhappy people can leave them feeling exhausted and overwhelmed. Many emotional intuitives have no inner shield or protective boundary and unknowingly feel and intuit both positive and toxic emotional energy, often to their detriment.

Due to the magnitude and volume of emotions that an emotional intuitive absorbs and feels, many suffer from free-floating stress and anxiety. Because of this, some withdraw from social interactions or situations in an attempt to avoid emotional overload. However, because they are intuitively connected to emotional energy, this is rarely effective. Even when sitting alone in a room, they can still absorb the emotional energy of others or situations. Some emotional intuitives unconsciously harden their heart in an attempt to protect themselves or intuitively try to shut off their emotional receptivity. When the pain, grief, and stress of others and the world becomes too much to bear, they attempt to shield themselves by withdrawing and closing their heart. However, this is not an effective solution and often creates a sense of inner emptiness and unhealthy detachment. An emotional intuitive needs the vibrations of love almost as much as they need oxygen to survive. When they close their heart, they can no longer feel and benefit from the rich waves of pure love that flow through them.

While some emotional intuitives shut down, there are others who reside at the other end of the spectrum. They are almost addicted to the ups and downs of emotional energy and crave emotionally charged interactions. These emotional intuitives often have a fair amount of drama in their lives. Their relationships may be marked by the extremes of love, hate, jealousy, passion, and other intense emotional states.

Emotional energy can be seductive and powerful. For some it is almost like a drug that they feel they need in order to feel alive and full of energy. Without powerful emotional experiences they can become depressed, tired, and anxious. Yet the constant craving for emotional intensity can eventually lead to emotional burnout and even physical illness.

Intuition as a Feeling

Emotional intuition surfaces primarily through the heart. Listening to our heart is not the same as allowing our emotions, feelings, and desires to dictate our perceptions and behavior. Underneath everyday feelings and emotions resides the wisdom of the intuitive heart. Beneficial guidance and insights that can help us through the everyday ups and downs of life flow from the heart, and when we listen to and trust our heart, we never regret it.

A good place to start developing and refining heart-centered intuitive awareness is to become aware of the emotions and feelings that you experience on a daily basis. Although our emotional energy is multilayered, we tend to be most conscious of our current and recent emotions and what we want to be feeling. We are usually aware of how we feel toward the people we regularly interact with, and we tend to be in touch with the emotions that we generate in our present condition. Our feelings guide us in developing our likes and dislikes and our preferences and assist us in making choices and decisions.

We are always feeling something. Our emotions are a part of us and are so important to our well-being that we can never not be feeling. We may be confused or not know how we feel, but emotional energy is still circulating and moving though us. When we experience emotions that are uncomfortable, such as anger, fear, and grief, we often repress and ignore them. Yet they are still a part of us and continue to have power in our lives. Awareness of our daily emotions and feelings increases our self-awareness and promotes positive feelings of well-being. A stronger connection to and appreciation of the wide range of our emotions can also help us to better identify and understand our intuited emotions.

To develop emotional intuition, it is essential to become aware of the differences between emotions that are self-generated from our ego and personality self and emotional energy that has been absorbed from others.

Emotions and feelings that come from the ego are usually reactive and protective and are connected to what is happening in our lives, our personal preferences, and our past experiences. They are intertwined with our thoughts and beliefs and what we encounter on a day-to-day basis and may be triggered by another or a particular situation. They vary in intensity and come and go.

When developing emotional intuition, it is important to be aware of our ego-centered feelings and emotions without trying to rid ourselves of them. This awareness aids us in identifying and separating our personal feelings from intuited emotions and feelings.

Emotions Intuitively Absorbed from Others

While it is important to feel and be aware of our self-generated emotions, it is also crucial to be aware of the feelings and emotions that we intuit from others. When we unknowingly absorb the emotional energy of others or of events, it can be confusing. Waking during the night feeling intense emotions that do not make any sense or suddenly feeling a wave of sadness or grief may leave us wondering. Feeling emotionally overwhelmed and not knowing why we feel this way or suddenly being worried or concerned about another for no known reason can be disconcerting and even have us questioning our sanity.

Day-to-day life for those with a primary and innate mode of intuiting through their emotions may at times feel like an emotional rollercoaster. If you have a high degree of emotional intuition, you may not be aware of the degree to which you intuit another's emotional energy. Because you were born with this innate sensitivity, you may not always be able to distinguish between your own feelings and the feelings that you have absorbed from others. When young, many emotional intuitives become the emotional barometer for the family and unconsciously try to balance and harmonize the emotional energy within the home. They may be viewed as overly sensitive and moody and may express the bottled-up and repressed emotions of other family members.

While our self-generated emotions and feelings can help us increase our self-awareness and make good decisions and choices, emotions that have been absorbed from others are not as beneficial. We cannot process and gain personal insight from intuited emotions. While they can help us understand and develop our intuition, intuited emotions do not provide us with insight into personal preferences, issues, and needs.

For instance, I gave a reading to a woman named Sara, who suffers from depression. A heavy shroud seemed to weigh her down. She was physically tired and had no enthusiasm for the activities that had once brought her joy. Antidepressants were not effective, and therapy and other alternative treatments brought only minimal relief. When I first psychically tuned in to Sara's energy, it was almost as if I were reading two people. I could feel Sara's emotions, and intertwined with them was her mother's emotional energy.

When I shared this with Sara, she didn't argue or dismiss this unusual idea. Instead, she told me that her mother had experienced a difficult childhood, and as far back as she could remember her mother had seemed unhappy, tired, and sad. In an attempt to help her mother, Sara thought that maybe she was absorbing her depressive emotions and had been doing this for a long time. However, this intuitive strategy was not working. Her mother was still depressed, and Sara was burdened with these same feelings and emotions that she couldn't do anything about.

You cannot change emotions that are not yours, and you cannot take another's emotions from them. However well-meaning your intentions are, when you intuitively absorb another's emotions, you only feel what they feel.

The Power of Love

Once you become aware of your emotions and feelings and the emotional energy that you are absorbing from others and the environment, you can release and let go of those emotions that are creating stress or are toxic to your mind, body, and spirit. As you do this, it becomes easier to tune in to the intuitive heart and further develop and use the psychic abilities of emotional intuition in beneficial ways.

The heart is the psychic center for emotional intuition and is your connection to divine and unconditional love. Love in its highest form is positive vital life force energy. This kind of love elevates our consciousness and shields us from lower toxic energies. When your intuition is aligned with the pure vibration of love, you are protected from the harsh effects of negative and potentially damaging emotional energy. Guided by the wisdom of your heart, you cease absorbing others' energy and instead become a force of positivity and healing. Psychic love is healing and compassionate awareness. It is a calming balm that allows us to be a source of healing for others.

If you have a high degree of emotional intuition, it is essential that you open and connect to the higher vibrations of love. We all need love. If you intuit primarily through emotional energy, the need is even greater. The higher vibration of unconditional and divine love restores and creates balance and harmony. It strengthens and protects you from the potentially debilitating effects of toxic and caustic emotional energy. It helps to soothe the effects of emotional sensitivity and enables you to intuit others' emotions without absorbing them. Love empowers you to embrace your intuitive gifts and use them in life-enhancing ways.

🪷 Exercise: Receiving High-Vibration 🪷 Love Energy

This exercise helps you to release toxic and negative emotions that you may have unknowingly intuitively absorbed from others and the environment. It also empowers you to release and heal any personal repressed emotional wounds and blocks. As you open your heart to the nurturing and enlightened energy of divine love, a cleansing flow of high-vibration energy releases toxic emotional energy and fuels psychic awareness.

To begin, get comfortable and breathe long, deep cleansing breaths. Imagine breathing white-light energy down through the top of your head. Send this energy through your body and exhale any stress or tension through the out-breath. Continue to breathe cleansing and clearing breath, releasing any stress or tension through the exhale. Imagine a protective white-light bubble of high-vibration energy completely surrounding you.

When you feel relaxed, imagine breathing white-light energy down through the top of your head, then send this breath into your heart. Feel your heart open as you continue to breathe in this way. If you have any difficult or repressed emotions that you are holding on to, allow them to surface. Continue to breathe into your heart and feel any emotions that emerge. As you ac-knowledge and feel your emotions, even the difficult and confus-ing ones, they release and dissipate. You do not need to know the origin of the feelings or why you are feeling them. If you find yourself beginning to overthink, go back to the breath. Inhale white light, sending the breath through the heart.

Feel your heart expand as the emotions surface. Breathe and let go of them. Allow your heart to become lighter and fully open. Ask for the energy of pure divine love to flow through you. Continue to breathe and imagine that you are connected to the highest form of love. Feel your heart expand.

Stay in the vibration of love as long as possible. Move this love energy through your entire body. As divine love moves through you, repressed, negative, or toxic emotions dissipate.

Breathe and feel the love that is within your heart. This love is timeless and connects you to higher benevolent forces. Listen to your intuitive heart. It has a message for you. Remain open and receptive.

When you feel complete, imagine that the white light of love is completely surrounding you. This love allows only positive and life-giving energy to enter your mind, body, and spirit.

Repeat this meditation as often as needed to release repressed or difficult emotional energy and the emotions and feelings that you may have absorbed from others or situations. You can also use this meditation before or after psychic development exercises to ensure that you are connecting to the highest vibrations of love and to release any energy that you may have unknowingly ab-sorbed. Make it a daily practice to invoke and surround yourself with the white light of love and protection to protect yourself from harmful energy.

CLAIREMPATHY

Clairempathy is the ability to psychically feel and become aware of another's past, present, and future emotions and emotional energy. Through clairempathy, which empowers you to feel and express compassion, you can detect repressed and toxic emotions and heal emotional wounds.

Empathy is the sensitive awareness of another's feelings, pain, and suffering. A conscious act of sympathy and caring, empathy helps you to form positive connections and relationships with others. Most people are born with this innate ability and are socialized from a young age to express concern and support for others who are experiencing emotional difficulties and challenges. Clairempathy is the superpower of empathy. It allows you to be aware of another's emotional energy even when the person is hundreds of miles or more away and to be a channel of divine love and healing.

Like most psychic skills, clairempathy often occurs spontaneously. For instance, my friend Laura was driving home from work one evening when a wave of sadness came over her. However, there was nothing in particular in her life that she was sad about. As she continued the drive home, her friend Meg came to mind and she intuitively realized that these feelings were connected to her. Laura knew that Meg had recently interviewed for what she believed was the job of her dreams. In this moment of sadness, Laura intuitively felt that Meg had not gotten the job. Her heart filled with compassion and love for Meg, who was having a difficult time in other areas of her life as well.

Not all of the feelings that we absorb from others and the environment are painful, distressing, or toxic. Clairempathy also enables us to feel the positive and joyful feelings of others and can be an uplifting and energizing experience. For instance, some political and charismatic leaders and spiritual and religious teachers can have this effect on others. When we hear them speak, read their writings, and follow their teachings, we absorb the energy of their love and inspiration. We also intuitively absorb the positive energy of others. We often do this randomly and without our conscious awareness. When we open our heart to love and positivity, they find their way in.

EMOTIONAL HEALING

With clairempathy comes the innate ability to help, comfort, and heal others. Quite often this gift goes unacknowledged and operates on an unconscious level. When we do not embrace our innate soul gifts, they can surface in confusing and unhealthy ways.

Those with a high degree of emotional intuition often unknowingly absorb others' difficult and painful emotions and feelings in an attempt to alleviate their suffering. Many loving and compassionate people do not recognize their innate intuitive gifts and unknowingly take on others' burdens and emotional stress and find that they continually feel overwhelmed and exhausted.

For instance, I recently did a reading for Claudia, a cosmetologist who has a busy hairstyling practice. Like many people who work in this industry, she is a natural healer. When I began our session, I could feel Claudia's exhaustion as an energetic heaviness in her body and energy field. As I intuitively looked for the cause, I became aware of her emotional intuitive nature and her desire to help others and alleviate their stress. As she washed, cut, and styled her clients' hair, she compassionately listened while they shared their difficulties and challenges. However, she did more than just listen. Because of her sensitivity and innate clairempathic ability, she was also absorbing their burdens. Her clients' emotional difficulties and stress clung to her energy field like a heavy shroud.

When I told Claudia that her exhaustion was in part due to her tendency to intuitively absorb others' problems and emotional difficulties, she agreed.

"I thought this might be happening but would then doubt myself. It seemed a bit far-fetched to believe that someone else's energy could affect me so much," she said. "But last week I had an experience that made me realize just how much others' emotions can drain me. I went in to work feeling well rested and full of energy. When my first client, a woman I have been working with for years, sat down in my chair, I could literally feel the energy draining out of me. Her daughter has leukemia and the whole family is suffering. My heart goes out to all of them. When she began to talk about her daughter's recent medical treatments, my heart opened and I wanted to help. I could almost feel their pain being absorbed into my body."

Becoming aware of the tendency to intuitively absorb others' energy and further developing the psychic ability of clairempathy acts as a protective energetic shield. Clairempathy is not simply feeling emotions and being aware of emotional energy; it is also the gateway for the healing higher vibrations of divine love to flow through you.

HELPING OTHERS WITHOUT HURTING YOURSELF

If you find yourself feeling physically and emotionally tired for no known reason or feeling confusing emotions that make no sense, you may be absorbing others' emotional energy. Feeling disoriented, exhausted, or ill during or after emotionally charged situations or when you are in the company of others who are experiencing emotional challenges is an indication that you have absorbed difficult or toxic energy from others or your environment.

❋ Exercise: Letting Go of ❋ Intuited Toxic Emotions

If you suspect that you have intuitively absorbed the difficult or stressful emotions or feelings of others and you are ready to release them, try this exercise.

Sit quietly and become aware of your feelings and emotions. As you allow your emotions to surface, name them. Being able to identify and name our emotions and feelings is not always easy, but it helps us to better understand them and increases our self-awareness.

As you focus on the most intense emotions and name them, ask if these emotions are yours or someone else's.

The answer will come as an intuitive feeling, insight, or awareness. Trust what you receive. Self-generated emotions feel intense, raw, powerful, and potent. You may want to stuff them down, and they may invoke memories or thoughts about a situation or another person. You feel them.

When you unknowingly intuit and absorb others' emotions, you may feel detached, numb, or confused. You are aware of the emotions, but they may feel heavy, muted, and confusing. Their origin is a mystery, and you may not be sure where the emotional force is coming from. There may not be anything you are currently experiencing that you can relate them to.

To process and transform self-generated feelings, fully feel them. Although it may be difficult and uncomfortable to allow their full intensity to surface, they will disperse and release as you feel them.

You do not need to understand or figure out why you are feeling what you are feeling. Simply accept your feelings and feel them. Be gentle and compassionate toward yourself. Allow the feelings to surface and at the same time become aware that love is present. Ask for the presence and power of the pure energy of love to soothe you as you feel and let go of the difficult emotions.

If the feelings or emotions that you are experiencing have been absorbed from others, ask them to return to their source—not in their present form, but transformed through the energy of love. Breathe into your heart and imagine it opening. Feel love flow through you. Send this love to the person, group, or situation that generated the feelings or emotions.

If you suspect that you may have absorbed the emotional energy of more than one person, you can repeat this process. Ask the feeling or emotion to return to its source, and send high-vibration love to the person or group that generated it. Feel the power of love flow through you, and trust that it is truly helping and healing others.

It is not necessary to know whose feelings you are feeling in order to help another. Just ask that this feeling go back to its source as positive energy.

Protecting Yourself

Once you embrace your emotional intuition and become aware that at times you may unknowingly absorb others' emotional energy, you can take steps to protect yourself and become a positive force of healing.

Make it a daily practice to become aware of your feelings and the emotional energy of your environment. If you are in an emotionally stressful situation or with others who may be experiencing emotional difficulties, take a moment to shield yourself. You can do this by simply imagining a white-light bubble of love energy completely surrounding you. Intend and imagine that this bubble of light allows you to absorb only positive energy that is in your highest good. Become aware of your desire to help alleviate others' suffering, and ask to be a channel through which divine love, healing, and compassion flow to them. If there is someone in particular whom you would like to help, imagine that divine healing energy uplifts and heals that person.

You can also ask for the angels or another divine presence to be with you and act as an intermediary. Years ago I began to become overwhelmed by the suffering and pain I felt with my clients and in the company of others. In a moment of emotional exhaustion, I looked up to the skies and asked for help. I suddenly felt the presence of Mother Mary. Even though I had not previously looked to her for support in this way, I felt uplifted and free of emotional burdens in her presence. I still feel her with me when I am with others who are in need. The suffering and difficult emotions of others bypass me and easily move into her vibration, where all is transformed into pure love energy.

How to Prevent Others from Absorbing Our Negative or Toxic Emotions

Do ever wonder if others may be intuitively absorbing your less-than-positive feelings and moods? In the same way that you intuit another's negative or toxic emotions, it is likely that others are intuitively affected by yours.

On a daily basis we all experience a range of emotions. We may wake up feeling excited about a new project at work. Then after sitting in traffic or spilling coffee on ourselves, we may show up at the office feeling grumpy and frustrated. Emotions and feelings come and go, the pleasant and uplifting as well as the angry and sad.

One of the best ways to ensure that others do not intuitively absorb your emotions and feelings is to acknowledge and own them. It is our unconscious and repressed emotions that have the most power to negatively impact others. When we take responsibility for our emotions, we can feel and process them.

Journaling, talking to a trusted friend or counselor, and meditating are other helpful tools that empower us to understand and let go of negative or toxic emotions. Accepting our feelings, feeling them, and having love and compassion for ourselves is usually all we need do to ensure that others do not intuitively soak in our less-than-pleasant emotions.

When we are suffering from a significant loss, grieving, struggling with depression, or working through past repressed emotions, the process of emotional healing may take longer. However, you are not necessarily adversely affecting others just because you feel lousy. As long as you are not denying your emotions or wanting and expecting others to take care of you and take on your feelings, you can still be a positive influence. Your courage and strength in accepting your feelings and processing them can be a valuable example and light the way for others when they are struggling.

We cannot control the actions and intuitive receptivity of others. There will likely be times when we are emotionally struggling and another may choose to detach from us or avoid our company. This does not necessarily mean that we are not taking responsibility for our feelings or that we are a negative influence. The other person may be dealing with their own issues and feeling emotionally vulnerable or intuitively sensitive and overwhelmed, and just need alone time.

🪷 Exercise: Meditation to 🪷 Release Your Toxic Emotions

This meditation can help you release and let go of negative emotions. Even if you are not able to release all of the negative or difficult emotions that you feel in one session, you have still made progress. It may take concentrated effort over a few days or weeks to feel our difficult emotions and let them go. Eventually you will feel lighter and more positive. Clearing our emotional energy of toxic emotions also boosts and increases our intuitive receptivity.

Begin by taking a deep breath, then relax and exhale any stress or tension. Inhale white-light energy down through the top of the head and send the energy of the breath down through the body. Exhale any negativity or pent-up emotions. Continue to breathe in this way for a few minutes.

When you feel relaxed, move your awareness through the body, starting at the top of the head. Become aware of any confusing or negative feelings and emotions anywhere in your body. Breathe into these emotions. As difficult as it may be, allow yourself to feel them.

Imagine that the emotion has a voice and can speak to you. What would it be saying? Listen and continue to breathe, feel the emotion, and exhale it. As you allow your feelings to surface and acknowledge them, they release.

Continue this process until the emotion or feeling begins to dissipate. Once the emotional intensity subsides, imagine breathing white-light energy down through the top of the head. Continue to inhale and allow white light to collect in your heart and solar plexus. Imagine that with every breath, this energy becomes stronger and expands throughout your entire body. As your body fills with white light, imagine that it forms an orb that completely surrounds you.

This white-light orb allows you to intuitively absorb only what is in your highest good. At the same time, it continues to help you to release negative or toxic emotions.

CLAIRSENTIENCE

Clairsentience is the ability to feel energy information and is another psychic skill of emotional intuition. On a daily basis we all have spontaneous episodes where we receive energy information in this way.

For instance, despite a lack of evidence, have you ever had a feeling that a plan or project would be a success and this feeling proved to be spot on? Are your feelings about how a future event will unfold generally spot on? Do you ever feel like you can trust someone, or are you ever wary of another without any factual evidence? Have you ever not listened to your feelings about something or someone and then later regretted it? These are common ways that clairsentience guides us and provides insights and information.

The two different types of clairsentience are physical and emotional. Physical clairsentience is an intuitive awareness that is felt in the body, usually in the solar plexus and gut or through a tingling up and down the spine or arms. Emotional clairsentience is heart-centered awareness. To be clairempathic is to intuit and feel the emotions and feelings of others without being in their presence and without conscious knowledge of their circumstances. To be clairsentient is to intuit energy information through pure heart awareness, unclouded by feelings and emotions.

The feeling energy of clairsentience is not the same as our self-generated emotions. The feelings associated with clairsentience are more neutral and may at times be in conflict with our personal emotions and desires. Instead of being reactive and ego-based, they emanate from within as a certainty or feeling of clear and sure awareness. Emanating from the heart, clairsentient feelings are intuitive signals that broadcast energy information and guidance.

For instance, from a young age, Glenda, a client of mine, had always felt an affinity for animals. In her youth she had a dog and cat, but after moving to the city she was pet-free. The condo where she lived did not allow them, and with her busy work schedule she knew it would not be fair to leave a dog or cat alone for long hours.

One morning on her way to work on the subway, she read an article about a woman who had started an animal rescue farm a couple hours north of the city where she lived. As she read of the pigs, sheep, horses, and other animals that now found shelter on this farm, her heart opened.

I would love to be doing this, she thought. However, her busy life went on as usual and she forgot about the article. Several months later the animal rescue farm that she had read about was featured on the local news. The owner was asking for donations and help as the need for her services grew. Again, Glenda felt a powerful feeling of connectedness stir her heart. However, this time she felt that she was meant to be involved with the farm. The feeling was so clear and strong that she could not dismiss or deny it.

The next morning Glenda called the owner of the animal rescue, and the following weekend she went up for a visit. After a couple of years of going back and forth and helping with the animals once a month, she decided to move north and become a partner with the owner. Her heart told her that this was the right decision, and she never questioned it or regretted listening to it.

Emotional Relationship Radar

The feelings of clairsentience often provide valuable information for and about others. One of the most common ways that we naturally use clairsentience is in our relationships. Intuitive feelings upon first meeting or being introduced to another are especially important to pay attention to. You most likely have experienced this yourself. For instance, have you ever met someone and felt instantly comfortable with them? Alternatively, have you ever felt uneasy and apprehensive when meeting another even though there was no known reason to be feeling this way? Do your feelings ever warn you about another or an event?

This happened to me several years ago while walking to a gazebo with my children in a secluded section of a park. My feelings of enjoying the day with my kids was interrupted by a strong feeling of danger and stress. As I got closer to the gazebo I noticed a lone man with his back to me. Although I tried to shake off my feeling of unease, the closer I got to him the more apprehensive I felt. With my two young children in tow, I realized that it was probably a good idea to listen to the feeling. I turned around and headed back to the playground. I will never know what might have happened if I had continued, but the feeling subsided as soon as I acted on it. We are all born with this natural intuitive insight and awareness. Unfortunately, we do not always truly listen to it and trust it.

Clairsentient feelings often let us know when we are meeting or about to meet a potential partner or romantic interest. For instance, have you ever first met someone and felt that you know them? Beyond physical chemistry, the feeling of being drawn to another and the intuitive awareness that someone has come into your life for a reason or purpose comes from the heart and soul.

However, it is important to recognize that when you listen to and act on these feelings, you may not always experience what you expect. People often tell me that they have felt an immediate soul-mate connection with another, but the relationship did not turn out to be the bliss they had hoped for. The feeling of connection that we instantly feel with another is a signal that there is something that this person has to share, teach, or experience with us, but it might not be a long-term or romantic relationship. If you have listened to and acted on the feeling that you were meant to be with another and the relationship did not turn out the way you wanted it to, it does not mean that you made a mistake. Continue to trust your feelings and know that there are important reasons that people are brought into our lives, even if we do not always know or understand what those reasons are.

Precognitive Clairsentience

Clairsentience often manifests as precognition, the psychic ability to intuit future events and manifestations. This may naturally occur as the feeling that you are meant to experience something in particular or the heartfelt awareness of your life purpose. It might also be a feeling that you need to make a life change, pursue a dream, or take action on something that seems contrary to the status quo.

For instance, my friend Sasha and I were born on the same day. With a master's degree in art history, Sasha's dream was to spend time in Italy going from gallery to gallery and soaking in the art and sculpture. When she was in her late twenties she landed a great job at a prestigious museum. It was a surprise to everyone when, after only a year of employment, she quit her job to go to Italy. Her vacation days did not allow much time off and she felt a strong desire to travel. We were all stunned, and more than one of her friends tried to talk her into waiting a few years for this epic trip. But Sasha was determined.

"I feel that I need to go now," she said and never wavered from this feeling.

Sasha spent two wonderful months in Italy seeing and doing all that she had wanted to do. Three months after her return, the car she was driving slid into a telephone pole on an icy road. She died instantly.

I think of Sasha often, and she gives me courage to follow my feelings, as crazy or inconvenient as they sometimes seem to be.

🪷 Exercise: Tuning In to the Intuitive Heart 🪷 Through Clairsentience

Clairsentience can help us to become aware of our deepest soul truth. Underneath our desires and ego-based emotions and feelings, the heart guides us to the people and experiences that are in our highest good.

In this exercise you can practice how to become more aware of heart-centered intuitive guidance.

To begin, think of an issue, condition, or concern that you would like to intuitively receive clarity and guidance on. Sit quietly and breathe. Imagine inhaling white-light cleansing breath and exhale any stress or tension.

Allow your feelings and emotions about this issue to surface.

For instance, you may feel anxious, hopeful, worried, or confused about your current job or relationship. Name the feelings as they surface.

Become aware of your desired outcome. What would you like to have happen? How would you like this concern or condition to be resolved? What would you like to be feeling in relation to this situation? Write down your feelings and responses.

Once you have written down your feelings and emotions surrounding your concern, sit quietly and breathe in cleansing and clearing energy and exhale any stress or tension. Feel the feelings and concerns that you have just written down. This helps to release them.

When you feel relaxed, take a deep breath and send the energy of this breath into your heart. As you exhale, imagine your heart opening. Visualize a high-vibration white-light orb of energy completely surrounding and protecting you from negative influences. Continue to breathe and open your heart and imagine the pure energy of love filling your heart. Feel this love and send it through your body.

Listen to your heart. Underneath the ego emotions and feelings that you have surrounding your issue or concern, the quiet presence of love is speaking to you.

Continue to breathe, open your heart, and listen. Take all the time you need. What is your heart saying to you? What do you feel?

Accept your heart's guidance, however it emerges. You may not intuit a specific outcome or a step-by-step plan of action. However, when you feel and allow the healing power of your heart to flow through you, its energy resolves and transforms your stress and fears. Conditions and difficulties begin to resolve and transform. Continue to listen, and when you are ready, open your eyes and write down your experience.

THE IMPORTANCE OF EMOTIONAL INTUITION

Emotional intuition is so common that we do not always recognize its psychic importance and potential. Emotions can be elusive and transitory. They are constantly changing, and their ability to provide solid insight and guidance may seem to be less effective than other forms of intuition. However, emotional energy is powerful. Our emotions and feelings guide our choices and decisions, dictate our behavior, impact our health, and create a life of happiness or misery. Our unconscious emotions are especially powerful. Emotions that we have stuffed away or are in denial of contribute significantly to what we create and experience on a day-to-day basis. Unhealed grief, anger, or stress impacts our well-being, and until we recognize our core emotions, they create havoc in all areas of our lives.

Intuitive emotional awareness can help you to tune in to unconscious and repressed emotions and feelings and provide you with insight into how they may be influencing what you are experiencing and creating in your life. It can also help you to release these emotions, heal, and create positive and fulfilling experiences.

For instance, Pauline, an attractive woman in her early thirties, came to me for her first reading. Soon into the session, I became aware that she had recently ended a relationship and was not sure if she had made the right decision. I talked about her ex-boyfriend and a few other issues. However, I knew that her biggest concern was if she would ever meet her soul mate and have the kind of loving relationship that she so longed for.

When I looked into the future, I saw a romantic partner whom I felt she would meet later that year. I shared this with her, and she asked questions such as *What kind of work does he do?* and *Where will we meet?* and I gave her my impressions.

There was, however, a bigger issue that had to be addressed. Just because I saw someone coming into her life did not mean that she would experience the love and joy that she hoped to experience with him. To be able to give her a more accurate reading, I needed to psychically tune in to Pauline's emotional readiness and ability to create and sustain a loving relationship. Even though she so much wanted such a relationship, if her unconscious emotional energy was not in alignment with this desire, the relationship would fail. She might also attract someone who would once again hurt or abandon her.

When I tuned in to Pauline's emotional energy, I felt feelings of unworthiness and unhealed childhood wounds. She felt abandoned by her father and was fearful of future disappointment. Pauline needed to become aware of these unconscious feelings and beliefs and heal them. Otherwise they would sabotage her efforts and desire. As much as she wanted a loving, long-term relationship, she would likely continue to attract the same kind of disappointing relationships that she had been encountering for years. When I told her this, she seemed committed to doing whatever it would take to attract a loving partner.

In my early years of psychic work with others, I may have intuited that Pauline would soon meet someone, but I might have either missed or underestimated the effect that her emotional energy would have on the success of the relationship. Over the years I have learned to tune in to my client's emotional energy before I give a prediction about what may or may not happen.

Although we may be able to intuit the success, abundance, and healthy relationships coming our way, if we feel unworthy or too emotionally wounded or fearful to accept these positive opportunities, they will pass us by. Many psychic predictions do not manifest for this reason. To manifest and live our highest good, our heart must be open and ready to receive.

It is important to remember that psychic accuracy will only be as good as your ability to tune in to the emotional energy of any situation or condition. This is true both when you intuitively tune in to yourself and what is coming your way and when you intuit for another.

If you intuitively detect and feel that you are sabotaging or preventing good and positive experiences and opportunities from coming into your life, take some time to intuitively listen to your heart. Emotional intuition is an effective tool for self-healing and mending your emotional wounds. Listen within without judgment and stay with the emotions that surface. Be kind and loving to yourself and ask your angels to guide and assist you in healing. To further release and heal negative and self-sabotaging emotions, you can practice the Letting Go of Intuited Toxic Emotions exercise in this chapter.

Fully developed emotional intuition is a powerful force through which you can create positivity and joy and receive all the good that life has to offer. The psychic skills of clairempathy and clairsentience empower you to receive heart-centered, soulful guidance and to heal and transform yourself and others.

CHAPTER 5

The Body as a Psychic Antenna (Physical Intuitive Type)

Physical intuition is the ability to receive energy information through the physical body, the sense of touch, the natural world, and objects and photographs. The physical body of someone with a high degree of physical intuition is a psychic antenna. Psychic energy information may be experienced as gut feelings, sensations of energy moving up and down the spine, or a tingling in the scalp or along the hair on the arms. Those with a high degree of physical intuition are often powerful and natural healers. When holding the personal object of another or a photograph of someone, a physical intuitive may be able to intuit information about that person.

INTUITION AS VIBES

Someone with a high degree of physical intuition may refer to their intuitive awareness as *vibes*. Grounded in the physical world, their intuition is more closely connected to the five physical senses. For this reason, a physical intuitive is not as likely to intuit energy as streaks of light or color or feel the presence of spirits, like a spiritual intuitive often does. Receiving intuitive feelings and emotions, like an emotional intuitive, or thought energy, like a mental intuitive, may also be less common.

For the physical intuitive, vibes are usually felt in the body, in the gut or solar plexus, or as sensations of energy moving through the body. Vibes might also be experienced as feeling positive, empowered, and lighter or heavier, stuck, and unable to move forward.

Going into a room full of people and feeling good, positive vibes helps a physical intuitive to relax and feel comfortable and connected to others. However, if the vibe doesn't feel right, they may turn around and leave, no questions asked. Physical intuitives feel vibes in all kinds of situations. For example, when first meeting someone they may experience a queasy sensation in their stomach. This may be a warning sign that tells them to be careful and cautious. When planning a trip and making a choice about the location, a physical intuitive might feel a positive, energizing vibe about one of the possible destinations and a heavier, uncomfortable sensation about another.

BEING A PHYSICAL PSYCHIC SPONGE

Those with a high degree of physical intuition tend to unknowingly absorb others' energy into their psychical body. For instance, in a stressful situation or in the company of angry or argumentative people, a physical intuitive may suddenly have a headache or back pain or feel lethargic. Then as quickly as they felt the pain or discomfort, it may dissipate once the situation is resolved. A physical intuitive may absorb and feel the pain of a coworker who complains of a physical problem or of a family member who has an ailment of some kind. However, they are usually unaware that their sudden aches and pains may be coming from others.

The ability to intuitively communicate through the physical body is evident in a physical intuitive's sense of touch. Many physical therapists, bodyworkers of all kinds, hands-on healers, and physicians, especially homeopathic and alternative medical practitioners, have a high degree of physical intuition. The hands of a well-developed physical intuitive move with the grace and fluidity of a master craftsman. As health and wellness practitioners, their hands know where there is discomfort or pain and how to bring relief and balance to the physical body. Through their intuitive connection to plants and the natural world, a physical intuitive is also especially adept at helping and healing others with herbs and flower and plant essences and other natural remedies.

In addition to their strong connection to the physical body, physical intuitives are also attuned to the vibrations of the natural world in a more profound way than the other psychic types. Because they often unknowingly absorb the energy of the people and situations they come into contact with, a forest, seashore, mountains, lakes, and open deserts can be a haven of calm and tranquility. Many physical intuitives have the innate intuitive ability to communicate with animals, birds, plants, and other inhabitants of the natural world. Even when they are unaware of their innate intuitive abilities, they experience a sense of oneness and connectedness in nature.

COMMON CHARACTERISTICS
OF A PHYSICAL INTUITIVE

Those with a high degree of physical intuition tend to be down-to-earth and practical. They accept their intuitive gifts in a matter-of-fact kind of way and do not overthink what they sense or experience. Although they often trust the vibes that they receive and have an intuitive connection to the physical body and the natural world, their innate intuition often goes unacknowledged. Those with a high degree of physical intuition rarely view themselves as psychic or believe that they possess extrasensory capabilities. Because they are centered in the physical body and connected to the earth, the natural flow of energy that moves through them is organic and grounded. It does not feel ethereal, mystical, or out of reach. A physical intuitive has a core trust in and acceptance of their gut feelings and instincts and may view their intuitive awareness as common sense.

Because physical intuition goes directly into the body, it often bypasses thought and emotion and conscious awareness. A highly sensitive physical intuitive may become overly energized and excited or depleted and tired and experience tightness and tension for no known reason. In order to release and calm the parade of energy that moves through their body, they might become physically active and enjoy all kinds of exercise, such as running or biking, or discover a special passion for extreme sports. Some go in the opposite direction and may overeat and become physically lethargic in an attempt to quiet the physical sensations they continually experience. Many psychics and mediums in past generations were overweight, possibly for these reasons. Those with a high degree of physical intuition might also experience extremes with sleep, either having insomnia or needing a lot of sleep. A child with a high degree of physical intuition can experience challenges in school and with learning. They can become agitated and fidgety when expected to sit quietly all day at their desk, as they often need to touch things and be physically active to learn and thrive.

Once those with a high degree of physical intuition become aware of their innate intuitive tendencies, they can find healthy ways to become physically balanced and centered. With this awareness, they can use their intuition in positive ways and become physically healthier in the process.

CLAIRSENTIENCE

A natural way to begin developing physical intuition is by becoming aware of the vibes that you spontaneously experience. Even if you do not have a high degree of physical intuition, you most likely have experienced intuitive vibes. A form of clairsentience, vibes are physical sensations that may be subtle or more discernible.

Clairsentience is the ability to receive energy information through the sense of feeling. For the emotional intuitive, clairsentience is emotional and heart-centered. For the physical intuitive, clairsentience is a more tangible and concrete feeling and sensation. Common clairsentient signs include vibes, gut feelings, a tingling energy up and down the spine, the hair on the arms or the scalp standing up, and body aches and pains.

Pay attention to the intuitive cues that your body sends you, as these signals tend to surface in everyday situations. For example, when meeting someone for the first time, feel what is happening in your body. When entering a room full of people or at the beginning of a new activity, job, or relationship or when making plans, tune in to the intuitive information that your body is sending you.

Because clairsentient sensations are so common, we often unconsciously tune them out. Make it a habit to check in with yourself when you feel the slightest little nudge. Just focusing and putting more effort into feeling and becoming aware of when your body is sending you a message will increase and strengthen your intuitive receptivity. Sometimes intuitive sensations and vibes are subtle. You may feel a twinge in your solar plexus or a slight tingling wave of energy move up your spine or arms or in your head. The sensations can also be more dramatic, like a tightening in your throat, a pounding in your head, or an upset stomach.

Listen to and Communicate with the Vibes

Once you become aware that you are receiving a psychic message through clairsentience, you can then begin to develop the ability to communicate with the vibe or sensation and interpret its meaning.

When you experience a feeling or sensation in your body that you think may be an intuitive vibe or message, listen and fully experience it. If the sensation is uncomfortable, like a headache or a tightening in your chest, there is likely a negative or stressful situation that you need to pay attention to. If the vibe is positive and energizing, such as feeling a burst of energy or feeling powerful and lighthearted, this indicates a beneficial situation, circumstance, or connection with another.

If the vibe or sensation is subtle and not easily identified as either positive or negative, or if you want to receive more information, you can dialogue with it. Psychic energy information is responsive to our requests, and when you interact with it, more information will come forward. Although it may feel silly to ask questions of energy, give it a try. Simply ask something like *What is the message behind this feeling or sensation?* Keep the questions simple and ask them one at a time. Then pause in between each one and listen. You might not receive the answer as soon as you would like, especially when you first start to communicate in this way. So be patient. Talking with energy and asking questions prompts the body, mind, and spirit to begin to work together and send information to the conscious self in a way that you can understand.

For instance, I recently had three contractors give me estimates on work that needed to be done on my house. All three of the bids were close in price. There were no obvious reasons to pick one company over another. They all had good reviews and the work that I needed done was not highly technical. However, I received clairsentient messages about each contractor that helped me make the decision.

While talking to the representative of one company, I felt like I needed to sit down. Just being in his presence made my stomach do a few flip-flops. I asked myself why I felt this way, and the insight came to me that this company would likely have hidden costs. The physical stress I felt was a sign to steer clear of this option. With the representative of another one of the companies, I experienced a calming sensation. My stomach, which is where most of my physical intuitive signals occur, was surprisingly relaxed. When I asked myself if this sensation had to do with the bid I'd received, I sensed a yes response. While talking to the third contractor, I felt restless and spacey. I couldn't focus on what he was saying and I was anxious to end the conversation. I was not sure if these feelings were related to my low blood sugar or were intuitive signs. I sat quietly for a moment and asked what these sensations were connected to. I received the immediate intuitive awareness that the sensations were coming from the third company. Because these feelings made me uncomfortable, I went with the second company and this was the right choice. The work went quickly and there were no hidden costs.

If you experience a spontaneous clairsentient sensation and are not sure why it is surfacing and what it may be related to, become aware of any current or pressing issues or concerns.

Take a moment to ask yourself if the sensation or feeling you are experiencing has to do with your current situation. If there are several different areas where you are experiencing concerns or questions, go through them one at a time. Once you ask a question, take a few minutes to feel and listen for any physical sensations and gut feelings.

The answer may come as a quick awareness, or the clairsentient sensation may increase in intensity. If you feel a stronger surge of energy, this is usually a yes sign. You may want to listen further for any other intuitive information or guidance. If you ask a question and then feel no increase in energy or a dull or flat response, this is a no sign.

If you would like to receive further insight and you are feeling more confident in your ability to discern and tune in to clairsentient sensations, ask the following question: *If these bodily sensations or feelings had a voice, what would they be saying?*

Then be patient. You might not get an immediate answer, but you will get one. Sometimes the intuitive information surfaces when you are not focusing on it.

Even when you follow these suggestions, there will be times when you experience clairsentient sensations but cannot discern their message or meaning. This is normal. Try not to rush the process, and let go of your expectations. Develop an open-minded, casual attitude that fosters intuitive awareness. If we assume that our intuition will surface in a particular way, we might unknowingly miss and disregard important information and intuitive insights that do not fit our expectations.

It is important to remember that physical intuition does not always provide the kind of understandable messages and explanations that you might receive with mental and emotional intuition. While you may recognize a physical intuitive signal, you may not always know what it is trying to tell you. However, physical intuition in the form of vibes and physical sensations is always significant and should be listened to. Unlike mental, emotional, and at times spiritual intuition, physical intuition bypasses the conscious self.

It takes observation and practice to become more familiar with the meaning and message behind the specific physical intuitive signals that you receive. There is a consistency and a pattern to your vibes, so give yourself some time to notice and fully understand them. Keep a journal of the intuitive vibes, feelings, and sensations that you receive. Document your interpretation and the actions or choices or changes that occurred as a result of the message. This will help you to further trust and develop a reliable dialogue with physical intuitive messages.

CLAIRSENTIENT ACHES AND PAINS

Some of the more puzzling physical intuitive sensations that we may experience come in the form of physical symptoms that appear to be connected to our health.

While it may be energizing to take on the positive and healthy vibes of another, absorbing unhealthy and problematic physical energy is confusing and potentially unhealthy. Those with a high degree of physical intuition are susceptible to absorbing the physical energy of coworkers, family members, friends, and even those they encounter on a daily basis. Although we are more likely to absorb the aches and pains of those we are emotionally and/or physically close to, it is possible to pick up the energy of another while riding the subway or during a meeting at work.

If you find yourself suddenly experiencing a headache, back pain, an upset stomach, unexplained pain, or some other form of physical discomfort, you may be experiencing another's physical issues. Not all unexplained and sudden aches and pains come from others. However, if your health suddenly changes after being with someone who is ill or in pain or if a physical symptom feels off, you may need to further investigate the source of these feelings.

🌸 Exercise: Understanding 🌸 Clairsentient Sensations

To intuitively tune in to the source of your physical pain or unexplained symptoms, sit quietly and listen within. Take a few relaxing breaths and draw your attention to the area where you are experiencing pain or discomfort. Dialogue with this area, then pause and listen.

Here are a couple questions you may want to ask:

Does this physical discomfort originate from within? Did I absorb it from another?

It is important to take time to listen and be patient. At times there will be a quick, direct intuitive response, and other times the message will take longer to understand. Keep in mind that your body may also communicate to you through your dreams or through synchronicities. Simply paying attention and listening to your physical intuitive sensations increases the free flow of intuitive communication with your body.

Communicating Further with Your Body

Pain that does not abate even when you are no longer in an environment where others may be ill or in pain or that does not seem to be related to another is likely coming from within yourself. Seek medical attention and continue to communicate intuitively with your body.

If you feel that the physical pain or symptoms you are experiencing are related to your personal health, talk to your body. Discomfort or pain is one of the ways that the body communicates with us and sends us messages. If you have physical symptoms or pain that you would like to better understand and begin to heal, here are a few questions to begin the dialogue:

What can I do to heal? What is this pain trying to tell me? What thought, belief, or emotion is connected to this pain or discomfort?

Ask one question at a time, then pause and listen within. Be patient and keep in mind that the answer or response may come at a later time. Sometimes when we are overly focused on receiving intuitive information, we block it from naturally surfacing. Try to stay in a relaxed, curious, and receptive mode.

Amie's story is a good example of intuitive listening. A few months after the first session of one of my year-long intuitive development classes, she began to experience headaches. At first she didn't think too much of them, but when they continued to persist off and on for several weeks, she went to her doctor. After the exam and tests, her doctor was unable to find out what was causing her headaches. Over the course of the next few months, they continued to occur off and on with varying degrees of intensity. She went to another doctor and then another, and still she did not get a diagnosis or relief from the pain. Then during one of my classes she had the intuitive realization that the headaches were connected to her attempt to develop her intuition and psychic and clairvoyant abilities.

I encouraged her to communicate with and ask questions of the headache. As she did this, images of her father surfaced. He was a conservative religious man who believed that psychic awareness was connected to the devil and temptation. Brought up in a household and church that feared and discouraged anything that had to do with intuition and psychic energy, Amie found that her attempts to develop her innate abilities were being met with inner resistance. As she continued to dialogue with her pain, the tension began to dissipate. She listened to her unconscious resistance and sent compassion to her fearful inner self that wasn't sure that developing intuition was the right thing to do. By the end of the class, her headaches began to dissipate and she was soon pain-free.

Common Signs of Absorbed Energy

If you feel that the physical symptoms you are experiencing are coming from another or from a situation, you can take steps to free yourself and feel better. Here are some common intuitive signs that the physical sensations you are experiencing have been intuitively absorbed from an outer source:

- The pain, discomfort, and other symptoms mimic the symptoms of another whom you are close to or spend time with.
- The physical symptoms come and go and intensify when in the company of certain individuals or in a specific environment.
- You are unable to heal the condition.
- You receive intuitive insight, gut feelings, etc., that the symptoms come from an outer source.

❁ Exercise: Releasing Intuited ❁ Physical Symptoms

If the pain and discomfort that you are experiencing has been absorbed from another or from a situation, you can intuitively communicate with the energy to release it and help the person in the process.

To communicate with and let go of energy that you have intuitively absorbed into your body from another, try this.

Find a comfortable and quiet place where you will not be disturbed. Take a deep, relaxing breath and let go of any stress or tension. Continue to breathe and relax.

Draw your attention to the physical discomfort or pain, and send compassion and love to this energy. Imagine the sensation, headache, pain, etc., surrounded by high-vibration white light.

Take a deep breath, then visualize a white-light ball of love energy and compassion and imagine sending it to the person or situation that generated this discomfort. You do not need to know precisely where or whom it came from. Just ask that this sensation go back to its source as positive energy.

PROTECTING YOURSELF FROM ABSORBING OTHERS' ENERGY INTO YOUR BODY

If you are absorbing others' physical energy, it is important to recognize this vulnerability and take steps to protect yourself. Those who habitually take on others' aches and pains tend to be compassionate and caring people and innate healers. They may not recognize their gifts and unconsciously try to alleviate others' pain, and in the process end up absorbing it into their body.

If you have a high degree of physical intuition, it is a good practice to visualize and imagine that you are surrounded by divine white-light energy, especially when you are in public or in the company of individuals who are ill or physically challenged. Intend that only positive energy that is in your highest good be allowed to enter into this bubble of light. If you notice any uncomfortable sensations or begin to feel tired or heavy around someone or in a situation, imagine that there is a white-light bubble protecting you. You can also surround those who are ill or in pain with white light.

I recently gave a medical intuition reading to Amanda. Her story is a good example of what can happen when we absorb the physical energy of another. As I intuitively scanned her body, I was drawn to her liver. It was full of toxins, and I was initially perplexed by the cause. She ate well and was generally healthy, and the source of the toxins was not apparent. As I continued to intuit the source of this energy, I saw an image of a man whom I could feel was a long-time drinker. I suddenly realized that this was Amanda's husband and that she was absorbing this toxic energy from him.

For over twenty-five years, Amanda had been in a codependent relationship with her alcoholic husband. Throughout the marriage, she tried to do all she could to help and heal him. Unfortunately this included absorbing his toxic physical energy.

I shared my intuitive impressions with Amanda, and she was not surprised at my findings. Over the years, her stamina and health seemed to decline as her husband's drinking increased. Although she had visited many doctors and tried different diets and supplements, nothing seemed to help. We talked about ways that she could both protect herself from her husband's toxicity and send him healing. Amanda seemed relieved that she could protect herself this way and wanted to stay in the marriage while practicing these techniques.

As she continued to shield herself from absorbing her husband's toxic drinking, she began to take better care of herself. Slowly she came to the realization and acceptance that her husband's drinking was destroying their marriage. In a tearful conversation, she told him that she wanted a separation. Not knowing what to expect, Amanda was surprised by her husband's reply. He told her that he had recently started going to an afternoon AA meeting near his work and knew that it was time for him to admit that he had a problem and get help. They are still together and working on improving their marriage.

VIBRATIONAL SENSITIVITY

Physical intuition surfaces from the mysterious divine mastery and intelligence of the physical self. It is no surprise that many bodyworkers, healers, and medical professionals possess a high degree of physical intuition. The body and particularly the hands of many physical intuitives are finely tuned intuitive sensors and transmitters. Many possess an innate sensitivity to the energy vibrations of the physical body.

Vibrational sensitivity can be used to sense and detect illness, disease, and discomfort in the physical body. A healthy physical body possesses a balanced and unrestricted flow of vital life force energy. The energy flow of someone suffering from an illness, disease, or pain is sluggish, heavy, and low-vibration and may feel dense and blocked. Through vibrational sensitivity, the hands can sense and tune in to the body's energy flow and intuit the areas of low vibration that are in need of healing and balancing.

You can practice this psychic sensitivity by tuning in to your own or someone else's body, or you can tune in to a pet or even something in nature.

✻ Exercise: Detecting ✻ Energy Health in the Body

This exercise will enable you to begin to sense and experience energy vibes in a more physical way. It opens up the psychic channels in the body and helps you to become more aware of different vibrational frequencies. Every living being has a unique vibrational imprint. As you become more sensitive to and familiar with vibes, you will be able to better intuit the energy information contained within them.

Place your palms on a part of your body that is strong, healthy, and problem-free. Breathe and relax while keeping your hands on this part of your body. You may want to close your eyes to better focus.

Feel the energy flow and vibration. At first it may feel subtle or barely discernible. Be patient and allow your hands to sense the flow of energy.

When you get a feel for the energy vibration flowing through you, move your hands to a part of your body that may be sore or tight or where you have pain or discomfort. Breathe and relax. Focus your awareness on the palms of your hands, and get a feel for the energy flow in this area.

You can switch back and forth, from a healthy and strong area of the body to an area of discomfort or tension.

You can use the same process with a friend or family member or with a pet. If you try this technique with something in nature, place your palms first on a healthy tree, flower, or bush, and then on a different tree, flower, or bush that appears to be weak or dying.

When you begin to feel more confident in discerning a healthy flow of energy through the body, you can practice on another. Without first being told which areas of the person's body feel weak or painful and which ones feel strong and healthy, allow your hands to intuitively guide you.

Be aware that while your hands are receiving the energy vibration, you may recognize it through another intuitive modality. For instance, if you have a high degree of emotional intuition, you may become aware of the vibration through feeling it emotionally. If you have a high degree of mental intuition, you may just know the flow of the energy vibes. If your spiritual intuition is predominant, you may see an image of the flow of energy.

For more information on communicating intuitively with your health and well-being, check out my book *Discover Your Medical Intuition.*

The Healing Abilities of Physical Intuition

Those with a high degree of physical intuition are often naturally adept at hands-on healing. Just as it is possible to innately receive and absorb the energy vibrations of others, it is also possible to absorb the vibrations of divine healing energy. As a natural conduit of energy, a physical intuitive may unknowingly transmit healing energy to others. Many massage therapists, acupuncturists, and other bodyworkers heal their clients this way. As they go about the business of touching the sore spots and practicing their craft, stress, tension, and aches and pains fall away. Even though they may not advertise and know the full extent of their healing ability, you will know the healing capacity of a health care worker by how busy and popular they are.

Everyone to varying degrees can channel healing energy. The simple intent and request for divine healing energy to flow through you activates vital life force energy. This high-vibration energy of love and healing is everywhere and always available. If you would like to increase your ability to channel healing energy, sit quietly, open your heart, and ask for healing energy to flow through you and for the ability to assist others in their healing. Practice placing the palms of your hands on your pets, children, loved ones, and even trees and plants while asking for healing energy to flow through you.

Practices such as Reiki, Healing Touch, and other energy healing modalities are rooted in the same principle of transmitting high-vibration energy healing to others.

🪷 Exercise: Hands-On Healing 🪷

This healing exercise is a simple and effective method that incorporates physical intuition and hands-on healing. You can practice this form of hands-on healing on your own aches and pains or with a friend, family member, or pet.

Begin by breathing long, deep, cleansing breaths and exhale any stress or tension. Continue to breathe and relax. Imagine breathing white light down through the top of your head and sending this energy through your body. As you breathe white-light energy through your body, ask a for a higher power, divine presence, or whatever higher source of pure healing energy you believe in to move through you. Continue to take long, deep breaths, sending the healing energy through your entire body.

As you continue to breathe, imagine a white-light bubble of energy completely surrounding you. With each breath, this bubble becomes more vibrant and flows with white-light energy. Imagine a constant stream of divine white-light energy flowing into the bubble and then into you. Breathe this energy into your physical body. You may begin to feel tingling or a heightened vibration in your hands, heart, and solar plexus.

When you are ready, place your hands on a part of your body that feels sore or tense or is painful. Imagine that white light flows through your hands to any discomfort or imbalance.

If you are working with another, allow your hands to guide you to the part of their body that needs healing. Place your hands where they are led, and imagine divine white light moving from your hands to any place in the person's body where healing is needed.

You can also place your hands on the top of your head or on the top of the head of the person you are working with. Imagine that white-light healing energy flows through your hands and then down through their entire body.

At this point there is an additional intuitive step that you can add to better tune in to the physical body. Once you become comfortable with allowing your hands to guide you to specific areas in the body that may need healing, you can begin to receive intuitive energy information and guidance.

The body is wise and communicative and ready to work with you to heal and improve health. With your hands placed on an area of pain, tension, or imbalance, intuitively tune in, listen, and be patient. If you do not receive any impressions, feelings, thoughts, or images, move your hands to another part of the body.

If you do receive some intuitive information, take note of it and continue to send healing. When you have received all that you can, move your hands to another part of the body, tune in, and send energy healing.

When you feel the energy flow begin to dissipate, remove your hands and come back to normal consciousness. Imagine a white-light bubble completely surrounding you and separate from the person you are working with.

If you have received any intuitive impressions or images, share them with the person you have been working with or write them down to reflect on later if the messages are for you.

PSYCHOMETRY

One of the more interesting psychic abilities is psychometry. An innate physical intuitive skill, it springs from the ability to intuit energy information through receiving vibes. Psychometry is the ability to hold a personal object of another or look at or hold another's photo and receive intuitive information about the person through it.

Items and objects such as watches, keys, jewelry, and clothing absorb our energy vibration. This is also true of photos. They are imprinted with our personal energy vibration. Through psychometry, it is possible to receive a broad range of intuitive information about the person whose photo or personal item is being read.

For example, years ago during a psychometry exercise in a psychic development class, everyone put a personal item in a bowl. We then passed the bowl around the room and each student took an item. After holding the object and meditating on it, we went around the room to share the intuited information.

When we got to Kari, a woman in her late twenties, she was a little hesitant to share what she had experienced. After some encouragement, she told the group that when she held the ring that she had picked out, she saw gray clouds and felt confused and disoriented. There was no one in the class who seemed to fit the energy that she had intuitively received, so she questioned her psychic abilities and didn't want to appear foolish.

However, Jake, the man who had placed the ring in the bowl, assured Kari that her intuitive impressions were on target. Jake explained that he had been in possession of the ring for only a few weeks. The ring was his grandfather's, and he had worn it for over sixty years. When he died of Alzheimer's a few months earlier, Jake had inherited the ring.

Because the ring still held the grandfather's vibrational imprint, Kari had correctly intuited Jake's grandfather's energy.

❀ Exercise: Using Psychometry ❀ to Read the Vibes

To develop psychometry skills, hold a personal item or a photo of someone you do not know very well. It is easier to trust the intuitive impressions you receive when you do not know much about the person whose item you are intuiting.

If you are having trouble finding another's items or photos to practice with, you can ask a friend to share something from one of their family members, or you can use a photo of someone unknown to you that you find on the internet or in a newspaper or magazine. If you use a public photo of another, make sure not to read anything about the person until you are finished with the exercise. You can also use items from a used clothing store or yard sale.

As an alternative psychometry exercise, you can also hold something from the natural world. Rocks, stones, crystals, and feathers work well, or you can place your hands on the trunk of a tree.

To begin, take a few deep cleansing breaths and exhale any stress or tension. As you breathe, imagine a white-light bubble completely surrounding you. This white-light bubble of protection allows only what is in your highest good to come close. When you are relaxed, hold an item or photo in your hands and continue to breathe and relax.

Be alert to any feelings, thoughts, or images that surface. They may be subtle, and what you receive may not always appear to be meaningful or significant. Do not dismiss anything that you feel, see, or sense or any impressions that surface. Write them down and continue to focus on the item or photo you are holding and breathe and relax.

When you feel that you have received all that you can, place the item or photo a few feet away from you. Continue to breathe and imagine a white-light cleansing shower of energy above your head. Imagine that this energy shower washes away and clears any energy that you may have absorbed from the object or photo.

If you used a public photo of someone from the internet or a publication, you may be able to read and discover more about the person. If the photo or item came from a friend, you can share what you received with them. Keep in mind that if you choose a public photo or an item of someone you do not know, you may not be able to verify your impressions. Remember to focus on the impressions, images, feelings, and other energy information that you receive, even if you're not able to obtain feedback and verification of accuracy.

If you are using a natural object like a rock or crystal, the energy information you receive may come in the form of surprising and unique physical sensations and awareness. Instead of intuiting another's characteristics or personality or some other identifying information, you may experience a sense of stillness or expansion. Feel how your body feels. For instance, when holding a rock, you may feel grounded, peaceful, and connected to all of life. Crystals can be particularly helpful with psychometry, as each one is an individual and usually has a story to tell and can express a wide range of information.

In generations past, it was common practice for a psychic to hold the hands of the person they were giving a reading to. This is a form of physical intuition that enables them to better tune in to and receive personal energy information. Some modern-day psychics still like to hold the hands of their clients, and many mediums ask for photos of loved ones who have passed over to better communicate with them. I am not a strong physical intuitive, so looking at a photo or holding a personal object is not as effective for me as it is for others.

Even if you do not naturally possess a high degree of physical intuition, developing the psychic abilities of physical intuition will support and enhance your overall psychic ability. Because physical intuition tunes in to the energy information contained within the material and physical, it can bring balance to the other psychic types. For those with a high degree of spiritual intuition, physical intuition can help to stabilize their naturally elusive and at times intangible connection to energy information. Physical intuition can decrease the mind chatter that can plague a mental intuitive and help those with a high degree of emotional intuition to transform and let go of intuited toxic emotions.

Chapter 6

Psychic Sight
(Spiritual Intuitive Type)

Spiritual intuition is the ability to receive energy information through the energy field, or aura, and through direct communication with spirit. Although it may be a little more difficult for our reasoning brain to fully understand this kind of innate intuition, you likely have unknowingly received energy information in this way.

For instance, have you ever seen flashes or sparkles of light or orbs? Have you ever had the feeling that a loved one on the other side is close? Does it ever feel as if an angel is guiding you? Has a dream ever revealed helpful information or valuable insights? Do you ever daydream and see images of future possibilities? Spiritual intuition spontaneously emerges through these kinds of experiences.

Spiritual intuition tunes in to energy information in its most minute, unseen, and intangible form. It may be easier to relate to the feelings of emotional intuition or the thoughts of mental intuition. Intuiting through the spirit or energy field may seem like an abstract concept. However, all things and living beings are composed of energy. At the most basic level, you are thousands and thousands of minuscule atoms of vibrating energy. Although you may appear to be solid and finite, this is just an illusion. At the core of your being, you are waves of energy vibration.

Characteristics of a Spiritual Intuitive

People who intuit primarily through spiritual intuition are sensitive souls who can become overstimulated by noise and sounds and may have food and other allergies. They may feel overwhelmed in crowds and be adversely affected by electromagnetic energy fields. While they often sense the energy around people, places, older homes, and open spaces, putting into words what they experience may be more difficult. Those with a high degree of spiritual intuition often seek spiritual and out-of-body experiences. Anything that empowers them to experience a reality beyond the confines of physicality can be appealing.

When it comes to finding their purpose and a sense of connectedness to others and the world, spiritual intuitives can struggle more than other types. Because of their innate connection to energy and spirit, they can resist the mundane and everyday. With an inner drive to immerse themselves in spiritual essence and the nonphysical, some may feel out of place and unconnected to the physical here and now. Their refined sensitivities and tendency to feel and sense the sublime and elusive can cause other types to view them as distant, lazy, or in their own world.

Mental intuitives derive a sense of self through their thoughts. Emotional intuitives' self-awareness comes by way of their feelings and emotions. Physical intuitives know themselves through their physical body and their presence in the world. Self-awareness can be a bit more confusing for spiritual intuitives. Their sense of self tends to be more ethereal and spiritual. Because of this, they can lack a cognitive understanding of who they are in relation to the material and physical world. In our culture, our awareness of spiritual presence and energy and nonphysical states of being is limited. For this reason a spiritual intuitive can feel out of the mainstream and innately different. Without an awareness of their intuitive and spiritual nature, they may continually put effort into knowing who they are yet feel that something essential is missing.

DREAMS

Those with a high degree of spiritual intuition often have a rich dream life. Depending on outer influences, a spiritual intuitive may go in and out of cycles of dreaming and non-dreaming. Many dreams are derived from the unconscious and express our repressed or pent-up thoughts, feelings, and experiences. Dreams can give us insight into issues in our lives and parts of ourselves that we need to further process or consciously understand better.

Some dreams are more intuitive in nature. They tap into the collective unconscious, the spirit realm, and our soul awareness. When we sleep, the conscious mind recedes and we are better able to receive psychic energy information. Intuitive dreams can reveal personal insights and guidance. They can help us to make a decision or uncover aspects about ourselves that may be limiting us and need to be healed. Dreams can also offer important guidance and serve to warn us of upcoming obstacles, danger, or health-related issues.

For instance, I had a client, Cari, who dreamt that she was standing in front of what appeared to be an X-ray machine. She couldn't understand what she was looking at, yet she had a sense that it was important and that something needed more attention. The next day she felt led to look at her calendar and realized that she had not had a mammogram in over a year. She made an appointment that day and a few days later was told that a small lump had been discovered. Fortunately the tumor was small and at a very early stage. Now, many months after treatment, she is cancer-free.

Not all intuitive dreams are about ourselves. Many provide insights and information about others and worldly events.

For instance, Ron, a client of mine, recounted a recent dream where he was in the company of a former girlfriend who appeared to be ill. The next day he called a mutual friend who confirmed that she was indeed suffering from an illness. Although Ron had not seen her in over fifteen years, in the dream he felt close to her. A few weeks after the dream he called her and asked her to forgive him for his insensitivity over their breakup. From his own experiences he knew the healing potential of forgiveness and wanted only the best for her.

Those with a high degree of spiritual intuition often knowingly or unknowingly commune with the spirit realm through dreams. Have you ever woken up in the morning and felt as if you have been busy all night? Maybe you've had the sense that you have been communicating or visiting with someone or something. Have you ever felt as if you were being taught while you slept? Although the physical body needs rest and recuperation, the soul and spirit do not. While the conscious self is sleeping, your soul may be engaged in communicating, visiting, and learning with the spirit realm. The home of spirits, angels, guides, and divine beings, the spirit realm is active and likes to visit, help, guide, and interact with us. Many people communicate and connect with their loved ones who have passed over through their dreams. They may see and feel their presence and feel their warmth and love. Loved ones on the other side may communicate concerns and messages through our dreams, either directly or through dream symbols.

Angels and other divine beings are often present while we sleep, bringing us comfort and helping us to heal. When we go through challenges, experience loss, or have difficulties, the spirit realm is especially close. Although we seldom remember these encounters when we wake, we may feel a sense of comfort or renewed hope and inspiration. However, there are times when we clearly remember a dream encounter we had with a divine being or angel.

For instance, my friend Stacy remembers a dream she had many years ago in vivid detail. An angel came to her and showed her how to earn feathers for her wings. In the dream Stacy was surprised to realize that she had transparent wings that she had not known about. The angel told her that through being kind and helpful to others, she would earn her feathers and get closer to heaven. This dream left such a strong impression on her that Stacy thinks of it often and does all she can to earn her feathers.

DAYDREAMS AND VISIONS

Along with nighttime dreaming, daydreaming is a common spiritual intuitive pastime. Although much of our daydreaming is fantasy and ego-created imagination, energy information can also be received while daydreaming.

For instance, my client Jonas loves science fiction and often imagines himself in different fantasy scenarios. When he is bored or tense, he floats off into space and imagines himself conversing with distant beings and visiting other realms. This both relaxes him and helps him to unwind. One afternoon while landscaping his backyard, he stopped for a short break, and while leaning against his shed he gazed off into the distance and saw a vision of himself planting blueberry bushes. He thought this was odd, as he was only going to do a little weeding and finish repairing some stonework near the patio. He didn't even have any blueberry bushes.

Later that afternoon after completing the work, he heard his wife pull up in the driveway after a shopping trip and went out to help her unload the van. As you may have guessed, among the items that she had bought on the way home from work were six blueberry bushes.

Although there are some commonalities between daydreams and visions, they each have a few distinct characteristics. While both provide us with the opportunity to intuit energy information, we often engage in daydreams to escape what is going on around us. Because most daydreams are created from our imagination, it is not always easy to detect any intuitive insights that surface. When we do notice them, we may quickly discount them, as they may feel made-up and unreliable.

Intuitive visions usually occur spontaneously and feel like they are coming from an outer source. Unlike daydreaming, visions can interrupt and break through the conscious mind. Often unexpected, they may contain a visual image that we do not understand, people we do not know, and unfamiliar situations. They can unexpectedly emerge when we are driving or taking a walk or anytime the conscious thinking mind is passive.

Some of the differences between daydreams and an intuitive vision are subtle but still discernible. Similar to dreams, in a vision you are an observer. You are not making things happen. Visions draw you into their activity. You may feel absorbed into their energy and curious as to what they mean and represent. In a vision you are often surprised or perplexed and not initially sure of what you are seeing and why. Psychic visions do not necessarily portray us in ego-gratifying ways or fulfill our desires by showing us what we want to see or hear. They simply provide us with energy information that may or may not be personal.

Although the meaning or purpose of an intuitive vision is not always initially clear, in time its meaning unfolds and is revealed. Some visions offer us guidance and connection with the spirit realm. For instance, many spiritual scriptures, such as the Bible and the Bhagavad Gita, recount stories of visitations by angels and archangels where messages and guidance were provided through dreams and visions. Although they are often fearful of appearing grandiose or a little eccentric, many people have told me of visions of angels or archangels. At times, physical sensations accompany a vision, such as the hair on the arms standing up or shivers or tingling all through the body. Some people may experience a heart opening or a sense of awe and a profound awareness. Visual encounters with divine spirit beings usually have a lifelong impact and may even inspire a life change or new career.

Visions That Involve Others

At times, the message of an intuitive vision is not meant for us. We are simply the conduit.

This is what happened to Fran. On an unusually warm winter evening, Fran decided to sit out on her patio. It was a dark and quiet night, and as she gazed up at the stars, she felt herself begin to gently doze off. When she was awakened by the call of an owl, a space in front of her seemed to open up and she saw a vision of a woman extending her hand to a man who seemed confused and lost. When the man noticed the woman's hand reaching out to him, he smiled and rushed into her arms. The vision quickly evaporated, and Fran realized that she did not recognize the man or the woman.

The next morning on her way into work, Fran was met by Sharon, a coworker. Visibly shaken, Sharon shared that her brother had unexpectedly passed over the day before of a heart attack. She told Fran that she had just come in to get a few things and would be taking the rest of the week off. When Fran offered her condolences, Sharon remarked that she hoped her brother was with their mother, who had passed over just a year earlier.

Fran was perplexed and thought it might be too much of a coincidence to think that this coworker's brother could be the man in her vision. Yet when she passed by Sharon's desk, she couldn't help but stop and look at her photos, one of which was of a family reunion from a few years earlier. Fran was stunned to see that one of the men in the photo was indeed the man she had seen the night before.

It took Fran several months to share this vision with Sharon, but when she did, Sharon started to cry and thanked her. Knowing that her brother was with their mother brought her peace and comfort.

THE THIRD EYE

With mental intuition, energy information is received through the mind and consciousness. Those with a predominance of emotional intuition receive intuitive energy through the heart, while physical intuition is received through the body. The psychic center of spiritual intuition is the energy field and the third eye.

The third eye—or the divine eye, as it is sometimes called—is located in the midpoint between the eyes. Many esoteric and spiritual traditions, among them Mahayana Buddhism and Taoism, have practices devoted to opening and perceiving enlightenment through the third eye.

When the third eye is open and activated, it becomes possible to see with psychic vision. The psychic ability of clairvoyance emanates from the third eye. This is the ability to receive energy information through figurative, symbolic, and realistic images. An important psychic tool, clairvoyance empowers you to perceive the past, present, and future through images and visions.

Unlike physical eyesight, clairvoyant sight is not always three-dimensional or true to physical form. Images may be symbolic, metaphoric, cartoon-like, flat, or full of color and movement. Clairvoyant sight might also not be highly visual. Images can be intuitively sensed, known, and felt. This might not initially seem to make much sense. Through our physical senses the nose smells, the ears hear, and the eyes see. Psychic senses are more intertwined and often rely on one another to interpret energy information in a way that we can fully understand.

Be careful not to ignore and pass over clairvoyant images if they surface in unexpected ways. Many people become frustrated when they do not readily perceive clear visual images when beginning to develop clairvoyance. For some, the expectation is to clairvoyantly see in the same way that the physical eyes see. However, instead of initially seeing an image, some may intuitively know what an image looks like through claircognizance. Others may intuitively feel an image through clairsentience. It is even possible to become aware of an image through inwardly hearing what it looks like through clairaudience. If you experience these kinds of images, do not dismiss or disregard them. Pay attention to what you receive and allow your psychic senses to converge and flow into one another. As you do this, they begin to work together and to provide accurate and understandable information.

Imagination

Along with intuitively feeling, knowing, and hearing images, your imagination plays an important role in developing clairvoyance. Not understanding the importance of imagination in the intuitive process can create stumbling blocks that inhibit the ability to receive and interpret psychic energy. At the beginning of developing psychic awareness, many people fear that their intuitive impressions are not valid because they used their imagination to help create them.

Psychic awareness is the ability to transform elusive psychic energy into a coherent form that the brain can decipher. With spiritual intuition this is accomplished by transmitting energy information through the third eye and energy field into the brain, which then goes to work to make sense of it. Calling on all of its resources, the brain employs imagination as an interpretation tool.

Consciously using our imagination to create a visual image is not making something up or intuitively cheating. It is a useful tool that integrates the functions of the brain and intuition and invites them to work together. Eventually they catch on and do this on their own. When you use your imagination, you are simply helping to introduce psychic energy to the brain and encouraging them to be friends and play nicely together.

In time it becomes more obvious when you are simply making something up and when your imagination is being employed to decipher and express energy information. Being psychic is a bit like exercising a muscle. You can feel it when it is working. When your mind is engaged in receiving and interpreting energy information, you may feel a bit tired or drained, like something is tugging on your energy. However, you are simultaneously also likely to feel energized and a slight buzzing sensation when you are connected to higher-vibration energy. When you are simply using your finite thinking mind to create images, you do not have that feeling of connection that comes with psychic energy, and you will continually need to keep thinking to produce images.

When you are beginning to develop clairvoyance, be patient with the process. It takes time to finely tune and synchronize your intuitive muscles to produce clear and accurate images. If you have ever tried to learn a new language, you know that it takes practice to understand and interpret words that initially do not make sense. When you develop psychic abilities, you are introducing a new way of receiving and interpreting information. Beyond the scope of the five senses and the normal way of thinking, this is a rich new world of energy that you are becoming familiar with.

❀ Exercise: Using Clairvoyance ❀ to Open the Third Eye

To develop clairvoyance, it is essential to open and activate the third eye. This is a natural and healthy process. Along with developing clairvoyant ability, an open third eye empowers us to increase our creative thinking ability and receive higher wisdom and knowing.

This activation exercise helps you to open the third eye and become familiar with how it feels to receive and transform energy information through clairvoyance. I recommend that you repeat this exercise often.

Get into a comfortable position where you will not be disturbed and close your eyes. (This exercise can also be done with eyes open, softly gazing at one spot on the floor or wall.)

Imagine a white-light bubble that completely surrounds you and allows only what is in your highest good to enter.

Place the tip of your tongue on the roof of your mouth and press slightly. As you do this, breathe in through the nose and out through the mouth.

Continue to breathe in this way, moving the inhale through the body and exhaling any stress or tension.

When you are relaxed, breathe down through the top of the head, drawing your awareness to the area between the eyes. This is the third eye area. Keeping the tip of your tongue on the roof of your mouth, inhale down through the top of the head and imagine exhaling through the third eye.

As you exhale, use your imagination to create an image of a rose or lotus bud in the third eye area.

Continue to inhale through the top of the head and then exhale through the third eye. As you exhale, imagine the petals of the rose or lotus flower softly opening one at a time.

Continue to breathe down through the top of the head, drawing your awareness to the space between the eyes, and exhale. Observe the petals of the rose or lotus flower softly opening. Once it is fully open, imagine high-vibration spiritual energy emanating from the center of the flower. Absorb this energy and move it down through the body to the soles of the feet.

Become aware of any other images or sensations that emerge. Take note of them and continue to breathe and exhale through the third eye.

When you feel complete, take a long, deep breath and move the energy of the breath through the body. Continue to breathe in this way. Feel energy move through the body and down to the soles of your feet.

Open your eyes when you are ready.

SIGNS OF THIRD EYE ACTIVATION

It is possible for the third eye to open spontaneously without any effort. Some of the activities that can trigger spontaneous third eye opening include meditation, psychic development, studying spiritual scripture, dreamwork, chanting, music, creating art, altered states of consciousness, dance, and spending time outdoors. The opening of the third eye can be gradual or more intense and rapid.

One common sign that the third eye has been activated and is beginning to open is when you see dots or sparkles of light or purple or violet energy when your eyes are either open or closed. For some, these colors and sparkles of light may transform into spontaneous cartoonish figures or faces of people you do not recognize. You may see flashing images, symbols, streaks, or patterns or shapes of light and color.

As psychic energy increases and begins to flow through the third eye, fragments of energy that have been blocked or stored in this area may surface. Childhood or repressed memories and images of past lives may emerge. What you perceive may not make any sense, and it is not necessary to understand everything that surfaces.

Visions of light, divine beings, and angels may also appear. Another common sign of the third eye opening is seeing an eye. It may appear as a symbol or as one similar to a human eye.

You may also experience physical sensations and changes such as a slight headache or pressure in your forehead, or you may feel lightheaded and dizzy. Your body may tingle with energy, and you may feel unusually warm or cold. These are signs that you are taking in a lot of energy and expanding your psychic capacity.

Grounding the high-vibration psychic energy moving into the third eye will help your body adjust to it. Good grounding activities include such things as taking a walk, practicing yoga, going outside in the sunshine, and digging in the dirt. It is also a good practice to end your clairvoyant sessions by imagining a white-light cord running from the top of the head to the third eye area, then down through the spine and through the soles of the feet, anchoring you to the earth. As you do this, imagine that the white-light cord is dissolving any intuited energy held in the body or energy field.

ENERGY RECEPTACLES

As you become more confident and familiar with receiving energy through the third eye, you can begin to use clairvoyant images to receive and understand energy information. Not only does an open third eye activate psychic seeing, but it also stimulates and triggers our innate and complex creative thinking ability. This is important because clairvoyant images are often symbolic in nature. With an open third eye, you will discover that your ability to intuitively understand symbols and other types of clairvoyant images is stronger.

One of the ways to encourage clairvoyance is to use and employ energy receptacles. Energy receptacles are images that provide a form through which psychic energy information can accumulate and be observed. They can assist you in deciphering and understanding intuited energy information. Once you use your imagination to create an image, it receives energy information and changes, shifts, and transforms the receptacle.

For example, in the dream state you are an observer. You may be watching yourself in the dream, but there is a part of you that is simply viewing what is happening. You are not consciously creating the dream or thinking about what is happening. You are in an aware state of observation. This is the optimum state to be in when using clairvoyance. You are not making something happen, you are simply watching it unfold. Patience and observation allow psychic energy information to emerge and evolve. Once you use your imagination to create an energy receptacle, you become an observer and allow energy information to manifest through it.

🪷 Exercise: Using Clairvoyant 🪷 Energy Receptacles

Use this exercise to become more familiar with psychically tuning in to energy information through clairvoyant energy receptacles.

It is important to remember that while clairvoyance is the ability to see energy information, you may initially feel, sense, or know what an image looks like and not see it in visual form. If this happens, don't resist. Go with the image however you receive it and continue to tune in to and receive energy information. Let go of your expectations and become the observer. Do not discount anything, even if it seems insignificant, and stay in an open and receptive state.

In this exercise, a tree is the energy receptacle. What happens with the tree is dependent on the intuitive energy.

Get comfortable and close your eyes. Begin to breathe long, deep, relaxing breaths, sending the energy of the breath through the body. Exhale any stress or tension. Continue to breathe in this way. Inhale deeply down through the top of your head and release any stress or tension through the exhale. Imagine a white-light bubble completely surrounding you, allowing only what is in your highest good to enter.

When you feel relaxed, breathe down through the top of the head and send the breath into the space between your eyes. Continue to inhale down through the top of the head, sending the breath to the third eye area. Exhale softly and imagine the third eye gently opening.

Using your imagination, create a blank screen in front of you. On this blank screen, imagine a healthy tree with its branches full of leaves. This can be any type of tree. Notice it in detail: its trunk, the color of its leaves, and its roots digging deep into the earth. Feel the strength and vibrancy of the tree. Take a few moments to observe the tree. This is your energy receptacle.

Now imagine an image of yourself leaning against the tree trunk or an image of a branch of the tree reaching out and touching you. Observe the tree and any changes that occur when it connects to your energy. Be patient, as the changes may be subtle.

Common changes that others have experienced in the tree include the leaves of the tree becoming more vibrant, changing color, or appearing to glow. More leaves may appear, they may fall, or they may multiply and grow. The tree itself may become a different type of tree or transform into an entirely different image or object. Just observe and notice any changes that occur when the tree responds to your energy. Be aware of any feelings or thoughts that surface.

To end the exercise, imagine the tree in a place in nature with the sun shining down on it, full and healthy.

It is not essential to interpret and understand the changes in the tree and all that occurs during this exercise. However, you may receive a spontaneous awareness, guidance, or insights about yourself or a concern.

As you continue to practice this exercise, you will strengthen your clairvoyant ability. You may find that each time you do the exercise you receive different images and energy information. This happens for a couple of reasons. Your ability to clairvoyantly see is strengthening, and each time you do the exercise the tree will express your changing moods, emotions, and other predominant experiences that you are presently involved with.

❀ Exercise: Using a Clairvoyant Energy ❀ Receptacle for Another

In this second exercise we continue to use a tree as an intuitive receptacle. However, instead of the tree expressing your energy, it receives the intuitive energy of another. This provides you with the opportunity to notice and observe the differences between intuiting another's energy and intuiting your own. Before you begin, think of someone you would like to tune in to. It is always a good idea to ask for permission before intuiting another's energy.

Begin by breathing long, deep, relaxing breaths, and send the energy of the breath through the body. Exhale any stress or tension. Continue to breathe in this way. Inhale deeply down through the top of your head and release any stress or tension through the exhale. Imagine a protective white-light bubble of high-vibration energy completely surrounding you.

When you feel relaxed, breathe down through the top of the head and send the breath into the space between your eyes. Continue to inhale and softly exhale, and imagine the third eye gently opening.

Focusing your attention on the third eye area, create an image of a healthy tree with its branches full of leaves. Notice it in detail: its trunk, the color of its leaves, and its roots digging deep into the earth. Feel the strength and vibrancy of the tree. Take a few moments to observe the tree.

Ask for the energy of the person you are tuning in to to enter this image. If you feel that this person does not want to be present or is resistant, choose someone else to do this exercise with. If this person is willing to be energetically present, imagine them leaning against the tree trunk. You can also imagine that the tree is reaching out and touching this person's essence or energy field. Observe the tree and any changes that occur when it connects to this person's energy. Be patient, as the changes may be subtle.

Similar to the first exercise, be aware of any changes in the color of the tree. Notice if the leaves change or fall away or if the tree itself transforms or becomes a different tree or some entirely different object or image when it connects with the person's energy. Also pay attention to any feelings or thoughts that surface while you are doing the exercise.

When you have received all that you can at this time, imagine the tree in the sunshine somewhere in nature, healthy and strong.

Compare the two exercises and take note of the differences and similarities between them. As you do this, become aware of any other intuitive information or interpretations of the energy that you received to surface.

Common Clairvoyant
Experiences and Questions

Here are a few common experiences and concerns that others have had after working with clairvoyance and energy receptacles.

Seeing Only Black

If you do not see an image, not even the tree, relax and slow down. This is not uncommon. Be patient, focus on your breath, and breathe into the third eye area. Eventually you will begin to sense and feel energy activity.

Remember that the image may not look like a three-dimensional tree that you see with your physical eyes. It may seem made-up, or you may know or feel the image and not visually see it. In visualization exercises it is helpful to use your imagination to create the image, then patiently intuit and observe.

Nothing Much Happened

Perhaps you saw the tree, but nothing seemed to happen or change. Again, slow down, focus on the breath, and be patient. Sometimes expectations become a block to further activity or we have an unconscious resistance to opening up psychically. Be aware of any intuited thoughts or feelings and eventually the energy will loosen up and flow.

Too Much Happened

Instead of nothing happening, perhaps you were overwhelmed with images, thoughts, feelings, and sensations, and you found that you could not discern the intuited energy information from mind chatter and random feelings.

If this happens, make a list of everything you received, then do the exercise again. Breathe and relax, and begin when you are feeling calm. If you start to overthink and feel overwhelmed, go back to breathing long, deep, relaxing breaths. Come into a receptive state and observe the energy information that surfaces. If you begin to feel overwhelmed, go back to the breath and relax. Go back and forth in this way. Eventually your body-mind-spirit will align with the process and settle into a receptive mode.

The Feeling of Making It Up
You may feel like you made the whole thing up. In time you will be able to discern the difference between connecting to energy information and making up images from the conscious self. Accept whatever you receive and continue to receive intuited energy information.

Not Knowing What Anything Means
You may have received, seen, and felt colors, changes in the tree, or other activity but have no idea what any of it means. In each meditation exercise in part 4, an image glossary is provided to help you better understand what you have intuited. For now, write down what you receive and pay attention to any thoughts or feelings that surface when you do this.

You may have a sense of what the different intuited images, thoughts, and feelings mean but have no verifiable evidence to support it, and so you may discount it. If this happens, trust your inner intuitive knowing and write down your interpretation. Notice evidence that supports what you received.

Fuzzy and Indefinable Images
When you begin to develop clairvoyant abilities, do not become overly concerned about the quality of the images and your ability to understand and interpret them.

When energy information emerges in a form that does not seem to make sense, don't discount it or give up. Instead, become aware of the subtle energy force behind what you are receiving. Even if you cannot put what you perceive into words or see clear images, continue to connect with the energy. Eventually your psychic senses will strengthen and improve and you will be better able to see and understand what you are receiving.

If the energy information that you are receiving feels flat or if you feel like you are trying too hard to make something happen, relax and get into the observing mode. Even though it may feel like the wrong thing to do, do nothing, wait, and be patient. Eventually you will begin to sense and feel energy. It may feel like a vibration, a buzzing sensation, or a pull on your third eye area. You may feel a bit tired and drained. It takes effort and energy to develop and use your psychic senses. Be alert to these types of feelings and sensations and stay connected to them, even if this initially does not yield any understandable images.

The Spirit Realm

Along with clairvoyance, another one of the psychic gifts of spiritual intuition is awareness of the spirit realm. Opening the third eye and practicing clairvoyance strengthens our intuitive ability to perceive and communicate with spirit beings. For some, this awareness may surface through seeing the presence of spirit as flashes of light, color, or orbs, while others may perceive an outline of a person or energy sparkles moving though a room. Alternating sensations of warm and cold air are another sign of an unseen presence. Because energy information is received through the energy field, or aura, sensing energy shifts and movement or tingling sensations of energy up and down the spine also lets you know a spirit being is close. Those who intuit primarily through spiritual intuition may sense and feel the presence of a spirit being but not realize that this is what they are experiencing. They may discount the sensations, visual apparitions, and other phenomena as their own personal quirkiness.

When a spirit being is present, we may experience uplifting and positive feelings or hear an inner thought message. Quite often we carry on an inner conversation with a loved one on the other side or with an angel or spirit guide without realizing what is really happening. It may feel as if we are talking to ourselves or simply coming up with good ideas and solutions to issues and problems.

Although it may seem like connecting with the spirit realm is a rare gift, most people have had some form of communication with the other side. When we are young, we are more aware and able to naturally connect with the spirit realm. We may have an invisible friend or see or talk to our loved ones on the other side or other spirit beings. This is natural and normal, and we feel quite comfortable and at ease doing this. By the age of five or six, many lose touch with this ability.

For instance, my client Lea told me that her four-year-old daughter, Bridget, often talks about her friend Kate. At first Lea thought that Kate was a friend from preschool. However, when Bridget mentioned that Kate was waiting for her in her bedroom, Lea realized that she was speaking about a very different kind of friend.

One afternoon, Bridget asked her mother if she would help Kate find her mommy. She said that Kate had been looking for her for a long time and that she really missed her. Bridget was visibly upset, and Lea told her that she would look for Kate's mom. A few days later while folding laundry, Lea saw a flashing image of a blond-haired little girl with a red dress on running down the hallway. As quick as she had appeared, she disappeared. A few days later, Lea saw the same little girl sitting at the foot of her bed and looking up at her. Again, the image quickly disappeared. Not knowing what to think, Lea asked Bridget what Kate looked like. Bridget told her that she had long blond hair with ribbons and she was wearing a red dress and black shoes.

"You know, Mommy," she said, "I told Kate that you could help her find her mom."

Lea realized that this was more than an imaginary friend. This is when she came to see me to help the little lost soul rejoin her mother in the spirit realm.

Spirit High-Rise

Because spiritual intuition absorbs energy information through the aura, or energy field, it is naturally aligned with nonphysical vibration and frequency. This awareness aids us in tuning in to the spirit realm. Think of the spirit realm as a very large and tall multi-story building. Each floor is a different vibration of energy: the lower the floor, the more dense the vibration, and the higher the floor, the higher the vibration. The ground floor of this high-rise is the physical and material realm. As you ascend into the higher vibrations, you come closer to pure divine God energy.

Most loved ones on the other side are on the floors close to the ground level. They still look very much like they did when they were still on Earth, and they retain much of their personality and memories of their life here. A few floors above, our loved ones are spirit guides. Above spirit guides are angels and then archangels and other divine beings.

Spiritual intuition is like an elevator that helps you to go from one floor to another. We cannot visit the spirit realm in our physical body, but our spirit can. Our aura, or energy field, is our travel suit and empowers us to connect and communicate with the different levels of vibration.

This spirit high-rise building is everywhere at all times. Your energy field has access to all these levels. Wherever you are, there are different levels of vibration, both within you and surrounding you.

❋ Exercise: Communicating ❋ with the Spirit Realm

In this exercise you can practice connecting to a spiritual being and receiving a message. When you begin to contact the spirit realm, it is best to be open to whoever comes forward. It is natural to want to ask for a specific loved one or an angel or guide. However, when you initially begin the process of spirit communication, it is better to be open to whoever is present. There may be a loved one on the other side who is particularly skilled at being able to communicate with those in the physical realm. Likely this will be who comes through first.

Before beginning this exercise, let go of your expectations. Like many people, you may want to know the name and other identifying characteristics of whoever you connect with. You might also want to receive a clear and understandable message. While it is realistic to want this type of information, it may take some time and practice to receive this kind of clarity. Be patient with the process. As you become more confident and accustomed to communicating with the spirit realm, more clearly defined information will surface.

To begin, get into a comfortable position. Close your eyes and take a long, deep breath and then exhale. Continue to breathe, sending the warm energy of the breath to any part of your body that is sore, tense, or tight. Then breathe out any tension or stress. Continue with this cleansing breath. Each time you breathe, draw in warm and relaxing white light and exhale any tension from the body.

Breathe in white-light energy down through the top of your head, then exhale it through your heart. Keeping breathing in white light and exhaling through the heart. As you do this, imagine a white-light bubble completely surrounding you. Continue to breathe as this bubble grows stronger and stronger. Imagine that you are completely protected in this bubble of light. Only what is in your highest good can enter. When you invoke the protection of white light, only loving and pure-vibration spirits come close.

As you continue to breathe in this way, you raise your vibration. Your body may begin to tingle, and you may feel lightheaded and sense a heightened vibration. Colors, sparkles of light, and images may surface.

Invite a loving being from spirit to come close. Continue to breathe and ask to become aware of the spirit's presence.

Pay attention to any feelings or sensations that surface. Notice any intuitive thoughts, words, or feelings of warmth or a shift in the energy around you. Become aware of any images, flashes of color or light, shimmering outlines, or energy vibration shifts.

Be calm and accept what you receive. Continue to breathe and relax. Stay in this receptive state for as long as possible.

When you feel the energy connection begin to fade, breathe and continue to open your heart and fill yourself with love.

Send gratitude to whoever has come close. Open your eyes. Record any intuitive impressions that you may have received.

Continue to practice this exercise to strengthen your intuitive ability to become aware of the spirit realm. As you become more comfortable and able to discern and communicate with spirit energy, you can ask for names and other identifying information.

In future sessions, you can invite a particular spirit into the session and further develop your intuitive ability by communicating with that spirit.

Spiritual intuition opens the door to spiritual adventures and possibilities. It governs both spirit communication and clairvoyance. These two areas amplify, refine, and boost your overall proficiency as a psychic. Even if you are not a natural spiritual intuitive, developing this area of intuition aids and enhances your ability to receive and interpret the energy information that you receive through the other psychic modalities.

PART 3
Increasing and Refining Psychic Power

CHAPTER 7

Practices and Techniques to Enhance Psychic Awareness

Developing psychic abilities is more than learning a set of skills. We may be attracted to psychic awareness for the insight and answers that it can provide. However, this is just a drop in the bucket. Psychic awareness leads us out of our soul slumber and wakes us to our potential. Like a well-sharpened knife, it carves away the fleeting rewards of the personality and ego self and delicately reveals the core of the self, soul, and spirit.

TAMING THE EGO

Once we begin to experience spontaneous psychic insights and desire to further develop our natural intuition, we are at a tipping point. Our spirit and soul are emerging and integrating into our conscious self. Our spirit is naturally psychic. It is not contained or limited by time or space and physical death. It is eternal and connected to the vast source of all love and wisdom. As our spirit bubbles up into our conscious awareness, it further strengthens our psychic awareness.

The work of psychic development is to activate our innate psychic awareness and integrate it into our conscious self and daily life. All too often we attempt to control psychic energy and fit it into what our ego feels and thinks it should be, but this rarely proves to be a successful strategy.

It can be difficult to give up the reins of control to the unseen inner force of psychic activity, as the ego continually wants to jump in and take over the process. However, the ego or personality self is not intuitive or psychic, and this aspect of our being is forever confined to the limitations of the five physical senses.

When we allow the ego to dictate and tell us what to expect when we intuit energy information and how to develop psychic abilities, we lose our way. When confronted with psychic energy, the ego reacts with apprehension, fear, and doubt. It has a preconceived idea of what it means to be psychic and what the intuitive information and guidance that we receive should look and feel like. Yet these assumptions and expectations are never correct and helpful. Too often people discount genuine psychic experiences and sabotage their progress because of unrealistic expectations.

Invite the ego to take a back seat. Allow your spirit, the eternal part of you that is trustworthy and always works in your best interest and highest good, to come forward. Intuitively listen to your spirit and observe, become aware of, and learn the unique ways that psychic energy manifests in your life. Unlike the ego, which operates through judgment and expectations, your spirit is gentle and guiding and meets you right where you are. It works through your individual strengths and weaknesses and helps you to develop your unique psychic gifts.

Spiritual Power

Although it is possible to develop psychic abilities with little or no focus on our spiritual development, we will only get so far. To go beyond the limitations of the five senses, we have to build the inner power that is needed to reach higher levels of psychic awareness. This power comes from our spirit.

Our spirit is a free agent, not able to be contained or defined by any one specific religious belief or devotion to a particular spiritual practice or understanding. It does not matter if you believe in God, divine beings, Jesus, Muhammad, or the Goddess. Whatever you believe or do not believe is up to you. The kind of spiritual power that psychic ability requires is not dependent on a religious orientation. Instead, the spirituality of psychic awareness is the recognition and acceptance of your integral connection to an invisible network of love, wisdom, and goodness. Wherever you are and whatever you are doing, there is a divine presence within you, assisting and guiding you like a star in the night.

To strengthen and deepen your psychic awareness, listen within to your spirit and allow it to lead you and reveal new truths and insights. When you have the courage to go beyond conventional perspectives and preconceived assumptions and listen within, you build spiritual power. All too often we try to wrangle our spirit into a three-dimensional, finite perspective that our ego self feels comfortable with. If you want to advance in psychic awareness, it is necessary that you let go of control and walk the unknown path. It is only when you open your heart and mind and embrace the mystery that new truths are revealed.

Psychic awareness is a natural expression of our spirit. Just as we grow and develop physically, mentally, and emotionally, so too do we spiritually evolve and advance.

For instance, as we get older, our bodies naturally grow and develop. Through exercise and a healthy diet we can increase our physical stamina and contribute to good health. Learning how to accept our emotions and feelings, forgive ourselves and others, heal our emotional wounds, and love ourselves increases emotional maturity, while mental and intellectual growth occurs through questioning, exploring, learning, and problem solving.

Spiritual growth is just as important. Listening to the voice of our spirit allows our understanding of who we are and what life is to evolve and transform. As our spirituality deepens, our ability to develop and use our psychic senses expands and strengthens.

Psychic Protection

As we listen to our spirit and open ourselves to receive nonphysical energy information, we increase our interaction with the spirit realm. A source of loving, wise, and positive energy, the spirit realm seeks to guide and help us. Through our intuition we connect and communicate with loved ones on the other side, spirit guides, angels, and other divine beings. At times we may recognize or receive the name or other identifying information about who we are communicating with. However, it is not always important and it can even become a distraction to focus too much on the identity of the spirit who is spiritually close. If the energy information that you receive is positive and affirming and if you feel comfortable and calm while intuiting, you can trust that you are connected to positive and beneficial spiritual forces.

However, even though the spirit realm is predominately positive and safe, there are lower-vibration nonphysical energies that can create confusion and provide inaccurate psychic energy information. Although they are rare, there are also nonphysical entities that can be disruptive and thrive on fear and negativity. However, in the spirit realm, the power is with the positive and the good. The light, or high-vibration divine and positive energy, is a stronger force, and once it is invoked, any dark forces scatter and diminish. Under normal circumstances, lower-vibration spirits cannot harm, hurt, invade, bother, or attach to us while engaged in psychic development.

With this said, there are a few things to be aware of and ways to further protect yourself during psychic activity.

Practice the following:

- Do not open yourself to psychic influences if you are under the influence of alcohol or drugs. This lowers your vibration and weakens your energy field, enabling harmful energies to draw close to you.

- If you are angry, fearful, anxious, or in a heightened emotional state, do not engage in psychic development work. First talk to someone who is understanding and compassionate and who can help you to discharge and release difficult emotions. Seek an inner state of tranquility through meditation and prayer. Engage in a physical activity like running, swimming, or a sport that will help you blow off steam. When you feel more of a sense of calmness, you can open your psychic channels.

- Never seek psychic energy information for revenge, to prove that you are better or more special than others, or to have power over another. This lowers your vibration and attracts negative energies that will offer you the information you want in order to create a bond with you. However, only the initial information you receive will be correct and helpful. Eventually you will become confused and disturbed by what you receive.

• Before you intuitively tune in to psychic energy information, it is always a good idea to say a prayer or invoke divine and positive, high-vibration light energy and presence. Before I begin a session I always say a short prayer. I ask to be surrounded by the white light of love and protection, and I ask to only receive information and guidance that is in my and my client's highest good. This activates protective high-vibration energy and repels negative or unhelpful spirit realm influences.

Raising your vibration, embodying the divine attributes of love and forgiveness, and being mindful of your spiritual growth activates a white-light bubble of protection that continually surrounds you.

🪷 Exercise: Intuitive Meditation 🪷

Meditation can help you to connect with your spirit and better receive clear and accurate intuitive guidance. During meditation, the active, conscious mind and emotions become less prominent. To varying degrees the inner chatter also becomes more subdued and quiet. Although the thinking mind never completely turns off, meditation allows you to differentiate between the voice of the thinking mind and conscious self and the deeper presence of your spirit, where psychic energy information emerges. A regular meditation practice can strengthen and accelerate psychic development.

Here is a simple meditation that will help you to increase your intuitive awareness.

To begin, find a quiet place where you will not be disturbed. It is best to have a dimly lit room. Turn off any electronics, and sit in a comfortable chair or on the floor with pillows. When beginning a meditation practice, you may want to set a timer for five to fifteen minutes.

Close your eyes and pay attention to your breath. Breathe long, deep inhales and exhale any stress or tension. Continue to breathe this cleansing breath, inhaling and then releasing any tightness or tension in the body through the exhale.

As you breathe, be relaxed yet attentive and notice random thoughts and emotions as they surface without overfocusing on them. Do not push away or ignore what surfaces. Simply take note of your thoughts, breathe, and let them go. Don't react and begin to overthink. Train your mind to notice a thought and then let it go. When an emotion surfaces, feel it and breathe and release it. Acknowledge whatever surfaces and continue to bring your awareness back to the breath.

When you feel relaxed, imagine your mind opening. Visualize, sense, or feel a white-light orb of energy above your head. Continue to breathe cleansing breaths, and slowly allow this light to fill and open your mind. Continue to imagine your mind merging with this light.

Breathe into your heart and imagine it opening. Allow the white light to expand from your mind into your heart. As your heart opens, imagine the light filling you with love. Move the energy of light and love through your body. Feel your body respond and soften and become receptive. Imagine this light and love extending from your body and filling your energy field.

As your mind, heart, body, and energy field merge with light and love, become aware of any psychic thoughts, feelings, images, and sensations that emerge. Accept whatever surfaces without overfocusing on it. Continue to breathe and invite and allow any psychic impressions to continue to emerge. Stay in a receptive mode, and take note of what you receive without trying to understand or overthink it.

When the energy begins to fade, gently open your eyes. Write down any psychic impressions, feelings, thoughts, images, and sensations that you experienced.

INTUITIVE TYPES AND SPIRITUALITY

As we continue to open to and become more familiar with listening to and connecting with our spirit, new connections and aspects of our authentic self emerge. Psychic development sets in motion accelerated growth and change. It pushes aside the mundane and inconsequential and moves our soul and spirit to the forefront. Although developing psychic abilities can begin as nothing more than an interesting pastime, it creates a subtle but significant shift in our consciousness. We become part of a rich world of energy, spirit presence, and spiritual exploration.

Spirituality and psychic development are intertwined. Each of the four psychic types connect with and express spirituality in slightly different ways. We all embody and have the seed of each type's spiritual gift within us. While you have the potential to experience and express the spirituality of each type, you may find a stronger connection with the spiritual energy of your predominant psychic type or types.

Consciousness (Mental Intuitive Type)

If you have a high degree of mental intuition, you likely have a natural spiritual understanding of and connection to higher consciousness, wisdom, and mindful awareness. Unlike an emotional intuitive, you are less likely to be swayed by emotional states and heightened spiritual longing. You are more interested in what makes sense, not necessarily logical sense but intuitive inner sense.

Because you are a truth seeker, you may investigate and try out different religions and spiritual paths. Always attracted to new ideas and knowledge, you may enjoy studying spiritual texts and investigating less mainstream spiritual thought. Many mental intuitives are attracted to spiritual practices that explore the power of the mind, such as using the mind to heal the physical body, create abundance, and intuitively explore and communicate with other dimensions and spiritual beings.

A mental intuitive may also be attracted to the study and research of different religions and spiritual practices, such as Buddhism, Science of Mind, and mindfulness.

The Lovers (Emotional Intuitive Type)

If you have a high degree of emotional intuition, your heart is the door-way to spiritual presence. You are intuitively connected to the energy of unconditional love, compassion, and forgiveness. With your tendency to feel deep feelings and create intense emotional connections with others, your spirituality is likely heart-centered and passionate.

You may be devoted to a particular spiritual leader or spiritual being with whom you experience a close, personal, and loving connection. The desire to feel and experience heightened states of longing and rapture and spiritually merge and become one with a soul mate or beloved part-ner may stir deep in your soul and motivate you.

For an emotional intuitive, feelings of love and the desire to heal the emotional wounds of others intensify psychic abilities. Through the combined forces of emotional intuition and spirituality, an emotional intuitive has the innate ability to connect and communicate with the angelic realm. Through this special connection to the angels, they are often able to lovingly heal and compassionately tend to those who suffer.

Earthwise (Physical Intuitive Type)

If you intuit primarily through physical intuition, you are naturally at-tuned to the divine presence within all of life. A bird in flight, the roar of sea waves, or a blooming flower may whisper to you of a greater divinity.

If you are a physical intuitive, you may feel a special spiritual connec-tion with nature. The walls of your church may be the trees, the wind, and the sky. You may be attracted to Wiccan and pagan practices and intuitively feel the power of your spirit through earth-based rituals, or you might instead be drawn to the time-honored rites and practices of more traditional religions.

As a physical intuitive, your spirituality may be expressed through action and service. Not content to meditate, like a spiritual intuitive, or contemplate truth and reality, like those with a high degree of mental intuition, you may feel more comfortable expressing your spirituality in more tangible and hands-on kinds of way. You may give to those in need, quietly take on the less-sought-after tasks of keeping an organization or family on track, and contribute your time and energy as a way to love and divinely serve.

If you possess a high degree of physical intuition, you may be a natural healer who is able to work with divine forces through hands-on and other forms of healing. Your physical self, particularly your hands, can be a conduit of higher-vibration spiritual energy. In this way you have the potential to penetrate and go beyond the limitations of physicality to transform and heal.

Essence (Spiritual Intuitive Type)

If you have a high degree of spiritual intuition, you likely have a natural appreciation and affinity for the unseen and spirit realms. Because of your awareness of nonphysical beings, you have the natural ability to discern and trust the positive guidance and love of the unseen. Through communicating with spirit, you have the potential to bring messages of hope, understanding, and guidance to others. You are also likely to intuitively tune in to the spiritual purpose and soul path of others and activate and support their spiritual gifts.

With a rich inner life, you may seek solitude or spiritual practices that assist you in achieving higher states of awareness. You might also be drawn to spiritual practices where you can lose your sense of self and merge into a greater feeling of oneness, beyond the physical body. Those with a high degree of spiritual intuition are often attracted to less conventional spiritual practices. Unlike a physical intuitive, who often experiences spirituality through nature, or an emotional intuitive, who enjoys heart-centered communication with others, you may experience your spirituality through an inner state of awareness. For a spiritual intuitive, spirituality may be a sense of connectedness to the unseen whole and a peaceful oneness with all of life. Although your ability to feel and be immersed in a wide range of spiritual states is highly refined, you may not necessarily be able to put your experiences into words.

FREQUENCY

As our connection to spirituality increases and intensifies, so does our vibration. The process of attuning our mind, emotions, body, and spirit to the energy of pure, wise, and loving divine presence is often referred to as *raising our vibration*. The higher your vibration, the easier it is to psychically receive accurate and helpful guidance. Fear, negativity, and similar emotions and states of mind vibrate at a lower density. When we receive psychic energy information through lower vibrations, it is more likely to invoke fear and confusion and be inaccurate. As we connect and align our consciousness with high-vibration energy, we are naturally protected from lower energies and psychic interference.

We can only psychically receive energy information at our level of consciousness. Higher consciousness awareness embodies the divine attributes of love, compassion, and wisdom. As our consciousness ascends to these higher levels, it becomes easier to receive accurate and crystal-clear psychic information.

It is important to raise your vibration before engaging in psychic work. However, this practice can also be done on a daily basis, as integrating higher levels of intuitive awareness into your everyday life is the ideal. Not only will your psychic abilities increase in strength and accuracy, but you will be happier and experience more inner peace. Some of the benefits of raising your vibration include improved mental clarity, an increase in personal power, improved physical health, and rapid healing of illness and other physical, emotional, and mental ailments.

There are many ways to raise your vibration. Here are a few:

- Practice meditation on a daily basis. Even if you have only five or ten minutes, tuning inward, focusing on the breath, and listening to your spirit can raise your vibration and increase intuitive receptivity.
- Spend time in nature. If you live in the city or are not able to be in a natural setting, look out the window at the sky, stars, and clouds. Sit on a porch or deck, watch the birds and squirrels, or tune in the energy of the trees.
- Be grateful. It can be helpful either in the morning or evening to have a daily practice of recognizing and having gratitude for three things that you experienced in the past twenty-four hours.

- Notice beauty. Beauty is an attribute of the divine. Spiritual beauty is not necessarily the same as what society deems attractive. The smile of a child, a cat sitting in the sun, a home-cooked meal, and other simple occurrences all radiate beauty.

- Be kind. Smile, forgive, do not react to provocation, let go of defensiveness, and give others the benefit of the doubt. These are all acts of kindness.

- Go on an electronic fast. Turn off your phone, television, computer, or music for a specific amount of time.

- Eat fresh, raw foods and drink water.

- Do more of what brings you joy. If you are not sure how to generate feelings of happiness, try different things. Gravitate toward what feels good.

- Help others. Be of service and give, and let others be there for you.

- Trust your intuition and act on your innermost truth.

- Releasing negative emotions and replacing them with positive ones quickly raises our vibration. Instead of ignoring and suppressing uncomfortable emotions, let yourself feel them. As you do this, they dissipate. However difficult it may be to let your feelings surface, it causes more harm to stuff them down and ignore them. Your emotions do not define you; they are simply feelings. They come and go. You are not your anger, fear, frustration, or grief. As you feel your negative emotions and let them go, you make room for the higher vibrations of love and compassion to fill you.

- One of the most effective ways to raise your vibration and accelerate your psychic development is to pay attention to your thoughts. Interrupt the cycle of mind chatter and negative self-talk. When you encounter fear-based, negative, critical, or judgmental thoughts, let them go. Acknowledge them and then choose to think a different thought. Replace negative or fear-based thoughts with a positive, reinforcing statement.

    For instance, imagine that you find yourself thinking thoughts such as these:

I don't know what is wrong with me.

I know I am going to be disappointed.

Last time I tried that I failed miserably. I am not going to take that chance again.

You can choose to counteract these negative thoughts with more positive ones. For instance:

I value my individuality and like doing things my way.

I know everything will work out for my highest good.

I learn a lot by trying new things. I am grateful that life is always providing me with new opportunities.

The first statements lower your vibration and drag you down. The second statements are more motivating and focus on good feelings. They raise your vibration and open you to positive energy.

❀ Exercise: Meditation to ❀
Raise Your Vibration

Raising your vibration prior to engaging in psychic activity will protect you from lower, negative energies and help you to receive higher guidance and insight. This is especially important if you are stressed or fearful or have been in a negative environment.

This meditation can be used to clear your mind, heart, and physical body in preparation for psychic development work, exploration, and practice.

To begin, find a quiet place where you will not be disturbed and sit in a comfortable position. Close your eyes and breathe a long inhale and exhale any stress or tension. Continue to breathe cleansing breaths, releasing any tightness or tension in the body. Focus on the breath and become aware of any random thoughts or emotions that begin to surface. Accept whatever thoughts or feelings surface without pushing them away or ignoring them. Simply take note of them and let them go. Anytime a thought or emotion surfaces, acknowledge it and continue to bring your awareness back to the breath.

Continue to breathe and imagine a beam of pure, high-vibration white-light energy above your head. This divine light is soothing and relaxing and at the same time energizing and nurturing.

Take a deep breath and allow this light to move down through the top of your head and into your third eye area. Breathe and imagine this light expanding and filling your head and neck with calm, soothing energy. Take a moment and continue to breathe in this energy. Move the beam of light down into your shoulders. Feel yourself relax. With the energy of this light, imagine that any burdens and stress in your jaw, neck, and shoulders release and dissipate.

Move this beam of light into your heart. Imagine your heart opening. Stuffed-away and suppressed feelings surface and easily dissolve as you breathe this light into your heart. Feel your heart expand and open like the blossom of a flower. Your heart grows larger and larger, filling with high-vibration love energy.

Allow this light to move down into your solar plexus. Feel this light filling you with strength and power. This high-vibration spiritual power enhances and supports your intuition. This light expands, and you feel spiritually grounded in the physical body.

Move this light into your organs. Feel this high-vibration energy releasing any toxins in the body as you fill with light. Feel this light nurturing and strengthening you.

Continue to breathe and feel the energy move down into your hips, legs, and feet. Feel your whole body energized and relaxed. In this high-vibration energy you feel lighter and at the same time grounded as the light reaches down into the earth and anchors you.

Continue to breathe and feel your body, mind, and spirit vibrating and expanding. Feel yourself move beyond and outside of the physical confines of your body. Imagine this light surrounding and protecting you.

Stay in this high vibration as long as possible. When you feel ready, breathe and come fully and completely into your physical body. Allow the white-light bubble to continue to surround and protect you.

ALTERED STATES OF CONSCIOUSNESS

Raising your vibrational frequency empowers you to reach the kind of altered state of awareness that supports and encourages psychic awareness. In an altered state of awareness, the personality and ego self recedes into the background as your intuitive soul self comes forward. To the overtaxed brain, altered states of awareness can feel soothing and relaxing. They are often experienced as expansive, loving, and tension-free.

Being in an altered state can be so pleasant that many people attempt to achieve it in false and potentially damaging ways. Alcohol and drug use weakens the energy field and makes us more vulnerable to negative spiritual influences. Although they can bring relief by numbing and quieting the personality and ego self, they give only temporary relief that cannot be sustained.

The best way to achieve an altered state is through training the mind to detach from ego-driven states of consciousness and reside in higher-frequency awareness. This can be accomplished by detaching from mind chatter and raising your vibration. The more adept and familiar you become with altered states of consciousness, the easier it is to access psychic energy information. Here are a few ways that you can achieve an altered state through raising your vibration.

Walking Meditation

Walk someplace where you do not need to be overly concerned about traffic and noise. A quiet street or path through nature is preferred. As you walk, pay attention to your breath and scan your environment. Continue to breathe, and if you find yourself overthinking or carrying on an inner conversation, go back to the breath. As you breathe, open your heart and become intuitively receptive. As you receive energy information, don't try to figure it out or overthink. Allow energy and awareness to flow in and out as you scan your environment, relax, and breathe.

Prayer

Prayer induces an altered state of awareness and connectedness to a higher presence and power. Invoking and talking to God, Goddess, Divine Spirit or Presence, or whatever higher energy you feel most aligned with is a powerful way to raise your consciousness and nurture your intuitive receptivity. Prayer puts things into perspective. It allows you to let go of control and accept grace and intervention. When your psychic awareness is aligned with higher forces, you become a messenger and intermediary for the divine.

Chanting

Chanting is an excellent way to raise your vibration. While speaking and singing are a projection of the voice in the external environment, chanting focuses the energy of the voice inward. This sound energy reverberates throughout the body and energy field and shifts your consciousness into higher states of awareness. Various spiritual practices and disciplines use chanting as an effective way to draw closer to the divine.

Here is a simple but effective chant. Sit with your back erect and close your eyes. Breathe in through your nose and exhale the *Om* sound. When you run out of breath, repeat. Breathe in through the nose and exhale the Om sound. Continue this breath and the repetition of Om.

Music

Listening to music relaxes the thinking mind, soothes the nervous system, and releases stress. Allowing the conscious self to recede and the intuitive self to come forward is the hallmark of an altered state of awareness. The best kinds of music to induce an altered state are polyrhythmic, monotonous drumming, chants, and New Age music. However, you may have a particular type of music you enjoy that induces an altered state.

Music can positively impact our brain waves and stimulate psychic receptivity and awareness. It may be helpful to listen to instrumental music and to close your eyes and relax. As you do this, allow images, feelings, thoughts, and sensations to emerge. Don't overfocus on what surfaces; just keep relaxing and listening.

Incorporating these kinds of activities into your daily life will help you to become more familiar and comfortable with shifting into an altered state. This is turn will make it easier to attain this state when you want to use your psychic abilities. If you are constantly rushing, overthinking, stressed, and anxious, it is difficult to quickly shift into the receptive and open awareness that is necessary to receive psychic energy information. Psychic awareness is a way of life, and the more you nurture and encourage altered states of awareness on a daily basis, the stronger your psychic muscle becomes.

Being Present

Along with raising your vibration and attaining an altered state of consciousness, being grounded in the here and now is essential for successful psychic development. Grounding is being fully centered, mind, body and spirit, and it encourages and supports you in receiving psychic energy and translating it into understandable and usable information. When you are not grounded, receiving psychic energy can create mental confusion and leave you feeling off balance and overwhelmed with sensations and foggy impressions.

At times, raising your vibration and engaging in psychic development can tip the scales and knock you off balance. Here are a few telltale signs of being ungrounded:

- Feeling spacey
- Physical awkwardness, bumping into things, tripping
- Forgetfulness
- Headaches
- Grogginess and laziness
- Staring into space for an extended period of time
- Feeling fearful, anxious, or stressed
- Inability to communicate your psychic impressions
- Feeling a constant stream of psychic information moving through you (even when you do not want to receive psychic energy)

- Experiencing emotional ups and downs for no known reason
- Constantly hearing words, phrases, and inner talk that do not make sense
- Constantly seeing orbs, colors, images, people, faces, and other images that others do not perceive (when not engaged in psychic work)
- Not eating or sleeping well
- Pounding in your head or dizziness
- A constant buzzing feeling of vibration moving through your body
- Being unable to focus
- Craving sweets or carbohydrates

When developing and engaging in psychic development work, it is helpful to include grounding as a part of your daily practice. Here are a few grounding activities:

- Practice mindful awareness. Notice your surroundings and the activity that is going on around you. Smells and sounds can bring us into the here and now. What subtle noises, fragrances, and colors do you notice in your environment? Move your awareness into your body and become aware of any tension or stress in the muscles and joints. Stretch and release any tightness or discomfort. Breathe and center your awareness in your solar plexus. Feeling your inner core of power centers your consciousness in the body.
- Being in nature, feeling the sun on your face, dipping your toes in a cool stream, or digging in the garden all help to ground your energy. Feeling a connection with nature is a good way to clear your head, open your heart, and feel your connection with the earth. All of these also help you to increase and build up your inner psychic reserves.
- Lifting weights, running, doing yoga, and most types of physical activity are good ways to ground. Psychic development work tends to increase our spiritual energy and expand our consciousness outside of the physical body. Physical activity helps this energy to move back into the body and nurtures the spirit as well.

- Eating protein such as beans and meat (if you are not a vegetarian) and red, orange, or yellow fruits and vegetables energizes the lower chakras.

- Take a bath or shower, sit in a hot tub or steam room, or go swimming. Water neutralizes energetic static and helps to connect and integrate the mind, body, and spirit.

- Practicing visualizations can help us connect our spiritual and physical energy centers with the earth and the elements. Here is an easy grounding visualization. Imagine a red cord of energy that extends from your lower spine down into the earth. White-light high-vibration energy moves down through the top of your head, through the spinal column, and into this cord. This cord extends into the ground and anchors itself deep in the earth, and moves the energy of the earth up through the cord and into the physical body.

The Clearing-Out Process

One of the most reliable ways to raise your vibrational frequency, ground yourself, and refine and sharpen your psychic abilities is through personal inner growth. As high-vibration energy enters your consciousness, whatever resides within you that is not in harmony with your highest good surfaces. Simply put, your stuff will rear its ugly head. Old emotions and emotional wounds will make their way to the surface, and beliefs, feelings, and thoughts that prevent you from growing psychically and embracing a new understanding of yourself may seem to become stronger. While you may feel and become more aware of your fears, stress, low self-esteem, vulnerabilities, and sense of worthiness, you may be at a loss as to how to heal and transform these feelings and issues. Psychic development does not happen in a vacuum. The shift to a higher psychic consciousness stirs up our fears, thoughts, and emotions and prods and pushes to the surface all that is preventing us from being clear channels of positive, high-vibration energy.

If you resist this growth and try to hold back the tide that wants to wash away all that is obstructing and preventing you from clear and accurate intuitive receptivity, you will hit a wall. Intuition will become fuzzy and unclear and you may feel blocked and unable to form a clear psychic connection to energy. If you continue to try to push through and work with psychic energy without addressing personal issues and releasing past emotional wounds and limiting beliefs, you may feel a heightened degree of anxiety, which for some people often becomes a feeling of panic.

The only way to continue on the psychic journey is to participate in the work of personal and inner growth. This is not the exciting work of psychic exploration and paranormal intrigue, but the tedious and often difficult work of purging and letting go of painful emotions, beliefs, prejudices, fears, suppressed anger, and all the other stuff that we try to avoid.

The good news is that your psychic awareness can assist you in this process. It acts almost like an intense cleansing agent. As high-vibration energy pours in, it stimulates and helps to flush out what needs to be let go of. The pace of this work can vary; sometimes it is slow and other times it happens more quickly. Trust the timing and rhythm of this detoxification process. Your soul and spirit working through your intuition are guiding you.

Subtle Clearing

The clearing process can happen at any time and any place, but it is more likely to occur when you are relaxing, meditating, or doing an intuitive exercise. During a gentle psychic clearing you may begin to experience subtle feelings of sadness or anxiety. You may become frustrated with your intuitive progress and want to give up, or you may wonder why you are even trying to become more psychic. You may feel blocked and unable to access your intuition. Although the feelings are not overwhelming, you may lose interest in developing your abilities or become restless, and your attention may become focused on something else. However, if you are able to sit with these feelings and probe deeper, you will discover that what you are experiencing is motivated by an inner resistance. There may be an unconscious belief about psychic development, or you may be fearful that you are changing and entering uncharted inner territory.

There may be suppressed pain or fear from the past that has nothing to do with psychic awareness and that you need to let go of.

As you become a clear psychic channel, the low-vibration energy of negativity and toxic emotions surfaces to be released. Instead of denying the uncomfortable feelings and thoughts, embrace them. Feel the emotions and allow the thoughts to surface, breathe, and then let them go. This is all that you need to do. You do not have to relive past events or be consciously aware of the origin of what surfaces. Just accept and feel and the energy will dissipate. As you do this, you heal and transform. High-vibration energy flows through you, and you experience better spiritual, mental, emotional, and physical health and well-being. Your psychic power increases.

When we move forward in our psychic development, it is inevitable that at some point we will take a step backward. Don't let setbacks alarm you, and don't give them more attention and meaning than they deserve. Take a deep breath, do what needs to be done, and keep moving forward.

Continually Purge the Psychic Channels

Clearing your energy is not a one-time event. It is important to continually acknowledge and become aware of the emotions, feelings, resistance, memories, and beliefs that get stirred up and brought to the surface during psychic development. To continue to receive clear and accurate psychic energy information, feel your feelings, let go of negative thoughts, and release any built-up stress or tension in the body.

Sometimes the process of clearing is obvious and other times it occurs in unexpected and more challenging ways.

For instance, you may be at home reading about intuition or spirituality or doing an intuitive exercise when a wave of sadness or other unexplained feelings comes over you. You may want to cry without knowing why. Or you might become anxious and it may feel like your skin is crawling, or you might all of a sudden feel a sense of fear or impending doom or that something is not right. Although these episodes are confusing and likely do not make sense, they are signs that something is surfacing from within and needs to be released or healed. If this or something similar to these experiences occurs, don't run from what is happening but instead stay with it.

For some people, confusing memories may surface. Events that you don't remember and that have been repressed and don't make sense may come into your awareness. You might recall past-life memories and feel the trauma or fear that you felt long, long ago. Feelings of anger or even rage may spontaneously come over you. You might find yourself mad at something that doesn't seem like a big deal. None of what is happening makes sense and you don't know what to do. You may dream of places and events that you do not recall but that invoke strong emotions, or you may awaken feeling an emotional intensity that you cannot identify.

While developing and increasing your psychic capacity, the clearing-out process is sure to happen to some degree. When it does, stay with the process, despite the feeling of wanting to shut down and avoid all that is surfacing. Becoming conscious is a big step in psychic and spiritual growth and awareness. If you resist this process, you will feel lost and ungrounded. Despite the intensity of the experience, allowing and not resisting it is healthy and positive. Not only will your intuitive abilities increase and become stronger, but your health and overall feeling of wellness will improve as well.

When confusing feelings or memories surface, stay mindful of the process. Allow a part of your awareness to experience the feelings and tune in to the memories and other sensations that need to surface while another aspect of you allows and invites positive, loving, and high-vibration energy in. Breathe and receive this energy, open your heart, and have compassion for yourself as you clear out and let go of what is not in your highest good. Stay with this process for as long as possible. Eventually the painful feelings, stress, and anxiety will begin to calm down and dissipate. Feelings of peace and love will flow in, and you may become aware of and feel a warm and loving angelic presence helping you.

Once you have let go of whatever may have been getting in the way of you receiving high-vibration, clear, and accurate psychic insights and guidance, other changes may occur. For instance, you may feel motivated to let go of people and activities in your life that are not supporting your highest good. Certain friendships may go by the wayside, and you may no longer find interest in past activities and pursuits. You may find that you are more sensitive to certain foods, like those high in sugar and carbs, and that crowds and loud noises are uncomfortable. As your vibration heightens, you may experience an increased interest in spending time outdoors, being with others who are on a spiritual path, and taking better care of yourself. Once activated and developed, your psychic awareness acts as an invisible radar leading you to the people, food, activities, and environments that support and nurture the best possible you. Being psychic is a way of life, and it leads to a good life of abundance, positive connections with others, inner peace, and joy.

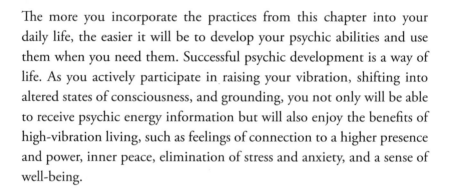

The more you incorporate the practices from this chapter into your daily life, the easier it will be to develop your psychic abilities and use them when you need them. Successful psychic development is a way of life. As you actively participate in raising your vibration, shifting into altered states of consciousness, and grounding, you not only will be able to receive psychic energy information but will also enjoy the benefits of high-vibration living, such as feelings of connection to a higher presence and power, inner peace, elimination of stress and anxiety, and a sense of well-being.

Reading Yourself

The path of psychic development leads to increased self-awareness. Our thoughts, feelings, expectations, desires, and personal biases all come to the forefront. Don't resist this process, as self-awareness creates intuitive clarity and trust. When we know ourselves, we are less likely to confuse intuitive receptivity with our personal biases, thoughts, and judgments. One of the most common concerns that surfaces with psychic development is the inability to trust where the energy information is coming from. Many people fear that what they believe to be intuitive feelings, thoughts, and sensations are coming from their non-intuitive personal thoughts, desires, expectations, and hopes. To be able to trust what you intuitively receive, it is essential to know yourself. This is true both when we seek intuitive information for our own personal needs and desires and when we intuit for someone else.

There is a difference between psychically tuning in to ourselves and our personal issues and psychically tuning in to another. The basic dynamics of receiving and interpreting psychic energy information are similar. However, there are specific factors and influences in each of these approaches that determine psychic accuracy.

GUIDELINES FOR SUCCESS

The motivation to develop psychic ability often comes from our desire to intuitively tune in to our personal issues, conditions, and concerns. When we need to make a decision or choice or when we have concerns or questions about our career, a relationship, or another area of life, many of us turn to our intuition for guidance and direction.

However, if you have been frustrated by your attempts to receive energy information or don't trust the intuitive guidance that you have received, you are not alone. Many people initially have the same experience and doubt their psychic ability. Before you become discouraged and give up, know that it is likely not your level of psychic awareness that is hindering you. Instead, it may be your approach and your personal baggage that are interfering.

Neutrality

Accurately intuiting energy information and guidance about our personal issues can be challenging. Our desire for certain outcomes and our biases can interfere with intuitive clarity. This is natural and normal. We are human after all, and we have desires, wants, and needs. Being able to detach from what we hope our intuition will tell us is not always easy to do. Yet psychic receptivity requires a state of neutrality. This is the ability to accept the energy information that you receive, whatever it may be. It may take some time to reach this level of acceptance. Achieving a state of neutrality may be easier to do for some issues than others.

When beginning to develop intuition, it can be helpful to stick to personal issues and questions whose outcomes you are not attached to. This allows you to develop psychic abilities without the pressure of your desires lurking in the back of your mind. Once you are more secure in your abilities, you can approach areas of more personal importance. It is also a good practice to write down your expectations, fears, and desires before intuitively tuning in to your concerns and the area in question.

Emotions

When it comes to accurately intuiting personal concerns and issues, our feelings and emotions influence receptivity. Strong emotions and potent unconscious emotions often generate energetic static and muffle intuitive impressions. They can also interfere with intuited information and sway how we interpret what we receive.

It is best not to try to receive intuitive information and guidance when feeling emotionally overwhelmed or triggered. Being fearful or anxious about the information that you might receive blocks intuitive receptivity. In a similar way, intuiting energy information about a current emotionally charged situation or problem can be difficult. Unfortunately, it is usually when we are confused, distraught, worried, or stressed that we most want to receive psychic energy information. However, this is when it is most difficult to access it.

If your emotions are getting in the way of receiving accurate energy information, take a step back. Focus on your feelings, allow them to surface, and feel them and then they will begin to dissipate. This may take some time, and you cannot necessarily rush the process. It may be helpful to meditate, write down your feelings, or process your feelings with someone you trust. Discharging your emotions will help you to achieve a more intuitively receptive state.

Thoughts

Another factor that affects intuitive receptivity is our beliefs and thoughts and what we think will happen. Our predictable ways and patterns of thinking often have an effect on what we intuitively receive and how we interpret it. What we believe is possible and likely to happen can be a self-fulfilling prophecy. If you are by nature more optimistic, the energy information you receive will be more positive. If you are more pessimistic, then you will likely intuit and interpret energy information through this lens.

Be aware of this unconscious bias. Trust energy information that surprises you and goes counter to your patterned way of thinking. This is a sign that what you are receiving is not coming from your personal biases. If something psychically surfaces that you did not expect, do not try to talk yourself out of it. It can take self-discipline to avoid trying to fit psychic information into what we think it should be. Trust your intuitive senses more and your analytical, rational thinking less.

The optimum state for psychic receptivity is to be free of personal influences and unbiased and receptive to what is. Not only is this state psychically beneficial, but this detached and open awareness releases stress and tension. It aligns us with our highest good and activates high-vibration energy.

Confidence

In order to successfully tune in to our personal issues and questions and receive accurate energy information, we must have confidence. Many people get hooked into the belief that they must first prove their abilities before they can trust them. While this may seem like a reasonable argument, it is trust and confidence that breed success. It is similar to the timeless question *What came first, the chicken or the egg?* Without confidence in yourself, it is difficult to psychically receive energy information, and if you do not receive accurate energy information, it is difficult to have confidence.

When I notice a lack of confidence in my students, I ask them to suspend their doubts and act as if they are receiving psychic energy information and then to take their time interpreting it. Although they may still be a little timid, this approach allows for increased psychic receptivity and accuracy.

Using the Ego

The ego constantly wants to influence and interfere with your psychic senses. Your personality and ego self will never truly allow you to be all of who you are. As long as you listen to and accept its perspective about who you are and what your life is, your psychic abilities will flounder. The ego wants to be in charge. However, the ego is a product of the human self and not the spiritual, soulful self. It does not have a broad range of awareness and access to psychic energy information. The ego is connected to the physical and material world. It relies on the five senses and defines what you experience through the mind and reasoning.

However, having a healthy and strong ego can be helpful to psychic ability. Your ego can help you to stay balanced in the physical world by protecting your vulnerabilities and shielding you from the judgments and opinions of others. Although psychic ability is becoming more mainstream and accepted, there are still some who are critical or judgmental of it. A healthy ego helps you to defend your right to be who you are and pursue your gifts and interests. In this kind of subordinate role, your ego can support your intuition and empower your psychic senses.

The ego can also support the intuitive process by encouraging and supporting your efforts. Its divine purpose is to help us function in this world and provide us with a base of support. When we want to give up, the ego can encourage us to keep going and try again. The ego's grounded approach can also help us by taking care of what needs to get done in the business of day-to-day life.

Self-Honesty

Being honest with ourselves is not always easy. We have a psychological tendency to shield ourselves from information that may challenge our desires and beliefs. To psychically tune in to our own issues and questions, we have to be able to accept the truth.

Before you ask for psychic energy information, ask yourself if you are ready and willing to be completely honest with yourself. If you are not, that is okay. Give yourself some time to explore your fears and desires.

When you are ready to be honest with yourself, don't settle for trite or shallow answers. Go deeper into the truth and be willing to explore what you may need to do or change that will empower you to be happier and create more of what you want.

For instance, I worked with a woman recently who wanted to know if she would ever meet her soul mate and long-term partner. She wanted a yes or no answer and she wanted to know when she would meet him and what he would look like. This is a fairly typical type of request. However, the answer is rarely as straightforward as what we would like it to be.

The truth is that there is a constant flow of abundance, love, joy, and fulfillment moving through the universe and into our lives. It is not simply what or who is coming our way but more importantly our readiness to receive it that determines what we experience.

Over the many years of giving readings and intuiting the future, I have learned that to give an accurate prediction, it is necessary to intuit personal readiness. As much as we may want psychic information to give us answers to questions about relationships, career, finances, and other issues with specific times, places, and descriptions, this may not come to pass if there is an unconscious factor preventing us from receiving information. Sometimes we are ready for the abundance and love of the universe to come our way, but not always. If there is a personal fear, unhealed wound, belief, or other hindrance getting in the way, it is important to become aware of this. In this way we can heal what needs to be healed and change what needs to be changed, and then we can receive and experience what we desire.

When intuiting personal information, be honest with yourself and be willing to receive the kind of helpful psychic information that will empower you to experience and create more joy and satisfaction. Explore your core truths and allow yourself to receive guidance about what you may need to confront and what may be inhibiting you. This is the kind of self-honesty that leads to clear intuitive receptivity, inner growth, and joy.

❀ Psychic Exercises ❀
You Can Use Throughout the Day

Make psychic awareness a way of life. Throughout your day, listen to and trust your intuition. Even if you are not sure if you are receiving a psychic message, pay attention to the intuitive impressions as they surface. Seize opportunities to strengthen and refine your psychic muscle. To be able to use your psychic awareness when and how you want to, it is necessary to develop an intimate relationship with it. You can do this by keeping a part of your conscious awareness alert to psychic insights and messages as they present themselves.

We are accustomed to focusing on the outer world and on our thinking mind. We habitually and overwhelmingly stay limited to being absorbed in our thoughts and our chattering mind. We also tend to continually scan the outer world and our environment through our physical senses. However, as you strengthen your connection to your spirit and become more familiar with listening within through meditation, you find a valuable inner resource that you can draw from.

As you tune in to your psychic awareness throughout the day, remember to pay attention to the signs and signals that accompany energy information. Psychic insights are even-toned, understated, and repetitious and may sound like a still, small voice. They may emerge through spontaneous images or unexpected knowing. Physical sensations like tingling up and down your spine or arms or a feeling of your heart opening may accompany them. Receiving psychic energy information is not stressful or anxiety-producing. It feels calm and eases tension and stress. Psychic insights can feel like an aha awareness. They do not come through linear thinking, and there will be no known evidence or reasons to back them up.

You can use your psychic abilities all day, every day. While you are driving to work, dropping off the kids at school, working, sitting in class, or even having dinner with friends, be aware of psychic feelings, thoughts, sensations, insights, and guidance. At first it might seem a little distracting to keep a part of your awareness alert to inner messages and guidance, but with a little practice and discipline it will begin to feel more natural and normal.

Here are a few ways that you can use your psychic muscle on a daily basis.

Finding a Parking Space

When driving to a location where crowded parking may be an issue, ask your inner psychic senses to guide you. It is best not to wait until you are stressed and searching for a parking space. Instead, ask for guidance when you are relaxed and have enough driving time to connect with your intuition. You may see an image of an open spot or hear the name of a street or landmark, or you may feel as if you are being directed to a particular location as you get close to your destination.

What Route to Take

Along with finding a parking space, your psychic awareness can also let you know the best route to take when driving or when taking a bus or public transportation. Again, it is best to ask inwardly for guidance when you begin your trip and not wait until you are anxious or run into a problem. Become aware of feelings, sensations, images, and other ways that you feel you are being led.

Stress and Anxiety

When we confront a challenge or problem, we tend to overthink, react emotionally, become stressed, or ignore or push through it. Whatever our unconscious strategy may be, we generally do the best we can at any given time. However, next time you feel stressed or anxious, ask your intuition for help and then go about your day.

It is not always easy to receive clear intuitive information when we are stressed or anxious. However, make the intention to be intuitively guided and trust that you will receive what you need, when you need it. Instead of focusing on receiving psychic insights, trust that the inner wise and loving intuitive you has this covered.

When I find myself becoming stressed or anxious or overthinking, I do my best to remember to ask within for guidance and insight. If there is some action I need to take, I ask to know and become aware of what I can do. I imagine high-vibration divine energy moving through me and releasing my anxiety and stress, and then I let it go. If I start to overthink the issue or become stressed, I focus my thinking mind on something else. I then inwardly listen and wait, knowing and trusting that I will intuitively receive what I need and I can rest in the assurance that there is a loving higher power at work.

Getting Things Done

If you are multitasking and feeling overwhelmed, ask your psychic awareness to tune in and guide you to what is most important. You do not need to specifically list all that you are doing; just ask for guidance on what is the best use of your time and energy. If you have a predetermined agenda of what you think is important and necessary, this may be difficult. You may feel pressured to accomplish certain tasks and projects and not want to leave it up to your intuition. However, the energy information that you receive may surprise you. If it conflicts with what you think is important, take a chance. Trust your intuition, act on what you receive, and see what happens.

What to Eat

Before you grab a snack or plan your meals for the day, take a moment to listen within as to what your body needs to be healthy and full of energy. If you suspect that you may have a food allergy or that a specific food may be interfering with your metabolism or digestion, hold the food in your hand or create an image of it and listen within. Your intuition may speak to you through feelings, thoughts, or sensations of physical depletion or positive waves of energy.

Meetings, Events, and Socializing

If you have an upcoming business or work meeting, take a moment to check in with your intuition. Create an image in your mind's eye of the room or the people attending the meeting, or if it is a remote meeting, imagine yourself during the meeting. Take a deep breath, relax, ask if there is anything you need to know or be aware of, and feel the emotional energy of the meeting.

You can also do this to intuit energy information about an upcoming event or social situation.

Once you have intuited information, be sure to send positive energy to the space and those who will be attending.

Self-Care

Before you start your day or if you are in a challenging situation, ask your intuition for help in self-care. All too often we forget about our own needs and struggle to come into balance when we are confronted with others' wants and desires or when we are busy. Even when we are alone and not necessarily overwhelmed or stressed, we are not always aware of what supports our highest good. Make it a practice to ask your intuition how to best care for yourself, emotionally, mentally, physically, and spiritually. Take a few moments and listen within, then act on what you receive. Even if it seems unfeasible or indulgent, trust your intuition to be your best and most supportive friend.

Psychically tuning in to yourself promotes self-awareness and a deeper communion with your authentic and higher self. Within you there is a wise and loving presence that seeks to draw close and empower you to live a life of abundance and love. Trust this presence and continue to listen within.

CHAPTER 9

Reading Another

Although we are often intimidated by the prospect of psychically tuning in to others' issues and concerns, in some ways it can be easier than intuiting for ourselves. When we know little about the person, we are more inclined to trust our psychic impressions. With little information to go on, the conscious thinking mind cannot interfere. Unless we have a close relationship with the person whom we are psychically reading, we are not emotionally invested in the energy information that we receive. We are less biased and will not be tempted by our hopes and desires or be inclined to want to interpret what we receive in any particular way. However, there are a few challenges to reading others successfully.

EXPECTATIONS

When you read another, it is necessary to manage your expectations and the expectations of the person you are reading. Don't expect to receive energy information in the manner that you desire. Every person you read is different, and you will likely receive energy information in a variety of ways. For instance, if you are primarily a mental intuitive, you might want to receive intuitive impressions through thoughts and knowing. However, if the person you are reading is more of an emotional intuitive, they may be broadcasting energy information through their feelings and emotions. This doesn't always happen, but it is common. Be prepared to receive energy information through all the modalities, even those that you may not have as much confidence in. If the person you are reading has a strong tendency to express energy through a certain modality, the energy information you receive from them will likely come through in this form.

The person you are reading will also have their own expectations. They may want to receive specific information, and they likely have a desired outcome. As much as you may want to provide the kind of information and guidance that the person wants, detach from their expectations as much as possible. Limit the amount of personal information that they give you. Although it may seem helpful, knowing too much about the person can be confusing and interfere with your intuition. Even though you are reading another, it is necessary to stay focused on your own psychic process. Make it your intent to provide clear, accurate, and helpful energy information. Be kind and compassionate toward the person, but do not let their expectations sway you from interpreting the energy information accurately or from trusting the energy information that you receive.

Emotional Stress

The emotional energy that most often interferes when psychically reading another differs from the types of emotions we may experience when reading ourselves. When we first begin to psychically read others, we may feel nervous, stressed, and anxious. We may be nervous about our performance and worried that our psychic awareness will fail. It is also common to doubt our ability and feel pressured to be correct and accurate about what we receive. This is normal, and as we build more confidence in our abilities, these kinds of stresses will begin to dissipate.

If you feel yourself becoming overly anxious when tuning in to another, take a few moments to breathe and relax. Keep it simple. Do not overemphasize your role in the person's life. Provide the energy information that you receive as best you can. Don't tell the person what to do or what not to do. This is not your responsibility. Whatever decisions or choices another makes is up to them. Be careful not to guarantee outcomes. We all have free will, and it is our individual responsibility to make personal choices.

Another common reason for experiencing emotional stress when psychically reading another is the tendency to intuit others' emotional energy. When you psychically tune in to another's issues, questions, and energy, you may unknowingly absorb and feel their feelings. Most people feel varying degrees of nervousness, anxiety, and vulnerability when receiving a psychic reading. Besides feeling nervous about having another person delve into their private issues and questions, they may be in the midst of a crisis or worried, anxious, or grieving. When you tune in to another, you may absorb this emotional energy and become stressed yourself. If you feel that this might be happening, take a few long, deep breaths and exhale any tension or stress. You may want to lighten the mood and make small talk with the person you are reading. When I sense that a client may be nervous, I try to lighten the mood and say something like "Don't be nervous. I'm doing all the work!"

INTERPRETATION

When beginning to psychically tune in to others, it is always best not to overinterpret or overanalyze what you receive. Share information the way that you receive it. If you are not sure of your accuracy, say so. Let the other person interpret the energy information if you are having a hard time understanding it. If you see images, share them the way you perceived them. Share the feelings, thoughts, words, impressions, and insights that come to you without any personal bias.

Most of the time, incorrect psychic information stems from misinterpretation of what we receive and not from a lack of psychic receptivity. It is often better to allow the person you are reading to interpret what you have intuited. You can give your impressions, but allow others to use it in the way that works for them. As you continue to psychically tune in to others, your ability and confidence in interpreting what you receive will strengthen.

RIGHT AND WRONG

A common stumbling block when reading another is the fear of being wrong. Saying something that is not true or does not make sense to the person you are reading is every psychic's nightmare. But it doesn't have to be. Every psychic makes mistakes. When you are met with a blank stare or the person you are reading tells you that they cannot relate to what you have said, don't panic. Stay calm and admit that you may have misinterpreted what you received. It may be helpful to describe what you experienced without interpreting it. You may also want to take a deep breath and further tune in to the energy and become aware of any new energy information. If you cannot understand or make sense of what you are receiving, you can simply say that you are going to move on and let it go for now. If there is something important that the person you are reading needs to know, it will come back to you, usually in another more straightforward way.

It is also possible that you are entirely correct about what you have received, but the person you are reading is too nervous to connect with what you have said or simply doesn't want to. This happens quite often.

For instance, I was giving a health reading to a client, and I told her that eating dairy, especially dairy combined with sugar, was creating unhealthy bacteria and she might want to eliminate this from her diet. She looked at me with a heavy stare and told me that she did not eat dairy. I was confused. I kept seeing her eating dairy, and I told her so. She maintained her opposition. I then asked her if she ate chocolate ice cream while watching television in the evening. After a short pause and with a look like she had just been caught with her hand in the cookie jar, she said, "Well, I do eat some chocolate ice cream at night."

It is helpful to pay attention to how it feels when you are correct and how it feels when you are incorrect. There is a certain tingling energy that you will likely feel when you are connecting with energy information and correctly interpreting it. In the same way, you will find that when your psychic connection is faulty, it is likely to feel flat and empty.

EGO

The ego can also interfere with your ability to psychically tune in to others. When others look to you for guidance and answers, it is tempting to feel more insightful, spiritual, or powerful. It is important to remind yourself that this does not necessarily mean that you are more special or infallible. These feelings come from the ego, as it longs to feel powerful, in charge, and in control. If you feel that your psychic insights are always right and that it is up to you to manage another's affairs and life, your ego has taken over.

For women, the ego often surfaces as a desire to help and heal everyone. Some women will experience feelings of guilt and stress if they are not able to fully help everyone and make others feel better and solve their problems. For men, the ego tends to surface more as feelings of power and control and the desire for recognition.

When you are centered in your spirit, you recognize that being psychic is a gift that empowers you to serve and help others. When you use your psychic abilities in service to others, you help yourself. You learn from the insights and increased awareness that psychic abilities provide. Working with high-vibration, loving energy is enjoyable and energizing. Your psychic abilities increase and provide unexpected feelings of well-being and connection to a higher power. When your ego attempts to hijack your psychic awareness, your abilities will diminish and suffer. The energy information that you receive will be focused on lower vibrations. While you still may be psychically accurate, what you receive may not necessarily be helpful and in the highest good.

MAINTAIN INTEGRITY

Intuiting energy information for others is a sacred responsibility that requires integrity, confidentiality, compassion, and wisdom. Never gossip or share intuitive information that you have received for another with others. Let go of how others accept what you receive. Do your best and accept constructive criticism if it is helpful, but be careful not to allow others to confuse the messenger with the message.

When you intuitively tune in to another's energy, they may feel exposed and vulnerable. Be kind, and at the same time maintain your focus. Be mindful of the feelings and expectations of the person you are working with, and remain intuitively neutral and receptive toward the energy information that presents itself. While you can be personally supportive and understanding of the person you are working with, the job of a psychic is to receive and interpret the energy information as objectively and accurately as possible.

✿ Exercises for Intuiting Another ✿

The following intuitive exercises can be done throughout the day. They will help you to become more familiar with intuiting others' energy. We often become overly serious and tighten up when we read another. It is important to stay loose, receptive, and open.

Meeting with Another

Next time you have a meeting, a lunch date, or an appointment scheduled with someone, take a few minutes to intuit something about that person's appearance beforehand. This can be anything from the color of the clothing they are wearing to their hair style or any jewelry or other accessories they may have. If you are meeting with someone you have never met and do not know what the person looks like, you can intuit their height, hair color, or anything else about their appearance.

You can use variations of this exercise. Before you leave for work, intuit the color of the clothing of the person you will first encounter at work. If meeting someone for a meeting or coffee, intuit the exact time they will arrive. You can also intuit what the person will want to talk about or discuss or any other random information that will surface during the meeting.

Intuiting Social Media

Before you check your Facebook, Instagram, or other social media site, take a moment to intuit an image or any other descriptive qualities of the first post or photo that you will encounter. Psychic insight might come in the form of colors, shapes, faces, or other fragments of images. You can also intuit the mood or emotional content of a post or photo, or the emotion that it is intended to invoke. Through a sense of knowing, you may receive energy information about the content of a post, such as if it is humorous, political, sentimental, or inspiring. Don't overreach as you intuit. Be content with the thoughts, feelings, images, and sensations that emerge. Pay attention to them, and when you are ready to look at the post or image, focus on the similarities, associations, and connections with your intuited information.

Be careful not to focus on what you did not correctly intuit. Instead, it is more helpful to notice the connections and associations that you intuitively received. In this way you will learn more about how your intuition naturally surfaces.

Insights about an Issue

Throughout the day, if you encounter a problem or challenge, think it through and then ask your intuition for input. Breathe and take a moment to relax. Then listen and pay attention to any intuitive messages or insights that surface. If your mind starts to race, continue to breathe and listen. If you are feeling stressed or anxious, this might be more challenging. If you do not receive any intuitive information and you become frustrated, let it go and do something else. Sometimes the intuitive guidance and insight that we are asking for does not surface until we are in a calm state or doing something entirely different. Be aware that you may receive an intuitive response later, perhaps while driving home or having lunch.

Insights about Another

Along with asking for guidance on a current challenge or problem, you can also ask for psychic insight about another or how to improve a relationship. Maybe you are perplexed by something your boyfriend, girlfriend, spouse, boss, coworker, or friend has said or done. Your mind is overthinking and your emotions have been triggered.

Do your best to relax, breathe, and let go. You do not need to know what kind of guidance you need or to ask a specific question. Simply ask within for insight and clarity and let go. Do something that will help you to release the emotions and feelings that have been triggered, and try not to overfocus on receiving psychic guidance. Keep part of your awareness open and receptive. In situations where you are feeling strong feelings, it may take a little longer to receive psychic insight.

Intuitive Communication with Another

Next time you get an email or message from a friend or coworker, or even when someone pops into your mind, intuitively ask that person what they want to communicate to you.

Take a moment to visualize this person or inwardly repeat their name. Send a thought message asking the person to communicate to you what they would like to say. Then listen, feel, sense, and see what comes to you. You may see fragments of images, have a sense of knowing, feel what is on their mind, or hear a phrase or words. However the information comes to you, receive it and continue to ask their energy for information and be aware of what you receive.

A variation of this exercise is to intuitively ask for insight into another's feelings and emotions. Then become aware of any emotions or feelings that you begin to feel. They may be subtle and feel as if they are your emotions. If this happens, ask within if these are your feelings or another's. Trust what you receive. If you feel emotions such as sadness, grief, anger, or anxiety, imagine high-vibration divine energy moving through you. Release and let go of these feelings and absorb this positive and soothing energy.

Invite psychic awareness to be an integral part of your day-to-day life. As you do this, it becomes a more natural and normal aspect of who you are. We like to dramatize psychic abilities as being surreal and outside the status quo. However, everyone has psychic ability. Claiming and developing your natural intuition empowers you to create a more fulfilling and abundant life. It is also a much more enjoyable and interesting way to go through the day.

PART 4
Your Practice:
Psychic Meditation Exercises

CHAPTER 10

Preparation for the Psychic Meditation Exercises and What to Expect

The psychic meditation exercises in the following chapters empower you to use your intuition to receive insight and guidance about the everyday issues of life. Now that you are aware of the four ways that intuition naturally surfaces and have had some practice with developing these different modalities, let's bring them together.

Although you may be more naturally proficient in one or more types of intuition and weaker in others, the ideal is to be balanced in all four psychic types. The meditation exercises help you to become more comfortable with and skilled at directing psychic energy through the four psychic modalities and receiving and interpreting guidance. When used together, mental, emotional, physical, and spiritual intuition strengthen one another and add depth and refinement to psychic awareness. Like a finely tuned musical quartet or your favorite recipe, the psychic types blend together harmoniously to form a cohesive whole.

Imagination and Integrating Psychic Abilities

The meditation exercises in the following chapters begin with clairvoyant imagery. If you do not readily see or become aware of spontaneous images, use your imagination to create them. As the meditation continues, remember that you might not always see clairvoyant images. Instead, you may feel them, know how they appear, have a sense of them, or even hear a description of the images. Psychic senses do not have rigid boundaries and are not as black and white and clearly defined as the physical senses. They can easily blend into one another, and one or more psychic abilities may occur simultaneously.

While you are engaged in the meditations, the symbols and images will evolve and change. As they do, be attentive to receiving energy information through claircognizance, the psychic sense of knowing and awareness through thoughts. In addition, psychic information will likely surface through clairaudience, which is inner hearing energy and tuning in to your inner voice. Also be aware of clairsentience, which is receiving psychic information through emotions and heart-centered awareness, and of receiving information through somatic sensations and awareness in your physical body.

Find a Balance Between Engaging In the Meditation Exercise and Remaining Neutral

While it is important to be neutral during the meditation exercises, psychic awareness is not a spectator sport. There is a fine line between observing intuitive impressions and projecting your desires and trying to make something happen. Be aware of your approach and continually practice receptivity, patience, and openness if you find your ego self becoming overly involved. The only way to find your optimum intuitive vantage point is through trial and error.

I encourage you to be an active participant and at the same time an observer. When you are asked to imagine an image of yourself in a specific scene, don't be overly tentative. Project your energy into the scene. Feel yourself there and be fully present to the experience. Open your intuitive senses and be present to the subtlety of energy and meet it halfway. Become aware of the sounds, smells, feelings, and sensations of the environment that each exercise creates. Use your energy. This may not make complete sense to you, but as you work with the meditations it will become clearer. Being psychic requires the active participation of your spirit and core energy self. Don't allow your logical thinking mind to take over. It will be there, critiquing and providing input every step of the way. Please don't listen to it. Let your psychic awareness handle this.

WHAT MAY HAPPEN DURING A MEDITATION EXERCISE AND HOW TO DEAL WITH IT

There is a vast array of psychic information that you will receive and experience while engaged in these meditation exercises. Every time you do an exercise, even the same one, different intuitive information will surface in a variety of ways. Sometimes your primary intuiting mode may be visual, and other times you may feel or hear energy information. There may be times when your psychic connection is strong and information glides into your consciousness with little effort. You intuitively receive and interpret your impressions with clarity and confidence. A moment later in another exercise, your intuition may seem to have diminished. Doubt replaces confidence and you wonder what you did wrong.

There are many moods of intuition. Don't become overly concerned and freeze up or become discouraged if the intuitive process is not going the way you expected it would. Learn how to dance with the flow of your psychic rhythms and not resist or try to control it. Go where your intuition leads you, follow it without restraint, and give it all you can.

However well prepared you are to receive energy information, you won't really know what it is like and what to expect until you jump in. While intuiting, you may feel overwhelmed and not understand what you receive and how to interpret it. This is normal, and the more you intuit, the more familiar and confident you will become in the often strange and uncharted territory of psychic impressions. Here is a rundown of what you may experience as you move through the meditation exercises.

No Information, Nothing Happens

You are ready to begin and have either read through the meditation exercise or recorded it. You settle in, breathe, and relax, but nothing happens. There are no images, sensations, feelings, or other intuitive insights. If this happens while doing the exercises, it may be an indication that you are not energetically engaged or lack trust in the process, or it may be that you just need to be patient.

If you are too much in your head, thinking about what you are doing, you are not engaged in the psychic process. To strengthen your intuitive connection, breathe and move the breath through your body. Then breathe and move energy through your heart and solar plexus. Wake up your energy with the breath.

If you do this and still nothing is happening, be patient. Sometimes we just need to wait for our brain to integrate energy information and express it to us in an understandable way. Similar to when we are learning a new language or other skill, it takes time for everything to come together. Keep applying focus and energy to the exercise and eventually the energy will begin to move and flow. Intuitive information may not come in the form that you would like it to or in a way that makes sense, but don't disregard it. At the beginning it is enough to identify intuitive energy information and accept it. The more often you do the meditation exercises, the faster, clearer, and more accurate your intuitive abilities will become.

If you continue to have difficulties receiving psychic energy information, scale back the meditation exercise. Begin by breathing and relaxing and then do the first step. Imagine whatever image the exercise begins with, become aware of any psychic information that surfaces, and then end the session. Next time you come back to the exercise, do one step at a time until the energy begins to flow freely and you feel more confident.

Disruptive Sensations

Imagine that after getting comfortable, breathing, relaxing, and beginning the meditation exercise, you become restless and unfocused. Your leg or arm begins to itch, you notice that your back is sore, you have a dull ache in one of your calves, or you just can't sit still. The more you try, the more restless you become.

If this happens, stop, breathe, stand up, and stretch. Shake your arms and legs, take long, deep breaths, and move energy through your body. If you have a high degree of physical intuition, it is likely that your body is reacting to the increase in psychic energy. Becoming physically overactive or overstimulated means that there is a lot of available energy that you can channel into psychic receptivity.

Once you have released energy through stretching, try again. Sit down, become comfortable, and breathe. However, instead of moving the breath through the body, imagine moving the energy of the breath to your heart, mind, and spirit. Breathe and send the energy through the heart and the third eye area and then exhale. Send the breath outside of the physical body to your energy field, and imagine your aura becoming larger and more luminous. This channels the energy to activate your psychic senses and prevents your body from becoming overstimulated. Continue to breathe in this way and continue with the exercise.

Emotional Avalanche

If your primary intuitive type is emotional, you may feel and receive an abundance of emotional energy. If this happens, accept all the emotions that you feel. Don't try to rush through the meditation exercise. Instead, slow down and feel. Name the feelings that surface, and discern if they are your personal feelings or if they are intuited feelings.

Sometimes, relaxing, breathing, and coming into an intuitive listening state opens the heart and repressed feelings surface. This is natural and beneficial. In order to receive intuitive guidance from the heart, it is necessary to let go of suppressed emotions and feelings. Simply allowing the feelings to surface is healing and makes way for intuitive energy information to surface. Take all the time you need to feel your feelings, as this allows them to dissipate.

Intuited emotions emanate from a quiet heart. They are repetitive and wise. Listen to them. When you identify an intuitive emotion or feeling, be patient and listen for further information. The initial intuited emotion opens the door for more psychic impressions to surface. You do not need to understand the origin of the emotion or feeling and what it may mean. Just take note of it and remain receptive to other energy information that surfaces.

Mind Chatter

Lets face it: the mind is going to talk and talk. It is not going to be quiet because you want it to. During the meditation exercises, don't try to shut down the mind. It will resist and become stronger. Don't give the mind chatter too much attention. Instead, listen for the intuitive messages that lie under the chattering mind. They are there. As you focus on intuitive energy, it becomes stronger. Be patient with the process. If you notice yourself engaging in thinking and listening to your mind ramble on, go back to the breath and a receptive mode.

Remember, intuitive thoughts are repetitive, nonlinear, and consistent and do not provoke emotion or engage the thinking process. They provide energy information in a somewhat flat and matter-of-fact way.

Personal thoughts are engaging. They pull you in, and one thought leads to another and another. They can be difficult to detach from because they can be enticing and feel productive.

Intuitive thoughts simply make a statement. Listen to these, even though they may feel less compelling and not as prominent as personal thoughts. The more you focus on intuitive thoughts, the easier they become to identify and understand. When you receive or hear an intuitive thought, take note of it and return to a receptive and open state.

Confusing Images

In addition to dealing with confusing emotions and thoughts, you may find yourself perplexed by the images you receive. You may feel that you are making them up, they are unreliable, or you are simply not seeing them in the way that you want to.

If you feel that you are making up the images or that you continually need to use your imagination to create them, slow down and be patient. It may be that your brain needs more time to interpret the energy information that you are receiving and express it in an image. Remember that your imagination is a tool that can help you to better understand and intuitively perceive what you are receiving. Find that balance between observing and projecting your energy into the meditation exercise and being patient and allowing an image to emerge in its own time. Eventually everything will line up and you will better understand how your clairvoyance operates.

If the images are unclear or fuzzy, don't panic or ignore them. This is common and normal. It may be that more energy information can be supplied by your other psychic senses. Don't rely too much on your clairvoyance. Tune in to how the images feel, what they are saying to you, or what you intuitively know in connection to them.

While many people feel that they experience difficulty receiving energy information through images, there may be times when you are overwhelmed with visual images and don't know what they mean. If this happens, go back to the breath, slow down, and imagine a blank screen. Instead of allowing the images to randomly float in and out, be more directive with them. Ask for an image to emerge that represents a specific aspect of the exercise or a question or concern. Keep asking for specific images one at a time. Then go back to the breath and a blank screen if you become overwhelmed with too many images.

The images are also likely to change and transform as you work with them. If this happens, simply observe. This might feel almost like a dream. You are engaged in the meditation exercise, but it seems to take on a life of its own. This is generally a good sign. It means that your intuition is flowing without restraint. However, it might also indicate that you are too personally involved. For instance, your mind may be overthinking, the images may be stimulating an emotional response, or you may be perceiving a visual scene that reflects your desires and preferred outcome. It may be that your imagination is not connected to your intuition but rather to your ego. If you believe that this is happening, slow down, go back to the breath, and imagine a blank screen. Ask for an image to emerge that represents something in the exercise that you would like to intuit. Keep going back to the breath and the blank screen if the images become too confusing or change or alter too quickly. Eventually you will find the right balance.

The Meditation Exercise Seems to Veer Off Course

As you proceed through a meditation exercise, everything seems to be moving along. Then instead of following the format, your intuition seems to steer you in an unexpected direction. You see, feel, or know things that don't seem connected to the question or issue, or you receive energy information in an unexpected way. Although this can feel disruptive and confusing, it can be a good sign.

Similar to what happens in your dreams, at some point your intuition will begin to lead you. When we are dreaming and are aware that we are dreaming, we are observing a scene unfold. We are not making anything happen and we do not know what is going to happen next. Eventually your intuition will begin to unfold in this same way. You simply observe, receive, and take note of what is happening. It is important to stay focused and aware when this happens. If you start to overthink or control the process, you will lose the energy and it will slip away.

Meditation Exercise Format

Like most people, you may be motivated to develop your psychic abilities to receive helpful guidance and insight into everyday questions and concerns and to be happier and more successful. The meditation exercises in the following chapters empower you to receive guidance and insight about relationships, career, finances, abundance, spiritual purpose, and manifestation.

Included with each meditation exercise is an image glossary to assist you in interpreting the energy information that you receive. Each glossary section includes signs and symbols and their meanings and guides you in interpreting intuited feelings, sensations, and thoughts.

Psychic Protection

It is always a good idea to set an intent before you psychically open to receive energy information that is in your highest good. Before you begin a psychic meditation, take a moment to imagine yourself surrounded with protective white-light energy. This will ensure that you receive only high-vibration, positive energy and that no negative spirit influences can affect you. If you like to work with a particular divine spirit being, such as Mother Mary or Archangel Michael, or you wish to ask for God's protection, you can say a short prayer.

Read or Record the Meditation Exercise

Some people find it challenging to read the meditation exercise text and practice it at the same time. If this is true for you, you may want to read through the meditation and then record it before you begin. Pre-recording the meditation may also assist you in getting into a deeper intuitive state. However, the meditations are not difficult or complex. They can be practiced by first reading them over and then getting into a relaxed state and going through the steps.

Intuiting for Another

Although these meditation exercises are designed for personal use, you can use them to practice receiving energy information for another. If you wish to intuit for someone else, become aware of your expectations, emotions, feelings, and beliefs about your intuitive abilities before you begin. If you are feeling nervous and unsure of your ability to receive and interpret useful information, take a few deep, relaxing breaths and have compassion for yourself. Know that this is not a test and you do not need to judge or criticize your performance. Being psychic is a learning process, so do the best you can and learn from the experience.

Begin each meditation exercise by setting an intention or saying a short prayer and asking to receive positive and helpful energy information for the person you are intuiting for. You can also inwardly repeat the person's name before beginning or use another personal identifying symbol to better connect to and receive their energy vibration. Before I intuit for a client, I ask them for their date of birth. This aligns me with their energy and allows me to more clearly and accurately intuit their soul vibration.

Once you start the meditation exercise, imagine the person you are intuiting for instead of yourself. The intuited feelings and thoughts that you experience during the exercises are connected to and express the energy of the person for whom you are intuiting.

Increasing Intuitive Receptivity

Before you begin the meditation exercises in the following chapters, please read through the clearing preparation exercise in the next section and answer the questions that it asks of you. This may seem tedious, and you may not feel that it is necessary. However, to successfully intuit, it is necessary to be as neutral as possible. When it comes to issues and questions that affect us personally, it can be easy to allow our expectations, emotions, beliefs, and desires to interfere and create doubt when intuiting.

To be successful with the meditation exercises, it is essential that you be able to discern intuited information from your own desires, feelings, thoughts, and expectations. As you answer the questions in the clearing preparation exercise, keep in mind that becoming fully aware of your thoughts, feelings, and desired outcome will enable you to more confidently recognize and discern intuited energy from your personal expectations and desires.

Clearing Preparation Exercise

In each of the meditation exercises you will be asked to formulate a question or focus on a specific question, concern, or issue. Once you have done this, take a deep breath and feel any emotions or feelings you have about this issue or concern. Write down the feelings and emotions that surface.

What are your thoughts surrounding your question and this area of your life? What are the factors affecting it, the facts as you know them, and your expectations? Write all of this down.

What is your desire in relation to your question or issue? What do you want to happen?

What do you fear may happen? How are you controlling the situation and any others involved? What do you want the outcome to be and why? Write all of this down.

Our personal biases can hamper our intuitive efforts. It is not possible to always be completely neutral about issues that personally affect us. However, by becoming conscious of our expectations, feelings, and desires, it is easier to recognize and trust what we intuitively receive. Awareness supports us in being a more open and clear channel for unbiased and pure energy information. If you feel that you are not ready or are too attached to the outcome to receive guidance that might be contrary to your wishes, it is best to wait until you are in a more neutral state to do the exercise.

CHAPTER 11

Rainbow Meditation Exercise to Intuit Abundance and Finances

The first intuitive meditation exercise is the rainbow meditation. It begins with activating your clairvoyance by imagining the different colors of the chakras. However, it is not essential that you see these colors like you see with your physical eyes. You may instead feel the colors, know how they appear, have a sense of them, or see flashes of them that fade and then become clearer. Accept whatever way they appear for you. The goal is not to judge your clairvoyant ability, but instead to become comfortable with combining your imagination and intuition and better discover how your clairvoyant ability surfaces. As you invoke the different colors of the chakras, you activate and strengthen your overall psychic energy and awareness.

If you would like to gain intuitive insight into your finances or abundance or how a particular project or opportunity might impact you financially, the rainbow meditation exercise may help. In this exercise you can ask a question about your finances or state of abundance in a specific area, such as the future outlook, an investment, or a career opportunity.

Pick one area of your life where you would like to gauge financial increase or decrease. Formulate a question, then do the clearing preparation exercise at the end of chapter 10 before beginning the meditation.

Before You Begin

Here is a review of the clearing preparation exercise from chapter 10 to do before you begin:

Take a deep breath and feel any emotions or feelings that you have about this issue or condition. Write down the feelings and emotions that surface.

What are your thoughts surrounding your question and this area of your life? What are the factors affecting it, the facts as you know them, and your expectations? Write all of this down.

What is your desire in relation to your question or issue? What do you want to happen?

What do you fear may happen? How are you controlling the situation and any others involved? What do you want the outcome to be and why? Write all of this down.

Rainbow Meditation Exercise

Once you have answered the questions in the clearing preparation exercise, get into a comfortable position and close your eyes. Begin to breathe long, deep breaths. Move the energy of the breath through the body and exhale any stress or tension. Continue to breathe in this way.

As you continue to breathe, imagine the colors of the rainbow swirling around you. Take some time to imagine the different colors and energy completely surrounding you. Let yourself feel this energy and become part of it.

Imagine a red ray of light emanating from the base of your spine and swirling around you. Then imagine that below your belly button there is a ray of vibrating orange light moving in unison with the red ray of light. From your solar plexus imagine a ray of yellow vibrating energy flowing with the red and orange energies. Then moving up the body, imagine a ray of green energy pulsating through your heart and allow it to flow with the other energy colors. Now imagine that from your throat area a vibrant blue energy joins them, while indigo swirls of energy flow from your head and surround you. Above your head imagine violet and white light flowing around your body in unison with the other colors.

Imagine all these colors of light—red, orange, yellow, green, blue, indigo, violet, and white—flowing as one energy and completely surrounding you. This is your rainbow energy self. Take a few moments to imagine and feel the high-vibration energy of your rainbow. You may hear a slight sound emanating from the rainbow or feel it as a buzzing or a vibration.

Continue to breathe and imagine the energy of the rainbow intensifying and increasing your vibration and frequency. Breathe and focus on your question or area of interest. If your thoughts begin to scatter, go back to the breath and stay centered in your question.

As the energy of the rainbow continues to surround you, imagine a blank screen. Using your imagination encourages clairvoyance. Remember, you may not see a three-dimensional blank screen. Instead, you might have a sense of it or know or feel it. It may appear cartoonish or made-up. All of this is fine.

Imagine on this screen a gold pot. Remember that you may not see a clear, three-dimensional image. Instead, you may have an awareness of the pot, a feeling of it, or a sense of knowing, or you may hear a message about it.

Stay with the image of the gold pot and notice it in detail. Is it old, new, worn, or broken? Notice anything that you can about it.

Imagine that the rainbow energy surrounding you moves in and out of the pot and back to you. As the rainbow connects with the pot, it absorbs your abundance and financial energy. Continue to breathe and relax.

Once you feel that the pot has absorbed the energy of the rainbow, notice and become aware of anything in the pot or any changes to it. Remember, intuitive information may come to you as an image, or you may intuitively know, sense, or feel what is inside of the pot. For instance:

- Is there an object inside the pot, such as money or gold or something else?
- Is the pot empty, upside down, or barely full? Is the pot filling or emptying?
- Does the gold pot change color or morph into another image?

Be aware of any intuitive energy information that you receive through a sense of knowing or your thoughts. What are your inner voice and heart saying to you? What emotions and feelings surface? Tune in to any sensations in the body and listen to them. Do you perceive any other images and symbols? Become aware of intuited energy information as you receive it. Do not try to understand or interpret it. Instead, stay in a receptive mode.

When you feel that you have received all that you can at this time, imagine a ray of light dissolving the images and the colors of the rainbow fading into your energy field. Slowly come back to normal consciousness and write down what you have intuited.

What to Do if Nothing Happened

If you did not intuit any thoughts, feelings, images, or sensations during the meditation exercise, relax and take your time. This doesn't mean that you are not intuitive.

Try again and alter the exercise by using your imagination to create an image of the pot. Notice anything about it and receive any other intuitive information. Once the image begins to fade, you have completed the exercise. Repeat this step at another time. Simply imagine an image of the pot and become receptive, and keep repeating this until the scene begins to come alive and you are able to intuit more energy information. When you begin to receive more intuitive information, start at the beginning and imagine the colors of the rainbow and go through the entire exercise.

INTERPRETATION

Intuited positive feelings and emotions such as happiness, joy, serenity, and peace indicate a positive outcome and increase.

Intuited negative feelings and emotions such as confusion, stress, and negativity can indicate possible financial loss, lack, or an undesired outcome.

Intuited physical sensations such as an increase in physical energy or feeling light, energized, and tingling can indicate a positive outcome and increase.

Intuited sensations of heaviness, low energy, or feeling blocked or tired can indicate an undesired outcome and can be a message to change or review your plans and expectations.

Intuited thoughts that surface in the form of a word, phrase, or song lyric may not initially make sense. However, don't ignore these or discount their significance, as they may contain insight and information. Thought messages can be auditory and sound like your own voice, or they can come in the form of an idea or insight.

Intuited thoughts and energy information that you receive through inner hearing are often straightforward and do not need any further interpretation. If thoughts surface that you do not understand, resist overthinking and do not discard them. Give them time to unfold. When you least expect it, the meaning will surface.

IMAGE GLOSSARY

You may receive intuited images visually, through a sense of knowing, or through feeling them. They may or may not be clear and detailed.

Colors of the Rainbow (as Related to Abundance and Finances)

Red is the energy color of your first chakra. It represents grounded energy, power, action, and security.

Orange is connected to the second chakra and represents the ability to manifest wealth and abundance. Orange can indicate an increase in finances through a grounded approach.

Yellow is the color of the third chakra. It corresponds to the power to listen to your gut intuition about finances. It can also represent the kind of confidence and healthy self-esteem that empowers us to manifest and create abundance.

Green is connected to your fourth chakra. It vibrates to the healing of money and abundance issues and can also represent money and wealth.

Blue is connected to the fifth chakra and vibrates to expression and use of the will. In the energy of abundance this may indicate the need or ability to express and communicate your ideas, desires, and truth. It can also represent the use of personal will to move forward and manifest abundance.

Indigo emanates from the sixth chakra. It represents the third eye, truth, and higher consciousness. It may indicate creative and inspired ideas and insight and the ability to trust your higher vision of manifesting abundance.

Violet is connected to the seventh chakra and flows with the energy of the higher self, our purpose, and our soul plan. It may indicate that you are being divinely guided or that you have positive karmic manifestation abilities.

Gold and **white** vibrate to divine spirit, abundance, wisdom, and compassion. They can indicate a financial gift from spirit coming your way.

Rainbow

The rainbow is your energy self and encompasses the vibrations of all the colors. When activated, the rainbow energy self is intuitively wise and receives psychic energy information. It is also able to heal and bring balance to the mind, body, and spirit. Related to finances and abundance, the rainbow represents wholeness and attainment.

Gold Pot

The gold pot is the energy receptacle that holds and expresses psychic information in this meditation exercise.

Coins or gold filling the pot: Coins or gold filling the pot is a positive sign of financial increase and abundance that may occur over a period of time.

Coins or gold spilling out: This indicates losing money on an idea or project. It may also indicate a need to pay attention to spending and avoid taking chances.

Cracked or broken pot: This symbolizes a flaw in your plan or expectations and is a sign to review and make changes to your current financial plan.

Empty pot: An empty pot indicates that future or present finances and abundance may not manifest in the way you want them to or at the desired time.

Empty scene; no pot or gold: This is a indication to be patient and use your imagination. It might take a little longer to receive psychic energy information. If you continue to be blocked, this may indicate that fear, doubt, or stress is getting in your way. If no images or psychic energy information surface, it may not be in your best interest to know the outcome or you may not be ready for it.

New pot: A new pot may be a suggestion to pay attention to a new idea, plan, or opportunity that will bring increase and abundance. It might also be a message to let go of the old and begin anew.

Pot full of gold: A full pot of gold symbolizes abundance, coming good fortune, and an increase in finances.

Pot half-full of gold: This symbolizes a measured increase in wealth and abundance. It may not be as much as you want, but it is a comfortable amount.

Something other than a pot of gold: If another symbol or image appears instead of a pot of gold, do not dismiss it. This is what you are meant to see and know. Focus on the image and intuitively receive more energy information and guidance.

Worn or old pot: A worn or old pot can indicate abundance coming from a past idea, investment, or project. It might also be a message to stick to the traditional way you have been doing things. It can also indicate a debt being paid.

KATE'S EXPERIENCE

The meditation exercises in this book engage your visualization abilities and help you to develop and trust the psychic skills of clairvoyance. If you are not comfortable intuiting in this way, you are not alone. When first beginning to use clairvoyance, it may feel as if you are making up what you receive, or the images may not be what you think they should be like. To help you to better understand and value your clairvoyant ability, I am including an example here of one of my students who had difficulty intuiting in this way. You can still receive valuable guidance even if you do not receive clearly seen visual images and even if the exercise takes an unexpected turn.

Kate, a project manager in a pharmaceutical company, was ready to leave the corporate world behind. After many years in the profession, she was ready to pursue her dream of opening an antique shop in the mountains with her husband. However, they were both nervous. After several years of planning and preparation, Kate and her husband were hesitating before taking the leap. Concerned about how this new venture would affect their current and long-term finances, they were exploring every option. Kate took my class to help her trust in and use her intuition to make good decisions and was ready to jump into the meditation exercises and learn more.

When Kate began to breathe and relax at the beginning of the exercise, she initially felt comfortable visualizing white light surrounding her. When I asked the class to see or feel the colors of the rainbow, she began to run into trouble. Wanting to develop clairvoyance and do the exercise correctly, she was disappointed when she couldn't clearly see visual images. Kate recalled me telling the class that they might see the clairvoyant images more through a sense of knowing, and that helped her. She knew that the colors of the rainbow were present, and even though she couldn't see them clearly, she continued with the meditation. When her body began to tingle with energy and she felt a slight vibration in her head, she took this as a good sign and trusted that she was still on track.

It was easier for Kate to visualize the blank screen than to see the colors. Excited when she saw an image of the pot of gold, she was disappointed when it faded and then disappeared. Thinking that she might have gotten too excited, she remembered to go back to breathing and relaxing and focusing on her breath. Eventually the image of the pot of gold returned. This time she noticed that there was something in it, but she wasn't sure what it was. As she tried to focus on the pot, it disappeared again. For a moment she thought she was doing something wrong, but fortunately she remembered to rely on her other psychic senses and went back to tuning in to her intuitive thoughts and listening.

This is where it got interesting. All of a sudden she felt as if her father were present. She could feel him. He had passed over many years earlier and she had not previously felt him close. Surprised that this was happening, she continued to feel her father's warmth and felt comforted by his presence. She heard the inner message that everything was going to work out with the antique store, and tears came to her eyes when she intuitively felt in her heart that this was true.

Then everything went blank again and she went back to breathing. This time as Kate was breathing and relaxing, she suddenly saw an image of the porch of the store that she was considering buying. At the front door there was the pot filled with gold.

Overall Kate was pleased and felt positive about the meditation exercise. It left her with the intuitive awareness and assurance that her father was close and was looking out for her. His presence was so unexpected that she felt it had to be her intuition at work.

❦

Although the meditation exercises in this book take you through a series of steps and actions, be flexible with what happens and where you are led. If you veer from the format, that is fine. The exercises stimulate and encourage your psychic energy to focus on a specific question, issue, or concern. However, it is not fundamentally important for you to stick to the steps one by one. As long as you are receiving intuitive energy information, continue with your personal process as it unfolds. Do what works and go back to the exercise format if you begin to feel lost or unconnected to your intuition or the energy information that you are intuiting.

CHAPTER 12

Path Meditation Exercise to Intuit Career and Life Path

This meditation exercise provides a format to intuitively receive energy information and insight into what may be unfolding and coming your way in your career or on your life path. Before you begin, determine if you would like to receive energy information about what is currently happening in your career or on your life path or if you would like to explore what may be coming your way with a new idea or plan that you are considering.

BEFORE YOU BEGIN

Here is a review of the clearing preparation exercise from chapter 10 to do before you begin the exercise:

Take a deep breath and feel any emotions or feelings that you have about this issue or condition. Write down the feelings and emotions that surface.

What are your thoughts surrounding your question and this area of your life? What are the factors affecting it, the facts as you know them, and your expectations? Write all of this down.

What is your desire in relation to your question or issue? What do you want to happen?

What do you fear may happen? How are you controlling the situation and any others involved? What do you want the outcome to be and why? Write all of this down.

🪷 Path Meditation Exercise 🪷

Get into a comfortable position and begin to breathe long, deep, cleansing breaths. Move the energy of the breath through the body and exhale any stress or tension. Continue to breathe in this way. This relaxes and increases your vibration.

When you are ready, imagine a blank screen in front of you. Using your imagination encourages clairvoyance. Remember, you may not see a three-dimensional blank screen. Instead, you might have a sense of it or know or feel it. It may appear cartoonish or made-up. All of this is fine.

On this screen imagine an image of yourself standing in front of a path. Relax and imagine yourself in the scene, feel it, and allow it to become vibrant and alive. Notice as much detail about yourself as you can: the clothes you are wearing, the expression on your face, etc.

Then focus on the path. How does it appear to you? Notice all that you can about it. What is it made of? Are there stones or boulders on it, or is it paved or made of lush vegetation? Feel the energy and activate your imagination to experience being in the scene. Let the sounds, colors, and sensual energy of this path unfold.

Imagine that you are walking down the path. Is the walking easy or difficult? Does the path change? Does it wind or is it straightforward? Does it split or fork? Do you know which way to go? Does the path end abruptly?

Notice what is on both sides of the path. Do the surroundings feel empty and like a spacious void? Are they dark or light? Are you surrounded by vegetation, or does the terrain seem to be empty and desert-like? If there is any water, is it clear or murky?

Continue to walk along the path, noticing and taking note of any changes that occur as you proceed. Are there any obstacles? Does it become harder to walk, perhaps as you head uphill, or is there a sense of making progress with ease?

Does anything or anyone show up to help you, such as an animal, a group of people, or one person? Does anything appear that seems to hinder you? Can you communicate with whatever or whoever shows up on your path? Do you feel like you are being guided?

What is the weather like? Does it change? Is it sunny or cloudy, windy or calm? Is it hot or cool? Is it daytime or night?

Continue to walk along the path, noticing everything that you can about it and anything on either side of the path.

Eventually the energy will begin to fade. This is a sign that you have received all that you can at this time. Before you end the session, ask if there is anything else that you need to know, feel, or become aware of. Pause and take a few moments to listen. Receive anything else that surfaces. Allow the energy to fade and imagine a ray of light dissolving the images.

Before you do anything else, write down any symbols and all that you experienced. More psychic information may come to you as you write.

WHAT TO DO IF NOTHING HAPPENED

If you did not intuit any thoughts, feelings, images, or sensations during the meditation exercise, relax and take your time. This doesn't mean that you are not intuitive.

Try again and alter the exercise by using your imagination to create an image of a path. Notice anything about this path. Once the image begins to fade, you have completed the exercise. Repeat this step at another time. Simply imagine an image of a path and keep repeating this until the scene begins to come alive and are you able to intuit more energy information. As you continue to practice this exercise, imagine yourself moving forward on the path little by little.

INTERPRETATION

Intuited positive feelings and emotions such as joy, enthusiasm, positivity, and contentment indicate that you are going with the flow and are on track with your career or life path.

Intuited negative feelings such as confusion or stress or the feeling that something is not right may indicate that your desires or plans or the outcome of your current path are not in keeping with your highest good.

Your feelings and emotions are likely to change during the meditation exercise, so pay attention to the predominant feelings and any images or other intuited information that surface simultaneously.

Intuited physical sensations such as feeling unable to move forward or feeling heavy, stuck, or lacking energy may indicate resistance, challenges, and a possible undesired outcome to your plans or on your current path.

Intuited physical sensations such as tingling, a feeling of ease, or feeling energized, powerful, or light are indications that you are on the right path or your plans are in keeping with your highest good.

Intuited sensations of flying or floating may indicate that you are being spiritually guided. Pay attention to any other intuited information, as flying may also indicate that you are not grounded and you might need to focus on what is possible to make your dreams a reality.

Intuited thoughts that surface in the form of a word, phrase, or song lyric may not initially make sense. However, such thoughts likely contain insight and information that will eventually become clearer. Thought messages can be auditory and sound like your own voice, or they can come in the form of an idea or insight.

Intuited thoughts and energy information that you intuit through inner hearing are often straightforward and do not need any further interpretation. If thoughts surface that you do not understand, resist overthinking and do not discard them. Give them time to unfold. When you least expect it, the meaning will likely surface. Trust the thoughts that come to you during the exercise. Take note of them, and when the exercise is complete, they may make better sense.

Image Glossary

You may receive intuited images visually, through a sense of knowing, or through feeling them. They may or may not be clear and detailed, but either way they are significant.

Animals

An animal may appear on your path as a spirit guide. Try to communicate with it and listen within for any guidance or direction that it may be transmitting to you. The kind of animal may also be important. You may want to research the symbolic meaning of the animal that comes to you.

Path

The path is the energy receptacle in this meditation exercise. It symbolizes what is coming into being in your career or in the area of concern you are inquiring about.

Blocked path: If the path is blocked, it is likely that obstacles are in your way. These may be emotional, psychological, or spiritual obstacles or an unknown outer or external issue or event. Notice if you can get around the obstacle and how much effort this requires. If you are able to get through the block, notice what is on the other side. If you cannot get through it, you may need to rethink your current career or life path.

Detour: A detour on your path indicates change is coming. This may be unexpected. Notice what the path is like after you make the detour. This will give insight into upcoming ease or challenges.

Fork in the path: A fork in the path represents a choice or decision coming your way. Explore both paths of the split and get a sense of which feels more comfortable and affirming. It may be possible to receive energy information related to the decision or choice that may soon present itself.

Rocks on the path: Large rocks and boulders indicate potential problems and issues in your career or in the area of concern. Depending on the other intuitive information you receive, rocks may also indicate a grounded, secure path or the need to be realistic in your expectations.

Stones on the path: Smooth rounded stones indicate small issues that you can overcome. Gems or colorful smooth stones can be a sign of spiritual help and the manifestation of spiritual gifts.

Sharp or jagged stones are a message to be careful, as there may be annoyances coming your way. Don't underestimate small issues. Notice how much of the path is covered with sharp, jagged stones. If they extend a long way, you may want to change your current plans.

Stop or dead end: If the path ends abruptly, this may indicate that your current plans are not viable or there may be an unexpected change. Alternatively, this can be a positive sign of fruition and completion. What is at the end of the path can supply more information.

Straightforward path: This is a positive sign that you are on the right track and may be a suggestion to stay focused.

Winding path: A path that winds is a sign that it may take longer to achieve and manifest what you would like to experience. Conditions may unfold slowly and there may be a delay in manifestation.

Vegetation

Barren, desert-like: These conditions can signal new beginnings or possibilities but can also indicate a lack of support and empty promises.

Flowers, flowering bushes: These are signs of happiness and can be indications of reaching a goal, fulfillment, or completion.

Fruit, fruit trees: Fruit or fruit trees are symbolic of attainment, abundance, and fruition. If there are fruit trees with no fruit on them, it can suggest that you may have to be patient and wait.

Grass: Healthy, lush green grass is symbolic of growth and abundance.

Overgrown vegetation: This can indicate that you may be trying to do too much. You may need to scale back your expectations and focus on one step or idea at a time. It can also indicate confusion.

Trees: Healthy trees full of leaves can be a sign of positive growth and long-term success. Frail-looking trees or trees with no leaves can symbolize loss and indicate that what once may have been a good idea is no longer viable.

Weeds: Weeds indicate a need to become focused and eliminate negative thoughts and fears.

Walking

Walking is symbolic of progress in your career or on your life path. If the walking is easy, this can indicate unencumbered advancement. If the walking is difficult or you are going slowly, this can indicate that things may take more time to manifest than you would like.

Water

Clear water: Translucent, clear water indicates spiritual clarity and is a sign of emotional peace and ease.

Flowing water: Flowing water represents progress and going with the flow of life and your highest good.

Murky water: Dark, cloudy, or murky water may indicate the lack of a clear vision, spiritual or emotional confusion, or the need to let go and free yourself from a burden or limitation.

Puddles: Symbolic of emotions that need to be let go of, puddles may be a sign to be patient, as events and conditions are in the formative stage.

Sea or ocean: A positive sign of spirituality, the divine, and love, the sea or ocean can symbolize that you are being divinely guided on your life path and purpose.

Stream: A stream symbolizes the beginning of a project or plan or going it alone.

Weather

The weather symbolizes feelings, emotions, and moods.

Clouds: These can indicate muddled thinking, confusion, and a lack of clarity.

Cold: Very cold weather indicates being frozen and unable to move forward and can symbolize fear. Mildly cold weather can indicate feeling alone and a lack of passion on your path.

Heat: Hot weather can indicate feeling overwhelmed and the need to slow down and not push yourself. Mildly warm weather is a positive sign of heart-centered warmth on your path.

Night sky with stars: This indicates that even though you may not be sure of where you are going, you are being led and guided.

Rainbow: A rainbow is symbolic of happiness and attainment in your career or on your life path.

Sunny blue sky: Sunny blue skies are a sign of adventure, positivity, and success.

Storms or dark sky: Stormy weather indicates potential difficulties or emotional stress.

Wind: A strong breeze or wind can indicate sudden changes or new ideas and may be a suggestion not to push yourself.

KEVIN AND CLARA'S PARTNER EXPERIENCE

In this example, Kevin, a student in one of my psychic development classes, shares his experience with the career and life path exercise. In this partner exercise, he is intuiting for Clara, another student whom he had not met prior to the class. When we completed the path meditation exercise, Kevin was the first to volunteer to share his experience.

When Kevin and Clara began the exercise, Kevin was a little nervous and didn't know what to expect. He shared that he wanted to help his partner and felt a little pressure, but Clara seemed kind, which put his fears to rest.

As soon as he began to breathe and relax, Kevin started to see different images. Not knowing if he was too anxious or was trying too hard, he felt himself wanting to think about what he saw and try to understand the images. He said that it took a lot of discipline not to give in to this. However, when he remembered to go back to breathing and relaxing, he felt more centered.

As he further relaxed, he saw the path and imagined Clara on it, but he didn't see much else. What he could visually see and feel seemed peaceful and gentle. It was sunny and he saw flowers and birds, and there was one bird, a blue jay, that seemed to be following Clara as she walked down the path.

As he was wondering if anything else was going to happen, Kevin became concerned that he was making up what he was experiencing. He said that the scene seemed like something you might see on a greeting card or poster. Realizing that he was again overthinking the process, he went back to breathing and relaxing.

Then everything changed and he became aware of a big boulder on the path. He visually saw it but mostly felt it and knew that it was there. Surprised when the bird, the blue jay, got closer, Kevin said that it felt as if the bird could communicate with him and he could hear it and knew what it was thinking. As he listened to the blue jay, he became aware that Clara could easily get around the boulder. She seemed to know this, because he then felt that she was on the other side and the scene felt open and positive again. Then it all seemed to fade.

When the exercise was over, he told Clara that overall her career path felt positive, and he described the flowers and the blue sky. Kevin then told her about the boulder and that it felt as if there was an upcoming obstacle that she might need to maneuver around. Trying to push through it didn't feel like it was going to work. He also shared his awareness of the intuitive blue jay and let her know that if felt like an animal spirit helper to him.

The feedback that Clara then gave Kevin was helpful to him. He didn't know if he was making up his impressions and felt a little silly telling her what he had received. However, Clara let him know that she likes her job, it is positive, and she feels fortunate. In this way, she said, the blue sky and flowers made sense. She thought that maybe the obstacle that he had felt coming her way had to do with a proposition that she was planning on presenting to the board of the organization where she worked: a request for an increase in funding for a special project. She knew that there would be some opposition to it. Clara also told Kevin that she feels a special connection to blue jays and loved that the bird seemed to help her get around the boulder.

Intuiting for another can sometimes feel like jumping off a cliff. If it is someone you do not know, all you have is the energy and your intuition to rely on. While this is ultimately the best way to further develop and better understand the power of your intuition, it can also be a bit intimidating. I encourage you to jump in. Be willing to be incorrect and downright wrong about what you receive and your interpretation. It will get better, and there is every reason to believe and trust that your intuition knows what it is doing.

CHAPTER 13

Rose Meditation Exercise to Intuit Relationship Insights

The focus of this meditation exercise is relationships. Similar to the other meditation exercises, it utilizes imagery as a psychic energy receptacle. However, in this one you invite another person to join you. Roses are used to symbolize you and the other person. Intuitive guidance and insight surface through obvious and often subtle changes and movement in the roses.

In this exercise pay particular attention to emotional energy and listen to your heart. Because this exercise is centered in relationship energy, intuited feelings and heart-centered awareness are key to becoming aware of insights and new understanding. If you begin to overthink, go back to the breath and open your heart.

Think of someone you have a relationship with, whether a romantic one or otherwise. If there is a question or concern or something that you would like to better understand about the relationship, write this down. You can also simply observe how the meditation unfolds.

It is possible that the person you want to invite into this exercise will not show up. There is nothing you can do about this. It is their free will choice. If this happens, ask for someone else to enter the imagery.

Before You Begin

Here is a review of the clearing preparation exercise from chapter 10 to do before you begin:

Take a deep breath and feel any emotions or feelings that you have about this issue or condition. Write down the feelings and emotions that surface.

What are your thoughts surrounding your question and this area of your life? What are the factors affecting it, the facts as you know them, and your expectations? Write all of this down.

What is your desire in relation to your question or issue? What do you want to happen?

What do you fear may happen? How are you controlling the situation and any others involved? What do you want the outcome to be and why? Write all of this down.

🌸 Rose Meditation Exercise 🌸

Get comfortable and breathe long, deep, cleansing breaths. Move the energy of the breath through the body and exhale any stress or tension. Continue to breathe in this way.

When you are ready, imagine a blank screen in front of you. Using your imagination encourages clairvoyance. Remember, you may not see a three-dimensional blank screen. Instead, you may have a sense of it, know it, or feel it. It may appear cartoonish or made-up.

On this screen imagine a rose. This rose represents you. Notice its stem and leaves, the bud or blossom, the color of the rose, and any other details.

Ask for the higher-self energy of the person you would like to be part of this meditation exercise to be present. Imagine another rose. This one represents the other person you are inquiring about. Notice everything you can about this rose: its color, stem, leaves, and bud or blossom.

Imagine the two roses side by side.

Observe how the roses interact and become aware of any changes that occur. For instance, do either of them wilt, open into a full blossom, turn the other way, come closer, or shed their petals? Does either rose change color, fade away, or transform into something other than a rose?

Continue to observe and feel the connection between the roses. If you have a question, project it as a thought message onto the screen.

After you have asked your question or projected your thoughts and feelings onto the roses, notice any changes that occur with the roses.

In addition to observing the roses, pay attention to energy information that you intuit through your thoughts, emotions, feelings in your body, a sense of knowing, or your inner voice. With this meditation it is especially helpful to pay attention to intuitive feelings and emotions.

Continue to intuitively receive energy information through the different psychic modalities. Do not try to interpret or understand what you receive. Stay in this receptive mode until the energy begins to fade.

Before you complete the meditation, send a beam of white-light love energy from your heart to the person you are inquiring about. This will help to heal any disharmony between the two of you and infuse the connection with love. Then imagine a ball of light shattering the image.

WHAT TO DO IF NOTHING HAPPENED

If you did not intuit any thoughts, feelings, images, or sensations during the meditation exercise, relax and take your time. This doesn't mean that you are not intuitive.

Try again and alter the exercise by using your imagination to create an image of a rose. This rose represents you. Notice details about the rose (the color, the bud, etc.) and become aware of any changes to it and receive any other intuitive information. Once the image of the rose begins to fade, you have completed the exercise. Repeat this step at another time. Simply imagine an image of a rose and keep repeating this until the scene begins to come alive and are you able to intuit more energy information. As you continue to practice this exercise, imagine another rose and keep moving forward with the exercise little by little.

INTERPRETATION

Intuited feelings and emotions are common in this exercise. At times you may feel overwhelmed or confused by the amount of emotional energy that surfaces. If this happens, take your time, slow down, and feel the emotions as they surface.

Some emotions will be expressive of your ego and others will be heart-centered intuitive messages; quietly listen for them. Remember that intuitive feelings and emotions are consistent and reside underneath more intense and dramatic ego-based emotions.

Intuited positive feelings equal positive outcomes and shared positive feelings between you and another.

Intuited feelings of sadness, anxiousness, or grief can describe the emotional energy of the past, present, or future between you and another.

Intuited feelings of disappointment or confusion may also indicate an unhappy outcome to or disharmony in the relationship.

Personal emotions and desires related to the relationship may surface and interfere with receiving energy information. It this happens, take it as a sign that you are not ready to proceed with the exercise. Let yourself feel these feelings. Don't push them down or ignore them. Give them all the space they need. When you are feeling more neutral, try again. If confusion and doubt persist, this may be an intuitive sign that this is the energy of the relationship.

Intuited sensations such as your heart opening or feeling energized can indicate a positive connection or a loving soul-mate relationship with another.

Intuited sensations of heaviness or stress or feelings of disconnection can be a message that the relationship may not be in your highest good.

Intuited thoughts that surface in the form of a word, phrase, or song lyric may provide insight and information. Thought messages can be auditory and sound like your own voice, or they can come in the form of an idea or insight.

Thoughts and energy information that you intuit through inner hearing are often straightforward and do not need any further interpretation. If thoughts surface that you do not understand, resist overthinking and do not discard them. Give them time to unfold. When you least expect it, the meaning will surface.

Image Glossary

You may receive intuited images visually, through a sense of knowing, of through feeling or sensing them. They may or may not be clear and detailed.

Rose

The rose is the psychic receptacle for love, compassion, and relationships, and through it you can receive energy information about your relationship with another.

Blossom: A fully open rose blossom is a positive sign of intimacy, an open heart, and a fulfilling relationship.

Bud: A closed rose blossom indicates a closed heart. A slow-opening bud indicates patience, a slow-moving relationship, or uncertainty about the relationship.

Changing color: If one or both roses change color, this indicates change and transformation in the relationship. Pay attention to the color that the rose changes into, as this will provide more information. If the rose continues to change color, it can also indicate chaos and uncertainty in the relationship.

Dying: If one or both roses die, this can indicate the end of the relationship or the waning of love and feelings of intimacy and affection toward another.

Shedding petals: This may indicate loss in the relationship or be a sign to let go of expectations. It might also indicate that you or the relationship needs to change and you need to let go of something or someone.

Turning away: If one or both of the roses turn in another direction, this may indicate emotional distance or a lack of intimacy or communication in the relationship. It may also indicate a lack of honesty or trust.

Wilting: If one or both roses begin to wilt, it may be an indication of a lack of interest and commitment or a sign that the relationship needs positive energy and healing to come back to life and be fulfilling.

Rose Colors

Blue: Blue indicates tranquility and emotional depth. Dark blue can symbolize depression or sad feelings. Blue might also indicate an increase in communication or the need to communicate in the relationship.

Green: Green indicates healing and growth as well as renewed feelings and the rejuvenation of a relationship. Fluorescent green can indicate jealousy.

Orange: Orange symbolizes positive feelings of enthusiasm, fun, and passion.

Pink: Pink can indicate new love, healing, and appreciation as well as angelic help and guidance.

Purple: Purple indicates a soul connection with another or that the two of you have been brought together for a purpose.

Red: Red symbolizes intense love, romance, and passionate feelings.

White: White symbolizes spirituality, pureness, and new beginnings and can also be a sign of divine connection and blessings.

Yellow: Yellow symbolizes friendship (but not romantic love) and joy and can be a sign of hope.

TAMMY'S MEDITATION EXERCISE EXPERIENCE

About to graduate with a master's degree in social work, my client Tammy always thought she would meet the love of her life at college. She assumed that she would marry young and have children, but this plan was not unfolding the way she had envisioned. Although she had been on plenty of dates during her college years, she had not been in a committed relationship. When she met Justin, she was hopeful. He was easy to be with and they had common interests and backgrounds. Tammy thought he might be the one, but he seemed to have some issues with intimacy. The closer they got, the more he would later pull away and become distant. Wanting to better understand and work through this issue, Tammy tried to talk to him several times about her feelings. However, whenever she brought it up, Justin would look at her with a blank expression, saying that he did not know what she was talking about.

Tammy attended an intuitive workshop in the hope that her intuition could help her to better understand herself, others, and relationships. She was excited to do the rose meditation exercise.

Before Tammy began the exercise, she wrote down her feelings, concerns, and desires about Justin and about relationships in general. Surprised by what it revealed, she realized that she was more anxious and stressed about her ability to be in a good, long-term relationship than she had thought. More feelings about Justin surfaced, such as confusion, sadness, and hopefulness, and she wrote them all down.

When she began to relax and breathe cleansing breaths, more feelings came up, but she continued to breathe through them. Eventually she felt calm and began to visualize the blank screen, which she could feel more than see. Because I had told her that this might happen, she knew that it was okay not to see a clear image of the screen and she kept going. On the screen she imagined a rose that represented her. It was initially red, but then the color began to fade and it became more yellow. Her rose seemed healthy and was fully open.

She then imagined a rose that represented Justin's energy on the screen. She also sent his higher self a thought message to make sure that it was okay with him to take part in this exercise The rose stayed and didn't fade, so she took that as a yes answer. His rose was also red to begin with, but then it seemed to become more dull. It looked healthy and was bigger than hers, and that struck her as interesting. As she was thinking about this, an inner voice told her that his rose was bigger because he had more power in the relationship. She was not too surprised by this insight, as she knew in her heart that she was giving him her power.

Tammy told me that there seemed to be a barrier between the two roses on the screen. When her rose tried to face his and get closer, his rose turned and moved away. That made sense to her, as this is what kept happening in real life in their relationship. She wanted to know why his rose turned away and what the barrier was that she often felt with him. Tammy sent a prayer to her angels and asked this question and also projected it onto the screen. She waited for something to happen, but not much did. Then she heard the inner voice again, which said that Justin's inability to be close was not her fault. As she felt and became aware of how much she wanted the relationship to work, she cried a few tears. The intuitive feeling and awareness that there was nothing she could do to change what was happening became stronger, and she knew she had to let go of him.

Feeling sad, she suddenly saw her rose again, but Justin's rose was no longer on the screen, and she didn't want it to be. As she was about to end the exercise, she felt a feeling of comfort and the intuitive awareness that there was a soul mate that she was meant to be with in this life. In her heart she felt and knew that when the timing was right, she would meet him. When she ended the exercise, she was still sad about Justin, but she also felt more hopeful and ready to move on.

Tammy's story is another example of diverging from the meditation exercise format and receiving valuable energy information and guidance. Let the format of the exercises be a jumping-off point and trust where your intuition takes you. Intuition is fluid, and it is best to trust it, remain open, and follow where it leads.

Intuiting guidance and information about a personal relationship can be challenging. Our feelings and desires can interfere, and we may not want to accept or even become aware of intuitive information that opposes our desires. Unlike when we are intuiting for another person, when we bring another's energy into an intuitive exercise in order to better understand our connection with them, the energy information we receive will likely invoke a personal reaction.

When you want to intuit information about a relationship, make sure you are ready and willing to accept whatever surfaces, and allow it to be a lesson in learning more about yourself, another, and what you may need to do to evolve and grow.

CHAPTER 14

Elevator Meditation Exercise to Intuit Spiritual Guidance

Although much of the energy information that we intuit is sent to us through angels, spirit guides, loved ones on the other side, or a divine presence, we are not always sure who is guiding us. In our haste to receive answers and guidance, we do not necessarily focus on the deeper spiritual meaning and importance of what we receive. This is understandable and not uncommon. However, there will be times when we feel ready to receive more spiritually based messages that help us to better understand our spiritual path.

Spiritual guidance is not always easy to understand, as it tends to be directed to our soul awareness and not the conscious ego part of us. For this reason it may seem that it is coded in mystery and wonder. Even when we receive and correctly interpret intuited energy information, it can be a puzzle and it may take us a while to truly take in the message in a logical way. Once our spirit and soul have had a chance to simmer and absorb spiritual guidance, the information tends to become clearer. However, be patient, as it usually takes time and patience for the meaning to be revealed. In the meantime, the intuited symbols, messages, feelings, or insights that we receive seep deep into the recesses of our soul and spirit and create inward change that is not always easy to recognize and understand.

This meditation exercise assists you in raising your vibration and receiving intuitive spiritual guidance from angels, a divine presence, and spiritual beings. With this exercise you can receive general guidance or insight about a question or area of interest.

BEFORE YOU BEGIN

Here is a review of the clearing preparation exercise from chapter 10 to do before you begin:

Take a deep breath and feel any emotions or feelings that you have about this issue or condition. Write down the feelings and emotions that surface.

What are your thoughts surrounding your question and this area of your life? What are the factors affecting it, the facts as you know them, and your expectations? Write all of this down.

What is your desire in relation to your question or issue? What do you want to happen?

What do you fear may happen? How are you controlling the situation and any others involved? What do you want the outcome to be and why? Write all of this down.

🪷 Elevator Meditation Exercise 🪷

Breath work can be helpful in reaching a higher vibration. It gives you the energetic boost you need to ascend to higher realms. Get into a comfortable position and close your eyes. Begin to breathe long, deep breaths. Move the energy of the breath through the body and exhale any stress or tension. Continue to breathe in this way.

When you feel relaxed, raise your vibration to a higher state of consciousness by breathing white light down through the top of the head and exhaling it through the heart. Continue to breathe in this way. Inhale white-light energy and, as you exhale, imagine your heart opening. You may begin to feel the signs of a higher vibrational state, such as tingling in the body, a buzzing feeling, a feeling of expansion and lightness, or feeling lightheaded. Breathe in this manner until you sense an increase in vibration.

When you are ready, imagine a blank screen in front of you. Using your imagination encourages clairvoyance. Remember, you may not see a three-dimensional blank screen. Instead, you may have a sense of it, know it, or feel it. It may appear cartoonish or made-up. All of this is fine.

Imagine an elevator on the blank screen. Notice as much detail about it as you can, such as its color, structure, size, and anything else.

As you pay attention to the elevator, imagine that the door opens and you step into the elevator. Within it there is a feeling of openness and space. It feels soothing and comfortable. Breathe and imagine your consciousness rising as you move energy through your body.

Once you are in the elevator, the door gently closes and you begin to ascend higher and higher. As you are lifted higher, continue to breathe and relax. Breathe and imagine your consciousness rising. Move the energy through you and allow it to lift you.

You may feel the sensation of the elevator rapidly ascending, or it may be a slower and more gradual lifting. Eventually the elevator comes to a stop.

When the door opens there is a message waiting for you. Become aware of any intuitive thoughts, feelings, messages, or insights. In addition, you may intuitively see or sense a spirit being or messenger or an object or symbol. Be patient and stay in a receptive mode. It may take some time to become intuitively aware of and receive guidance and energy information.

When you have received all that you can at this time or if the image begins to dissipate, imagine a beam of light dissolving the image.

WHAT TO DO IF NOTHING HAPPENED

If you did not intuit any thoughts, feelings, images, or sensations during the meditation exercise, relax and take your time. This doesn't mean that you are not intuitive.

Try again and alter the exercise by using your imagination to create an image of the elevator. Notice any changes in this image and receive any intuitive information. Once the elevator begins to fade, you have completed the exercise. Repeat this step at another time. Simply imagine the elevator and keep repeating this until the scene begins to come alive and you are able to intuit more energy information. As you continue to practice this exercise, imagine yourself moving upward little by little.

It is also possible that you may receive a spiritual message through a dream.

INTERPRETATION

Intuited emotions such as love and compassion usually accompany spiritual guidance. The message may come as an emotional healing or a feeling of comfort or deep peace, and you may feel a heart-centered opening and new awareness.

Intuited physical sensations of higher-vibration energy such as a buzzing sensation or an increase in energy in your body, particularly in your head, are a positive sign. This indicates that you are increasing your frequency and raising your vibration.

Intuited thoughts may come in the form of a word, a phrase, or a complete understanding. You may have a sense of knowing and become aware of spiritual insights. Some of what you receive may be difficult to put into words and fully grasp. If you do not understand a message, give it time to unfold.

Spiritual messages often speak to our soul and can be difficult to comprehend cognitively. However, their deeper meaning eventually makes sense. Keep in mind that the message and the deeper connection with spirit forces has a positive and healing influence on us even when we cannot mentally decipher the message.

IMAGE GLOSSARY

You may receive intuited images visually, through a sense of knowing, or through feeling them. They may or may not be clear and detailed.

Elevator

In this meditation exercise, the elevator is the psychic energy receptacle that assists you in reaching a higher state of consciousness in order to receive spiritual guidance.

Intuited Images

You may see or sense an image that embodies the message. Be aware of other energy information that surfaces along with an image. The images that you receive may be unique and may reveal more insight and meaning over time.

Intuited Symbols

The message may come as a symbol that you see, feel, sense, or know. You may want to write down or draw the symbol and search for its meaning in a dream dictionary. Some symbols are unique and are meant to speak to and invoke the energy of our soul. They bypass our conscious understanding and work on deeper levels.

Some spiritual symbols may be more universally understood. For example, common positive spiritual symbols include a dove, a ring, gems, being pregnant, a house with a new room that you didn't know about, the sea, pure flowing water, a fountain with water gushing, a sunrise, flowers, clouds parting and the sun shining through, hearing music, and anything white or gold. These indicate the presence of spirit, so pay attention to the feelings and thoughts that may emerge along with them.

Spirit Messenger or Being

You may see or sense a spirit being or divine presence. This may be a loved one in spirit, an angel, or a spirit guide. Although you will likely want to know more about the being that is present, try to focus on the message and the feelings that emanate from the spirit presence.

My Dream

This meditation exercise is based on a dream I had a few years ago. In the dream I was in an elevator that was shooting straight up into the air at lightning speed. As I went higher and higher, I felt a tingling of vibration and movement all through my body. The elevator eventually came to a stop on its own, and the door opened. Standing before me was an Asian man dressed in the kind of clothing that you would see in Tibet. He bowed and handed me a yellow hat that had faint embroidered designs on it. He said nothing. Then the elevator door closed and I woke up.

This was one of those dreams that felt significant, but I didn't know why. The next day I felt an intuitive nudge to research Buddhist yellow hats. It seemed silly and I didn't expect to find much. However, I was surprised to discover that the dominant tradition of Tibetan Buddhism today is the *Gelugpa*, or the Yellow Hat school. The Dalai Lama is the head of this sect. I am not sure why I was given this gift in my dream, but I felt honored. This may be an example of a spiritual message that bypassed my conscious thinking mind and instead spoke to a deeper part of me, my soul and spirit. The dream left me with a sense of peace that I still feel whenever I think of it.

❧

Spirit guides, angels, and loved ones on the other side have their own way of doing things. While we may desire a specific answer or guidance in a form that makes sense to us, their agenda may be quite different. When working with higher energy, remember that you are the student. It will not work to try to control the process or the spirit realm. Let yourself be led and humble yourself in the process. There is much greater goodness and love waiting for you than you can imagine. Spirit plays big.

CHAPTER 15

Going Backward Toward a Goal Meditation Exercise to Intuit Steps to Attain a Goal

Do you ever want to achieve a goal but you don't know where to begin? Maybe you have a sense of where to start, but you are not sure what is necessary and required to manifest your desire. One of the gifts of intuition is that it can provide us with a complete big-picture awareness. We can perceive past, present, and future events through a bird's-eye view and feel and experience a sense of completion that carries us through a project. When we know and feel that something will succeed, we are more likely to go forward with enthusiasm.

In this meditation exercise you employ your psychic awareness to intuit the necessary steps to achieve a goal or something that you would like to manifest or experience. Like all of the exercises in this book, it makes use of clairvoyance (see), claircognizance (know), clairaudience (hear), and clairsentience (feel and sense). There are four steps to this process, and we will be working our way backward through the steps. Although initially this may seem confusing, reversing perception diminishes the power of the thinking mind and aids in psychic receptivity.

Become aware of something you would like to experience, a goal you would like to attain, or something you would like to manifest.

Before You Begin

Here is a review of the clearing preparation exercise from chapter 10 to do before you begin:

Take a deep breath and feel any emotions or feelings that you have about this issue or condition. Write down the feelings and emotions that surface.

What are your thoughts surrounding your question and this area of your life? What are the factors affecting it, the facts as you know them, and your expectations? Write all of this down.

What is your desire in relation to your question or issue? What do you want to happen?

What do you fear may happen? How are you controlling the situation and any others involved? What do you want the outcome to be and why? Write all of this down.

🌸 Going Backward Toward a Goal 🌸
Meditation Exercise

Get into a comfortable position. Begin to breathe long, deep breaths. Move the energy of the breath through the body and exhale any stress or tension. Continue to breathe in this way. This will both relax you and increase your vibration.

In as much detail as possible, imagine what you want to experience or the goal or achievement that you want to manifest. Notice what you are doing and how you feel. Imagine an image of yourself doing and experiencing this in as much detail as possible. What do you see, sense, or know about your desired outcome? How does it feel to be successful? Focus on the positive feelings that come with achieving what you desire.

Finding Step 4

Once you see, feel, or sense yourself having achieved the desired outcome, ask your intuition what step you took right before you manifested this outcome. This is step 4 in the process of achieving your goal. What action, thought, feeling, awareness, or perception leads to this success? See and feel this, and imagine it in as much detail as possible. Use your imagination to create an image of what is happening and what you are experiencing.

Finding Step 3

Once you see, feel, or sense the step that led to your achievement, intuitively tune in to the step that came before it. This is step 3. See and feel step 3 in as much detail as possible. What is the action, thought, awareness, or perception that you are experiencing in this step?

Finding Step 2

Take a deep breath, then release the breath, and now intuitively tune in to the step that led to step 3. This is step 2. What are you doing, feeling, and experiencing in this step? Use your imagination to create an image of yourself engaging in this step's activity. See and feel it in as much detail as possible.

Finding Step 1

Continue to breathe and relax. Ask yourself what step you can now take that will set in motion the steps to success. This is step 1. What awareness, action, perception, feeling, or decision can you presently take to initiate the process of manifesting what you desire? Ask yourself what you need to know or feel or any action you need to take now. Feel this energy flow through you. What do you feel? What do you know? What awareness inspires and empowers you to move forward?

Stay in this energy for as long as possible. Then write down the intuited steps toward manifestation of your goal in as much detail as possible.

WHAT TO DO IF NOTHING HAPPENED

If you did not intuit any thoughts, feelings, images, or sensations during the meditation exercise, relax and take your time. This doesn't mean that you are not intuitive.

Try again and alter the exercise by using your imagination to create an image of what you want to manifest. Notice any changes and intuit any information about this goal. When the image begins to fade, you have completed the exercise. Repeat imagining your goal at another time. Simply imagine the goal and keep repeating this until the scene begins to come alive and are you able to intuit more energy information. As you continue to practice this exercise, imagine yourself moving forward step by step.

INTERPRETATION

Intuited positive emotions, especially heart-centered emotions, may reveal insight into what will bring you joy, inner peace, and feelings of deep satisfaction.

Intuited negative emotions such as fear or frustration may indicate that unconscious or stuffed-away emotions may be hindering you from moving forward. They may also indicate that you may experience these feelings as you move forward but you should keep going. Sometimes we have to move through resistance and difficulties to manifest what we desire.

Intuited thoughts that emerge through a word, phrase, insight, idea, or a complete understanding can provide valuable information. Insights and information about the steps to take or what is required for you to move forward may surface through an inner knowing, or you might also hear a quiet inner voice guiding you.

Intuited images may spontaneously emerge that provide information about the step. They may describe places, people, objects, and other realistic and identifiable information. Instead of visually seeing images, you might feel or sense them or have a feeling of what you may need to do or experience to manifest your goal.

It is not essential to see and work with images in this meditation. If you see an image that you do not understand, don't rush to try to interpret it, but don't discard it either. In time its meaning may become clearer.

Physical sensations such as feeling light, tingly, and full of energy may indicate unencumbered progress and positive results.

Intuited sensations such as feeling heavy, blocked, or tired may indicate some inner resistance about the steps or the goal. You may need to review your goal and make sure that it is in keeping with your heart's desire and highest good.

Intuited symbols may also surface that may or may not make sense. Most likely they will be personal to you or point you in the right direction to attain your goals. If you receive a symbol that you do not understand, write it down or draw it, and its message and meaning will either gently or spontaneously unfold.

To achieve your goal, it is important to act on the information that you receive as best you can. Do not wait until you fully understand everything that you received. This can lead to procrastination. As you act on the steps, continue to listen to your intuition for more guidance and direction. As you move forward and take action on the energy information that you received, the steps will begin to fall in place and make more sense.

RESTAURANTEUR JOSH

My friend Josh went to culinary school, and he loves to cook and create new ways to prepare and combine spices in traditional food dishes. After working in a few different restaurants, he was ready to branch out on his own, either with a catering business, a food truck, or a small restaurant. Although he was willing to pursue any of these options, he wasn't sure which was best for him. After several months of indecision and time spent researching, he had a lot of information but was no closer to knowing where to begin.

When he told me that he was having trouble making up his mind, we did the Going Backward Toward a Goal meditation exercise.

Almost as soon as we started the meditation exercise, Josh began to see images and feel and hear information. Intuitive insights flowed in so easily that he wondered if he was making it all up.

In the image that represented his goal, he saw himself happily at work in a kitchen. It smelled great, with an aroma of spices, fresh cilantro, and nutmeg filling the air. This was his restaurant and it felt good to be there. There were others with him cooking, serving food, washing dishes, and taking care of the many things that needed to be done. It was a small place but attractive, with lots of color and a bistro look. There were lots of people who seemed to be enjoying themselves, and he could hear laughter and conversation.

When he intuitively tuned in to the step before his goal came to fruition, he saw himself getting ready to open the restaurant. He was painting the walls and putting together tables and seating. There were others in the kitchen installing restaurant equipment and stocking the shelves. He didn't feel stressed or worried, just excited. It all felt like it was coming together. Josh realized that opening the restaurant was a team effort. Although he had always known that he could not do this alone, he now better understood that even before the restaurant opened he would need to enlist the help of others.

In the step before this awareness, step 2, he saw an image of himself looking for a location. Someone was helping him and pointing out possible spots. It intuitively felt as if he had a strict budget, and he saw himself having to pass on a few potential locations for financial reasons. He then became aware of a smaller space in the downtown area that fit within his financial limits. Wondering how he got the money to lease anything, he projected this question to the image and quickly had the sense that he had a partner and there were others who were involved with the financing.

In the first step, what he could do in present time, Josh saw himself talking to the owner of a restaurant that he used to work for. His previous boss was giving him the name of someone else to talk to. He didn't know if it was a business associate of his or a financial advisor, but he knew it was a helpful contact.

As Josh continued to wonder how he would be able to afford to open the restaurant, he felt an odd physical sensation, almost as if someone or something was giving him a strong energetic nudge. With this feeling came the awareness that he needed to get to work on this now. With an intuitive sense of knowing, he became aware that it was time to seek out and talk to some of the people who had been supportive and had offered to help in the past. He didn't need to figure everything out on his own. Although it now seemed obvious, he became aware that he had not been accepting the offers of advice and support that others had been extending to him. The intuitive images, thoughts, and feelings all made it clear how important it was to network and follow up with others when they offered help, advice, or helpful contacts. Feeing more confident and enthusiastic, Josh had a better sense of where to begin.

This meditation exercise can reveal important and essential information to empower you to achieve your goal that you may have overlooked or not been aware of. More than in the other exercises, in this one you may find yourself lapsing into overthinking and trying to figure things out. If this happens, gently guide yourself back to the breath and relax, clear the mind, and continue to receive energy information. If you receive images, thoughts, sensations, or feelings that seem counter to what you believe is possible or seem beyond your ability to carry out, continue to intuit without judgment or overthinking. This exercise can expand and move us beyond our finite sense of what we can achieve and open us to new possibilities and ways of proceeding that may be out of our comfort zone. Spirit knows us as unlimited beings and may be attempting to encourage us to perceive ourselves this way.

Each time you use these meditation exercises, the depth and quality of the intuitive insights and guidance you receive will strengthen and increase. The ability to combine the different psychic modalities and form a more complete and cohesive psychic understanding will become more natural, and interpreting intuited information will be easier and more intuitive. Continue to practice the exercises, open your heart and mind, become receptive, and be willing to be surprised.

CHAPTER 16

How to Receive and Interpret Psychic Information

It is no small feat to channel the wispy, elusive psychic energy that surrounds us and manipulate it into a neat, comprehensible, and accurate package of information. To be a psychic is to be an energy engineer, scientist, translator, and developer. In addition, psychic awareness requires the sensitivity and wisdom of a seer, shaman, spiritual guide, and diviner.

As we come to the end of the book, I wonder, how are you doing? Are you a bit overwhelmed, or are you more excited and motivated to continue learning, practicing, and developing your psychic abilities? Perhaps you feel a mix of emotions: optimistic and inspired by the increased awareness of your innate psychic potential and energized by the possibilities yet not quite sure where to go from here. All of this is understandable. If you feel a bit wobbly after reading and trying out the information contained in this book, it might be helpful to go back to the basics.

Here is a summary of the psychic development process for easy reference.

Awareness

On a daily basis, notice and identify spontaneous intuitive impressions, hunches, and insights as they surface. Tune in to your intuitive feelings, thoughts, dreams, daydreams, spontaneous images, and physical sensations. Notice the difference between psychic energy information and your day-to-day personal thoughts, feelings, and other non-intuitive processing. Hone in on the different intuitive modalities as they naturally surface.

Practice

We improve and get better at anything we do often and consistently. Establish a time and place to tune in to and pay attention to your intuition on a consistent basis. Life goes on; we all have a lot to do and we get busy and distracted with many things. However, committing to a daily, weekly, or monthly psychic practice pays off in many ways. Psychic awareness is centering and connects us to our wise and loving soulful self. The insight, guidance, and information that we intuitively receive enables us to make positive choices and act from a place of inner power and awareness. The calm inner peace that comes with psychic awareness is a balm to our soul in this overstimulated, busy, and sometimes lonely world. We all need this inner light to warm, shelter, and guide us.

A regular practice of tuning in and listening to your intuition makes psychic awareness an integral part of your life. When you need psychic guidance and direction, it becomes more readily available and you become better able to identify, trust, and utilize it. Consistent practice empowers you to become a more proficient and accurate psychic.

Neutrality

All too often we jump into attempting to receive psychic information before we are fully ready. Although becoming aware of our state of mind and emotions prior to tuning in to our intuition may seem like a waste of time or unnecessary, it actually speeds up the process by eliminating doubt and confusion.

Before you intuitively tune in to your own or another's energy, take some time to become aware of anything that might interfere with or influence your ability to be neutral. If you are receiving energy information for yourself, examine your thoughts, feelings, desires, and beliefs about the area of interest or question. Once you are consciously aware of these, it becomes easier to discern intuitive information from self-generated hopes and desires. Becoming clear of personal influences prior to receiving energy information is the best way to trust what you intuitively receive.

If you are receiving energy information for another, become aware of your expectations. Do not put undue pressure on yourself to be "right." Even if you feel that someone is depending on you to be accurate and helpful, being psychic is a learning process. Do your best and try not to let another's expectations weigh on you. Accept what you intuitively receive, even if you are having a difficult time interpreting it. Share the feelings, images, sensations, and other psychic energy information as you have experienced it.

PROTECTION

Before you intuitively open to and receive energy information, surround yourself with white-light energy. Simply make the intent to receive only positive and helpful energy information and imagine white light surrounding you. Depending on your spiritual or religious beliefs and practices, you can call on divine energy, positive energy, God, the Goddess, or a divine being for protection. Although under normal conditions it is rare to encounter negative or harmful energy influences, it is always a good practice to ensure that you are receiving only what is in your and others' highest good.

RECEPTIVITY

To receive energy information, breathe, relax, open your mind and heart, and simply listen and notice. Let go of what you think energy information will be like, and accept the feelings, impressions, thoughts, images, and physical sensations that surface. If you begin to overthink or judge what you receive, go back to the breath and relax. If you find yourself trying to understand and interpret your impressions, go back to the breath. Once you receive intuitive information, take note of it and move on; do not try to understand or evaluate it. Above all else, stay in an open and receptive mode. Be a sponge and a collector of energy information. If the energy information feels subtle or if you can barely detect it, raise your vibration by imagining the breath coming in down through the top of your head and then exhale through your heart.

Once the energy begins to fade and you feel like you have received all that you can, write down the feelings, thoughts, impressions, images, physical sensations, and anything else that you have experienced. Writing down your intuitive impressions allows more energy information to surface and helps clarify what you received.

Why Did I Intuit This?

You may find yourself wondering why you intuitively received certain information, especially if it does not seem to address your concerns or reflect the kind of guidance you were hoping to tune in to. We tend to intuitively pick up on energy information that has the strongest vibration. Sometimes there is no specific reason for this happening. The information is simply present and we intuit it. Other times there may be unconscious or higher consciousness information that is in our best interest to receive, or there may be someone on the other side who is trying to give us a message. Go through the process of interpreting what you intuit even if it does not make sense. This is the best way to clear your psychic channels and eventually receive intuitive information and guidance that is easier to understand and relate to.

Interpretation

You will likely receive all kinds of impressions and psychic energy information. Sometimes you will receive more energy information than at other times. You likely will also quickly understand some information that you receive, while other intuitive impressions may be more perplexing. However, the accuracy of a reading is not dependent on the amount of energy information that you intuit or the specific modality through which it surfaces. It is more important to be a clear channel and not personally influence or project your opinions onto your intuitive impressions.

Take your time with your interpretation. If you are intuiting personal information for yourself, you can allow the interpretation to unfold over time. There is no need to rush. Putting pressure on yourself to figure everything out right away is not helpful in the long run.

If you are giving another person a reading, you may need to interpret energy information more quickly. If you feel confident in your interpretation, share it. If you are not sure, share what you received exactly how you received it, and allow the other person to help you interpret it.

INTERPRETATION TIPS

Intuited emotions and feelings reflect and describe the emotions and feelings connected to a question or concern, a future event, or another's emotions. They are often precognitive and foretell the emotional outcome of your concern, or how you or another is likely to feel in the future. They might also indicate emotions that are repressed and are negatively impacting the desired outcome.

Positive feelings such as love, happiness, and peace equal a positive future outcome. Negative feelings such as stress, anxiety, and sadness equal a negative or unfavorable outcome. Interpret whatever emotion surfaces, such as confusion, excitement, fear, joy, etc., as a straightforward indicator of the emotional energy that is influencing your question or concern or that you will be experiencing in relation to your question or concern.

You may also receive psychic guidance, insights, and messages through feeling them. For example, you may have a feeling of what, why, and when something is going to happen or experience a more heart-centered feeling of what is in your or another's highest good.

Interpret intuited physical sensations and feelings as indicators that describe the future outcome of the question or concern or what is influencing the outcome. Sensations that feel soothing, energizing, and stimulating indicate positive outcomes. Feelings of heaviness or fatigue, a lack of energy, or feeling blocked indicate negative or unfavorable outcomes. Experiencing a stomachache, pounding in the head, random pain, or other psychic physical sensations only while intuiting are indicators of blocked energy, or they may be reflective of your or another's physical health. If they are not health-related, they usually foretell problematic outcomes and can be a psychic warning in relation to the question or area of concern. However, pressure in the head and feeling stimulated, light, and open can also indicate the presence of high-vibration, positive energy.

Most intuited thoughts and messages are straightforward and need no further interpretation. If you receive a word that you do not understand, research it or look it up in a dictionary. If intuited thought information does not initially make sense, this does not mean that it is not accurate. Resist overthinking it and trying to figure it out. Give it some time to unfold. Most of the confusing intuitive mental thoughts that we receive, such as initials, phrases, or other random mental messages, become clearer in time.

Psychic images can surface in a variety of ways. In addition to seeing them, we can think them, feel them, know what they look like, or sense them. They can be cartoonish, colorful, black and white, realistic, or symbolic. If an image is symbolic and you do not understand the symbolism, take your time and consider different meanings and interpretations. Use your intuition to get a sense of what feels right or correct. You may want to consult a dream interpretation book to better understand the possible interpretations and meanings of symbols. Some images may be straightforward, realistic descriptions, and you can interpret them in this way. Most of the images that I receive are true-to-life images of people, places, and what is to come.

Journal

Keep a journal of your psychic experiences and look for patterns in the way you receive energy information and how you interpret it. Become aware of your intuitive strengths and weaknesses and the personal issues that may repeatedly get in your way. As good as it feels to interpret energy information correctly, we can learn as much from our mistakes as from our successes. Journaling is a tool that can help you keep track of your development. Don't use it to rate your performance or judge if you are psychic or not, because you are. Accept this and move on.

THE MOODS OF INTUITION

There will be times when your intuition is spot on and gently surfaces without effort or constraint. There will also be times when it seems to fail you. Just as we go through emotional ups and downs for no apparent reason, so do we experience intuitive moods and changes. Our intuition may be easy to access, clear, and accurate, then despite our best efforts it may become distant, confusing, or even blocked. This can happen for several reasons, some of which we have no control over.

Changes in the Skies

Energetic and planetary shifts and changes can enhance or interfere with intuitive receptivity. During a full moon, your intuition is likely to be stronger and easier to access. Being in nature, particularly near water, can also enhance intuitive receptivity. Thunderstorms can interfere with, confuse, and stifle psychic energy. I once had to cancel a reading during a thunderstorm because it felt as if the electricity in the air was absorbing my psychic energy and channeling it into the lightning and the skies. Changes in barometric pressure can also lead to issues with psychic receptivity. As the air becomes denser, it can take more energy to intuitively receive. I tend to get headaches if I do several readings on days when the barometric pressure is in flux.

Discover Your Optimum Time to Intuit

There is likely a time of day when your psychic awareness is stronger. Mine is in the morning, the earlier the better. Because I live on the East Coast, this can be tricky with my West Coast clients and with those who want me to work with them later in the evening. I can give readings at all times of the day, but the quality may not be as good as that of a morning session. As much as I would like to change myself to suit others' schedules, this is beyond my control. Find what works for you. Like the seasons and the natural shifts that all of life flows with, there is a rhythm and pattern to psychic receptivity. Find out what yours is and work with it.

Others' Opinions

We can change and influence some of the factors that affect psychic awareness. In previous chapters we discussed how emotions, thoughts, beliefs, and desires can hinder clear intuitive receptivity and what we can do to minimize their interference. Along with our personal state of mind and emotions, others' thoughts and emotional energy can also affect our intuitive clarity.

It is likely that you have family members or friends who support and share your interest in psychic phenomena. It is equally likely that there are people in your life who do not understand and may be fearful or apprehensive of the psychic world and your connection to it. If those closest to you—a partner, spouse, parent, or best friend—oppose your psychic development, it can affect you more than you may be aware of. While you may not be concerned about what another thinks or feels, you may be energetically affected by their thoughts and feelings. Interestingly, when it comes to psychic awareness, the unspoken fear and resistance of others can affect us more than what they say. Unexpressed feelings and thoughts are more easily absorbed when we are not consciously aware of them. It is similar to what happens when a friend or family member is keeping something from us. We likely feel that something is off or not quite right, but we do not know what it is. This secret can block intimacy or feelings of closeness.

If you feel that another's fear or opposition is weakening or creating static with your intuitive receptivity, acknowledge this as a possibility and protect yourself. Create the intent and imagine that there is a web of white-light energy surrounding you that allows you to absorb only positive energy. There is no need to confront others or try to get them to change their mind or be supportive. Once we become conscious of another's thoughts and feelings, we can quickly minimize the effect that they have on us. Not everyone has to support our interests. However, it is our responsibility to take care of ourselves and create an energetic boundary that protects us from absorbing others' fear and stress.

Physical Space

The energetic quality of our physical conditions can also impact the quality and ease of our intuitive receptivity. It can be difficult to intuit in a negative, chaotic, or cluttered environment. Emotions are powerful energy, and feelings such as anger, negativity, and fear create intuitive confusion and blocks. These kinds of emotions can also attract low-vibrational interference. They bring the energy down and increase the risk of intuitively receiving confusing and negative energy information. An environment that is cluttered with electronic equipment or television or electronic game noise can interrupt the psychic flow of information. Chaos of any kind, clutter, disruptions, loud noises, or a crowded space all impact clear psychic receptivity. Keep in mind that objects and things absorb and collect energy. Antiques in particular can emit confusing and possibly negative vibes. If you collect antiques or enjoy objects from secondhand stores or yard sales, you may want to smudge them or put them outdoors in the sunlight to purify them before placing them in your home or office.

The optimum environment for intuiting information is a quiet, clean, and organized space where you will not be interrupted. However, while this is preferred, it is not always possible. I have given readings in stressful and chaotic conditions. I once worked on a murder investigation while in the back of a police detective's car, where one of the two detectives believed that I was a complete sham. Another time I gave a long-distance reading to a man in India who was standing on a crowded bridge with cars, buses, and other vehicles whizzing by him. While it is possible to intuit anywhere and at any time, it takes a fair amount of psychic power to move through the energetic crosswinds.

YOUR PSYCHIC COMPANION

Psychic awareness can be an invaluable companion. Through the ups and downs of everyday challenges and in quiet times of loneliness, questioning, and doubt, listen and draw close to your intuition. Allow its quiet whisper to guide you through day-to-day minor areas of concern and through more significant upheavals and life changes. Let your intuition surprise and astound you with information about things that you may not have ever considered or thought were possible.

Your intuition is as unique as you are. Allow its expression to unfold unhindered by your expectations or what you want it to be. Intricately connected to your soul, your psychic awareness knows your life purpose and is always steering you in the direction of what your heart desires and what brings you joy. Even when you may not believe this to be true, lean into and trust your innate and authentic wisdom. Your intuition is your soulful support system and is intertwined with every aspect of your life. You can trust it to be a positive presence in all that you experience.

As you continue to develop your psychic abilities, you may feel led to become a professional psychic and help others. If this is not presently a part of your soul purpose, you may instead want to use your intuition to better understand yourself and navigate through more personal issues. You might also use your psychic skills with friends and family and continue to grow and learn all that you can about intuition, spirituality, and related areas. Pursue what is right for you. The key is to allow your intuition to guide you and to trust where you are led. If you are not sure whether to share your psychic abilities with others, know that this will become clearer when the timing is right. The best way to prepare to intuitively work with others is to use your intuition to become more self-aware, heal old wounds, and receive daily guidance. If you have the desire to psychically work with others and you feel called by spirit to take this step, trust your intuition to guide you and be there for you every step of the way. Obstacles will fall away and all that you need to fulfill this mission will come to you naturally and without strenuous effort.

Remember, there is more to developing our psychic awareness than simply sharpening our intuition and becoming psychic. Inner changes occur as we allow our psychic senses to reshape our view of reality, our self-perception, and our sense of what is possible. To live the best life possible, it is necessary to evolve and change the habits and patterns of thinking and acting that sabotage our happiness and keep us from achieving all that we are capable of. Intuition provides us with the awareness and power to do this.

Not only does intuition help us to know, feel, and become aware of useful energy information, but it also connects us to a greater force of love, wisdom, and care. As we allow our intuition to be an ever-present and active participant in our life, its wise and loving influence infuses us with new perceptions and the awareness to make positive choices and experience our best self. This awareness arises from the soul and is unstoppable.

Release yourself into the universal life force current and flow with it. Intuition is the language of the cosmos, and the journey has no end. All of life is engaged in intuitive conversation, so join the party!

Bibliography and Reading List

Albertsson, Alaric. *To Walk a Pagan Path: Practical Spirituality for Every Day*. Woodbury, MN: Llewellyn, 2013.

Andrews, Ted. *Animal-Speak: The Spiritual & Magical Powers of Creatures Great and Small*. St. Paul, MN: Llewellyn, 2002.

———. *How to See and Read the Aura*. Woodbury, MN: Llewellyn, 2006.

Anodea, Judith. *Wheels of Life: A User's Guide to the Chakra System*. St. Paul, MN: Llewellyn, 1987.

Barnum, Melanie. *Psychic Abilities for Beginners*. Woodbury, MN: Llewellyn, 2014.

Brandon, Diane. *Intuition for Beginners*. Woodbury, MN: Llewellyn, 2013.

Brennan, Barbara Ann. *Hands of Light: A Guide to Healing Through the Human Energy Field*. New York: Bantam, 1988.

Browne, Sylvia. *Contacting Your Spirit Guide*. Carlsbad, CA: Hay House, 2015.

Chapman, Gary. *The Five Love Languages: The Secret to Love That Lasts*. Chicago, IL: Northfield Publishing, 2015.

Choquette, Sonia. *Ask Your Guides*. Carlsbad, CA: Hay House, 2006.

Cirlot, J. E. *A Dictionary of Symbols*. Mineola, NY: Dover Publications, 2014.

Dale, Cyndi. *The Complete Book of Chakra Healing: Activate the Transformative Power of Your Energy Centers.* Woodbury, MN: Llewellyn, 2009.

Eden, Donna. *Energy Medicine: Balancing Your Body's Energies for Optimal Health, Joy, and Vitality.* New York: Jeremy P. Tarcher/Penguin, 2008.

Holmes, Ernest. *365 Science of Mind: A Year of Daily Wisdom from Ernest Holmes.* New York: J. P. Tarcher/Putnam, 2007.

Kornfield, Jack. *Meditation for Beginners.* Louisville, CO: Sounds True, 2008.

Lennox, Michael. *Llewellyn's Complete Dictionary of Dreams: Over 1,000 Dream Symbols and Their Universal Meanings.* Woodbury, MN: Llewellyn, 2015.

Mason, Henry M., and Brittani Petrofsky. *Crystal Grids: How to Combine & Focus Crystal Energies to Enhance Your Life.* Woodbury, MN: Llewellyn, 2016.

Montgomery, Sy. *The Soul of an Octopus: A Surprising Exploration into the Wonder of Consciousness.* New York: Atria Books, 2016.

Nhat Hanh, Thich. *The Miracle of Mindfulness: An Introduction to the Practice of Meditation.* Boston, MA: Beacon Press, 1999.

Orloff, Judith. *Emotional Freedom: Liberate Yourself from Negative Emotions and Transform Your Life.* New York: Harmony Books, 2010.

Pollack, Rachel. *The Complete Illustrated Guide to Tarot.* New York: Gramercy Books, 2004.

Ruiz, Don Miguel. *The Four Agreements: A Practical Guide to Personal Freedom.* San Rafael, CA: Amber-Allen Publishing, 1997.

Todeschi, Kevin J. *The Encyclopedia of Symbolism.* New York: Berkley Publishing Group, 2009.

Virtue, Doreen. *Healing with the Angels: How the Angels Can Assist You in Every Area of Your Life.* Carlsbad, CA: Hay House, 1999.

Waite, Arthur Edward, and Pamela Colman Smith (illustrator). *The Rider-Waite Tarot Deck.* Stamford, CT: U.S. Games Systems, 1971. Originally published in 1910.

Webster, Richard. *Spirit Guides & Angel Guardians: Contact Your Invisible Helpers.* St. Paul, MN: Llewellyn, 1998.

Index

To Write to the Author

If you wish to contact the author or would like more information about this book, please write to the author in care of Llewellyn Worldwide Ltd. and we will forward your request. Both the author and the publisher appreciate hearing from you and learning of your enjoyment of this book and how it has helped you. Llewellyn Worldwide Ltd. cannot guarantee that every letter written to the author can be answered, but all will be forwarded. Please write to:

Sherrie Dillard
⁒ Llewellyn Worldwide
2143 Wooddale Drive
Woodbury, MN 55125-2989

Please enclose a self-addressed stamped envelope for reply,
or $1.00 to cover costs. If outside the U.S.A., enclose
an international postal reply coupon.

Many of Llewellyn's authors have websites with additional information and resources. For more information, please visit our website at www.llewellyn.com.

Discover *your* Psychic Type

Developing and Using Your Natural Intuition

SHERRIE DILLARD

Discover Your Psychic Type
Developing and Using Your Natural Intuition
SHERRIE DILLARD

Intuition and spiritual growth are indelibly linked, according to professional psychic and therapist Sherrie Dillard. Offering a personalized approach to psychic development, this breakthrough guide introduces four different psychic types and explains how to develop the unique spiritual capabilities of each.

Are you a physical, mental, emotional, or spiritual intuitive? Take Dillard's insightful quiz to find out. Discover more about each type's intuitive nature, personality, potential physical weaknesses, and more. There are guided meditations for each kind of intuitive, as well as exercises to hone your psychic skills. Remarkable stories from the author's professional life illustrate the incredible power of intuition and its connection to the spirit world, inner wisdom, and your higher self.

From psychic protection to spirit guides to mystical states, Dillard offers guidance as you evolve toward the final destination of every psychic type: union with the divine.

978-0-7387-1278-9, 288 pp., 5 ¼ x 8   **$15.99**

To order, call 1-877-NEW-WRLD or visit llewellyn.com
Prices subject to change without notice

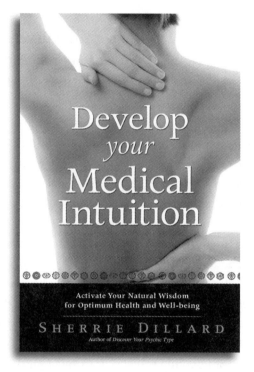

Develop *your* Medical Intuition

Activate Your Natural Wisdom
for Optimum Health and Well-being

SHERRIE DILLARD

Author of *Discover Your Psychic Type*

Develop Your Medical Intuition
Activate Your Natural Wisdom for Optimum Health and Well-Being
Sherrie Dillard

Use your intuition to tune in to your body and improve your health. Discover the four types of intuition (mental, emotional, physical, spiritual) and the five basic medical intuitive skills (clairvoyance, clairsentience, clairaudience, claircognizance, and vibrational sensitivity) and how to apply them for better health.

Medical intuition is the ability to intuit health energy information without reliance on an external source. This book explains step by step how to intuitively scan your own body and how to intuitively scan friends and loved ones to help them with their health concerns. *Develop Your Medical Intuition* includes essential tips for sharing health information with others, the importance of informing instead of diagnosing, understanding illness and disease as a metaphor, and the ethics of medical intuition.

978-0-7387-4201-4, 312 pp., 6 x 9   **$16.99**

Discover *your* Authentic Self

Be You, Be Free, Be Happy

SHERRIE DILLARD

Author of *Discover Your Psychic Type*

Discover Your Authentic Self
Be You, Be Free, Be Happy
Sherrie Dillard

Embrace your authentic self and let your soul's light shine forth with guidance from 150 lessons meant to inspire, motivate, and teach. This empowering book helps you shed what is false and come to know, accept, and express your true self.

With essays to uplift and engage you through personal stories, meditations, exercises, affirmations, and question prompts, *Discover Your Authentic Self* shows you how to live according to your passions and purpose. Explore a range of topics for self-discovery, including intuition, spirit animals, recognizing personal abilities as related to archetypes, living your purpose, spirit essence and energy (chakras and auras), and more. With this remarkable book, you'll unlock your truth and set yourself free.

978-0-7387-4640-1, 360 pp., 5 x 7   **$16.99**

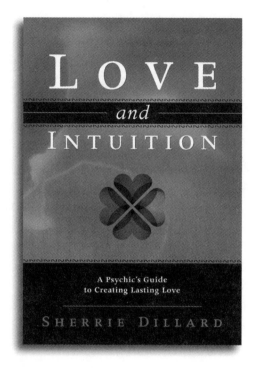

LOVE
and
INTUITION

A Psychic's Guide
to Creating Lasting Love

SHERRIE DILLARD

Love and Intuition
A Psychic's Guide to Creating Lasting Love
SHERRIE DILLARD

Love, by its very nature, is profoundly spiritual. Each of us can harness this transformative emotion by embracing our own natural intuition.

Building on the success of *Discover Your Psychic Type*, professional psychic Sherrie Dillard presents a life-changing paradigm based on the four love types. This unique book teaches you to develop your intuition to attract and sustain love, while enriching your relationship with your spouse or partner, friends, and yourself.

Once you find out your intuitive love type—emotional, spiritual, mental, or physical—you can then determine your spouse or partner's love type, and learn practical ways to strengthen your relationship and heighten intimacy.

978-0-7387-1555-1, 336 pp., 6 x 9   **$16.95**

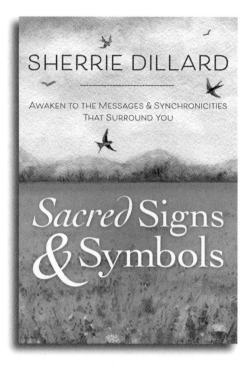

SHERRIE DILLARD

AWAKEN TO THE MESSAGES & SYNCHRONICITIES
THAT SURROUND YOU

Sacred Signs
& Symbols

Sacred Signs & Symbols
Awaken to the Messages & Synchronicities That Surround You
SHERRIE DILLARD

Everyone receives sacred signs, messages, and synchronicities, but we don't always notice or know how to interpret them. With *Sacred Signs & Symbols*, you'll develop the ability to recognize, understand, and be guided by the signs all around you.

Featuring a glossary of hundreds of signs and their meanings, this comprehensive guide helps you build a personal oracle system for invoking messages in your daily life. Explore a variety of methods for increasing your awareness, including exercises and divination techniques that you can personalize to your needs. You'll also discover ways to connect with loved ones in the spirit realm and expand your perception of the world. No matter where you are or what you're doing, a loving, wise, spiritual presence is offering you advice and comfort through divine messages.

978-0-7387-4968-6, 264 pp., 6 x 9   **$16.99**

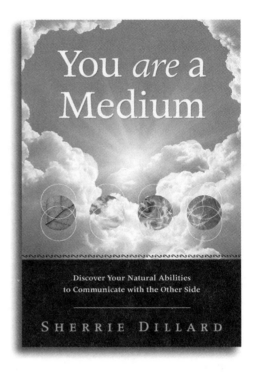

You *are* a Medium

Discover Your Natural Abilities
to Communicate with the Other Side

SHERRIE DILLARD

You Are a Medium
Discover Your Natural Abilities to Communicate with the Other Side
SHERRIE DILLARD

Discovering your natural abilities to communicate with the other side is as simple as taking a unique quiz to determine your medium type. Once you know how your subtle abilities work, you can develop your skills with the simple exercises and techniques presented in *You Are a Medium*.

Everyone has the innate ability to communicate with those who have passed on. As you become more confident with your medium abilities, be prepared to make a breathtaking discovery: Not only do our deceased loved ones help us from the other side—we also help them! Sharing inspiring case studies from her work with clients and students, Sherrie Dillard shows that when we succeed in learning our soul lessons, we become beacons of light to those in the beyond.

978-0-7387-3792-8, 288 pp., 6 x 9   **$16.99**

· LLEWELLYN'S ·

· COMPLETE BOOK OF ·
MINDFUL LIVING

AWARENESS AND MEDITATION PRACTICES
FOR LIVING IN THE PRESENT MOMENT

Including Michael Bernard Beckwith, Jack Canfield,
Cyndi Dale, Guy Finley, Rolf Gates, and Thomas Moore

ROBERT BUTERA, PhD and ERIN BYRON, MA

Llewellyn's Complete Book of Mindful Living
Awareness & Meditation Practices
for Living in the Present Moment
Robert Butera, PhD, and Erin Byron, MA

Enhance your awareness, achieve higher focus and happiness, and improve all levels of your health with the supportive practices in this guide to mindful living. Featuring over twenty-five leading meditation and mindfulness experts, *Llewellyn's Complete Book of Mindful Living* shows you how to boost your well-being and overcome obstacles.

With an impressive array of topics by visionary teachers and authors, this comprehensive book provides inspiration, discussion, and specific techniques based on the transformative applications of mindfulness: basic understanding and practices, better health, loving your body, reaching your potential, and connecting to subtle energy and spirit. Using meditation, breathwork, and other powerful exercises, you'll bring the many benefits of mindfulness into your everyday life.

978-0-7387-4677-7, 384 pp., 8 x 10   **$27.99**

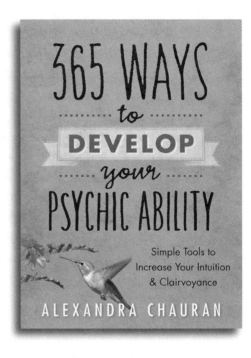

365 Ways to Develop Your Psychic Ability
Simple Tools to Increase Your Intuition & Clairvoyance
ALEXANDRA CHAURAN

Unlock and strengthen your innate psychic potential with 365 fast, effective ways to develop your abilities. Beginning with simple observation skills and moving forward to trance and divination techniques, this book's step-by-step practices guide you to psychic mastery.

Formatted to fit your personal pace and learning style, *365 Ways to Develop Your Psychic Ability* shows you how to build your psychic muscles day by day. Learn meditation, trance techniques, divination, and how to perform readings. Discover extensive exercises on scrying, clairvoyance, intuition, empathy, and more. Using quick and accessible methods that build upon one another, this comprehensive book helps you become a proficient psychic.

978-0-7387-3930-4, 360 pp., 5 x 7   **$16.99**

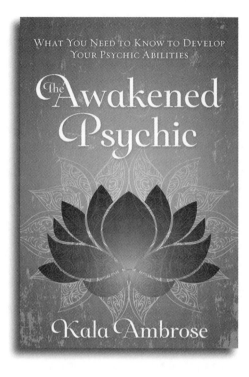

WHAT YOU NEED TO KNOW TO DEVELOP
YOUR PSYCHIC ABILITIES

The Awakened
Psychic

Kala Ambrose

The Awakened Psychic
What You Need to Know to Develop Your Psychic Abilities
Kala Ambrose

The Awakened Psychic is a guide to developing your inner psychic and tuning in to your intuitive wisdom. With hands-on exercises and stories from the author's practice, this book is all about lifting the veil between the worlds, seeing into the future, and connecting with spirits and loved ones on the other side. Join Kala Ambrose as she explores ideas and techniques for enhancing your psychic abilities and making the most of your intuitive talents, including:

- How to build a powerful energy field for psychic self-defense
- The difference between being psychic and being a medium
- Techniques to heighten your psychic abilities
- How ghosts and spirits are different
- How to awaken your powerful inner intuitive oracle
- The difference between an intuitive hunch and being psychic
- Techniques to connect with spirit guides and your higher self

Everyone has intuitive ability at some level, and those abilities can be helpful tools in making decisions, following your dreams, enhancing your relationships, and building a business or career that you enjoy. In this book, you'll discover the different kinds of psychic abilities and how they work together so that you can manifest your destiny and live a spiritually fulfilled life.

978-0-7387-4901-3, 216 pp., 5 ¼ x 8   **$15.99**

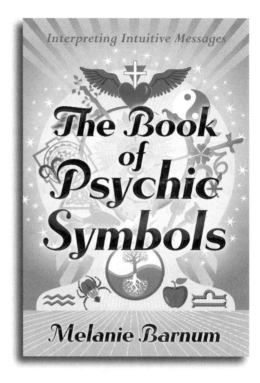

Interpreting Intuitive Messages

The Book of Psychic Symbols

Melanie Barnum

The Book of Psychic Symbols
Interpreting Intuitive Messages
Melanie Barnum

A strong feeling, a remarkable coincidence, a strange dream…What may seem ordinary could actually be an important message—a helpful hint or a warning from a deceased loved one or spirit guide. Open yourself to a wealth of guidance and opportunities by learning how to recognize and interpret the signs and synchronicities all around us.

The Book of Psychic Symbols can help you decode dreams, intuitive flashes, and all psychic impressions. Intuitive counselor Melanie Barnum explains what psychic symbols are, how we receive them, and where they come from. She also shares amazing stories from her life that clarify how the wondrous intuitive process works. In addition to a comprehensive dictionary of 500 symbols, there are many practical exercises for exploring symbols in your life, fortifying your natural intuition, and using psychic symbols to manifest your desires.

978-0-7387-2303-7, 288 pp., 6 x 9   **$16.99**

To order, call 1-877-NEW-WRLD or visit llewellyn.com
Prices subject to change without notice

LLEWELLYN'S
Little Book of
PSYCHIC
DEVELOPMENT

MELANIE BARNUM

Llewellyn's Little Book of Psychic Development
Melanie Barnum

Your psychic gifts are just waiting to be explored, and this pocket-size guide makes it easy! Discover how to tune in to your intuition, deepen your spirituality, and improve your relationships with simple techniques for developing your psychic senses.

Fill your life with abundance and positivity by engaging in your psychic birthright. This little book is packed with ways to help you, from hands-on exercises and journaling prompts to true stories from Melanie Barnum's clients and personal experiences. If you want to feel more connected to your spirit, make changes in your career, or receive help when making decisions in every area of your life, this is the right book for you!

978-0-7387-5186-3, 192 pp., 4⅝ x 6¼   **$12.99**

A PERSONAL EMPOWERMENT BOOK

CLAIRVOYANCE
FOR
PSYCHIC
EMPOWERMENT

THE ART & SCIENCE OF "CLEAR SEEING"
PAST THE ILLUSIONS OF SPACE & TIME
& SELF-DECEPTION

Includes

DEVELOPING PSYCHIC CLARITY & TRUE VISION

The Tattva Connection Meditation & Visualization Program
Microcosm to Macrocosm & Macrocosm to Microcosm

Based on the Ancient Tantra Tradition
An Eastern Gift to Western Psychic & Paranormal Science

25 Developmental Practices for Accurate Clairvoyance
Divination · Dream Interpretation · Invocation · Magick

CARL LLEWELLYN WESCHCKE
JOE H. SLATE, Ph.D.

Clairvoyance for Psychic Empowerment
The Art & Science of "Clear Seeing" Past the Illusions of Space & Time & Self-Deception
Carl Llewellyn Weschcke and
Joe H. Slate, PhD

This magnificently comprehensive resource combines little-known spiritual techniques of the East with Western scientific practices and research, providing readers with the best methods to develop clairvoyant abilities. More than just an interesting phenomenon, the insightful writing and clarifying illustrations reveal how the skills the book teaches can be applied to every level of your spiritual and daily life. Its breadth makes this an instant classic. All other books on this subject will compare themselves to this, but only the wide-ranging knowledge of Weschcke combined with the scientific rigor of Slate could produce this book.

978-0-7387-3347-0, 864 pp., 7 x 10   **$29.99**

Contributors

Rox Ann Sparks, RN MSN, MICN, LNC, ENPC
Contributing Writer

Alexander Schubert, BFA Fine Art
Product Developer

Mandy Tallmadge, BS Communication
Product Developer

Allen Croswhite
Illustrator

Nicole Hicks, BA Film & Video
Media Developer

Printed in September 2012.

IMPORTANT NOTICE TO THE READER

Assessment Technologies Institute®, LLC is the publisher of this publication. The publisher reserves the right to modify, change, or update the content of this publication at any time. The content of this publication, such as text, graphics, images, information obtained from the publisher's licensors, and other material contained in this publication are for informational purposes only. This publication is not providing medical advice and is not intended to be a substitute for professional medical advice, diagnosis, or treatment. Always seek the advice of your provider or other qualified health provider for any questions you may have regarding a medical condition. Never disregard professional medical advice or delay in seeking it because of something you have read in this publication. If you think you may have a medical emergency, go to your local emergency department or call 911 immediately.

Table of Contents

Safety

Professional Responsibilities

Infection Control

Phlebotomy

EKG Monitoring

INTRODUCTION

Learning Objectives

After reading this study guide, the CPCT student will be able to demonstrate an understanding of:

- *Patient care*

- *Safety*

- *Professional responsibilities*

- *Infection control*

- *Phlebotomy*

- *EKG*

Introduction

Welcome to the National Health Career Association's (NHA) Certified Patient Care Technician (CPCT) study guide. This study guide will help you prepare for the CPCT examination.

NHA will issue your CPCT certification after you pass the national certification exam. The NHA's CPCT certification provides a foundation for future training, and it can lead to additional employment opportunities in the health care field.

CPCTs are health care professionals who work under the supervision of a nurse or a physician. As a CPCT, you will not give orders or make clinical decisions without the assistance of a nurse or physician. As a CPCT you will:

- Respond to patient calls and requests.

- Assist patients with personal hygiene tasks.

- Tidy patients' rooms.

- Serve meals and feed patients.

- Monitor vital signs.

- Draw laboratory specimens.

- Perform EKGs and other clinical tasks.

- Set up equipment.

- Assist the physician or nurse with therapies.

As a CPCT, you are responsible for a number of duties, from maintaining your patients' personal hygiene, to providing emotional support for your patients and their families – as well as manually lifting and transferring your patients. You also must assist with the admission and discharge of patients, as well as the necessary room equipment and therapy techniques, such as tube feeding, catheters, peripheral IVs, and ostomy care.

Many CPCTs use their knowledge and training as a stepping stone toward becoming an LVN, LPN, or RN. Annual salaries for CPCTs range from $18,000 to $35,000.

The CPCT certification establishes a standard of care among CPCTs. In order to sit for the CPCT examination, you must have a high school diploma or a GED and complete a training program. However, you may substitute one year of CPCT experience in lieu of attending a formal training program. With this option, you must provide documentation that you worked as a CPCT for at least one year. If you meet these criteria, you may register for the examination online at www.nhanow.com.

The Patient Care Tech and the Patient Care Assistant proctored certification exam consists of 110 multiple-choice questions, with 100 scored items. If your school is a registered NHA test site, you may be able to take your exam there via computer or in a paper-pencil format. You also have the option to take your exam via computer at a PSI testing center. You have 110 minutes to complete the exam and you must achieve a scaled score of 390 out of 500 to pass. If you take the exam electronically, you get your score immediately after completing the exam. If you take the exam with paper and pencil, you get your results online in two business days. NHA mails hard copies of all score reports within 7 to 10 business days.

This study guide focuses on the concepts tested in the certification exam. It is not intended to replace the instruction, training, or experience needed to complete the exam.

Chapter 1: Patient Care

Chapter 1 of this study guide explains the importance of patient care skills and represents the majority of the course content. It begins with caring for your patient's hygienic needs; setting up the equipment for examinations; taking vital signs and monitoring for changes; documenting all the care you give your patient; communicating changes in your patient with the physician or nurse; and performing procedures on your patient, such as removing an IV catheter before discharge.

Chapter 2: Safety

Chapter 2 explains how to prevent injuries to patients and other health care workers. This chapter teaches you how to recognize and respond to abuse, including neglect, sexual harassment, substance abuse, and domestic violence. It also explores techniques for safely transferring patients, maintaining a safe environment for patients, preventing workplace injuries, and responding to emergencies. Lastly, the focus turns to the safety of your coworkers in the topics related to workplace injuries, fires, hostage situations, and biological hazards.

Chapter 3: Professional Responsibilities

In Chapter 3, you will learn your professional responsibilities as a CPCT. You will read about Basic Cardiac Life Support (BCLS) certification and the Health Insurance Portability and Accountability Act (HIPAA). Other topics include the use of proper medical terminology, the chain of command, and the use of therapeutic communication.

Chapter 4: Infection Control

Chapter 4 covers infection control. This includes universal, standard, and transmission-based precautions. This chapter also discusses the methods for disposing of biohazardous materials, performing aseptic technique, and performing sterile technique.

Chapter 5: Phlebotomy

Chapter 5 teaches you how to perform basic venipuncture and details the proper technique, including patient identification, preparation, troubleshooting, and potential complications. In addition, the chapter describes finger and heel stick blood collection, special collections, and the procedure for processing specimens.

Chapter 6: EKG Monitoring

Chapter 6 presents the information necessary to systematically approach an EKG and interpret arrhythmias encountered in the clinical setting. You also will learn how to correctly record an EKG.

Case Studies

Following these 6 chapters, there are 3 scenarios that test your cumulative knowledge in all areas of the study guide. Each scenario represents a real-life situation and requires critical thinking skills to effectively complete the discussion questions that follow.

NHA Certified Patient Care Technician/Assistant (CPCT/A) Detailed Test Plan
100 scored items, 10 pretest items

		# items
1. Patient Care		**48**
A. General Patient Care		**38**
1. Provide basic patient care under the direction of nursing staff (e.g., bathing, bedmaking, catheter care, transfer, assisting with ADLs).		
2. Provide emotional support for patients and their families while performing patient care.		
3. Support the coping mechanisms of patients and their families who are dealing with grief, death, and dying.		
4. Set up equipment to be used by the patient (e.g., oxygen, alternating pressure mattresses).		
5. Provide patient care for a patient with a feeding tube (e.g., aspiration precautions, observe tubing for kinks or problems).		
6. Perform care related to the special needs patient (e.g., physically, sensory, cognitively or mentally impaired).		
7. Report any new changes in the patient's condition (e.g., level of consciousness, shortness of breath).		
8. Monitor and record functions related to digestion (e.g., bowel movements, percentage of meal eaten).		
9. Monitor, record, and accurately measure intake/output (e.g., urine, emesis, wound drainage).		
10. Assist in admission, discharge, and/or transfer of patient to another unit or facility.		
11. Follow the established restorative plan of care ordered for the patient.		
12. Perform passive Range of Motion (ROM) for the patient.		
13. Assist with restorative rehabilitation activities (e.g., bowel and bladder retraining).		
14. Use adaptive devices for activities of daily living (e.g., feeding and dressing devices).		
15. Keep patient area clean.		

NHA Certified Patient Care Technician/Assistant (CPCT/A) Detailed Test Plan
100 scored items, 10 pretest items

	# items
16. Remove peripheral IVs.	
17. Perform dressing changes.	
a) Sterile	
b) Aseptic	
18. Transfer a patient using a mechanical lift.	
19. Manually lift and transfer a patient.	
20. Apply immobility splints to patients.	
21. Provide one-on-one care for patients who are at risk for suicide.	
22. Provide skin care (e.g., repositioning, creams, moisture barrier).	
23. Identify and report changes in skin integrity.	
24. Utilize devices to prevent skin breakdown (e.g., air mattresses, draw sheets).	
25. Apply sequential compression boots.	
26. Apply anti-embolitic stockings (e.g., TED hose).	
27. Assist the patient with coughing, deep-breathing exercises.	
28. Perform first aid, CPR, and rapid response procedures.	
29. Report critical values to the appropriate nurse in charge of the patient.	
30. Assist the patient with incentive spirometry.	
31. Check dressings for increased saturation and changes.	
32. Follow the 5 Rights of Delegation.	
33. Prioritize patient care based on patient needs.	
34. Recognize visual abnormalities in patient specimens (e.g., stool, sputum, urine, emesis).	

NHA Certified Patient Care Technician/Assistant (CPCT/A)
Detailed Test Plan
100 scored items, 10 pretest items

	# items
35. Monitor vital signs and patient status during blood transfusions.	
36. Assist patient with taking self-administered prescribed medications.	
37. Apply oxygen therapy (e.g., nasal cannula, mask).	
38. Assist with patient-administered nebulizer treatments.	
39. Weigh a patient (e.g., standing, wheelchair, or bed scales).	
40. Assist patients with orthotic or prosthetic devices (e.g., hearing aids, dentures, artificial eyes, or extremities).	
41. Perform home health aide services.	
42. Perform hospice/palliative aide care services.	
43. Perform ostomy care (excluding irrigation).	
44. Assist with ostomy care.	
45. Perform postmortem care.	
46. Observe for and report edema.	
47. Observe and report patient pain using a pain scale.	
48. Monitor and record vital signs.	
a) Blood pressure (manually)	
b) Blood pressure (electronically)	
c) Pulse (manually)	
d) Pulse (electronically)	
e) Apical pulse	
f) Apical-radial deficit	
g) Respirations (manually)	

NHA Certified Patient Care Technician/Assistant (CPCT/A)
Detailed Test Plan
100 scored items, 10 pretest items

	# items
h) Respirations (electronically)	
i) Pulse oximetry	
B. Patient Care and Preparation Related to Phlebotomy and EKG	**10**
1. Conduct appropriate introduction to the patient.	
2. Explain the phlebotomy procedure to be performed to the patient.	
3. Review the requisition for testing requirements and patient identity.	
4. Receive implied or informed consent from the patient.	
5. Determine venipuncture site accessibility based on patient age and condition.	
6. Verify patient compliance with testing requirements (e.g., fasting, medication, basal state).	
7. Prepare the patient.	
a) EKG monitoring (e.g., patient history, cardiac medications, patient positioning).	
b) Holter monitoring	
c) Stress testing	
d) Telemetry monitoring	
8. Apply electrodes on patients.	
a) EKG monitoring	
b) Holter monitoring	
c) Stress testing	
d) Telemetry monitoring	
e) Pediatric patients	
f) Patients with special considerations (e.g., right-sided heart, posterior chest, amputations)	

NHA Certified Patient Care Technician/Assistant (CPCT/A)
Detailed Test Plan
100 scored items, 10 pretest items

	# items
9. Respond to signs and symptoms of cardiopulmonary compromise.	
10. Monitor patient condition during stress testing.	
11. Respond to complications during stress testing.	
12. Verify patient understanding of Holter monitor procedures.	
2. Safety	**10**
A. **Identify and report**	
1. Abuse or neglect of patients	
2. Sexual harassment involving patients or staff	
3. Substance abuse involving patients or staff	
4. Domestic violence/intimate partner abuse involving patients or staff	
B. **Transport patients using proper body mechanics.**	
C. **Transfer patients using proper body mechanics.**	
D. **Monitor patients' environmental safety (e.g., fall precautions, faulty equipment).**	
E. **Prevent workplace injuries by following OSHA guidelines.**	
F. **Recognize and respond to emergency situations (e.g., fire, hostage, biological hazard).**	
G. **Follow the proper procedures for identifying patients.**	
H. **Follow the Joint Commission's (TJC) patient safety guidelines.**	
I. **Practice safety procedures when using medical supplies and equipment (e.g., lock the hospital bed, lock wheelchairs, raise stretcher side rails, apply safety belts and restraints).**	
J. **Report and document work-related accidents.**	

NHA Certified Patient Care Technician/Assistant (CPCT/A) Detailed Test Plan
100 scored items, 10 pretest items

		# items
3.	**Professional Responsibilities**	**5**
A.	Obtain and maintain Basic Cardiac Life Support (BCLS) certification for health care providers.	
B.	Adhere to HIPAA regulations regarding Protected Health Information (PHI).	
C.	Communicate with other health care professionals using appropriate medical terminology.	
D.	Observe the chain of command in a healthcare setting.	
E.	Use therapeutic communication when talking to patients (e.g., interpersonal skills).	
F.	Adhere to regulations regarding operational standards (e.g., TJC, CLSI).	
4.	**Infection Control**	**4**
A.	Use universal, standard, and transmission-based precautions.	
B.	Dispose of biohazardous materials properly, as dictated by OSHA (e.g., sharps containers, red bags).	
C.	Follow exposure control plans in the event of occupational exposure.	
D.	Wear personal protective equipment while following standard precautions (e.g., gloves, gowns, masks, shoe covers).	
E.	Perform aseptic technique.	
F.	Perform sterile technique.	
5.	**Phlebotomy**	**23**
A.	Primary Collections	15
1.	Demonstrate proper insertion and removal techniques for venipuncture.	
2.	Perform capillary collection method based on patient age and condition.	

NHA Certified Patient Care Technician/Assistant (CPCT/A)
Detailed Test Plan
100 scored items, 10 pretest items

		# items
3.	Ensure patient safety throughout the collection process.	
4.	Perform venipuncture steps in correct order (e.g., evacuated tube system, syringe, winged collection set).	
5.	Perform capillary (dermal) puncture steps in correct order.	
6.	Recognize common complications from primary collection (e.g., lack of blood flow, hematoma, petechiae, nerve injury).	
7.	Identify problematic patient signs and symptoms throughout collection (e.g., syncope, diaphoresis, nausea, seizure).	
8.	Follow order of draw.	
	a) Venipuncture	
	b) Capillary collection	
9.	Ensure that tube additives are appropriate for testing requirements.	
10.	Assemble equipment needed for primary blood collections.	
11.	Invert evacuated tubes with additives after collection.	
12.	Verify quality of equipment (e.g., sterility, expiration date, manufacturer's defects).	
B.	**Special Collections**	**3**
1.	Prepare peripheral blood smears.	
2.	Perform blood culture collections.	
3.	Assist other healthcare professionals with blood culture collections.	
4.	Collect blood samples for inborn errors of metabolism (e.g., PKU, galactosemia).	
5.	Perform phlebotomy for blood donations.	
6.	Calculate volume requirements to avoid causing iatrogenic anemia.	

NHA Certified Patient Care Technician/Assistant (CPCT/A)
Detailed Test Plan
100 scored items, 10 pretest items

		# items
C.	**Processing**	**5**
	1. Label all specimens.	
	2. Perform quality control for CLIA-waived procedures.	
	3. Transport specimens based on handling requirements (e.g., temperature, light, time).	
	4. Explain non-blood specimen collection procedures to patients (e.g., stool, urine, semen, sputum).	
	5. Handle patient-collected, non-blood specimen.	
	6. Avoid pre-analytical errors when collecting blood specimens (e.g., QNS, hemolysis).	
	7. Adhere to chain of custody guidelines when required (e.g., forensic studies, blood alcohol, drug screen).	
	8. Prepare samples for transportation to a reference (outside) laboratory.	
	9. Coordinate communication between non-laboratory personnel for processing and collection.	
	10. Use technology to input and retrieve specimen data.	
	11. Report critical values to point of care testing.	
	12. Distribute laboratory results to ordering providers.	
6.	**EKG Monitoring**	**10**
	A. Calculate patient heart rate from the EKG tracing (e.g., 6-second method, R to R, sequencing).	
	B. Identify artifacts from the tracing (e.g., wandering baseline, somatic, electrical).	
	C. Resolve artifacts from the tracing (e.g., wandering baseline, somatic, electrical).	

NHA Certified Patient Care Technician/Assistant (CPCT/A)
Detailed Test Plan
100 scored items, 10 pretest items

		# items
D.	Record leads on a patient.	
	1. 3- lead	
	2. 5-lead	
	3. 12-lead	
E.	Verify the leads recorded on an EKG.	
F.	Upload a completed EKG to a patient's electronic medical record.	
G.	Mount a completed EKG for a patient's chart.	
H.	Measure a patient's heart rhythm from the EKG tracing.	
I.	Inspect the waveforms of a cardiac cycle for symmetry, direction, and amplitude (e.g., P waves, QRS complexes, ST segments, T waves).	
J.	Measure a patient's heart conduction from the EKG tracing (e.g., PR-interval (PRI), QRS duration, QT-interval).	
K.	Identify the major classifications of arrhythmias from the EKG tracing (e.g., sinus, atrial, ventricular, junctional).	
L.	Identify the major variances to waveforms related to ischemia, injury, or infarction.	
M.	Respond to potentially life-threatening arrhythmias.	
N.	Verify EKG machine paper speed (e.g., 25mm, 50mm).	
O.	Verify EKG machine sensitivity (e.g., h, 1, 2).	
P.	Maintain EKG equipment and the work environment.	
Q.	Recognize pacemaker spikes on an EKG tracing.	

Learning Objectives

After reading this chapter, the CPCT student will be able to:

- *Provide basic patient care under directions of the nursing staff.*
- *Provide emotional support for patients.*
- *Support coping mechanisms for those dealing with grief, death, and dying.*
- *Set up equipment.*
- *Provide patient care for a patient with a feeding tube.*
- *Monitor and record functions related to digestion.*
- *Monitor, record, and accurately measure intake/output.*
- *Assist in admission, discharge, and/or transfer of patient to another unit or facility.*
- *Follow the established restorative plan of care ordered for the patient.*
- *Perform passive Range of Motion (ROM) for the patient.*
- *Assist with restorative rehabilitation activities.*
- *Keep patient area clean.*
- *Remove peripheral IVs.*
- *Perform dressing changes.*
- *Transfer a patient using a mechanical lift.*
- *Manually lift and transfer a patient.*
- *Apply immobility splints to patients.*
- *Provide one-on-one care for patients who are at risk for suicide.*
- *Provide skin care.*
- *Apply sequential compression boots.*
- *Apply anti-embolitic stockings.*
- *Perform first aid, CPR, and rapid response procedures.*
- *Assist the patient with incentive spirometry.*
- *Check dressings for increased saturation and changes.*
- *Follow the Five Rights of Delegation.*
- *Prioritize patient care based on patient needs.*

- *Monitor vital signs and patient status during blood transfusions.*

- *Assist patient with taking self-administered prescribed medications.*

- *Apply oxygen therapy.*

- *Assist with patient-administered nebulizer treatments.*

- *Weigh a patient.*

- *Perform home health aide services.*

- *Perform hospice/palliative aide care services.*

- *Observe for and report edema.*

- *Observe and report patient pain using a pain scale.*

- *Monitor and record vital signs.*

- *Obtain the patient's social, medical, surgical, and medication history.*

- *Educate patients about the EKG, Holter monitoring, stress testing, and telemetry.*

- *Properly apply EKG electrodes to acquire a 3-, 5-, and 12-lead EKG and Holter monitor.*

- *Discuss modifications to EKG lead placement in pediatric patients, right-sided EKG, and patients who have limb amputations.*

- *Discuss the signs and symptoms of cardiopulmonary compromise.*

- *Discuss the Health Insurance Portability and Accountability Act (HIPAA) and protected health information (PHI).*

- *Monitor a patient's condition during stress testing.*

- *Respond to complications during stress testing.*

- *List expected reference range vital-sign parameters for different age groups.*

Introduction

In the following chapter, we will explore basic concepts related to patient care. You will learn about the use of specific equipment, including feeding tubes, peripheral IVs, mechanical lifts, and sequential compression boots. The chapter concludes with a five-question self-assessment drill.

GENERAL PATIENT CARE

Provide Basic Patient Care Under the Direction of Nursing Staff

The certified patient care technician (CPCT) is responsible for performing tasks assigned by the nursing staff. Tasks can include bathing patients, bed making, room preparation and cleaning, and assisting patients with activities of daily living (ADLs). The CPCT is also responsible for obtaining vital signs, transferring a patient from a bed to a wheelchair or other assistive device, and reporting changes in the patient's condition to the nursing staff.

Assisting with ADLs

Patients admitted to the hospital often require assistance when performing tasks they would normally do on their own—such as eating, getting dressed, bathing, going to the bathroom, and ambulating. It is important for the CPCT to enable patients to do as much of their own care as possible and to offer assistance when needed. The CPCT must ensure patient safety at all times and work with the patient and family to determine the appropriate level of assistance needed to complete each ADL. For example, patients sometimes require no assistance brushing their teeth, but need assistance ambulating to and from the bathroom.

Bathing

Bathing is essential for maintaining personal hygiene and ensuring patient comfort. The CPCT is responsible for gathering the supplies necessary for bathing and for delivering the supplies to the patient's room. Supplies needed for bathing include a water basin, bath blanket, bath towels, washcloths, soap, gown, clean bed linen, bedpan or urinal, and a laundry bag.

While the patient is bathing, it is important for the CPCT to assess the condition of the patient's skin and take note of any rashes, cuts, open sores, and pressure ulcers. The CPCT should also note any range-of-motion difficulty reported by the patient. The CPCT should also evaluate the patient's ability to tolerate the activity. Any changes in skin condition, range of motion, and activity tolerance should be reported to the nursing staff immediately.

Remember to empower the patient by allowing him or her to complete as much of the bathing and dressing as possible. Offer assistance with any tasks he or she cannot perform. This promotes patient independence and ensures a more enjoyable hospital stay.

Bathing Procedure

When bathing patients, the CPCT must consider the following:

- Water temperature – The bath water should not exceed 105°F (41°C). Water that is too hot or cold can be uncomfortable for the patient and can cause injury. Always ask the patient to feel the water and to determine if the temperature is appropriate.

- Privacy – The CPCT must ensure patient privacy at all times. Close the door to the patient's room when the patient is bathing. If the patient is sharing a room with another person, ensure that curtains are closed and that no one can see into the patient care area. Use a bath blanket to keep the patient covered.

- Body mechanics – Adjust the bed's height to a comfortable working position. This can prevent back strains.

- Safety devices – Always keep the bed rails up to prevent falls. Ensure bed sheets are stretched tightly over the mattress and eliminate bunching of linens under the patient. Use moisture barriers where appropriate and follow the facility's guidelines for applying lotion or powder after bathing.

- Patient position – Patients should be repositioned after bathing and again every 2 hours (unless specified by a provider). Repositioning has been shown to reduce the risk for developing skin breakdown and pressure sores. If the patient has the ability to reposition himself, encourage him to change positions periodically.

The CPCT should take note of the patient's overall ability to bathe. The CPCT should look for the following signs: shortness of breath, increased pain, reduced range of motion, inability to stand, and the inability to follow instructions. The CPCT should report these to the nursing staff immediately. The CPCT should also report any changes in the patient's skin condition.

Bed Making

The CPCT should gather all of the necessary equipment for bed making prior to entering the patient's room, in order to care for the patient more efficiently. Items include a fitted sheet, a flat sheet, pillowcases, draw sheet, absorbent pad, blankets, and a linen bag.

The patient's bed should be raised to a comfortable working height for the CPCT. Follow the facility's policies for making the bed, replacing linens, and disposing of soiled items. As previously mentioned, it is important to ensure that linens are tightly pulled across the mattress. Bunched materials can create pressure points and promote skin breakdown and ulcer formation. Follow manufacturer recommendations when changing linens on specialty mattresses.

The CPCT will often have to replace linens while the patient is in the bed. Prior to changing the linens, be sure to complete any tasks that could soil the sheets. For example, bathe the patient and then change the sheets. The easiest method for changing linens while the patient remains in the bed is to:

1. Roll the patient to one side of the bed

2. Change the sheets on the unoccupied side

3. Roll the patient to the fresh side

4. Complete the linen change

Always ensure the bed rails are up and locked to prevent falls and injury to the patient.

Provide Emotional Support for Patients and Their Families

The CPCT must be aware and considerate of the emotional needs of the patient and patient's family. The CPCT must be empathetic at all times. He or she should encourage the patient to communicate feelings of fear and anxiety. Providing emotional support always includes being a good listener. Often, patients and their families simply need to express feelings of anger, frustration, fear, or anxiety.

Support the Coping Mechanisms of Patients and Their Families

Patients and their families deal with dying and death differently. The CPCT provides support for their coping mechanisms. The CPCT must never judge a patient or family member for the coping mechanisms demonstrated. Patients can deny their illnesses, turn to faith and religion for comfort, or express grief in another way. The CPCT must be a good listener and allow patients and their families to openly express their feelings. Everyone involved in health care must empathize with patients, encourage expression of feelings, and provide comfort.

Set Up Equipment to be Used by the Patient

Alternating pressure mattresses are special beds designed to circulate air or water under patients and reduce the risk of developing pressure ulcers. The CPCT should read the manufacturer's recommendations for proper set-up, use, and maintenance.

Provide Patient Care for a Patient with a Feeding Tube

Patients that have difficulty swallowing due to a medical condition can require the use of a feeding tube to facilitate passage of food into the stomach. The CPCT will encounter several types of feeding tubes, including nasogastric and gastric tubes. Nasogastric tubes are inserted through the nose into the patient's stomach. Gastric tubes are surgically inserted through the abdominal wall. Both are used to place food into the stomach without involving the mouth and throat. The CPCT is responsible for ensuring proper patient positioning during and after meals to minimize the risk for aspiration. The CPCT should elevate the patient's head to at least a 45° angle at all times to prevent aspiration. The CPCT must also monitor the tubing for kinks and report any problems with the feeding equipment to the nurse.

Monitor and Record Functions Related to Digestion

The CPCT should monitor and document the amount, color, and consistency of the patient's stool. Terms such as loose, soft, formed, and hard are used to describe the consistency of the stool. Patients should have at least one bowel movement every 3 days. The CPCT is responsible for notifying the nursing staff if the patient has not had a bowel movement over a 3-day period. The CPCT should also inform the nurse of any abnormal findings in the stool such as green, red or dark tarry-looking stool, and diarrhea.

Monitor, Record, and Accurately Measure Intake/Output

The CPCT is responsible for monitoring, recording, and measuring fluid intake and output. The CPCT must record everything the patient eats and drinks, as well as the administration of any intravenous fluids. The CPCT must also record the patient's total daily urine, fecal, and vomit volume (if any).

Assist In Admission, Discharge, and/or Transfer of Patient to Another Unit or Facility

The CPCT must prepare the patient's room prior to the patient's admission to the medical facility. The CPCT should ensure that the room is clean, stocked according to facility policy, and free of any tripping hazards. Nurses may ask the CPCT to obtain baseline vital signs, to weigh the patient, and to assist with documentation.

Some patients will need to be transferred to another medical or surgical unit within the hospital (or to an entirely different hospital) for specialized treatment or rehabilitation.

The CPCT will assist the nursing staff with such transfers. This includes obtaining vital signs, gathering patient belongings, and assisting transport crews.

When a patient is discharged, the CPCT will need to obtain vital signs, remove any peripheral intravenous devices, gather the patient's belongings, remove ECG stickers from the patient's skin, and assist the nursing staff with other functions. The CPCT can be required to assist the patient to a wheelchair or other assistive device. The CPCT can also be required to bring the patient to the facility's entrance for pick up.

Follow the Established Restorative Plan of Care Ordered for the Patient

The CPCT is integral to restorative care. Restorative care is care given to patients to help them become as independent as possible, following a medical or surgical event. It is critical for the CPCT to allow patients to do as many ADLs as possible, without interference. For example, if a patient is trying to get dressed or organize something, but is taking a long time to do so, the CPCT should not interrupt. Instead, the CPCT should encourage the patient and only provide assistance if absolutely necessary.

Perform Passive Range of Motion (ROM) for the Patient

Patients confined to a bed for long periods of time are at risk for developing contractures. Contractures are the abnormal shortening of the muscle or tendon, causing flexion of joints and the inability to move the affected extremity. Passive movement of the joints through their full ROM has been show to prevent contractures. The CPCT is responsible for performing ROM exercises with patients. The passive part of this exercise means moving the joint through its full ROM without assistance from the patient. Active ROM means the patient performs the motions independently. ROM exercises should be performed at least twice daily, moving each joint five times before returning it to its neutral position. Never push a joint further than it can move.

Assist with Restorative Rehabilitation Activities

Following certain medical conditions or surgical procedures, patients can lose control of their bladders or bowels. Physicians can order exercises to help patients regain control of their bodily functions. The CPCT is responsible for providing reminders on when to perform these exercises. Nurses are responsible for educating the patients on how to perform each exercise.

Keep Patient Area Clean

The patient's room should be clean and organized at all times. It is especially important to keep walkways free of clutter, trash, and other trip hazards. The CPCT should wipe down all horizontal surfaces with disinfectant wipes, especially before the patient eats and after the patient bathes. The CPCT should also ensure that bedside tables are within the patient's reach.

Remove Peripheral IVs

The CPCT is responsible for removing intravenous catheters prior to patient discharge. Removing an intravenous catheter requires a gauze pad, a piece of tape, and a pair of gloves. Ensure that the nurse has turned off the intravenous fluid prior to removing the catheter. While holding the catheter, remove any tape securing the catheter to the patient's skin. Next, place the gauze over the puncture site and remove the catheter by pulling straight back on the device, making sure the catheter is still intact. Tape the gauze in place and hold pressure over the taped gauze for several minutes. If the area around the catheter insertion site appears discolored, swollen or otherwise infected, notify the nurse immediately.

Perform Dressing Changes

Sterile dressing

Sterile dressings are applied and removed by a nurse or physician. Typically, sterile dressings are reserved for the operating room and are rarely applied in another setting. The CPCT cannot remove any sterile dressings without specific direction from a nurse or physician.

Aseptic dressing

Aseptic dressings are commonly encountered in medical settings. The CPCT is often tasked with changing patient dressings. Dressings are designed to protect and cover wounds and incision sites. To reduce the risk of causing infection, the CPCT must strictly adhere to facility policies and guidelines for changing dressings. There are many accepted methods for changing dressings, but most include the following steps:

1. Wash hands.

2. Place the patient in a comfortable position.

3. Don gloves.

4. Remove soiled dressings.

5. Assess the wound and note the amount, color, and odor of any drainage.

6. Remove gloves.

7. Wash hands.

8. Establish an aseptic working area.

9. Open replacement sterile dressing and saturate with sterile water.

10. Cleanse the wound.

11. Assess the wound size, depth, color, and odor.

12. Apply a new aseptic dressing.

13. Wash hands.

Transfer a Patient Using a Mechanical Lift

Mechanical lifts are special devices used for lifting and moving heavy patients. To prevent injury, the CPCT should become familiar with the specific device the facility uses. Lifting devices typically have a sling and a metal frame with a hydraulic lift mechanism. The sling is placed under the patient and is connected to the metal frame. The CPCT engages the lifting mechanism. Patients should only be lifted high enough for the CPCT to safely perform the required task, then slowly lowered back to the bed. Many lifting devices are equipped with wheels to enable the CPCT to move the patient from one bed to another. While lifting and lowering the patient, the wheels must be locked.

Manually Lift and Transfer a Patient

The CPCT should be familiar with the three most common types of patient transfers: independent, assisted, and dependent.

Independent transfer is used when a patient is able to move freely. The CPCT should monitor the patient during independent transfer, remove any obstacles the patient could trip on, and be prepared to assist the patient.

If the patient has trouble getting up, is unsteady on his or her feet, or requires assistance when moving, use an assisted transfer. The CPCT should discuss the procedure with the patient prior to moving him or her. The CPCT should also ask for help if the patient is too heavy to safely move alone. Several commercial devices exist to facilitate assisted transfer, such as the transfer or slide board. To prevent injury, the CPCT should be trained in the use of such a device prior to using it.

The dependent transfer involves moving patients that are completely incapable of helping during the transfer. The CPCT should never attempt to perform the dependent transfer of a patient alone. To prevent injury, two to three people should be used for dependent transfers.

Apply Immobility Splints to Patients

A splint is used to stabilize an injured extremity and provide temporary support to broken bony structures. If applied correctly, splints minimize pain associated with dislocations, fractures, and soft tissue injuries.

There are numerous types of splints and multiple manufacturers, each requiring specific application techniques. However, there are a few rules common to all splints. Splints should always be applied from the distal part of the extremity to the proximal part. For example, when applying a splint to the forearm, start at the wrist and work your way to the elbow. Always remove jewelry on the affected limb prior to applying a splint. After applying the splint, assess for circulation, movement, and sensation (CMS) in the areas beyond the splint. For example, after applying an elbow splint, assess the fingers for CMS.

Provide One-On-One Care for Patients who are at Risk for Suicide

The CPCT may be assigned to provide one-on-one care for patients who are at risk for suicide. The CPCT is responsible for creating a safe environment for the patient by watching over him or her continuously and removing any items that could cause injury. For example, patients at risk for suicide must not have razors, IV tubing, telephone cords, glass bottles, or medications. Any threats of suicide made by the patient should be reported to the nurse.

Provide Skin Care

The CPCT plays a vital role in preventing skin breakdown in hospitalized patients. The CPCT must ensure that patients are repositioned at least every 2 hours, in order to minimize the risk of developing pressure sores. Some facilities encourage the use of lotion or powder to prevent skin breakdown, while others preclude their use. Refer to your agency's policies on the use of skin protectants and follow the established guidelines.

Apply Sequential Compression Devices

Sequential compression devices, often referred to as boots, are used to prevent blood clots from forming in the lower legs. The devices are placed on each leg and may extend to the knee, thigh area, or just placed on the feet. The devices are connected to an air compressor that inflates and deflates them around the legs or feet. This continuous compression-decompression device promotes blood flow in the legs and feet, preventing blood clot formation.

Apply Anti-Embolitic Stockings

Anti-embolitic stockings prevent blood clots from forming in the deep veins of the legs. Blood clots are dangerous, because they can travel to the lungs and cause death. The stockings can also prevent fluid buildup in the legs.

Anti-embolitic stockings are commonly referred to as TED hose. They are made of elastic material that is designed to apply firm pressure to the lower legs. The CPCT is often responsible for applying the stockings. The stockings have a hole at the toe area to allow for assessment of circulation. The CPCT should remove stockings prior to bathing the patient, so that a thorough assessment of the skin can be performed.

Perform First Aid, CPR, and Rapid Response Procedures

The CPCT may be asked to assist the nurse or physician with providing first aid or to be part of a rapid response team. Follow your agency's policies and guidelines for providing first aid. Never perform tasks that are not permitted by your scope of practice. Many agencies require health care workers to have a current CPR card. Refer to Chapter 3 for information about CPR.

Assist the Patient with Incentive Spirometry

The incentive spirometer is a device that promotes circulation to the lungs and the movement of air into the lungs. The device is designed to minimize the risk of getting pneumonia in patients that are confined to a hospital bed, are immobile, or have had recent surgery, by forcing them to forcefully inhale through the device. The provider will prescribe the treatment frequency and determine the appropriate target number the patient should achieve while using the device.

Check Dressings for Increased Saturation and Changes

The CPCT may be asked to determine the level of saturation in a dressing. The CPCT must examine the dressing and determine if the dressing is dry, has blood soaking through, and if the dressing is securely taped to the skin. It is also important for the CPCT to note the amount, color, and odor of any drainage.

Follow the Five Rights of Delegation

The CPCT must always function within his or her scope of practice. Always consider the following when performing any task delegated by a nurse:

1. The Right Task – Is this in your job description? Were you trained for the task? Is this task approved by the state?

2. The Right Circumstances – Can you perform the procedure safely under the present circumstances? Do you have the right tools?

3. The Right Person – Are you the right person for the task? Does this task fall within your scope of practice?

4. The Right Directions – Did you understand the nurse's directions? Did the nurse provide you with enough information to complete the task safely?

5. The Right Supervisor – Is the person delegating the task to you allowed to do so? For example, did a nurse delegate the task or was it a fellow CPCT? Only nurses can delegate tasks to CPCTs.

Prioritize Patient Care Based on Patient Needs

The CPCT has many competing priorities that need to be dealt with throughout the shift. The nursing staff is responsible for delegating tasks to the CPCT and for prioritizing delegated tasks. However, the CPCT must be able to prioritize the tasks assigned to him or her. The CPCT should always ask for direction and clarification if he or she doesn't understand a task.

Monitor Vital Signs and Patient Status During Blood Transfusions

Nurses are responsible for starting, maintaining, and discontinuing blood transfusions. The CPCT is responsible for monitoring vital signs before, during, and after the transfusion. The CPCT is also responsible for reporting the vital signs measurements to the nurse. Every facility has different rules governing the administration of blood products. The CPCT should be familiar with his or her agency's rules. When measuring vital signs or reporting abnormal findings, be sure to follow any directions provided by the nursing staff.

Assist Patient with Taking Self-Administered Prescribed Medications

The CPCT can assist patients with taking self-administered prescribed medications by handing the patient the medication and reminding the patient when he or she should take it. The CPCT must never prepare, prescribe, or directly administer any medications to the patient.

Apply Oxygen Therapy

A provider or nurse may order oxygen for a patient. If directed to do so, the CPCT may apply oxygen therapy. There are numerous commercial oxygen delivery devices and the CPCT should be familiar with the specific devices used in his or her facility. The most common oxygen delivery devices are the nasal cannula, simple facemask, and the non-rebreather facemask. Nasal cannulas have two nasal prongs that are inserted into the patient's nostrils. The oxygen tubing is placed around the patient's ears and the adjustment tab is moved into position near the patient's neck.

Simple facemasks and non-rebreather facemasks are placed over the patient's mouth and nose. They are secured with an elastic band around the back of the head.

Once the delivery device is applied to the patient, the nurse, respiratory therapist, or physician sets the oxygen flow rate.

Assist with Patient-Administered Nebulizer Treatments

The CPCT may assist with a patient-administered nebulizer treatment by handing the patient the device and properly positioning the patient in bed. Patients should sit up when using their inhalers. The CPCT must never administer the medication to a patient.

Weigh a Patient

It is important to weigh patients accurately, because many treatments and medications are weight-based. The patient's weight is typically recorded in kilograms. The CPCT should tare ("zero") the scale prior to use. Each scale is different, so the CPCT must be familiar with the device. The CPCT must also ensure the patient's safety by eliminating any tripping hazards near the scale. Encourage patients to use safety features such as ramps and handrails to get on and off the scale. The CPCT may use a chair or bed scale to weigh patients that are unable to ambulate.

Perform Home Health Aide Services

The CPCT may be required to work in a patient's home and function as a home health aide. In the home health setting, some of the duties of the CPCT include:

- Assisting with ADLs

- Assisting with patient ambulation

- Performing housekeeping duties

- Transporting patients to doctor or other appointments

- Offering companionship

- Training family members to care for the individual

- Measuring vital signs

- Changing linens

- Emptying bedpans

The CPCT must always remember that they are working in a patient's home and must be respectful of the patient, the patient's family, and the patient's belongings.

Perform Hospice/Palliative Aide Care Services

Hospice care is designed to allow the patient to die in the comfort of their home. Typically, the patient's family and a hospice nurse are present in the home. It is a privilege for health care providers to be in a patient's home, and the CPCT must always remember to be compassionate, respectful, and comforting with the patient, family members, and other members of the health care team. The CPCT is a part of a comprehensive team that cares for the patient and family. The team is comprised of a physician, a registered nurse, a home health aide, social workers, a spiritual caregiver, counselors, bereavement services, nutritionists, and volunteers. The role of the CPCT includes many of the same functions as the home health aide listed above.

Observe for and Report Edema

Edema is the inappropriate accumulation of fluid in body tissue. The CPCT can assess for edema by gently pressing on the patient's legs and determining if the pressure creates a "pit." The CPCT should immediately report findings of edema to the patient's nurse. Edema can also be observed in all of the dependent areas of the body. Dependent areas include the arms and legs, the back of the shoulders, sacrum, buttocks, and thighs.

Observe and Report Patient Pain Using a Pain Scale

As part of the vital signs assessment, the CPCT should assess the patient for pain. Several different tools are available to assist patients and health care providers in determining the intensity of the patient's pain. The Numeric Rating Scale is one of the most common tools used to determine the level of pain in adults. The patient is shown the scale and asked to associate a number with the intensity of their pain.

The Wong-Baker FACES Pain Rating Scale is another scale used to determine pain intensity in children. Similar to the numeric rating scale, the patient is shown the FACES scale and asked to point to the face that best represents the way he or she feels.

Monitor and Record Vital Signs

Blood pressure (manually)

Blood pressure can be measured manually using a stethoscope and a blood pressure cuff. The blood pressure cuff is typically placed on the patient's left upper arm, an inch or two above the crease of the elbow. The patient should sit comfortably with the left arm placed at the level of the heart. Next, locate the radial pulse and inflate the cuff until the pulse is no longer detected. The cuff is then inflated an additional 10 to 20 millimeters of mercury (mm Hg). Place the stethoscope over the left brachial artery and slowly release the pressure in the blood pressure cuff. The first sound heard through the stethoscope as the pressure is being released is the systolic (top number) pressure. Continue to listen over the brachial artery and release pressure in the cuff. Record the pressure on the blood pressure cuff the moment no more sound is heard through the stethoscope. This is the diastolic (bottom number) pressure.

An important point to remember is that blood pressure cuffs come in different sizes. It is critical to use the correct blood pressure cuff on each patient. Using a cuff that is too large or too small will cause errors in blood pressure measurement. Refer to the manufacturer's instructions for determining the proper cuff size for each patient.

Blood pressure (electronically)

The CPCT will often use an electronic blood pressure monitor to measure the patient's blood pressure. Electronic blood pressure devices typically measure the patient's heart rate at the same time, providing both results simultaneously. The electronic blood pressure devices are reliable and efficient. The CPCT should measure the patient's blood pressure manually if the electronic device measures an abnormal blood pressure, or if the patient has an irregular heart rate.

Pulse (manually)

The CPCT can measure the patient's pulse rate by palpating the area over an artery. The most commonly used sites for measuring the pulse rate are the radial, brachial, and carotid arteries. The radial site is located on the thumb side of the back of the wrist. The brachial site is located on the inside of the elbow closest to the body. The carotid site is located in the neck to the right and left of the windpipe at the level of the Adam's apple. The CPCT should locate the pulse site, count the number of pulses felt during a 30 second time interval, and then multiply the result by 2 to calculate the patient's heart rate. The normal adult pulse rate ranges between 60 and 100 beats per minute. If the pulse feels irregular, the CPCT should measure the pulse rate for a full 60 seconds and report the findings to the nurse. Report pulse rates outside the normal range to the nursing staff immediately.

Pulse (electronically)

The CPCT will often use an electronic vitals monitor to measure the pulse rate. The device usually measures the heart rate in conjunction with the blood pressure or oximeter.

Apical pulse

The apical pulse can be felt over the left chest in the area of the fifth intercostal space at the mid-clavicular line. The CPCT should measure the pulse rate at the apical site if the heart rate is irregular. The CPCT can palpate the pulse or use a stethoscope to listen to the heart and measure the rate over a full 60-second time interval.

Apical-radial deficit

The apical-radial deficit, or pulse deficit, is the difference between the apical and radial pulse rate. This measurement requires two health care workers to simultaneously measure the pulse at the apical site and at the radial site. If the difference between the two measurements exceeds 8 to 10 beats per minute, the finding should be reported to the nursing staff.

Respirations (manually)

The CPCT can measure the patient's respiratory rate using a variety of techniques. These include watching the movement of the patient's chest, placing the palm of the hand on the patient's back, or listening to respirations with a stethoscope. The CPCT should count the number of respirations during a 15-second interval then multiply by 4 to calculate the respiratory rate. Also, the CPCT should note the depth of respirations (shallow, deep) and the rhythm of respirations (regular, irregular).

Pulse oximetry

Pulse oximetry is a noninvasive method of measuring the oxygen saturation of hemoglobin. Typically, the pulse oximetry probe is placed on one of the patient's fingers. Alternatively, the probe can be placed on a toe or earlobe. The device uses infrared light to measure oxygen saturation and the test is painless. Certain conditions may cause false oximetry readings such as cold fingers, edema, nail polish, acrylic nails, and certain toxic exposures such as carbon monoxide. The normal oxygen saturation range is 94 to 100%. Certain diseases such as COPD may alter the normal oxygen saturation range. The CPCT should report any abnormal oxygen saturation results to the nursing staff immediately.

PATIENT CARE AND PREPARATION RELATED TO PHLEBOTOMY AND EKG

Conduct Appropriate Introduction to the Patient

During your initial contact with the client, use a warm and inviting voice to introduce yourself. Ask patients to identify themselves by name and solicit any additional information needed to ensure you are speaking to the right client. Always make sure you ask patients for their personal information; never state patients' personal information and then wait for them to confirm that the information is correct.

Explain the Phlebotomy Procedure to be Performed to the Patient

- If patient has never had blood drawn, explain the procedure by following these steps:

- Tell the patient that the physician has ordered blood tests.

- Go through the steps of the procedure:

  - Examination and preparation of a site

  - Application of a tourniquet

  - Insertion of the needle

- ○ Filling the blood tubes

- ○ Applying a bandage to the venipuncture site (after the blood is obtained and the needle is removed)

- Advise the patient that she or he will experience a slight bit of pain when the needle is inserted.

- Tell the patient that, if he or she is experiencing any severe pain or feels sick in any way, to let you know immediately.

- Inform the patient about complications of venipuncture, including excessive bruising, hematoma, infection, prolonged bleeding, and pain.

Do not use technical language when explaining the procedure. After you have told the patient about the complications of venipuncture, it is helpful to ask the patient to repeat this information back to you to confirm patient understanding.

Review the Requisition for Testing Requirements and Patient Identity

Physicians, physician assistants, and nurse practitioners order laboratory tests. The laboratory order form should contain the following information:

- Full name

- Date of birth

- Gender

- The tests to be drawn

- Who ordered the tests

In addition, there should be space on the form for the phlebotomy technician to document when the blood sample was obtained.

Receive Implied or Informed Consent from the Patient

Prior to performing any procedure on a patient, you must obtain consent to do so. After educating the patient about the procedure, confirming that the patient understands the procedure and the possible complications, ask the patient for permission to perform the procedure.

Determine Venipuncture Site Accessibility Based on Patient Age and Condition

The preferred location for venipuncture is the antecubital fossa. The antecubital fossa is the area of skin that is between the forearm and the upper arm. It is commonly known as the bend of the elbow, and it can be seen when the patient extends his or her arm and turns the arm palm up. The antecubital fossa is a good site for venuipuncture, because there are several large veins there that are close to the surface and easily seen. Alternatively, the back of the hand is another good place to find veins.

Verify Patient Compliance with Testing Requirements

After you confirm the patient's identity and introduce yourself, verify that the patient has properly prepared for the procedure. Tests such as fasting glucose or cholesterol require the patient to fast for at least eight hours prior to the test. If the patient has not properly prepared for the blood collection, contact the ordering provider. Confirm that it is okay to perform the collection. If you are unable to reach the provider, be sure to document that the patient did not fast.

Prepare the Patient

EKG monitoring

- The static EKG is a diagnostic test that allows the physician to assess the electrical activity of the heart.

- It is a non-invasive, painless procedure that takes only a few minutes to complete.

- Ask the patient if he/she has ever had a reaction to latex or rubber.

- Apply sticky electrodes that can be easily removed to the patient's chest, arms, and legs. Clean the skin and trim hair to ensure proper contact between the skin and electrode.

- Instruct the patient to remove any electronic devices from his or her pockets, as they may interfere with the test.

- Instruct the patient to lie flat, or with the head slightly elevated, and avoid touching anything that conducts electricity, such as the handrails of the bed.

- Instruct the patient to remain as still as possible for approximately 10 seconds during the test while the machine acquires the EKG.

- Advise the patient to notify the CPCT if he or she experiences itching, swelling, or redness where the electrodes contact the skin.

- There are no significant side effects to this procedure.

Holter monitoring

- The ambulatory care (Holter) monitor is a device used to monitor the electrical activity of the heart over a period of 24 to 72 hr and is used to detect problems that occur transiently.

- Instruct the patient to bathe prior to his or her appointment, because the patient cannot remove the electrodes or immerse the device in water after it is in place.

- Instruct the patient to wear loose-fitting clothing so the monitor can be worn under a shirt or blouse. The ambulatory care (Holter) monitor can be worn with a bra.

- Ask the patient if he or she has ever had a reaction to latex or rubber.

- Place sticky electrodes on the patient's chest and keep them in place for the duration of the test. The skin may need to be cleaned to ensure that the electrodes adhere securely.

- The doctor's office should be notified if the patient experiences itching, swelling, or redness where the electrodes contact the skin

- Instruct the patient to continue his or her normal daily routine, including work, exercise, and sleep. Tell the patient to keep the ambulatory care (Holter) monitor in place continuously.

- Instruct the patient to keep a journal for the duration of the test. The patient should note the date, time, and duration of any symptoms, such as lightheadedness, palpitations, chest pain, and breathing problems. The patient should also record the date and time that he or she takes any medications, engages in physical activity, and sleeps.

- Instruct the patient to call the physician's office if the electrodes fall off.

- Tell the patient to call 911 immediately if any of the following occur: fainting, weakness, unexplained sweating, or unrelieved chest pain that radiates to the arms or jaw.

- Instruct the patient to return the monitor to the physician's office.

- Although wearing the ambulatory care (Holter) monitor may be inconvenient, there are no significant side effects to the test.

Stress testing

- A stress test is used to determine how the heart functions under the increased workload caused by physical exercise. Specifically, the stress test is designed to provoke myocardial ischemia under controlled settings. If heart disease is suspected, symptoms may manifest during exercise that are not present at rest.

- The stress test takes approximately 10 minutes to complete. Apply electrodes to the patient's chest, and if necessary, clean the skin and/or remove hair to ensure the electrodes adhere. Place a blood pressure cuff on the upper arm to monitor blood pressure during the test.

- If the patient experiences itching, swelling, or redness where the electrodes contact the skin, he or she should notify the technician.

- Take the patient's baseline EKG at rest. Then instruct the patient to walk on a treadmill or use a stationary bike to gradually increase physical activity until you detect symptoms, the patient becomes fatigued or ill, or a target heart rate is reached.

- Instruct the patient to wear comfortable walking shoes and loose-fitting, lightweight clothing for the test.

- Instruct the patient not to eat, drink, or smoke for 3 hr before the test.

- Tell the patient to continue their normal medication routine unless the physician tells him or her otherwise.

- Ask the patient about any previous reactions to rubber or latex. Ask the patient about any history of exercise-induced asthma or respiratory distress, or if he or she routinely uses an inhaler.

- Tell the patient to immediately report fatigue, lightheadedness, dizziness, shortness of breath, or chest pain.

- After exercising, the patient may need to sit or stand still for a few minutes while the machine continues to record heart activity.

- Potential complications include low blood pressure and abnormal heart rhythms. These symptoms usually are alleviated when the patient stops exercising.

Telemetry monitoring

- Telemetry is used to continuously monitor the electrical system of the heart in patients who are at high risk for cardiac complications in the in-patient setting.

- Telemetry monitoring is non-invasive and painless.

- Determine if the patient has had a reaction to rubber or latex.

- Place electrodes on the patient's chest and abdomen, and keep them in place continuously. If necessary, clean the skin and trim hair to ensure the electrodes adhere securely.

- Advise the patient to notify the CPCT if he or she experiences itching, swelling, or redness where the electrodes contact the skin.

- Registered nurses or CPCTs monitor the EKG. The monitors are programmed to alarm if the EKG detects a dangerous rate or rhythm.

- If the electrodes fall off at any time, the patient should notify hospital staff.

- Instruct the patient to notify hospital staff if they experience dizziness, lightheadedness, weakness, chest pain, nausea or vomiting, shortness of breath, or profuse sweating at any time during his or her stay.

Apply Electrodes on Patients

EKG monitoring

The 3-lead EKG configuration is generally used to continuously monitor the patient's heart rhythm. Review the 3-lead configuration to the right:

- White lead – Right shoulder or clavicle area

- Black lead – Left shoulder or clavicle area

- Red lead – Left lower abdominal area

- Green lead – Right lower abdominal area

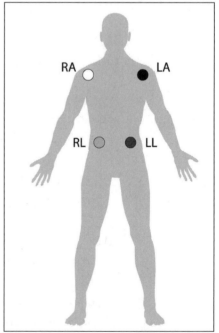

3-Lead EKG – *Electrode placement*

Holter monitoring

The 5-lead EKG configuration refers to the standard Holter monitor setup or the 5-lead rhythm monitor setup. The Holter monitor setup varies depending on the type of monitor. The 5-lead setup is the most common configuration employed:

- White lead – Right sternum/clavicle area

- Black lead – Left sternum/clavicle area

- Red lead – Left lower thoracic area

- Green lead – Right lower thoracic area

- Brown lead – Just below and to the right of the bottom of the sternum

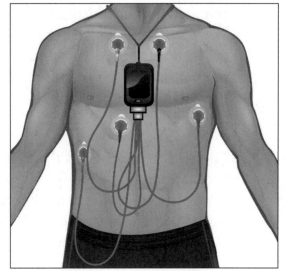

5-Lead EKG – *Most common electrode placement*

Stress testing

Stress testing requires slight modification of limb lead electrode placement to minimize limb motion artifact. Place the six precordial leads – leads V1 through V6 – in the same locations required for the standard 12-lead EKG. But place the four limb lead electrodes on the patient's torso, rather than on the arms and legs, as shown in the diagram at right.

- White lead – Right clavicle/shoulder area

- Black lead – Left clavicle/shoulder area

- Red lead – Left lower abdominal area

- Green lead – Right lower abdominal area

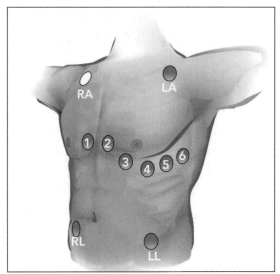

Stress testing – *Electrode placement*

Telemetry monitoring

Telemetry monitoring can be executed in either a 3-lead or a 5-lead setup. The diagram at right shows the most commonly employed electrode placement for each.

The picture on the left illustrates the standard 3-lead configuration. Place the white electrode on the right shoulder area; the black electrode on the left shoulder area, and the red electrode on the lower left abdominal area.

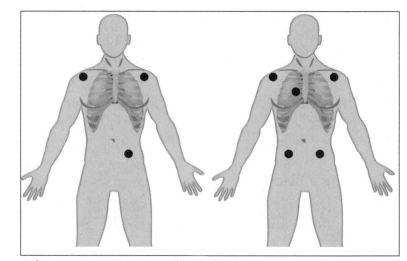

Telemetry monitoring – Electrode placement: 3-lead and 5-lead

The picture on the right illustrates the standard 5-lead configuration. Lead placement follows the 3 lead configuration exactly with the addition of a green electrode, placed on the lower right abdominal area, and a brown electrode placed just to the right of the bottom of the sternum. The brown lead provides similar information to lead V1 in the standard 12-lead tracing.

Pediatric patients

Patients younger than 2 years old require a right-sided, 12-lead EKG. For patients who are ages 2-8, you can use either left- or right-sided EKGs. After age 8, you can no longer use the right-sided EKG. You can also use the right-sided EKG for patients with certain conditions, including inferior wall ST segment elevation and myocardial infarction.

For a right-sided, 12-lead EKG, you place limb leads in the normal fashion, but place the precordial leads as illustrated in the diagram at right.

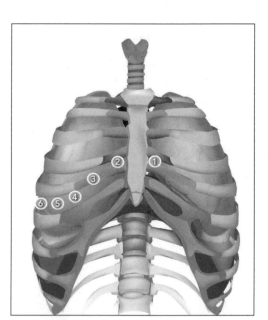

Pediatric patients – Electrode placement

Precordial leads – Right side

- V1 – 4th ICS, L of sternum

- V2 – 4th ICS, R of sternum

- V4 – 5th ICS, midclavicular (R) (most sensitive and specific to R ventricular infarction)

- V3 – between V2/V4

- V5 – 5th ICS between V4/V6

- V6 – 5th ICS, midaxillary

Patients with special considerations

Inferior wall infarction – When there's an inferior wall infarction, you always need to consider posterior wall involvement. This diagram shows proper placement of leads V7, V8, and V9 for a posterior EKG. You will rarely perform the posterior EKG. Using the concept of reciprocal change, you can glean the same information from viewing leads V1 to V4.

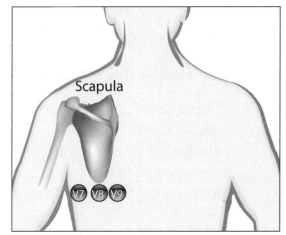

Posterior EKG – Electrode placement

Amputation – Lead placement must be modified in patients who have extremity amputation. Leads can be moved to an area just above the knees and elbows in patients who have distal extremity amputation. If the patient's amputation is close to the torso, EKG electrodes can be placed on the patient's torso.

Respond to Signs and Symptoms of Cardiopulmonary Distress

Signs and symptoms of cardiopulmonary compromise can include the following:

- Tachycardia or bradycardia

- Pallor

- Diaphoresis

- Low blood pressure

- Fast, labored, shallow, or slow respirations

- Anxiety or confusion

- Cyanosis

- Chest pain that radiates to the back, arms, or jaw

- Chest tightness (squeezing sensation)

- Shortness of breath

- Nausea and vomiting

- Lightheadedness

- Weakness

- Syncope

Immediately notify the physician if the patient experiences any of the above symptoms before, during, or after stress testing.

Monitor Patient Condition During Stress Testing

During stress testing, monitor the patient for abnormal vital signs, dysrhythmias, and signs of cardiopulmonary compromise. The heart rate increases with physical activity, but extremely high rates may be of concern. Observe the EKG for arrhythmias such as unifocal or multifocal PVCs, ventricular tachycardia, supraventricular tachycardia, and heart blocks. Look for signs of ischemia, including T wave inversion and ST segment changes.

If the patient complains of dizziness, lightheadedness, nausea, severe shortness of breath, chest pain, or fatigue, stop the test and notify the physician.

Respond to Complications During Stress Testing

Complications of stress testing include hypotension and dysrhythmias. These usually resolve with rest. If hypotension persists, have the patient lie supine with legs elevated and notify the physician. Also notify the physician of persistent dysrhythmias. On rare occasions, patients suffer cardiac arrest or ventricular dysrhythmias requiring resuscitation. Continuously monitor the patient during and after the stress test, and immediately report any concerning findings to the physician.

Verify Patient Understanding of Ambulatory Care (Holter) Monitor Procedures

Patients undergoing continuous heart monitoring in the outpatient setting should receive information about the device and how to troubleshoot common problems. To ensure patient understanding of ambulatory care (Holter) monitor procedures, ask the patient to verbalize the correct response to the following question:

- Is it okay to remove the electrodes? (No.)

- Is it okay to remove the battery? (No.)

- Is it okay to disconnect the leads or move them to a different location? (No.)

- What should you do if you experience itching, swelling, or redness at the site of electrode placement? (Call the physician's office.)

- Is it okay to go to work or to exercise while wearing the ambulatory care (Holter) monitor? (Yes.)

- What do you need to do when you experience any symptoms while wearing the ambulatory care (Holter) monitor? (Write the date, time, and duration of symptoms, and what the symptoms were.)

- What should you do if your symptoms include chest pain, shortness of breath, unexplained profuse sweating, or passing out? (Call 911.)

Summary

This chapter covered the basics of patient care. You learned about emotional support and coping mechanisms. You found out how to admit a patient and how to monitor changes in condition, digestion, and intake/output. The text also covered a number of devices commonly used in patient care, including feeding tubes, peripheral IVs, mechanical lifts, and sequential compression devices. Finally, you learned about patient care related to Phlebotomy and EKG.

Drill Questions

1. Which of the following statements made by the CPCT about taking a patient's blood pressure demonstrates the need for further teaching?

    A. "I will apply the cuff to the upper arm."
    B. "I will use the arm with the dialysis shunt."
    C. "I will locate the brachial artery with my fingers."
    D. "I will have the patient sit while I take the blood pressure."

2.

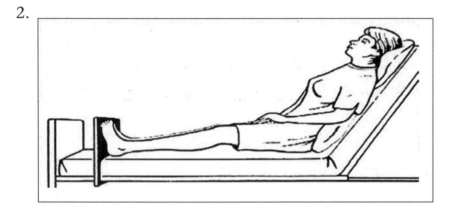

    Which of the following positions is illustrated in the figure above?

    A. Trendelenberg
    B. Prone
    C. Fowler's
    D. Recovery

3. In which of the following situations should the CPCT place the patient in the lithotomy position?

    A. Nasal exam
    B. Head pain
    C. Stomach ache
    D. Rectal exam

4. Which of the following statements made by the CPCT demonstrates the need for further teaching?

    A. "I will use hand sanitizer before and after the examination."
    B. "I will place instruments near the examination table."
    C. "I will leave the room during the examination to ensure privacy."
    D. "I will assist the doctor by drawing blood and urine samples."

5. Which of the following test results should the CPCT report to the nurse immediately?

    A. Blood pressure 102/62 mm Hg
    B. Heart rate 104/min
    C. Temperature 32.7° C (90.9° F)
    D. Respirations 18/min

Drill Answers

1. Which of the following statements made by the CPCT about taking a patient's blood pressure demonstrates the need for further teaching?

    A. "I will apply the cuff to the upper arm."
    B. "I will use the arm with the dialysis shunt."
    C. "I will locate the brachial artery with my fingers."
    D. "I will have the patient sit while I take the blood pressure."

    The arm with the dialysis shunt should never be used to record a blood pressure. The other choices are correct.

2.

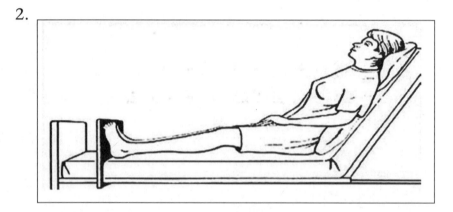

    Which of the following positions is illustrated in the figure above?

    A. Trendelenberg
    B. Prone
    C. Fowler's
    D. Recovery

    The figure illustrates Fowler's position.

3. In which of the following situations should the CPCT place the patient in the lithotomy position?

    A. Nasal exam
    B. Head pain
    C. Stomach ache
    D. Rectal exam

    The lithotomy position is used for genital and rectal examinations.

4. Which of the following statements made by the CPCT demonstrates the need for further teaching?

    A. "I will use hand sanitizer before and after the examination."
    B. "I will place instruments near the examination table."
    C. "I will leave the room during the examination to ensure privacy."
    D. "I will assist the doctor by drawing blood and urine samples."

The CPCT needs to stay in the room during the examination to assist the physician or nurse with the examination and treatment of the patient.

5. Which of the following test results should the CPCT report to the nurse immediately?

    A. Blood pressure 102/62 mm Hg
    B. Pulse rate 104/min
    C. Temperature 32.7° C (90.9° F)
    D. Respirations 18/min

The temperature is very low and should be reported to the nurse immediately.

Terms and Definitions

Afebrile – Absence of fever

Anuria – Absence of urine formation

Apnea – Cessation of breathing

Aspiration – The drawing of fluid and other substances into the lungs

Auscultation – Listening to sounds from the lungs, heart and other organs, often with the use of a stethoscope

Blood pressure – The tension exerted on the walls of the arteries by the contraction of the heart

Bradycardia – Slow heart rate

Bradypnea – Slow breathing

Diarrhea – The passage of fluid, unformed stool

Dyspnea – Difficult or labored breathing

Dysuria – Painful or difficult urination

Edema – Excessive fluid buildup in body cavities or tissue

Enuresis – Involuntary discharge of urine after the age at which bladder control should have been established

Hematuria – Blood in the urine

Hyper – Prefix meaning above, excessive, or beyond

Hypo – Prefix meaning below, under, beneath or deficient

Hypoxia – An oxygen deficiency in the tissues of the body

Inspection – Visual examination of the external surface of the body

Manipulation – To move or feel a part of the body with the hands

Melena – Black, tarry stool caused by digested blood in the GI tract

Nocturia – Excessive or frequent urination after going to bed

Orthopnea – Labored breathing that occurs while lying flat and improves when standing or sitting up.

Ostomy – A surgically formed fistula connecting a portion of intestine or urinary tract to a site outside the body

Palpate – Examine by touch

Percussion – Tapping a body part (usually with a finger or a small hammer) to determine position, size, or density of underlying organs

Polyuria – Excessive production of urine

Position – The manner in which the body is arranged

Pyrexia – Elevated body temperature

Pyuria – Pus in the urine

Tachycardia – Rapid heart rate

Tachypnea – Rapid breathing

02 SAFETY

Learning Objectives
After reading this chapter, the CPCT student will be able to:

- *Report physical abuse, sexual harassment, substance abuse, and domestic violence.*

- *Transport and to transfer a patient using proper body mechanics.*

- *Monitor a patient's environmental safety.*

- *Prevent workplace injuries – including biological, chemical, radiological, electrical, fire, explosive, and physical hazards.*

- *Recognize and respond to emergency situations.*

- *Explain the guidelines established by the Joint Commission (TJC).*

Introduction

In this chapter, we will discuss the basics of safety in health care. You will learn how to protect yourself, your patients, and your coworkers. The chapter concludes with a five-question self-assessment drill.

IDENTIFY AND REPORT

Abuse or Neglect of Patients

Health care workers must always report abuse according to agency, state, and federal guidelines. There are several kinds of abuse, including the following:

- Physical abuse – Intentionally inflicting harm on the patient

- Financial abuse – Spending the patient's money or using his or her assets for reasons other than that patient's wellbeing

- Psychological or emotional abuse – Intentionally inflicting harm through insults or verbal assaults

- Sexual abuse – Nonconsensual sexual activity

- Basic rights abuse – Violations of basic rights that are protected by state and federal law (e.g. privacy or freedom of religion)

Evidence of abuse includes the following:

- Lack of personal care – Uncombed hair, wrinkled clothing, poor oral care, and dirty fingernails

- **Malnourishment** – Poor skin condition, muscle wasting, or weakness

- **Dehydration** – Lack of fluids results in dry mucous membranes, sunken eyes, and dry skin

- Pressure sores – Open areas on bony prominences, coccyx, elbows, or hips

- Overt physical signs of trauma – Scratches or bruises

- Restraint trauma – Rope burns or welts

- Inconsistency in the explanation of how an injury occurred

- Undue anxiety, trembling, helplessness, thoughts of suicide, evasiveness, and lack of eye contact

- A caregiver will not read mail to a patient

- A patient is not given the opportunity to speak without the presence of a caregiver

- Overmedication or oversedation

If you identify any of these signs, report them to a nurse and follow agency, state, and federal guidelines.

Recognize that sometimes abuse appears to be occurring, but it is not. Be aware that caregiver stress can cause unintentional abuse. Lack of education regarding patient care can also account for some of the symptoms. Different lifestyles can account for other behaviors. Ask a professional to assess any questionable signs of abuse.

Education by your agency can help stop the abuse. In addition, inform the patient's family about resources that help with patient care.

Sexual Harassment Involving Patients or Staff

Sexual harassment occurs when a person of power makes unwanted sexual advances that relate to the victim's employment, academic status, or success. This includes sexual advances, requests for sexual favors, inappropriate touching, or inappropriate comments. Remember that both males and females perpetrate sexual harassment.

According to the Equal Employment Opportunity Commission (EEOC), there are four forms of sexual harassment. These are determined by whether or not submission to the perpetrator:

1. Is a condition of employment

2. Interferes with job performance

3. Is the basis for an employment decision

4. Creates a hostile and intimidating work environment

If a patient acts inappropriately towards you, clearly ask the patient to stop. Some neurological disorders, delirium, confusion, and psychiatric problems cause patients to act inappropriately. If you feel you are being harassed, immediately report it to your supervisor and to human resources. If a supervisor is causing the harassment, contact human resources.

Substance Abuse Involving Patients or Staff

A health care worker under the influence of drugs or alcohol is a danger to patients and to other workers. If you suspect drug or alcohol abuse from a coworker, inform the nurse. Most facilities and agencies have a no-tolerance policy. Supervisors can ask workers to undergo drug testing at any time.

There are noticeable symptoms of substance abuse:

- Lack of concentration

- Inability to complete tasks

- Signs of withdrawal (e.g. shaking or sweating)

- Emotional changes during a shift

- Deteriorating personal appearance

- Complaints of verbal abusiveness or roughness

- Unexplained errands during work hours

- Excessive absenteeism

- Excessive, long breaks

Patients must be protected from health care workers with substance abuse problems. Many certification boards will revoke the certification of such an individual until he or she has completed a rehabilitation program.

Domestic Violence Involving Patients or Staff

Domestic violence happens at all levels of society. It can include verbal abuse, physical abuse, or sexual abuse. It is very complex issue, because of the nature of the relationship between the victim and the abuser; victims are often financially or emotionally dependent upon their partners. Report any such abuse to a nurse. Be sure to include all details needed for further evaluation.

Transport Patients Safely Using Proper Body Mechanics

When lifting and moving patients, proper positioning is extremely important. Back injuries are a very common problem related to body mechanics. Keep the following points in mind:

- Keep your body centered when lifting patients

- Do not lock your knees

- Use your thigh muscles to move the weight

- Point your forward-most foot in the direction to which you are transferring the patient (for a better center of balance)

- Keep your abdominal muscles tight (to strengthen your spine)

- Always wear appropriate footwear (not high heels or platform shoes)

- Always keep your spine straight

- Use available assistance when transferring patients (e.g. slide boards, gait belts, or other staff members)

Stand straight when pushing wheelchairs or gurneys. This puts less stress on your back and other musculoskeletal areas.

Struggling to reach a falling patient can cause injury to the patient and to the health care worker. Be ready to stabilize yourself and your patient at any time.

Transfer Patients Safely Using Proper Body Mechanics

The most important precaution to take when transferring a patient is to make sure the equipment is locked. When transferring a patient from a wheelchair, make sure the wheelchair is locked. When transferring to a bed, make sure the bed is locked. When transferring from a bed to a gurney, make sure the bed and gurney are locked (to prevent their separation).

Monitor Patient's Environmental Safety

Darkness, obstacles, and sickness can cause falls. Furthermore, health issues can cause falls. Such issues include poor vision, hypotension, dizziness, substance abuse, poor gait, strokes, cognitive impairment, and advanced age.

Putting safety features into a home can help to prevent falls. For example, the patient could install bath tub rails and remove any throw rugs. Educating patients to rise slowly when taking antihypertensive or diuretic medications can prevent dizziness. Walkers, canes, and crutches can also be used to help with stability.

There are a number of other precautions that can improve a patient's environmental safety. If a patient is using an electric bed, the bed should be checked annually by a biomedical technician. Blood pressure equipment should also be checked frequently for accuracy. Patients should be taught how to take their own vital signs and how to interpret the results.

Prevent Workplace Injuries by Following OSHA Guidelines

The Occupational Safety and Health Administration (OSHA) regulates all workers' safety. OSHA requires the following basic safety practices.

Biological hazards – Danger caused by infectious agents such as bacteria, viruses, fungi, or other parasites. Remember your patients' body fluids contain biohazards.

Chemical hazards – These hazards involve damage caused by chemicals used in a medical laboratory. This includes exposure to toxic, carcinogenic, or caustic substances. All chemicals and reagents containing hazardous ingredients in a concentration greater than 1% must have a Material Safety Data Sheet (MSDS) on file. The MSDS contains information on physical and chemical characteristics, including:

- Safe handling
- Clean up
- Primary routes of entry
- Exposure limits

- Carcinogenic potential

- Fire, explosion, reactivity, and health hazards

- Emergency first aid

Radiological hazards – These hazards involve x-rays and other radioactive materials. If x-ray equipment is being used, wear a lead apron. If caring for a patient with radioactive implants, consider time, distance, and shielding. If a health care worker frequently encounters these hazards, he or she will be issued a radiation badge.

Electrical hazards – High-voltage equipment can cause burns and shock. The following steps can prevent electrical injuries:

- Avoid extension cords

- Ground and maintain electrical equipment

- Dry hands before using electrical equipment

- Position electrical devices away from sinks, faucets, and other sources of water

Electrical equipment cannot be used in a hospital without biomedical engineering examining and approving the device. If you find a frayed cord or a malfunction, immediately tag the item. Most facilities have an area where equipment that needs cleaning and checking is placed. Never use equipment that has been tagged for repair.

Fire or explosive hazards – Bunsen burners, oxygen, and chemicals can cause burns or other injuries. To prevent damage from fire, follow the policies of the facility. These policies will include routes of exit and evacuation. Be aware of the location of all fire extinguishers and fire alarms. Furthermore, smoking is not allowed in any facility.

Physical hazards – Heavy lifting can cause sprains, back injuries, and strains. To avoid physical injury, you should wear proper attire, do not overextend your reach, use a gait belt, lift with your legs, and move objects closer to your body before lifting.

Wet floors can cause falls. If water or moisture is on the floor, clean it up, or have it cleaned.

Should you become injured, report the injury to a supervisor and make out an incident report. If the injury is serious, have a physician treat the injury. Most facilities have a time frame in which you can report such an injury.

Recognize and Respond to Emergency Situations

All facilities give orientation for fire, biohazard, and hostage situations. Follow your facility's guidelines, as well as those listed below.

If you are involved in a fire, remember the acronym RACE:

- R – Rescue
    - Rescue anyone in immediate danger from the fire (if it does not endanger your life).

- A – Alarm
    - Sound the alarm and dial 911.

- C – Confine
    - Confine the fire by closing all doors and windows.

- E – Extinguish or Evacuate
    - Use a fire extinguisher or evacuate the area (if the fire is too large).

To use fire extinguishers correctly, remember the acronym PASS:

- P – Pull
    - Pull the pin on the fire extinguisher.

- A – Aim
    - Aim the nozzle at the base of the fire.

- S – Squeeze
    - Squeeze or press the handle.

- S – Sweep
    - Sweep from side to side, at the base of the fire (until it is out).

Hostage situations

For hostage situations, policies vary by facility. Know your facility's policy and what actions you are expected to take.

If you are safe from the situation, call 911 for assistance. If you have patients, keep them safe. Hide until help arrives, and stay as calm as possible.

Biological hazards

As a health care worker, you are exposed to bacteria, viruses, and fungi that are biological hazards. Washing hands frequently and maintaining personal protective equipment (PPE) are both extremely important. Dispose of PPE in an appropriate container within the room and wash your hands thoroughly. All sharps should be placed in the biohazard container. Do not fill the container above the safe level. When stuck by unknown sharps, seek immediate medical attention and notify your supervisor.

Follow Proper Procedure for Identifying Patients

The first step in any medical procedure is always identification. Identification (ID) bands are the standard. The ID bracelet contains the patient's name and date of birth, the physician's name, and the hospital identification number. Use the identification band to make sure you have the right patient.

According to the Joint Commission, you should always use at least two methods to identify a patient. Be sure to use the patient's name and date of birth as the primary means of identification.

A three-way ID is done by comparing the ID bracelet, the patient's verbal identification, and a visual comparison of a labeled specimen.

If an unconscious and unidentified patient is admitted to an emergency room, use a three-part label. The first part contains the ID number, the second part is attached to the specimen, and the third part is attached to the chart.

Follow the Joint Commission's (TJC) Patient Safety Guidelines

The Joint Commission's rules regulate all health care facilities. Each type of facility has its own National Patient Safety Goals (NPSGs). Hospitals, long-term care facilities, and hospice must teach their personnel these standards. In turn, these personnel are asked to relate these standards during inspections.

- While some standards vary, all facilities use the following guidelines:

- Use at least two forms of ID.

- Use hand-washing guidelines from the Center of Disease Control and Prevention (CDC) or the World Health Organization (WHO).

- Safely administer medications.

- Provide additional precautions to patients on blood thinners.

- Record and pass along information about patients' medications.

- Make sure patients know which medications they are to take at home.

Practice Safety Procedures When Using Medical Supplies and Equipment

Make sure you know how to use all safety devices correctly. Chart any device's application and the patient's tolerance.

When a patient is placed on a gurney, the side rails must be up for transport. During transport, make sure that extremities are kept within the side rails to prevent injury. Make sure IV poles and equipment are not too tall for doorways.

Most facilities are restraint-free, but seat belts are common. Another common restraint is a side rail. For safety, one side rail is raised to enable patients to turn themselves. If a patient rolls out of bed, the opposite side rail is half-raised.

Report and Document Work-Related Injuries

You should know your facility's policy regarding the reporting of a workplace injury. Report all injuries immediately, and fill out any necessary forms. An improperly filled out form can void workers' compensation coverage. If the injury is serious enough, you can also visit a doctor, urgent care, or an emergency room. The facility will then investigate the incident to avoid future injuries.

Summary

This chapter explained how to provide safety to patients and health care workers. You learned how to recognize and respond to signs of abuse – including sexual harassment, substance abuse, and domestic violence. You found out how to transfer and transport patients using proper body mechanics. You learned how to monitor a patient's environmental safety. The text also covered workplace injuries, emergency situations, and the guidelines established by the Joint Commission.

Drill Questions

1. Which of the following most frequently causes the spread of infection in healthcare facilities?

    A. Other patients
    B. Family members
    C. Health care workers' hands
    D. Health care equipment

2. A CPCT is assisting a patient who is ambulating. The patient states, "I feel so dizzy and weak," and her knees buckle. Which of the following actions by the CPCT is most appropriate?

    A. Guide the patient to a seated or lying position on the floor.
    B. Grab the patient under the arms and hold her up while calling for help.
    C. Release the transfer belt. Place a wheelchair behind the patient.
    D. Instruct the patient to grab the rail in the hallway while calling for help.

3. While caring for an 87-year-old female patient, a CPCT notices the IV infusion pump is cracked. Which of the following actions should the CPCT take?

    A. Complete the infusion.
    B. After discontinuing its use, place the pump in the utility room.
    C. Ensure that bioengineering performs maintenance on the pump.
    D. Monitor the pump and see if the crack worsens.

4. During a mercury thermometer exchange, someone drops a mercury thermometer and it shatters on the floor. How should the CPCT intervene?

    A. Have the person pick up the thermometer and place it into a plastic bag.
    B. Use a gloved hand to pick up the glass. Use a paper towel to pick up the mercury.
    C. Notify the hazmat team. Clear the area immediately.
    D. Put on gloves, a gown, and a mask before picking up the spill.

5. A patient has endometrial cancer and has been placed in isolation because of her radiation implants. The patient states that she is lonely and needs extra attention. Which of the following actions should the CPCT take when caring for this patient?

    A. Limit contact and have family members bathe the patient.
    B. Organize all care in short periods. Promise to return.
    C. Make frequent visits to the room and talk with the patient.
    D. Prevent all visitors from entering the room.

Drill Answers

1. Which of the following most frequently causes the spread of infection in health care facilities?

    A. Other patients
    B. Family members
    C. Health care workers' hands
    D. Health care equipment

    Health care workers' hands cause the spread of infection more frequently than the other options.

2. A CPCT is assisting a patient who is ambulating. The patient states, "I feel so dizzy and weak," and her knees buckle. Which of the following actions by the CPCT is most appropriate?

    A. Guide the patient to a seated or lying position on the floor.
    B. Grab the patient under the arms and hold her up while calling for help.
    C. Release the transfer belt. Place a wheelchair behind the patient.
    D. Instruct the patient to grab the rail in the hallway while calling for help.

    In this situation, the CPCT should guide the patient to a seated or lying position on the floor.

3. While caring for an 87-year-old female patient, a CPCT notices the IV infusion pump is cracked. Which of the following actions should the CPCT take?

    A. Complete the infusion.
    B. After discontinuing its use, place the pump in the utility room.
    C. Ensure that bioengineering performs maintenance on the pump.
    D. Monitor the pump and see if the crack worsens.

    In this situation, the CPCT should ensure that bioengineering performs maintenance on the pump.

4. During a mercury thermometer exchange, someone drops a mercury thermometer and it shatters on the floor. How should the CPCT intervene?

    A. Have the person pick up the thermometer and place it into a plastic bag.
    B. Use a gloved hand to pick up the glass. Use a paper towel to pick up the mercury.
    C. Notify the hazmat team. Clear the area immediately.
    D. Put on gloves, a gown, and a mask before picking up the spill.

    In this situation, the CPCT should use a gloved hand to pick up the glass and a paper towel to pick up the mercury.

5. A patient has endometrial cancer and has been placed in isolation because of her radiation implants. The patient states that she is lonely and needs extra attention. Which of the following actions should the CPCT take when caring for this patient?

    A. Limit contact and have family members bathe the patient.
    B. Organize all care in short periods. Promise to return.
    C. Make frequent visits to the room and talk with the patient.
    D. Prevent all visitors from entering the room.

    Care in short periods gives the patient stimulus and prevents the health care worker's overexposure to radiation.

Terms and Definitions

Abuse – Injurious, pathological, or malignant treatment of another person. Such abuse includes physical, mental, sexual, or financial factors.

Dehydration – The clinical consequences of a negative fluid balance. Marked by thirst, orthostatic hypotension, tachycardia, delirium, falls, hyperthermia, renal failure, and death.

Domestic violence – Mistreatment or injury in a domestic setting. This includes physical violence as well as psychological, emotional, and economic abuse.

Malnourishment – A condition resulting from either an inadequate or excessive exposure to nutrients. Common causes are inadequate calorie consumption and the inadequate intake of essential vitamins.

Neglect – Inattention to one's responsibilities (especially those related to a dependent person)

Pressure sore – Damage to the skin or underlying structures caused by tissue compression and inadequate perfusion. The most common sites of breakdown are bony prominences. If left untreated, the area can slough off all the skin, muscle, and tissue to the bone. This can result in gangrene.

Sharps container – A container used for medical articles that may cause a puncture or cuts to those handling them. This includes broken medical glassware, syringes, needles, scalpels, and disposable razors.

03 PROFESSIONAL RESPONSIBILITIES

Learning Objectives

After reading this chapter, the CPCT student will be able to:

- *Obtain BCLS certification.*
- *Adhere to HIPAA regulations.*
- *Use appropriate medical terminology.*
- *Observe the chain of command.*
- *Use therapeutic communication.*

Introduction

In this chapter, you will learn about professional responsibilities. The text will cover some of the duties required of a CPCT, including the use of appropriate medical terminology and therapeutic communication. The chapter concludes with a six-question self-assessment drill.

Obtain and Maintain Basic Cardiac Life Support (BCLS) Certification for Health Caregivers

You can obtain a CPR card from any properly authorized health educator. The American Heart Association certifies instructors to train health care workers in this procedure. You must request the class for certification as a health care worker, because there are many classes for laypeople that are not suitable for health care workers. To review the adult CPR procedure, refer back to Section 1 (Performing First Aid, CPR and Rapid Response). The course is initially one 6-hour day. Following the completion of this course, students will be issued a CPR card. A 4-hour class is required to renew the card. You must renew this card every 2 years, and – in order to work in the health care field – it must be current at all times. If you let it lapse, you must repeat the 6-hour class. Call your local American Red Cross to find out about classes.

In 2010, new guidelines for CPR went into effect. If you have not had the new class, the changes to this procedure are described by the acronym DR. C-A-B:

- D – Danger

    - Check for danger.

- R – Respond

    - Check for response of the victim.

- C – Compressions

    - Deliver 30 compressions hard and fast – this is 100 beats per minute, followed by 2 rescue breaths.

- A – Airway

    - Open the airway using chin lift or jaw thrust.

- B – Breathing

    - Check for breathing. Do not deliver rescue breathing.

After following these steps, direct rescuers to attach the automated external defibrillator (AED) as soon as it is available and to follow the prompts. Then continue 30 compressions to 2 breaths cycles until help arrives.

For all individuals over the age of 1, a 2-inch compression of the chest is recommended. For infants less than 1 year, a depth of 1½ inch is recommended. For a lone rescuer (regardless of the patient's age) the rate is a 30:2 compression-to-breath ratio. Two or more rescuers caring for an adult should use a 30:2 ratio. Two or more rescuers caring for an infant should use a 15:2 ratio.

It has been proven by evidence-based practice that the compressions are the most effective part of CPR. Fast but effective compressions with recoil of the chest between compressions correlate with the highest survival rate.

Although there are renewal classes available online, most facilities and health businesses do not allow them. Instead, they prefer hands-on demonstrations in front of instructors.

Adhere to HIPAA Regulations Regarding Protected Health Information

The Health Insurance Portability and Accountability Act (HIPAA) law was enacted in 1996. The law became effective in 2001, and it allowed facilities 2 years to comply. As of 2003, all those handling health care information must abide by the law or suffer stiff, monetary penalties. Violation of the law can result in civil and criminal penalties including:

- Fines of up to $25,000 for multiple violations of the same standard in a calendar year; or

- Fines up to $250,000 and/or imprisonment up to 10 years for knowing misuse of individually identifiable health information.

Patients have a right to keep their information confidential. Minimal information should be given. Disclosure of information – either written or verbal – about a patient must be accompanied by a consent form signed by that patient. Giving such information without a patient's consent is a violation of the HIPAA law. This can result in dismissal from your job, criminal charges, civil charges, and the removal of your certification.

More recently, congress passed the Health Information Technology for Economic and Clinical Health (HITECH) act of 2009. This act brought forward the technology for health care facilities to electronically record information of patient care – including computerized charts. All facilities and clinics were required to comply by 2011. By 2015, penalties will be given if a facility is not in compliance.

By using the Electronic Health Record (EHR) software, clinicians are able to retrieve information about a patient's condition more easily. With this new technology comes the possibility for lack of confidentiality. That is why HIPAA regulations are so strictly enforced.

Some hospitals offer patients the ability to look at their own records. Because these records are not available to unauthorized persons, only employees with access to the system can get this information. Should a breach occur, these actions can be traced. If a person accessed these records illegally, he or she can be reprimanded, counseled, fired, fined or otherwise penalized per HIPAA.

Recently, such information was leaked through the website Facebook where a nursing student discussed a patient's confidential information. The nursing student was dismissed from the nursing program and faces penalties from HIPAA. All health care and personal information about a patient needs to stay in the facility. This is an ethical issue, because medical personnel are present when a patient is the most vulnerable.

Communicate with Other Health Care Professionals Using Appropriate Medical Terminology

In today's health care arena, a patient may come into contact with 50 medical personnel during any given hospital stay. As technology advances, these health care workers may not even see each other. Communication is at the center of safe patient care. Lack of communication can cause medical errors that may result in severe injury or death. In 2005, The Joint Commission (TJC) reported communication failures as the leading cause of medication errors, delays in treatment, and wrong-site surgeries. Remember that communication and team collaboration are important aspects of good patient care.

You must communicate professionally with other health care workers. Layperson's terminology is not acceptable. Remember you are a professional and will work with many types of patients in your daily activities. You must display professional language. Some rules to follow are:

- Do not use profanity or vulgar language.

- Never use slang.

- Always speak clearly, so you are not misunderstood.

- Use a soft tone and speak gently.

- When caring for a patient who is deaf or hard of hearing, drop the tone of your voice to a lower register (higher tones usually hardest to hear), speak clearly, and face the person.

- Never shout or yell.

- Never argue or fight with patients or their families. Always maintain a soft voice. If the patient or a family member begins getting upset maintain a soft voice.

When communicating with professional staff (nurses, doctors), always use medical terminology. If you do so, you will get more respect from the nurses and doctors.

Always dress professionally. If your uniform is dirty and wrinkled, you may be seen as an unprofessional person. Most facilities have a dress code, so be sure to follow it. Shoes should be clean and polished. Long hair should be tied back. Most facilities do not allow excessive body jewelry or visible tattoos. Seek out the advice of a professional on these issues before applying for a job.

Observe the Chain of Command in a Health Care Setting

In any organizational structure, a chain of command is meant to create a clear line of responsibility from the bottom to the top of the organization. A good organizational structure lets everyone know to whom to report and what their responsibilities are.

If an employee has a complaint, this chain of command gives him or her a direction to turn for assistance. However, if an employee is having trouble with his or her boss, this causes conflict. Furthermore, some employees do not report problems for fear of retaliation. Doctors are usually the boss or the one giving orders; an employee of the hospital may not agree with the order or there may be a conflict with hospital policy. If this occurs, the employee can go to their supervisor report the offense. Human resources can also be used for some complaints and will have any necessary paperwork.

The chain of command in any facility or agency is very much the same. It includes a Chief Nursing Officer (or Director of Nursing), Registered Nurse in Charge, Licensed Vocational Nurse, or Licensed Practical Nurse, then the CPCT. Every facility has an organizational chart that shows this chain of command. You can usually find it in the policy book. If you need to complain or report something – and you feel your supervisor is not giving the information to the people in charge – make an appointment with the next person in the chain of command. If you still cannot resolve the issue, go to the next person – and so on. Giving each person in the chain of command a chance to fix any situation is a professional courtesy. Don't stop until the problem is resolved. If a patient is involved and his or her health is at stake, you will assume the role of a patient advocate. Health care providers that know the chain of command can protect themselves, other nurses, and their facilities.

If a patient's life is at stake, there are a number of steps you must take:

1. First, call the nurse. If he or she does not respond, go to the charge nurse. The charge nurse has the power to get a response from the physician or whoever needs to be involved.

2. Should this action fail (or there is no charge nurse), move on to the Unit Director or Director of Nursing. These individuals are always on call.

3. If there is still a problem, contact the Medical Director or the Chief Executive Officer (CEO).

4. As always, document every move and why it was made. Complete incident reports if possible.

5. Finally, if the problem persists, involve the state's Department of Welfare.

Remember, it is not a weakness to ask for help. Solving problems is what the chain of command is designed to do. Many careers have been ruined and many patients have been harmed because the chain of command was not used. You should always be your patient's advocate.

Use Therapeutic Communication When Talking to Patients

To effectively communicate with a patient, a CPCT should ask open-ended questions that require more than a "yes" or "no" answer. Furthermore, the CPCT should focus on the patient's feelings, restate the patient's comments, and make sure that all responses are neutral. Remember that effective communication is appropriate, simple, adaptive, concise, and credible.

There are a variety of interpersonal communication techniques that a CPCT can use. These include the following.

1. Offering self – Express interest and concern.

2. Active listening – Pay close attention to verbal and nonverbal cues.

3. Exploring – Ask questions related to comments made by the patient.

4. Giving broad openings – Begin conversations with open-ended questions.

5. Silence – Pause during verbal comments to allow for introspection.

6. Stating the observed – Verbalize the patient's comments, allowing for validation and discussion.

7. Encouraging comparisons – Find similarities and differences between feelings and events.

8. Identifying themes – Ask the patient to identify repeated thoughts and behaviors.

9. Summarizing – Reiterate the discussion and draw conclusions.

10. Placing the event in time or sequence – Ask the patient to describe the relationship between events.

11. Voicing doubt – Express any uncertainty about the patient's comments.

12. Encouraging descriptions of perceptions – Have the patient describe his or her opinions.

13. Presenting reality or confronting – Express the reality of any situation.

14. Seeking clarification – Ask the patient to reiterate any unclear statements.

15. Verbalizing the implied – Rephrase the patient's comments for clarification.

16. Reflecting – Present the patient's statement in the form of a question.

17. Restating – Repeat the patient's words.

18. General leads – Use neutral expressions (such as "Go on").

19. Asking questions – Use open-ended questions to allow for discussion.

20. Empathy – Acknowledge the patient's feelings.

21. Focusing – Pursue any relevant topic.

22. Interpreting – Offer a new point of view to provide clarity.

23. Encouraging evaluation – Ask patients about the importance of various subjects.

24. Suggesting collaboration – Offer help to patients.

25. Encouraging goal setting – Ask patients to determine needed changes.

26. Encouraging formulation of a plan of action – Invite the patient to determine are needed.

27. Encouraging decisions – Have the patient choose among options.

28. Encouraging consideration of options – Have patients weigh the pros and cons of any action.

29. Giving information – Provide all the information needed.

30. Limit setting – Discourage nonproductive actions.

31. Supportive confrontation – Push for action, while acknowledging any difficulty.

32. Role playing – Practice specific situations.

33. Rehearsing – Have the patient verbally describe upcoming situations.

34. Feedback – Point out specific behaviors.

35. Encouraging evaluation – Invite the patient to appraise their actions.

36. Reinforcement – Offer positive feedback.

Summary

In this chapter, we covered a CPCT's professional responsibilities. You read about Basic Cardiac Life Support (BCLS) certification and the Health Insurance Portability and Accountability Act (HIPAA). We also covered the use of proper medical terminology, the chain of command, and the use of therapeutic communication.

Drill Questions

1. A CPCT is caring for his neighbor's mother. The neighbor asks the CPCT if her mother is undergoing physical therapy. Which of the following responses by the CPCT is appropriate?

    A. "She is a family member, so I can let you know after I return to work."
    B. "I can call the staff and get the answer for you."
    C. "I'm sorry, but I cannot discuss patients."
    D. "Why don't you call tomorrow and ask for that information?"

2. A CPCT is caring for a patient who is agitated. The best way to handle this patient is to

    A. speak louder.
    B. put the patient into a chair.
    C. speak softly and clearly.
    D. ask the patient to be quiet.

3. A CPCT's patient's blood pressure is 80/38 mm Hg, heart rate 112/min, respirations 26/min. The CPCT tells the nurse, but she is busy. The CPCT retakes the vital signs and finds they are now blood pressure 78/30 mm Hg, heart rate 120/min, respirations 28/min. The CPCT's next action should be to

    A. call the charge nurse of the floor and report the patient's vital signs.
    B. report these findings to the nurse .
    C. prop the patient up and check him or her again later.
    D. call the doctor to report the vital signs.

4. A CPCT enters the nurse's station to find a nurse lying on the floor. Which of the following actions should the CPCT take first?

    A. Shout her name to see if she is conscious.
    B. Feel for a pulse.
    C. Begin CPR immediately.
    D. Give two breaths and begin CPR.

5. Two nurses are in an elevator going to lunch. A CPCT overhears them talking about a patient. Which of the following responses is appropriate?

    A. "Tell me about that patient. I think I know her."
    B. "You shouldn't talk about patients in public places."
    C. Ask questions about the care being given.
    D. Ignore what is being said.

Drill Answers

1. A CPCT is caring for his neighbor's mother. The neighbor asks the CPCT if her mother is undergoing physical therapy. Which of the following responses by the CPCT is appropriate?

    A. "She is a family member, so I can let you know after I return to work."
    B. "I can call the staff and get the answer for you."
    C. "I'm sorry, but I cannot discuss patients."
    D. "Why don't you call tomorrow and ask for that information?"

    The CPCT's neighbor must go through proper channels to find this information.

2. A CPCT is caring for a patient who is agitated. The best way to handle this patient is to

    A. speak louder.
    B. put the patient into a chair.
    C. speak softly and clearly.
    D. ask the patient to be quiet.

    Speaking louder, grabbing the patient, or ignoring him or her could cause further agitation.

3. A CPCT's patient's blood pressure is 80/38 mm Hg, heart rate 112/min, respirations 26/min. The CPCT tells the nurse, but she is busy. The CPCT retakes the vital signs and finds they are now blood pressure 78/30 mm Hg, heart rate 120/min, respirations 28/min. The CPCT's next action should be to

    A. call the charge nurse of the floor and report the patient's vital signs.
    B. report these findings to the nurse .
    C. prop the patient up and check him or her again later.
    D. call the doctor to report the vital signs.

    This patient is in a shock state and cannot wait for more vital signs, so the charge nurse should be contacted. Furthermore, a CPCT would not call the doctor; the nurse should take this action.

4. A CPCT enters the nurse's station to find a nurse lying on the floor. Which of the following actions should the CPCT take first?

    A. Shout her name to see if she is conscious.
    B. Feel for a pulse.
    C. Begin CPR immediately.
    D. Give two breaths and begin CPR.

    In this case, the nurse may have fainted. Shouting may awaken the nurse.

5. Two nurses are in an elevator going to lunch. A CPCT overhears them talking about a patient. Which of the following responses is appropriate?

    A. "Tell me about that patient. I think I know her."
    B. "You shouldn't talk about patients in public places."
    C. Ask questions about the care being given.
    D. Ignore what is being said.

    Because this is a HIPAA violation, the CPCT should tell the nurses not to discuss patients in public places.

Terms and Definitions

Automated external defibrillator (AED) – A device that identifies cardiac arrhythmias and stops them by applying an electric charge to a patient's heart, which interrupts the arrhythmia and gives the patient's heart a chance to reset to a normal rhythm

Cardiopulmonary resuscitation (CPR) – A manual procedure involving chest compressions and rescue breathing that provides air exchange and blood circulation to a person whose heart has stopped beating

Chain of command – A military term that refers to the formal hierarchy within an organization; it is a pathway of communication, responsibility, and authority; it is important that each person in an organization be aware of their place, whom they report to, and whom reports to them

Compressions – The act of pressing down on the sternum of a patient in a rhythmic and intentional manner to stimulate the heart to circulate, or pump, blood throughout the patient's body; these are done in response to a patient who has no pulse, and is usually accompanied by rescue breathing; also known as chest compressions

Electronic health records (EHRs) – Computer systems for the storage, manipulation, and retrieval of patient information; replaces the traditional paper-based medical record; EHR generally refers to a system-wide application, such as in a hospital or across a health system, whereas an electronic medical record (EMR) is a single provider electronic record usually seen in a physician's office or a small clinic setting

Health Insurance Portability and Accountability Act of 1996 (HIPAA) – Legislation that established the foundation for privacy protection of health information (HIPAA Privacy Rule) and set the standards for the transmission of electronic health information (HIPAA Security Rule) to ensure its confidential transmission

HITECH Act of 2009 – Legislation that further delineates privacy and security issues around patients' protected health information and raises the penalties for any breach; it also changes the accountability to include individuals, not only organizations; in addition, it sets a goal for the transition to electronic records across all health care organizations and provides for an incentive, or financial program, to encourage quick adoption and use of electronic health record technology; the act is part of the American Reinvestment and Recovery Act of 2009 (ARRA)

Joint Commission (TJC) – An independent, nonprofit organization that accredits more than 19,000 health care facilities in the U.S.; accreditation is granted upon review of each facility's adherence to a set of standards around patient care, documentation, organization leadership, facilities, and more; although there are other accrediting agencies, accreditation by the Joint Commission remains the gold standard in hospital and health care accreditation; the Joint Commission was formally known as the Joint Commission on the Accreditation of Health Care Organizations (JCAHO)

Organizational chart – A graphical representation of the hierarchy, or chain of command in an organization, with names and titles in boxes that link to other boxes in vertical orientation to signify reporting structure or in horizontal orientation when duties are shared or exist outside the command structure; also known as an org chart; the chief executive officer or president of a firm appears at the top of an org chart; large organizations have multiple organizational charts that break into departmental hierarchies to show the details across the organization

Therapeutic communication – A face-to-face communication process; the goal of therapeutic communication is to promote a patient's physical and emotional well-being; specific techniques help the health care professional gather information they need to identify illness, assess patient behavior, evaluate for modification when necessary, and provide patient education

04 INFECTION CONTROL

Learning Objectives
After reading this chapter, the CPCT student will be able to:

- *Explain the benefits of adhering to universal precautions.*
- *Differentiate between the different types of isolation precautions.*
- *Understand the rationale for precautions.*
- *Define aseptic technique and sterile technique.*
- *Understand the different types of isolations.*
- *Understand how to maintain isolation.*
- *Understand biohazard bags and containers.*

Introduction

In this chapter, we will discuss concepts related to infection control. You'll learn about universal, standard, and transmission-based precautions. The chapter concludes with a 5-question self-assessment drill.

Use Universal Precautions, Standard Precautions, and Transmission-Based Precautions

The Centers for Disease Control (CDC) determine how infections are transmitted and record the symptoms of the exposed person. The CDC lists the methods health care workers use to prevent the spread of a particular disease. As late as 1996, health care workers called isolation and prevention "universal precautions" and used these precautions for bloody drainages. Today, these methods are called "standard precautions" and they include all body fluids, open skin lesions or wounds, and all mucous membranes or moist surfaces of the skin. All health care settings use standard precautions.

The isolation categories have also changed. These are now known as transmission precautions. Droplet precautions are used for influenza or airborne infections. When following these precautions, the health care worker must wear a mask to protect themselves from inhaling the infection of the patient. Under airborne precautions, workers must wear an N-95 respirator when entering the room with a suspected or confirmed tuberculosis patient or any airborne infection. To comply with contact precautions, you must wear a gown and gloves when working with patients. This protects the worker from contaminating their clothing when they come in contact with the patient and their environment.

If a health care worker fails to observe the policy and procedures of infection control, he will face charges of misconduct. If he is a licensed health care worker, his licensure or certification can be revoked by the issuing state.

To stop an infection from spreading, you must break the chain of transmission. The best method is sterilization and disinfection. Patients cannot be sterilized or disinfected, but CPCTs can keep their environments cleaned daily, control draining wounds, stop bleeding, and keep any body fluids from leaking. If this happens, the environment must be cleansed with a disinfectant. Use a mask when the infection is airborne, and using contact isolation when the infection is transmitted by contact. Vaccinations should be encouraged for compromised patients and health care workers.

To control transmission:

1. Undertake good hand-washing hygiene (using alcohol-based hand rubs) before and after touching patients. This is the single most effective means of stopping infections.

2. Use barriers, such as gloves, mask, and gowns, appropriately.

3. Sterilize or disinfect environments and equipment.

4. Isolate communicable patients.

5. Clean the patient's environment through appropriate ventilation, waste management, and frequently-washed linen.

6. Use sharps and biohazard containers to prevent injuries.

7. Use needleless devices as much as possible.

8. Use standard infection-control techniques.

All facilities must monitor infection control, to make sure patients, community members, and staff are safe.

Dispose of Biohazardous Material Properly, as Dictated by OSHA

Items that have sharp edges (such as razors, needles, and broken glass) should be disposed of in a sharps container. A sharps container is puncture-proof, fluid-impervious, sealable case. When the container is full, lock the lid and have housekeeping replace it.

A number of federal agencies have mandated the use of biohazard bags in the disposal of hazardous waste, including the Environmental Protection Agency (EPA) and the Occupational, Safety and Health Administration (OSHA). Some states and local government agencies have regulations enforcing these policies. If a facility fails to follow the regulations, it can be fined, penalized, or even closed.

Red bags or containers usually have the biohazard sign on the side. The Material Safety Data Sheets (MSDS) manual explains where these are disposed and how they should be handled. Dispose of all bio-hazardous waste in an EPA-approved waste recycling center.

Performing Aseptic Technique

Asepsis means the absence of contamination. Aseptic technique and medical asepsis are the same technique, so the terms are interchangeable. This may also be referred to as clean technique. The technique reduces the chances of contamination and the spread of infections.

Hand-washing is an aseptic technique used to prevent the spread of infection. Health care workers attain asepsis in many other ways. For example, they may disinfect (or remove all pathogens) from rooms, surfaces, and objects used during a hospital stay. This can be done by using chemical, gas, steam, heat, or ultraviolet rays. When changing a wound dressing, aseptic (clean) technique is used – unless sterile technique is ordered (see below). For a dressing change, aseptic technique is performed as follows:

1. Wash hands.

2. Don clean gloves.

3. Remove dirty dressing.

4. Remove gloves and discard along with the dirty dressing.

5. Wash hands.

6. Apply new gloves.

7. Grasp sterile dressing on one side and apply the sterile underside of the dressing to the wound.

8. Tape the clean dressing.

9. Remove gloves and wash hands.

Performing Sterile Technique

Sterile means without life. The terms sterile technique and surgical technique are interchangeable. No item that is clean can touch the sterile field, because even clean items have germs. A sterile technique is used during a Foley catheter insertion. Surgery is also performed using sterile technique. Surgical suites are sterile and all health care personnel must put on sterile clothing and sterile gloves to go in the suites and assist with surgery. In these situations, sterile equipment is used, including sterile gloves. A sterile field is set up to prevent the spread of germs. All sterile items must be kept above the waist to prevent possible contamination. If an item should touch within an inch of the edge of the sterile field, it is considered contaminated.

Summary

In this chapter, we covered infection control. Infection control includes universal, standard, and transmission-based precautions. You also learned how to dispose of bio-hazardous materials, to perform aseptic technique, and to perform sterile technique.

Drill Questions

1. A CPCT is inserting a urinary catheter. He creates a sterile field between the legs of the patient, but the patient moves his leg onto the sterile field, touching everything. Which of the following actions should the CPCT take next?

   A. Remove the sterile field, get a new catheter set, and start over.
   B. Remove only the items the patient's foot touched and begin the insertion.
   C. Continue to do the catheterization and make sure to tell the doctor what happened.
   D. Ask a coworker to retrieve the contaminated items and continue with the procedure.

2. A CPCT enters a room with contact isolation and finds a doctor standing at the bedside without a gown or gloves. Which of the following actions should the CPCT take next?

   A. Remind him that the patient is in contact isolation.
   B. Ask if the patient has been removed from isolation.
   C. Give the doctor a gown and gloves.
   D. Assume a gown and gloves are not necessary.

3. A CPCT is teaching a family member how to change a patient's dressings. Which of the following actions by the family member indicates a need for further teaching?

   A. The family member does the technique quickly.
   B. The family member forgets to tell the patient that they are changing the dressing.
   C. The sterile field is set up correctly and sterile gloves are applied.
   D. The family member does not wash her hands after removing the dirty dressing.

4. To prevent back strain or injury, a CPCT should perform which of the following actions when changing the dressing on a patient's abdomen?

   A. Have a wide base of support.
   B. Raise the bed to a working height.
   C. Move the patient to the side of the bed opposite the CPCT.
   D. Position yourself near the head of the bed.

5. A patient has a viral infection that is spread through by touch. The CPCT should take which of the following precautions when working with this patient?

   A. Airborne precautions
   B. Droplet precautions
   C. Isolation precaution
   D. Contact precautions

Drill Answers

1. A CPCT is inserting a urinary catheter. He creates a sterile field between the legs of the patient, but the patient moves his leg onto the sterile field, touching everything. Which of the following actions should the CPCT take next?

   A. Remove the sterile field, get a new catheter set, and start over.
   B. Remove only the items the patient's foot touched and begin the insertion.
   C. Continue to do the catheterization and make sure to tell the doctor what happened.
   D. Ask a coworker to retrieve the contaminated items and continue with the procedure.

   Beginning with a new kit guarantees the procedure's sterility.

2. A CPCT enters a room with contact isolation and finds a doctor standing at the bedside without a gown or gloves. Which of the following actions should the CPCT take next?

   A. Remind him that the patient is in contact isolation.
   B. Ask if the patient has been removed from isolation.
   C. Give the doctor a gown and gloves.
   D. Assume a gown and gloves are not necessary.

   This is the most professional way to handle the situation.

3. A CPCT is teaching a family member how to change a patient's dressings. Which of the following actions by the family member indicates a need for further teaching?

   A. The family member does the technique quickly.
   B. The family member forgets to tell the patient that they are changing the dressing.
   C. The sterile field is set up correctly and sterile gloves are applied.
   D. The family member does not wash her hands after removing the dirty dressing.

   Hand-washing is the most crucial part of this procedure.

4. To prevent back strain or injury, a CPCT should perform which of the following actions when changing the dressing on a patient's abdomen?

   A. Have a wide base of support.
   B. Raise the bed to a working height.
   C. Move the patient to the side of the bed opposite the CPCT.
   D. Position yourself near the head of the bed.

   In this case, raising the bed is the most effective method of reducing strain.

5. A patient has a viral infection that is spread through by touch. The CPCT should take which of the following precautions when working with this patient?

    A. Airborne precautions
    B. Droplet precautions
    C. Isolation precaution
    D. Contact precautions

In this case, the CPCT should use contact precautions, because the virus is transmitted through contact.

Terms and Definitions

Aseptic – A condition free from germs or infection

Biohazard – Anything that is potentially harmful to humans, other species, or the environment

Compromised host – A person who lacks resistance to infection, owing to a deficiency in any of their defenses

Environment – The surroundings, conditions, or influences that affect an organism or the cells within it

Exposure – Contact with an agent able to cause disease or injury, such as bacterium or other contagious microbes

Infection – A disease caused by microorganisms, especially those that release toxins or invade body tissues

Isolation – The physical separation of individuals with certain infections from others; used to prevent or limit the transmission of this infection

Nosocomial – Pertaining to or occurring in a health care setting (such as a nursing home or hospital)

Pathogen – A microorganism capable of producing a disease

Precaution – An action taken in advance to protect against danger or possible failure

Standard precautions – Guidelines recommended by the CDC used to reduce the risk of the spread of infection in hospitals

Sharps – A colloquial term for medical articles that may cause punctures or cuts to those handling them; includes broken medical glassware, syringes, needles, scalpel blades, suture needles, and disposable razors

Transmission – Transfer of anything, including a disease or hereditary characteristic

CHAPTER 05 PHLEBOTOMY

Learning Objectives

After reading this chapter, the CPCT student will be able to:

- *Understand how to perform venipuncture correctly and safely.*

- *Understand how to obtain and process special collections correctly and safely.*

- *Understand how to process specimens correctly and safely.*

Introduction

This chapter is designed to provide the learner with the information needed to successfully perform basic venipuncture, and finger and heel stick blood collections; how to obtain and process special collections (e.g., blood cultures); and how to process patient specimens correctly and safely. The learner will be introduced to the concepts of sterility, patient identification and assessment, identification and management of complications, and safe and correct ways to transmit information.

This chapter is divided into three sections:

1. Primary Collections

2. Special Collections

3. Specimen Processing

Each section contains a list of key instructional content that will be discussed.

At the end of the chapter there will be nine multiple choice test questions. Answers and rationales will be provided as well. A list of terms and definitions also will be provided.

PRIMARY COLLECTIONS

The key instructional content for this section is:

- Venipuncture technique

- Capillary specimen collection

- Finger sticks and heel sticks

- Patient safety

- Complications associated with venipuncture

- Order of the draw

- Identifying and managing adverse reactions

- Blood collection tubes

    - Identifying the proper tube for specific tests

    - Proper handling of tubes after blood collection

- Equipment needed for blood collection

- Quality control of blood collection equipment

- Infection control

- Safety during venipuncture

- Medical emergencies

Venipuncture Technique

Venipuncture is defined as the puncturing of a vein to obtain a blood sample; another commonly used term for this process is phlebotomy. Most venipunctures are performed to obtain a blood sample that can be used to measure specific blood components such as creatinine, electrolytes, hemoglobin, or to measure drug levels. Venipuncture then is used to

- Diagnose an illness

- Determine the health of an individual or the health of a particular organ system

- Determine the effectiveness of a treatment and/or therapy.

Venipuncture is a relatively simple procedure. However, there are complications associated with venipuncture. Venipuncture must be performed correctly, so that the blood specimen can be accurately measured.

Correctly performing a venipuncture requires:

- Patient identification, patient assessment, and using the right equipment

- Patient preparation

- Proper technique

- Maintaining patient safety

Patient Identification and Assessment, Using the Right Equipment

Correctly identifying the patient is the first step in the venipuncture procedure, and it is critically important. However, you should always identify yourself as well. Patients have a right to know who is taking care of them, and you should always tell them who you are and what you are going to do.

Next, identify the patient. This should always be an active process. Always ask the patient to tell you his or her identifying information. Example: "Could you please tell me your full name and your date of birth?" Never tell the patient this information and wait to see if he or she agrees. Example: "Is your name John Smith? Is your date of birth November 20th, 1949?" The patient may not hear you correctly. You should use a minimum of two forms of identification (full name and date of birth are the most commonly used). Depending on where you work, you may be required to use a third form, such as the last four digits of a patient's Social Security Number. A patient's full name, date of birth, and Social Security Number are acceptable for identifying a patient. Addresses and telephone numbers are not; these can change, but the other information doesn't.

The identifying information the patient tells you should match the information on the laboratory requisition form (this will be explained later) and on the patient's medical record. If the information does not match, do not perform the venipuncture. Also, patients will often be wearing a disposable wrist band that has identifying information on it. You should never use the wrist band as the only way of identifying a patient. It is possible that the wrist band was applied to the wrong patient.

The next step is to assess the patient. The purposes of patient assessment are to determine if the patient

- Can understand what will happen during the venipuncture

- Can tolerate the venipuncture

- Is at risk for the complications associated with venipuncture

Patients must have the mental acuity to understand what will happen during the venipuncture. If they do not, the venipuncture procedure will be unnecessarily painful and frightening, the patient will not be able to cooperate, and the procedure could be dangerous. This part of the assessment is simple. Listen and watch carefully when the patient identifies himself or herself. If the patient cannot do this quickly and accurately, ask several questions to determine if the patient is oriented to time, place, and person. Example: "What is your doctor's name? Why are you here today?" If there is any reasonable suspicion that the patient does not have the mental acuity to understand what the venipuncture is and what will happen during venipuncture, do not perform the procedure. Do not leave the patient alone, but notify a supervisor immediately.

In order to know if the patient will be able to tolerate the venipuncture, ask these questions:

- "Have you ever had blood drawn?"

- "Have you ever had problems during a venipuncture?"

    o   If the patient says yes, find out what happened. If the patient cannot remember, ask these questions.

        - "You say that you had a problem the last time someone took your blood."

        - "Did you have a lot of pain, a lot of bruising, or bleeding?"

        - "Did you have chest pain, dizziness, fainting, or nausea?"

Use your eyes and ears. Is there anything about the patient's body language, posture, tone of voice, or what he or she says that indicates the patient is anxious or frightened?

Following that, you should always check to see if the patient is at risk for complications associated with venipuncture. There are many complications associated with venipuncture, but when you are performing patient assessment focus on patient factors that might increase the risk of excessive bleeding. Check the patient's chart – and ask the patient – to see if the he or she is taking any medications that would increase the risk of bleeding. Is the patient taking aspirin, warfarin (Coumadin), or any other medication that can increase bleeding? This information should be on the patient's record, but it may have been omitted.

Collecting and using the right equipment will help the venipuncture process to be completed quickly and efficiently. Gather everything you will need and put it in a convenient place next to the patient. Most clinics and laboratories use large amounts of equipment with high turnover rates, so expired equipment would be very unlikely. However, you should check the sterility expiration date on the blood collection tubes, needles, and any other equipment. The basic equipment for needed for venipuncture are as follows.

Personal protective equipment

Use disposable latex gloves when performing a venipuncture. Use one pair for each venipuncture; do not reuse them and never wear the same pair of gloves when caring for more than one patient. You can use vinyl gloves if you (or the patient) have a latex allergy. Using gloves when performing a venipuncture is mandatory. Gloves will help protect you in the event that blood is spilled, and they are also another level of protection for the patient.

You should also wear a laboratory coat or some sort of covering to prevent skin contamination with blood. Other personal protective equipment (PPE) (such as shoe covers and hair covers) are not needed. Face masks or respirators are only needed if the patient has an illness that is transmitted by the respiratory route. Protective eye wear and a face shield are not needed, unless there is a clear risk of blood splatters.

Isopropyl alcohol swabs

These are used to clean the skin before inserting the needle. They will be discussed in more detail later in the chapter.

Gauze pads

One-inch-by-one-inch gauze pads are used to cover the venipuncture site after the needle has been removed. These do not have to be sterile. They should never be reused.

Tourniquet

Tourniquets used for venipuncture are typically latex, but non-latex tourniquets are available. Although tourniquets can be reused, they should be discarded if they are soiled, obviously contaminated, or come into contact with blood.

Needles

Needles used for venipuncture are sterile and disposable. Venipuncture needles (and all needles that break the surface of the skin) should never be reused, even if the needle will be used again for the same patient. Sterile means that the needles have been processed, so that there are absolutely no microorganisms on the needle.

Blood collection tubes

These glass or plastic tubes hold approximately 6-10 mL of blood. The inside of a blood collection tube is sterile, but the outside is not. The tubes have an opening at one end that is sealed with a rubber stopper. When the tubes are manufactured, the air in the tube is removed, and the rubber stopper is placed over the opening to seal the tube. The tubes then have enough vacuum (negative pressure) so that when they are attached to a needle that has punctured a vein, blood will be drawn into the collection tube. The tubes are identified by the rubber stopper that seals the tube. The color of the stopper indicates what additive is inside, and the additive determines which specific blood test the tube should be used for. For example, a blue top collection tube is used to obtain blood for a prothrombin time (PT) test. The PT test measures the ability of the blood to clot, and a blue top tube has sodium citrate inside. Sodium citrate prevents the blood from clotting in the tube, which ensures that the PT test is accurate. Phlebotomy technicians must know and use the proper tube for each test.

Pediatric blood collection tubes

Blood collection tubes used for children are smaller than those used for adults. The reduced size results in less vacuum inside. The vacuum inside adult blood collection tubes is much higher than the pressure inside the blood vessels of a child. This vacuum would collapse a child's vein, and make it impossible to collect blood. Pediatric blood collection tubes are proportional to adult tubes (i.e., color, specific tubes for specific tests, etc.), but they are approximately half as big.

Winged infusion set

A winged infusion set is commonly known by the term Butterfly needle. (Note: Butterfly is a brand name, but the term Butterfly has become common usage for all winged infusion sets). A winged infusion set consists of:

- A sterile needle

- A short length of flexible plastic tubing

- Another sterile needle at the other end of the plastic tubing

The second needle is covered with a rubber sheath. After the first needle has been inserted into the vein, the second needle is used to puncture the rubber collection tube. As the second needle punctures the stopper, the rubber sheath slides back, the lumen (the inside of a needle or tube) of the second needles is exposed, and blood flows from the vein into the collection tube.

Vacutainer

Vacutainer is like Butterfly needle in that it is a brand name, but the term is commonly used for all similar phlebotomy equipment. Vacutainer phlebotomy equipment consists of a double-ended sterile needle with one end covered by a plastic protective cap and the other end covered with a rubber sheath. The two needles are joined by a threaded plastic connector. The needle is screwed into a plastic sleeve that has a small opening in one end for the needle and another, larger opening into which the blood collection tubes are inserted. The Vacutainer system works like the winged infusion set.

Lancets

A lancet is a small sterile blade that is used to perform a finger stick or heel stick phlebotomy. The lancet is used to puncture the skin and collect blood from a capillary.

Patient Preparation

There are two parts to patient preparation:

1. Patient education

2. Finding and preparing a site for the venipuncture

Patient education does not need to be lengthy or complicated, and you do not need to use technical terms. Tell the patient what you are going to do, what to expect, and what to do if complications occur after the venipuncture. Follow these steps.

- Tell the patient the steps of the procedure.

- Tell the patient that during the venipuncture he or she will feel slight pain when the needle is inserted and while the tubes are being filled.

- Tell the patient to let you know immediately if he or she is experiencing any severe pain or feels sick in any way.

- Tell the patient about the possible complications of venipuncture (excessive bruising, hematoma, infection, prolonged bleeding, and serious pain) and tell the patient what to do if these should occur. Do this before the venipuncture, but do so briefly. After the venipuncture you should repeat this information.

- Ask the patient if he or she has any questions or concerns.

Finding and preparing a site for venipuncture begins with hand washing. Wash your hands with soap and water or an alcohol-based hand sanitizer. Hand washing must be done before and after performing the procedure. After you have washed your hands, put on disposable gloves. Ask the patient to extend an arm and turn it so the palm is facing up. Then search for a vein by visual examination and by palpation.

The first place to look for a vein is the antecubital fossa. The antecubital (AC) fossa is the area of skin between the forearm and the upper arm, commonly called the "bend" or the "crook" of the arm. The AC fossa is the preferred site for venipuncture, because there are several large veins close to the surface there that can easily be seen. The three veins located in the AC fossa that can be used for phlebotomy are:

1. Median cubital vein – This vein is often the first choice of phlebotomy technicians. It is a large vein located in the center or near the center of the antecubital fossa, and it does not usually move when punctured. If the patient is obese, the median cubital vein may not be visible, but it can usually be palpated.

2. Cephalic vein – The cephalic vein is usually the second choice for venipuncture. The cephalic vein is located in lateral aspect of the antecubital fossa. It is a large vein and it can usually be seen. However, it tends to roll and cannot be easily stabilized.

3. Brachial vein – The brachial vein should be the last choice when performing a venipuncture. The brachial vein is located in the antecubital fossa on the medial aspect of the forearm. It is a large vein, but it is located very close to the brachial artery. It is not usually visible, and it tends to roll.

Examine the antecubital fossa. When you see a vein that looks suitable, palpate the vein. Palpation is a medical term that means touching with the fingers. Palpation will help you avoid puncturing an artery (arteries have a pulse, veins do not) and let you know if there is any condition of the vein you can't see that would make the it unsuitable for a venipuncture. A vein suitable for venipuncture should be soft, flexible, and non-tender. Veins may not be hardened, inflexible or tender (thus unsuitable for venipuncture), due to one or more of the following conditions.

- **Sclerosis** – Sclerosis is a process that happens to the blood vessels as people age. The blood vessels gradually become hard, inflexible, and narrowed, and they cannot be used for venipuncture.

- Tortuous veins – Tortuous veins do not run in a straight line, but twist and turn. Because of that, it can be easy to push the needle completely through the wall of the vein.

- Thrombotic veins – A thrombus is the medical term for a blood clot inside a blood vessel. A vein with a thrombus may feel hard and inflexible, and may be tender to the touch.

- Fragile veins – Fragile veins are quite thin and not strong. When they are palpated, they collapse very easily and do not refill very quickly. Many elderly people have veins that are fragile. Fragile veins are often very close to the surface, very dark, very thin, and collapse easily when palpated. They can rupture easily during a venipuncture.

- **Phlebitis** – Phlebitis is the medical term for inflammation of a blood vessel. A vein that is phlebitic will be tender and warm to the touch, and the area around the vein may appear red.

Venipuncture should not be performed on a vein that falls into one of the aforementioned categories. The venipuncture will be painful, the veins will be easily damaged, the vein will be difficult or impossible to puncture, and the blood supply through the veins may be poor.

If you cannot see or palpate a vein, there are several techniques that may be helpful. Place the patient's arm below the level of the heart for several minutes. This decreases the return of blood to the heart and allows the veins to fill. A warm compress may help, too. The heat will dilate the veins, and you may be able to see or palpate them. However, perhaps the most helpful technique is to slow down. Take your time, and you will almost always find a suitable vein. More often than not, you will find a suitable vein if you wait a few minutes.

If you cannot find a vein, ask another technician to try, ask your supervisor for advice, or notify the physician.

What should you do if you cannot see or feel a vein in the antecubital fossa? And what if neither the left nor right arm can be used for a venipuncture? The patient may have an IV line in his or her left arm and a dialysis shunt in his or her right arm.

There are other veins that can be used for venipuncture. However, these veins should only be used as a "last resort," and only if the person performing the venipuncture is experienced and very skilled at venipuncture. The other veins that may be used for venipuncture are as follows.

- **Hand and wrist veins** – Veins in the dorsum of the hand are easily seen and palpated, but they also tend to be more fragile than the veins in the antecubital fossa. They tend to roll because they are very superficial often small. Venipuncture of the veins on the dorsum is also more painful than venipuncture of a vein in the AC fossa. Even if the veins of the dorsum are large and can be stabilized, accessing these veins is difficult. They are often short, so it is difficult to achieve a good angle. They are also thin, so it is easy to push the needle completely through the vein. Veins on the underside of the wrist can be used, but they are very close to arteries and nerves. Because their location, they are physically difficult to access.

- **Ankle and foot veins** – The veins of the ankle or the foot should be the last choice for a venipuncture. These veins are difficult to access and easy to injure, and venipuncture of these veins is painful. Also, the circulation of the lower extremities may also be compromised by common medical problems such as diabetes or peripheral vascular disease. Venipuncture could cause an infection, phlebitis, or a hematoma. If your only option is an ankle or foot vein, check with the nurse before performing the venipuncture.

Never perform venipuncture in an arm:

- That has an IV line with IV fluids infusing

- That has a dialysis shunt

- On the same side of the body where a mastectomy was performed

Intravenous fluids can mix with the blood sample and affect the results. The circulation in an arm with a dialysis shut may be compromised. If a venipuncture causes a hematoma or excessive bleeding, the arm could be damaged. Lymph nodes may be removed during a mastectomy, so the circulation in the arm on that side may be compromised and a venipuncture could be risky.

Cleaning the site is the next step. Venipuncture is an invasive procedure; when you are performing a venipuncture you are breaking the surface of the skin. The skin is one of the body's major defenses against infection. Venipuncture potentially provides an entry point for microorganisms and puts the patient at risk for the transmission of diseases.

In almost all clinics, hospitals, and laboratories, the standard method for cleaning a venipuncture site is to scrub the area with 70% isopropyl alcohol. Isopropyl alcohol kills microorganisms by damaging cell walls, and it is most effective when the concentration is between 60% and 90%. The most common concentration used is 70%. Other germicides (e.g., chlorhexidine and iodine) can be used for a routine venipuncture, and they may be used for special collections. Isopropyl alcohol is preferred, because it dries quickly, does not leave a residue, is not highly irritating, does not obscure the venipuncture site, and does not dry the skin.

The isopropyl alcohol is supplied as a sterile swab. These swabs are one-inch-by-one-inch pieces of thin gauze or paper that are saturated with isopropyl alcohol and individually packaged. The swabs are sterile, disposable, and intended to be used once for one patient. Never reuse a swab. If you must re-clean a venipuncture site, use a new swab. Open the alcohol swab package, remove the swab, and scrub the venipuncture site. Use a circular motion and start from the inside and work out. Clean an area 3 to 4 inches in diameter and then discard the swab. Wait approximately 30 seconds for the alcohol to dry. Do not touch the site after it has been cleaned; doing so will contaminate the area. When the area is dry, you are now ready to perform the venipuncture.

After the alcohol has dried, apply a tourniquet. Wrap the tourniquet around the patient's upper arm approximately 3 to 4 inches above the antecubital fossa and then tighten it with a slip knot. The tourniquet will partially occlude blood flow through the veins. This will dilate the veins and they will be easier to see, making the venipuncture easier to perform. The tourniquet should be tight, but it should not be painful. Always ask the patient if it is too tight. A tourniquet that is too tight is not only painful for the patient but can also alter test results.

How tight should the tourniquet be? The tourniquet is used to dilate the veins, so it should be tight enough to accomplish this, but should not cause pain or interfere with the accuracy of a test. The best way to know when the pressure is correct is with a "hands-on" demonstration from an experienced professional. Once the correct amount of tourniquet pressure has been demonstrated, it will be easy to understand and duplicate.

You may see some technicians ask patients to make a fist after a tourniquet has been applied. This is not an acceptable technique, and for some blood samples it is contraindicated. Clenching the hand to make a fist may dilate the veins and make them easier to see, but there is evidence that it can change the blood concentration.

Proper Venipuncture Technique

Performing a venipuncture correctly takes practice. Performing a good venipuncture requires good hand-eye coordination and tactile feedback.

Performing a venipuncture correctly also requires knowledge of standards and practices (e.g., infection control; and, recognizing, preventing, and managing complications). These standards and practices help reduce the incidence of adverse effects and injuries. They also ensure that the venipuncture will be safe and relatively painless.

The step-by-step process of the venipuncture is as follows. Begin with the steps already discussed:

- Introduce yourself.

- Identify the patient.

- Check the laboratory requisition form.

- Have the patient sit or lie down. Do not perform venipuncture if the patient is standing. If the patient loses consciousness, he or she will fall and could be injured. (This will be discussed in the section on complications).

- Assemble the equipment, wash your hands, and put on disposable gloves. Make sure the equipment sterility expiration date has not passed.

- Locate a suitable vein.

- Clean the venipuncture site.

- Apply the tourniquet.

After completing these steps, move on as follows.

Stabilize the vein

Do not touch the area that was cleaned. Use your fingers to spread the skin around the site to make it tight. This will stabilize the vein, prevent it from rolling, and make the venipuncture less painful. If you push a needle through skin that is loose and flaccid, it will be very painful and the likelihood of a successful venipuncture is much lower.

Uncap and inspect the needle

Remove the cap from the needle and inspect the needle tip for burrs and a blunt edge. Discard the needle if it is found to be defective.

Insert the needle

The needle should be inserted at an angle between 15 and 30 degrees. This angle is used because it:

- Allows the phlebotomy technician room to work

- Reduces the risk of pushing the needle through the back wall of the vein

- Allows the best blood flow through the needle

The needle should be inserted with the opening (the beveled side) be facing up. If it is inserted with the opening facing down, the venipuncture will be more difficult and more painful. Also, if the needle is inserted with the bevel facing down, there is a slight possibility that the opening of the needle could be occluded by the back wall of the vein.

Determining how much force should be used when inserting the needle requires hands-on practice. However, it is not too difficult and most people quickly become comfortable with inserting the needle.

Most patients easily tolerate venipuncture, and the majority of patients would say that the needle insertion causes only minor and temporary pain. Regardless, the needle insertion does hurt, so you should always tell the patient when you are going to insert the needle and check with the patient several times during the procedure.

Release the tourniquet

Once the needle has entered the vein, and you have attached the first tube to the infusion set or the Vacutainer holder, release the tourniquet. The tourniquet should not be left on for longer than 1 minute. If the tourniquet is not released three complications are possible:

1. **Hemolysis** – This means destruction of blood cells. If blood cells become hemolyzed, the laboratory test result may be inaccurate because electrolytes and other intracellular components that are normally contained inside the cells will now be circulating in the serum. Laboratory tests are intended to measure electrolytes and blood components that are normally found in the serum.

2. **Petechiae** – These are very tiny hemorrhages that look like small red or purple spots on the skin. Petechiae are not dangerous, but they are unpleasant and upsetting for the patient.

3. **Hemoconcentration** – Prolonged application of a tourniquet can force fluids out of the blood. Concentration of the blood components will be artificially increased and the blood test will be inaccurate.

Attach the collection tubes

After the venipuncture has been made, attach the blood collection tubes to the Vacutainer or the infusion set and fill each one in turn. It's not uncommon for patients to become concerned at the amount of blood that is being removed, especially if 5 or 6 collection tubes are needed. If this happens, simply tell the patient that the amount of blood being taken in relation to total blood volume is very small and that no harm will be done. At most, you would be removing less than 6 teaspoons or so of blood, and the body has at least five liters. Each tube takes about 5 seconds to fill. The tubes must be filled in the correct sequence, and the tubes must be handled correctly after they have been filled.

Order of the draw

Filling the blood collection tubes in the correct sequence is called **the order of the draw.** The order of the draw is important for several reasons, including that it prevents preservatives or additives that are contained in one blood collection tube (e.g., lavender top collection tubes contain EDTA, a chemical that prevents blood from clotting) from being introduced into another blood specimen and affecting test results.

The correct order of the draw for standard phlebotomy collection is:

1. Blood cultures or sterile specimens

2. Blue top tube

3. Red top tube

4. Green top tube

5. Lavender top tube

6. Gray

Some facilities may routinely order special testing that requires additional (different additive) tubes to be drawn. These would most likely be sequenced after the lavender top tube. In addition, depending on the venipuncture method used, extra care may be required when drawing blue top tubes for coagulation testing. Be sure to check for the standard procedures at your facility so you can be prepared for any patient phlebotomy request.

Inverting the tubes

Once the tubes have been filled, they must then be inverted. Most people do this with one hand during the venipuncture, but it can be done after the venipuncture has been completed. Invert the tube by holding it in your hand and then turning your wrist, so that the bottom of the tube is pointing upwards. To complete the inversion, simply reverse this movement. To put it another way, an inversion is one complete turn of the wrist; the bottom of the tube is pointed up and then pointed down. Blood collection tubes are inverted in order to mix the additives in the collection tubes with the blood sample. This is necessary to mix the additives with the blood, to prevent the blood from clotting, and to make sure the test result is accurate. The number of inversions will vary depending on the color of the tube. Follow these guidelines:

- Blue top tubes: 3-4 inversions

- EDTA and heparin containing tubes (lavender top and green top): 8-10 inversions

- Serum separator tubes (SST, red tops) and serum tubes (red tops without the separating gel): 5 inversions

Removing the needle

After the last tube has been filled, place a gauze pad gently over the needle. Quickly remove the needle and immediately apply firm pressure to the venipuncture site. Always use a gauze pad and always wear gloves. If possible, remove your fingers from the gauze pad and have the patient apply the pressure. This will allow you to invert the tubes or do another task. If the patient cannot help, apply firm pressure for approximately 30 seconds and then place the adhesive bandage over the gauze. Instruct the patient to leave the bandage on for 15 minutes.

Labeling the specimens

Labeling specimens correctly is critically important. The labels have the patient's name and identifying information, and they should be attached to the blood collection tubes. They should not be attached to a bag or a container that the collection tubes are carried in. Most laboratories require the phlebotomy technician to place the date, time, and initials on the label. Be very careful when labeling specimens. Mislabeling can have serious consequences.

Handling and transporting specimens

Specimens also must be handled correctly. Most blood specimens require only the recommended number of inversions and being stored at room temperature, but there are exceptions. Some specimens must be stored on ice and transported to the laboratory within a certain period of time. Familiarize yourself with the facility's protocols for transporting blood specimens. If you are transporting specimens to the laboratory, there should be documentation for when the specimen arrives in the laboratory and who receives the specimen.

Finishing the procedure

Discard the needle and any other hazardous waste items in a hazardous waste disposal container. Remember that needles are disposable and should never be reused. Never recap needles – this is the No. 1 cause of needle sticks in health care settings. Remove your gloves and wash your hands.

Reporting test results

There may be occasions in which you will be asked to transmit laboratory test results. The keys to doing this accurately and correctly are repetition and confirmation.

After the Venipuncture

Check the patient after you have finished. Do this visually and by asking the patient how he or she is feeling. If the patient has tolerated the procedure, the next step is to tell the patient about potential complications and what to do if they should occur. These complications include:

- Excessive bleeding – A small amount of bleeding after a venipuncture is normal. However, if the gauze pad used to cover the venipuncture site becomes completely soaked with blood, that would be considered excessive. Tell the patient to return to the laboratory or ask a physician or a nurse for help if this occurs.

- Excessive pain – Venipuncture should not cause excessive pain. The patient should seek help if he or she has any severe pain after a venipuncture or if the pain from venipuncture lasts more than a few minutes after the procedure has been completed.

- Lack of sensation – The patient should be instructed to immediately return to the laboratory or ask a physician or nurse for help if he or she has numbness or tingling in the arm that was used for a venipuncture.

- Excessive bruising – A small bruise at the venipuncture site is normal. However, if the bruising is larger than the size of the gauze pad, the patient should ask a physician or nurse for advice.

- Signs of infection – If the venipuncture site becomes red, swollen, or painful, or if there is pus at the site, there may be an infection in the tissue. Patients should see a physician if this occurs.

- Patient feels unwell – Patients who need blood tests often have an ongoing illness or a chronic medical condition, and they may develop signs or symptoms as a reaction to a venipuncture. You cannot anticipate all possible problems patients may have after a venipuncture. The best approach is to simply tell patients that, if they feel sick in any way, they should ask a physician or a nurse for help.

After you have told the patient about the complications of venipuncture and what to do if they should occur, it is helpful to ask the patient to briefly repeat this information back to you. This confirms that the patient understands what you have said.

Troubleshooting Technical Problems during Venipuncture

Most venipunctures can be performed quickly and easily, but technical problems can occur.

What if you are performing a venipuncture and the blood flow stops? This happens because:

- There is not sufficient vacuum in the system.

- The patency of the system has been compromised (the system is blocked).

Blood collection tubes rarely malfunction, but it is possible for the vacuum in the tube to be insufficient to withdraw blood, or you may have incorrectly punctured the rubber stopper on the tube. Try another tube. If this does not work, check to make sure you have released the tourniquet. You should also make sure that the needle has not been advanced too far – if so, it may be touching the back wall of the vein. It is also possible that the needle has not been advanced deep enough into the vein.

Complications of the Venipuncture Procedure

Complications associated with phlebotomy are not common and are rarely serious.

- Nerve damage – This is a very rare complication. If a patient tells you that he or she has a sensation of numbness or a feeling of pins and needles immediately during a venipuncture, you may have hit a nerve.

- **Hematoma** – This is the most common complication associated with phlebotomy. A hematoma is defined as a "localized collection of blood." A hematoma can happen when the wall of the blood vessel is damaged during a venipuncture. The needle is pushed through both walls of the vein, and blood leaks into the tissue. Hematomas look like bruises but are raised from the surface of the skin. Most hematomas disappear in a few days and no harm is suffered. However, a hematoma can become infected. If a hematoma becomes very large, it can put pressure on a nearby nerve.

- Infection – This is always a risk with any invasive procedure, but infection from a venipuncture is very unusual.

- **Phlebitis** – This is an uncommon complication of venipuncture. It usually occurs when the same vein has been accessed many times.

- **Petechiae** – These are very tiny hemorrhages that look like small red or purple spots on the skin. Petechiae are not dangerous, but they are unpleasant and upsetting for the patient.

- **Thrombus** – A thrombus can occur if the phlebotomy technician does not apply sufficient pressure to the venipuncture site.

- **Physical reactions** – Minor physical reactions such as diaphoresis (sweating), dizziness, and nausea are relatively common during and after venipuncture. These reactions are not serious, and they will go away without treatment in a few minutes. Syncope (fainting) is uncommon – it happens in less than 1% of all patients undergoing phlebotomy – but when patients lose conscious they can fall and suffer a serious injury. On rare occasions, a patient who has serious cardiac disease may develop an arrhythmia or a cerebrovascular accident during a syncopal episode.

- **Collection or processing errors** – Paperwork errors are more common than physical complications, and the consequences of a collection error can be very serious. Examples of collection and processing errors include:

  - Misidentification of the patient

  - Improper site selection and preparation

  - Using the wrong tube

  - Incorrect order of the draw

  - Under-filling the tubes

  - Failure to invert the tubes

  - Failure to document when a specimen was obtained and when it was received

  - Mislabeling specimens

The physical complications of venipuncture are noticeable to the patient, but they are rarely serious. Collection and processing errors can cause more harm.

Proper technique will not prevent syncope, but syncope can be anticipated. Ask the patient if he or she has ever fainted during a venipuncture. Also, if the patient seems very anxious or if he or she is elderly, that patient may be at risk for a syncopal episode.

Needle Sticks and Contact with Body Fluids/Secretions

Good technique and the proper use of PPE ensure that you will not come into contact with blood and bodily secretions when you are performing a venipuncture. If contact does occur, do not wait. If there is skin contact, wash the area with soap and water. If you are splashed in the eye, rinse your eye for 15 minutes with lukewarm tap water or any other suitable solution. If you suspect that you could have inhaled a body fluid, immediately leave the area and seek fresh air. When you have finished these basic first aid measures, report the exposure as soon as possible.

If you suffer a needle-stick injury, wash the area with soap and water, cover the wound with a sterile dressing, and report the needle stick as soon as possible. Do not wait to report the needle stick any longer than is absolutely necessary to perform the first aid.

There is a real risk of disease transmission from needle sticks and exposure to body fluids/secretions. It may seem that the needle stick or the exposure to a body fluid/secretion was insignificant, and many people think that transmission of disease only happens if there is contact with blood or if the surface of the skin is obviously broken and there is contact with blood or body fluids/secretions. However, bacteria and viruses can find an entry point through ocular exposures, by inhalation, and through breaks in the skin (for example, in and around the nail beds on the hands). Always report any contact with blood or body secretions. This is especially important to do after a needle stick.

In these situations, there is a risk for the transmission of serious diseases such as hepatitis B, hepatitis C, and HIV. This risk can be reduced by prompt treatment.

First Aid, Medical Emergencies, and the Phlebotomy Procedure

You are a medical professional, and you should be prepared to respond to medical emergencies. However, you are not expected to provide anything beyond CPR and basic first aid. To prepare for medical emergencies, know:

- What to do if a patient is bleeding excessively. Apply direct pressure to the area and call for help.

- What to do if a patient faints. Call for help right away, try to prevent injury if the patient falls, and check to see if the patient is breathing and has a pulse.

- How to perform CPR.

- Who to call if an emergency happens. If a medical emergency develops, you will need help quickly so you don't want to waste time looking for phone numbers or trying to find out who can help.

Finger and Heel Stick Phlebotomy

Sometimes a blood sample is needed, but a venipuncture may be contraindicated, unnecessary, or impossible. In these situations, a finger stick or a heel stick can be used to obtain a blood sample. These procedures are not venipunctures, because they access capillaries, not veins. There are procedural differences between finger and heel sticks and venipuncture, but you you should use the same basic techniques.

Finger Sticks

Finger sticks are done when only a small quantity of blood is needed, when venous access would be very difficult, or when small blood samples are needed very frequently. Finger sticks are commonly performed on children because accessing their veins can be difficult and traumatic, and they have a smaller blood volume. Finger sticks also are performed on adults who need to have their blood frequently checked. Finger sticks also can be used to check blood levels of lead, hemoglobin, and other blood components.

The finger stick procedure described here follows the all of the basic principles of preparation, infection control, and patient safety. The basic techniques are outlined below.

- Assemble the equipment. This includes disposable gloves, isopropyl alcohol swabs, adhesive bandages, gauze, lancet, and collection tubes.

- Position the patient.

- Wash your hands and put on gloves.

- Identify the site. Use the middle or ring finger for a finger stick. The little finger is too thin, and the bone is too close to the surface. The index finger and thumb are likely to be too sensitive and to have thick calluses. Use the side of the finger for the stick. The tip of the finger is more sensitive, has fewer capillaries, and may have calluses. Never perform a finger stick on a finger that is very cold, cyanotic (blue), scarred, swollen, or has a rash. If you are not sure if a finger is suitable for a finger stick, use another finger or check with your supervisor. If a finger is thickly callused, choose another finger.

- If the patient's fingers are cold and the blood supply is limited, have the patient open and close the hand a few times.

- Clean the site with isopropyl alcohol.

- If you suspect that the blood supply to the finger is restricted, you may gently and briefly massage or "milk" the area. (Be sure not to touch the area that has been cleaned). Hold the finger, squeeze gently and then pull down towards the tip of the finger. Do this 5 or 6 times. Do not use excessive pressure, because it may affect the results.

- Puncture the fingertip with the lancet. Make the puncture perpendicular to the fingerprint lines. This will help the blood to form into a large drop that is easy to collect. Cuts made parallel to the fingerprint lines cause the blood to flow down the finger, making it will more difficult to collect.

- Wipe away the first drop of blood.

- Allow the blood to drip into the collection tube. Cap the tube when it is filled. If the blood flow is very slow or stops, you can have the patient drop the hand below the level of the heart and you may gently massage the finger to increase the flow. If you are collecting multiple tubes, you should have a container that can be used to hold the filled but uncapped tubes while you are collecting other tubes.

Heel Sticks

- A heel stick is used to obtain capillary blood from infants. Infants' veins are too small for a standard venipuncture, and infants do not have sufficient tissue on their fingers for a finger stick. Heel sticks can be used for almost any blood test. The basic heel stick procedure described here follows all basic principles of preparation, infection control, and patient safety.

- Assemble the equipment: Disposable gloves, a heel-warming device (optional), isopropyl alcohol swab, lancet, blood collection tubes, and a gauze pad.

- Choose the right lancet. Lancets used to perform heel sticks on infants do not depend on the technician to manually puncture the skin. These lancets are placed on the surface of the skin, the technician pushes a trigger, and the lancet blade pops out and punctures the skin. Each lancet will puncture the skin to a specified depth, and you must choose the correct one. For example, if the child is less than 1 kg (2.2 lb), choose a lancet that punctures the skin to a depth of 0.65 mm.

- Position the patient. If possible, the infant should be supine. Check with the patient's nurse or a physician to see if there are restrictions about positioning.

- Apply the heel warmer for 3 to 5 minutes.

- Wash your hands and put on gloves.

- Select a site. The best sites for a heel stick are the lateral and medial sides of the heel. The skin between the lateral and medial sides should be considered a secondary site. Do not use the back of the heel. There is too little tissue in that area and a lancet puncture may hit bone.

- Clean the site.

- Place the lancet on the skin and make the puncture. After the puncture has been made, use your thumb and fingers to gently squeeze the heel. Do not squeeze for a long time or use excessive pressure; doing so can affect the accuracy of the tests results.

- Wipe away the first drop of blood.

- Touch the open tip of the collection tube to the puncture site. The blood should drip into the tube. Allow the blood to passively drip into the tube. Do not "scoop" the blood to speed the collection time, as this may affect the accuracy of the test results.

- If the flow of blood stops, wipe away any surface clots with a gauze pad and stop squeezing the heel. These actions will allow the capillaries to refill.

- When the tubes are filled and capped, use a gauze pad to apply pressure to the site to stop further bleeding.

- Label the specimens, check to see if the patient is okay, discard all the equipment, remove the gloves, and wash your hands. Lancets should never be reused.

SPECIAL COLLECTIONS

A special collection refers to blood samples that are collected using techniques that are a bit more complicated and involved than a normal venipuncture. You may be required to perform or assist in a special collection.

Peripheral Blood Smears

A peripheral blood smear is a blood collection that is used most often to diagnose a hematologic disorder. In these cases, the smear is used to examine different types of white blood cells (WBCs). This is called checking the differential. Peripheral blood smears also are used to detect malarial parasites in the blood.

The peripheral blood smear can be done using capillary or venous blood. The blood can be collected at the bedside or using blood from an EDTA collection tube. You will need the following equipment:

- Lens cleaner

- Lens paper

- Glass slides

- Gloves

- An EDTA tube

Take two clean glass slides. Make sure they are not chipped. Put a drop of lens cleaner on each slide and use the lens paper to rub the slides until they are dry. Invert the EDTA tube 8-10 times. Then, open the stopper and, using a wooden stick, capillary, or other pipette, remove a small amount of the blood, and place a drop of blood 2 mm in diameter onto the slide. The drop should be in the center of the slide and approximately ¼ inch from the back edge of the slide.

Make the smear immediately after the blood has been applied. A delay will affect the accuracy of the test. Do this by using the end of the other slide (often called the "spreader" slide), holding it at a 30° angle just in front of the drop of blood, and then pulling the slide until it just touches the blood. The blood will begin to spread towards the edge of the bottom slide. Wait until the blood has almost reached the edges of the bottom slide. Maintaining the 30° angle, push the spreader slide rapidly forward across the bottom slide. Do not press down. Instead, use only the weight of the spreader slide. The smear should be across ¾ of the bottom slide, and the leading edge should be straight or feathered. There should be a smooth appearance and no holes or lines. It should also have a "rainbow" sheen when it is reflected in the light.

Allow the smear to air dry. Label the specimen appropriately.

Blood Culture Collection

Blood cultures are obtained to detect the presence of microorganisms in the blood (bacteremia). Bacteremia can have very serious consequences. Because the purpose of a blood culture is to detect bacteria and viruses, these samples must be collected by using specific procedure. This procedure is not difficult, but it does differ from the standard venipuncture procedure.

- Assemble the equipment. You will need blood culture bottles or blood culture collection tubes, one aerobic and one anaerobic. You will also need a tourniquet, gloves, isopropyl alcohol swabs, a small gauze pad, an adhesive bandage, and a chlorhexidine (preferred) or iodine swab. Blood cultures can be collected using a syringe or a winged infusion set.

- Clean the tops of the collection tubes with isopropyl alcohol. Do not use chlorhexidine or iodine. Allow the tops to dry for about 30 seconds.

- Find a suitable vein and clean the site with chlorhexidine. Firmly scrub a 5 cm area for 30 seconds. Allow the area to dry, and do not touch it after it has been cleaned.

- Make the venipuncture and obtain the blood. In an adult, you need 20 mL. The amount needed from a child depends on age and weight.

- Transfer the blood to the tubes. Do not change needles to transfer the blood. This is not necessary to prevent contamination, and it can cause a needle stick. Fill the aerobic bottle first, and then fill the anerobic bottle. The total blood volume obtained should be evenly divided between the bottles.

Occasionally, blood cultures may be collected from a peripheral or a centrally placed IV catheter. This procedure is normally performed by a nurse or a physician, but you may be asked to assist. The basics of the procedure and the principles involved are the same.

Blood Samples for Inborn Errors of Metabolism

Inborn errors of metabolism are genetic disorders that affect the way the body metabolizes certain nutrients. These disorders affect enzyme systems, and they often are diagnosed using specific blood tests. Three common blood tests that are used for this purpose are:

1. Serum ammonia

2. Serum lactate

3. Serum pyruvate

A venipuncture for these blood tests must be performed correctly to ensure the test's accuracy. In order to do so, follow these guidelines.

- Use the standard venipuncture procedure, but do not use a tourniquet. Also, make sure the patient does not make a fist when the blood sample is being drawn.

- The patient should be fasting before the blood test for serum pyruvate. Check the laboratory protocols to determine the duration.

- These blood specimens must be collected in special collection tubes. After they have been filled, the tubes must be immediately placed on ice.

- These blood samples must be transported immediately to the laboratory. Delays in transporting mean delays in processing. This can affect the accuracy of the tests.

Phlebotomy for Blood Donations

Aside from the use of some specific equipment and some screening issues, performing phlebotomy for blood donations is no different than a standard venipuncture. The same principles of patient identification, patient assessment, site preparation, vein access, and infection control would be used.

The screening issues are age, weight, and the possibility of a blood-borne disease. Guidelines for these are universal. Your workplace should have protocols in place that outline who can and who cannot donate blood.

In most cases, the maximum amount of blood that is taken is 525 mL. However, each individual must be assessed to determine how well he or she will tolerate a specific amount of blood donation. The American Academy of Blood Banks recommendation for blood donation is a maximum of 10.5 mL of blood removed per kg of body weight. This recommendation assumes a minimum body weight of 50 kg (110 pounds). The amount of blood removed should be determined on a case-by-case basis.

PROCESSING

Specimen processing is a critically important part of your job. If specimens are not correctly processed, test results may not be accurate. This can have serious consequences for patients. The key instructional content for this section is:

- Specimen labeling and transporting

- CLIA quality control

- Non-blood specimen collection and transporting

- Pre-analytical errors

- Chain of custody

- Communication and specimen collection and processing

- Entering and retrieving laboratory values

- Reporting routine and critical laboratory results

Specimen Labeling and Transporting

Specimens must be properly labeled. The labels are pre-printed and should have the following information: patient name, date of birth, and medical record number. The specimen must also be labeled with the date and time it was collected. You must write your name or initials on the label. All of this information must be on a specimen. A specimen that does not have this information cannot be processed.

Each facility has a protocol for transporting specimens. The two key parts of this protocol are:

1. The time from collection to transport

2. Storage requirements for the specimen during transport

For most routine specimens, the time it takes to transport a collection to the laboratory is not critical. However, for some specimens, the accuracy of the test will be affected if the specimen is not processed within a specified period of time. Also, some specimens are for stat (immediate) tests. If a blood test is stat, the specimen must be taken to the laboratory as soon as possible after it has been collected.

Most specimens can be stored at room temperature during transport, but some need to be transported on ice. If a specimen you are collecting is for a blood test with which you are unfamiliar, check to see if there are any special requirements for its transport.

Some specimens need to be processed in a specialty laboratory. If this is the case, you must make sure the specimen is properly labelled, arrange for a courier to transport the specimen, and speak with the laboratory before sending the specimen. Make sure to document when the specimen left the laboratory and the full name and telephone number of the person you spoke to. Arrange for the outside laboratory to call you to confirm that the specimen has been received.

CLIA Quality Control

Clinical Laboratory Improvement Amendments (CLIA) are federal regulatory standards for laboratories that perform testing of human samples. CLIA standards stipulate that certain simple, low-risk laboratory tests may be waived; there does not have to be any direct, routine oversight of the laboratories in regards to how they perform these tests.

This does not mean that these laboratories are exempt from quality control. If a laboratory has a CLIA waiver, it must observe good quality control practices, such as:

- Using the most recent package insert from the testing kit's manufacturer.

- Doing quality control and or calibration of the test kit according to the manufacturer's instructions.

- Documenting quality control.

- Storing and handling testing kits according to manufacturer's instructions.

- Providing laboratory personnel with appropriate training in the use of testing kits, and documenting this training.

- Using the OSHA regulations that pertain to laboratory testing.

Because they do not have direct, routine inspections, laboratories with a CLIA waiver must be especially vigilant with quality control. Your workplace should have a quality control manual, and it is your responsibility to know the quality control rules and to follow them.

Non-Blood Specimen Collection and Transport

You may be responsible for explaining non-blood specimen collection to patients. These specimens can include semen, sputum, stool, or urine. The collection procedures for these samples are simple. Except for a sterile urine specimen collection (often called a clean catch urine sample), no preparation is necessary. The patient simply places the specimen in a pre-labeled container and delivers it to the laboratory.

The following steps are used for collecting a sterile urine sample:

- Wait until the urine has been in the bladder for 2 to 3 hours.

- Wash hands with soap and water.

- For men – Clean the head of the penis with a sterile wipe. After cleaning, urinate for several seconds into the toilet, stop the flow, then urinate into the specimen container. Do not touch the inside of the container or the inside of the lid.

- For women – Separate the labia and use a sterile wipe to clean the area, moving from front to back. Then use a second sterile wipe to clean the area around the urethra, moving from front to back. After cleaning, urinate for several seconds into the toilet, and urinate into the specimen container. Do not touch the inside of the container or the inside of the lid.

Pre-analytical Errors

Pre-analytical errors are specimen collection errors. The most common errors are:

- Insufficient specimen quantity

- Hemolysis

- Hemoconcentration

- Specimen contamination

An insufficient specimen quantity error can be prevented by knowing exactly how much is needed for any specific test. If you are obtaining a sample for a test you are not familiar with, check the protocol before obtaining the sample. If you don't know the answer, check. Hemolysis and hemoconcentration errors can be prevented by using the tourniquet correctly and making sure the patient does not make a fist during the collection. Specimen contamination errors can be prevented by applying principles of sterility and infection control, and by using the proper procedures for site preparation.

Chain of Custody

Chain of custody is the process through which specimens used for legal purposes must be obtained, processed, and transported. It also refers to the documentation that must be done when these specimens are obtained, processed, and transported. The chain of custody would be used when specimens may have a legal impact. Examples would be blood alcohol levels, tests for the presence of illicit drugs, workplace drug testing, and specimens that may play a part in a criminal case such as a sexual assault.

In order to maintain the chain of custody, carefully document each of the following:

- When, how, and by whom a specimen was collected

- When, how and by whom a specimen was transported

- Who received a specimen and when; where and how it was stored

- How and when the specimen was processed

- When, by whom, and to whom the results were reported.

Most laboratories that handle specimens that require a chain of custody have chain of custody forms and a protocol.

Communication and Specimen Collection and Processing

Communication during specimen collection and processing is very important. Accurate communication is vital, and the best way to ensure accurate communication is to use repetition and confirmation.

Entering and Retrieving Laboratory Values

Laboratory values must be entered correctly. Doing so requires you to pay special attention to the values and the units that are used to report them. You also need to have a basic knowledge of normal and abnormal values. Entering and retrieving values incorrectly could have serious consequences.

Reporting Routine and Critical Laboratory Values

When you are reporting routine and critical laboratory values, use repetition and confirmation. You must also document to whom you report the values and when. Doing this is especially important when you are reporting critical laboratory values.

Summary

In this chapter, you learned how to perform basic venipuncture. You learned the proper technique – including patient identification, preparation, troubleshooting, and potential complications. In addition, the chapter described finger and heel stick blood collection, special collections, and the procedure for processing specimens.

Drill Questions

1. Which of the following are considered acceptable for identifying a patient?

   A. Full name and date of birth.
   B. Address and telephone number.
   C. Identifying wrist band.
   D. Work telephone number and place of employment.

2. Before performing a venipuncture, you should determine if the patient is taking

   A. calcium supplements.
   B. digoxin.
   C. aspirin.
   D. insulin.

3. Medical equipment that is free of microorganisms is said to be

   A. clean.
   B. disinfected.
   C. pyrogen-free.
   D. sterile.

4. The most commonly used disinfectant for venipuncture preparation is

   A. alcohol-based soap.
   B. isopropyl alcohol.
   C. iodine.
   D. chlorhexidine.

5. You should never leave a tourniquet on for longer than

   A. 5 minutes.
   B. 15 seconds.
   C. 1 minute.
   D. 10 minutes.

6. Using the correct order of the draw is important because

   A. it makes the venipuncture process more efficient.
   B. it ensures that additives in one tube do not contaminate another tube.
   C. it reflects the size of the collection tubes.
   D. the vacuum in each tube is different.

7. When obtaining a blood culture you should prepare the skin with

    A. alcohol-based soap.
    B. isopropyl alcohol.
    C. iodine.
    D. chlorhexidine.

8. Finger stick collection is done on children because

    A. accessing their veins can be difficult and traumatic.
    B. it takes less time than a routine venipuncture.
    C. site preparation is easier.
    D. a larger volume of blood can be obtained.

9. Chain of custody refers to the procedures and documentation

    A. used for reporting laboratory results.
    B. used for obtaining special collections.
    C. associated with forensic specimens.
    D. used for obtaining blood cultures.

Drill Answers

1. Which of the following are considered acceptable for identifying a patient?

   A. Full name and date of birth.
   B. Address and telephone number.
   C. Identifying wrist band.
   D. Work telephone number and place of employment.

   A patient's address and telephone number can change, an identifying wrist band can be put on the wrong patient, and people change their place of employment. A client's date of birth and name do not change.

2. Before performing a venipuncture, you should determine if the patient is taking

   A. calcium supplements.
   B. digoxin.
   C. aspirin.
   D. insulin.

   Aspirin affects the ability of the blood to clot, and the patient may bleed excessively after a venipuncture.

3. Medical equipment that is free of microorganisms is said to be

   A. clean.
   B. disinfected.
   C. pyrogen-free
   D. sterile.

   The term sterile refers to a lack of microorganisms.

4. The most commonly used disinfectant for venipuncture preparation is

   A. alcohol-based soap.
   B. isopropyl alcohol.
   C. iodine.
   D. chlorhexidine.

   In some cases, iodine or chlorhexidine can be used, but for routine venipunctures isopropyl alcohol is preferred.

5. You should never leave a tourniquet on for longer than

    A. 5 minutes.
    B. 15 seconds.
    C. 1 minute.
    D. 10 minutes.

    A tourniquet can be left on for up to 1 minute. If it is left on longer than
    1 minute, the accuracy of the blood test may be compromised because of hemolysis.

6. Using the correct order of the draw is important because

    A. it makes the venipuncture process more efficient.
    B. it ensures that additives in one tube do not contaminate another tube.
    C. it reflects the size of the collection tubes.
    D. the vacuum in each tube is different.

    If the tubes are not collected in the proper order, an additive from one tube can enter
    into another and affect the test result.

7. When obtaining a blood culture you should prepare the skin with

    A. alcohol-based soap.
    B. isopropyl alcohol.
    C. iodine.
    D. chlorhexidine.

    Blood cultures are used to detect the presence of microorganisms in the blood, so
    special care must be taken to make sure that the venipuncture site is as free from
    microorganisms as possible. Chlorhexidine is the best disinfectant for this purpose.

8. Finger stick collection is done on children because

    A. accessing their veins can be difficult and traumatic.
    B. it takes less time than a routine venipuncture.
    C. site preparation is easier.
    D. a larger volume of blood can be obtained.

    Finger stick collection is done on children because their veins are small, difficult
    to access, and easy to damage, and the venipuncture process is more traumatic for
    a child.

9. Chain of custody refers to the procedures and documentation

      A. used for reporting laboratory results.

      B. used for obtaining special collections.

      C. associated with forensic specimens.

      D. used for obtaining blood cultures.

Chain of custody is the process with which specimens that may be used for forensic purposes must be obtained, processed, and transported. It also refers to the documentation that must be done when these specimens are obtained, processed, and transported.

Terms and Definitions

Antecubital (AC) fossa – The area between the upper and lower arm, when the arm is palm up. It is the area most often used for venipuncture.

Bevel – The angled part of a venipunture needle

Blood culture – A blood specimen used to detect the presence of microorganisms in the blood.

Capillary – The smallest type of blood vessel, located in the periphery of the body

Chain of custody – Documentation, handling, and transport of a specimen

Chlorhexidine – A disinfectant used to clean skin before venipuncture. It is used specifically when cleaning the skin prior to obtaining a blood culture.

CLIA – Clinical Laboratory Improvement Amendments. These are federal regulatory standards for laboratories that perform laboratory testing of human samples.

Cyanosis – Blue coloration of the skin caused by lack of oxygen or decreased circulation

Finger stick – A method of obtaining blood samples when veins cannot or should not be used

Heel stick – Method of obtaining blood samples when veins cannot or should not be used

Hematoma – A localized collection of blood; the most common complication associated with venipuncture

Hemoconcentration – A concentrated blood sample caused by excessive pressure forcing fluids from the blood

Hemolysis – Destruction of red blood cells

Inversion – The process of turning blood tubes back and forth after they have been collected. Inversion is done to mix the blood sample with additives in the tubes.

Isopropyl alcohol – A disinfectant that is used to clean skin prior to a venipuncture

Lancet – A small sterile blade that is used to puncture the skin when performing a finger stick or a heel stick

Lateral – A medical term that refers to parts of the body away from the center

Medial – A medical term that refers to parts of the body that are at or near the center

Palpation – Touching or examining the body with the fingers

Peripheral smear – A specialized blood collection, used most often to check the white blood cell differential

Petechiae – Tiny hemorrhages that look like small red or purple spots on the skin.

Phlebitis – Inflammation of a blood vessel

Phlebotomy – The process of accessing a blood vessel to obtain a blood sample

Sclerosis – A narrowing and scarring of blood vessels

Stat – A medical term that means immediately or without delay

Sterile – Absence of microorganisms

Syncope – A sudden loss of consciousness, more often called fainting

Thrombus – A blood clot inside a blood vessel

Tortuous – Twisted

Tourniquet – A medical device wrapped around arm prior to performing a venipuncture

Vacutainer – A brand name of a piece of phlebotomy equipment; a plastic sleeve that holds a venipuncture needle and a blood collection tube.

Venipuncture – The process of puncturing a blood vessel to obtain a blood sample

Winged infusion set – A piece of medical equipment that is used to perform veinpucture; commonly called a Butterfly set.

Learning Objectives

After reading this chapter, the CPCT student will be able to:

- *Describe proper lead placement when acquiring various EKG tracings.*

- *List the EKG waveforms.*

- *Identify specific waveforms on the EKG.*

- *Measure the duration of waveforms on the EKG.*

- *Identify the direction of wave deflection.*

- *Determine T wave symmetry.*

- *Determine P wave symmetry.*

- *Measure the heart rate from the EKG tracing.*

- *Differentiate artifact from expected EKG tracing waveforms.*

- *Describe how to eliminate artifact from an EKG.*

- *Interpret arrhythmias originating in the sinus, atria, junction, and ventricles.*

- *Recognize pacer spikes on the EKG.*

- *Identify ischemic changes on the EKG.*

- *Describe the proper response for life-threatening arrhythmias.*

- *Describe how to maintain the EKG machine.*

Introduction

This chapter provides the information necessary to systematically approach the EKG and interpret arrhythmias encountered in the clinical setting. In addition, the chapter includes pictures and real EKG tracings to promote rhythm recognition. Important terms are located at the end of the chapter in a special section, enabling students to locate definitions quickly. The chapter concludes with a 10-question self-assessment drill.

Calculate a Patient's Heart Rate from the EKG Tracing

Heart rate can be measured from the EKG using a variety of different approaches. The following are the most commonly employed methods.

The 1500 method – Calculate the heart rate using the 1500 method by counting the number of small boxes between the P-P interval (for atrial rate) or R-R interval (for ventricular rate), then dividing 1,500 by that number. Fifteen hundred represents the number of small boxes, or the number of mm of paper consumed in one minute of time at the standard 25 mm/second paper speed. For example, if there are 15 small boxes between two R waves (R-R interval), the heart rate equals 1500/15, or 100/min. This is a great method for very precise measurements and is best applied to fast rhythms.

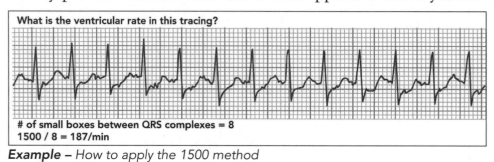

Example – How to apply the 1500 method

Sequence method – The sequence method (also known as the 300 method) is derived from the 1500 method. There are 300 large, 5 mm boxes in every minute of EKG tracing at the normal 25 mm/second print speed. Remember the pattern 300-150-100-75-60-50. Calculate these numbers by dividing 300 by the number of large boxes between QRS complexes. Find an R wave and start counting away from it moving towards the right of the tracing in 5 mm segments (one large box). With every move, apply the number in the pattern you memorized. This is a wonderful rule to apply most of the time, with one exception: irregular rhythms.

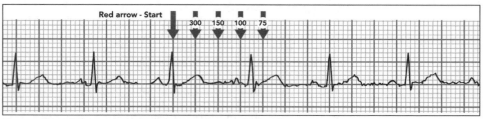

Example – How to apply the sequence method

6-second rule – The 6-second rule is simple and works well in any situation. It is the gold standard for estimating the rate of an irregular rhythm. At the top of the tracing, there are small hash marks indicating 3-second intervals. Count the number of QRS complexes in two of the sections (6-second period) and multiply by 10. For example, you count six QRS complexes in 6 seconds. 6 X 10 = 60/min.

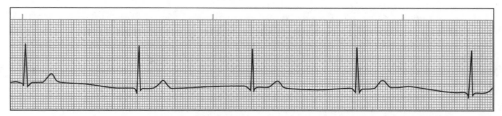

Example – How to apply the 6-second rule

Identify Artifacts from the Tracing

Artifact can come from a variety of both patient and nonpatient factors. The most common reasons for artifact on the EKG caused by the patient include seizure, trembling, fast breathing, dry or wet skin, and shivering. Nonpatient causes include use of electrodes with dry gel, damaged patient cables, electromagnetic frequency, and interference from cell phones and other medical and nonmedical devices.

Resolve Artifacts from the Tracing

Wandering baseline – A wandering baseline often appears on the EKG when the electrodes are improperly placed on the patient's torso. The wandering baseline artifact can result from a variety of causes that include movement of the cables or leads during the reading, patient movement, loose electrodes, dry electrodes, a patient's labored breathing, or improper skin preparation, leaving traces of lotion, oils, or gel on the skin. An easy way to eliminate the wandering baseline is to move the limb leads to the wrists and ankles. Another way to reduce the artifact is to have the patient relax and breathe more slowly , or to clean the skin where the electrodes are placed to remove lotion or oil, which cause a poor connection between the skin and the leads.

Seizure – Seizure activity will cause huge artifact problems on the EKG. Seizure activity must be controlled prior to acquiring the EKG tracing.

Trembling – Some patients may be anxious, cold, or have an essential tremor. The technician must reassure the patient to keep him/her calm, provide warm blankets to control shivering, and attempt to move the electrodes to an area with minimal tremor.

Dry skin – If the patient's skin is very dry, the electrodes and gel won't adhere well to the skin. The gel will be unable to have the appropriate surface area contact to ensure a strong signal. The technician can reduce artifact from dry skin by gently abrading the skin and using tincture of benzoin to promote good adhesion and surface contact.

Wet skin – Some patients will be diaphoretic during EKG acquisition. The technician can wipe the patient off with a towel and apply tincture of benzoin to the patient's skin before placing the electrodes. The benzoin needs to completely dry prior to applying the EKG electrodes.

Cold patient – If the patient is very cold, they may shiver, and in some cases, the electrodes won't adhere to the skin. The technician should provide the patient with warm blankets. Some patients may be unable to stop shivering, and the EKG may have to be acquired with the artifact.

Dry gel – The gel on the EKG electrodes is specially designed to interface with the patient's skin. The gel is able to sense extremely low levels of energy and requires the full surface area to make contact with the patient. Electrodes with dry gel should not be used.

Cell phone interference – Cell phone interference can cause lots of artifact on the EKG. It may appear as flutter or P waves on the tracing at a rate of 300/min. Though the cell phone artifact morphology is different than normal P wave or flutter wave morphology, take special care to ensure the patient's cell phone is off or moved away from the patient during the procedure.

Medical device interference – Medical and other electronic devices can interfere with the EKG tracing. Ensure that all unnecessary devices are moved away from the patient or turned off. Medical devices are often designed to minimize interference with other devices, so the technician should consider nonmedical devices as the source of interference first.

Record Leads on a Patient

3-lead

The 3-lead EKG configuration is generally used to continuously monitor the patient's heart rhythm.

- White lead – Right shoulder or clavicle area

- Black lead – Left shoulder or clavicle area

- Red lead – Left lower abdominal area

- Green lead – Right lower abdominal area

5-lead

The 5-lead EKG configuration refers to the standard Holter monitor setup or the 5-lead rhythm monitor setup. The Holter monitor setup varies depending on the type of monitor. The 5-lead setup pictured here is the most common configuration employed.

- White lead – Right sternum/clavicle area

- Black lead – Left sternum/clavicle area

- Red lead – Left lower thoracic area

- Green lead – Right lower thoracic area

- Brown lead – Just below and to the right of the bottom of the sternum

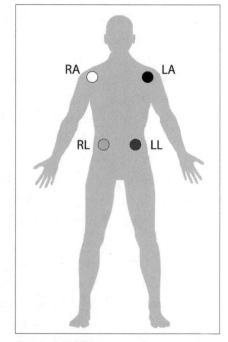

3-Lead EKG – *Lead placement*

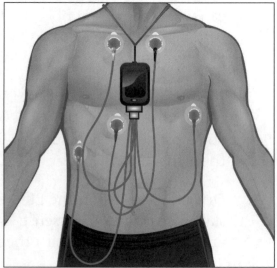

5-Lead EKG – *Most common lead placement*

12-lead

The standard 12-lead EKG requires placement of 10 electrodes; the standard 4 limb leads, plus 6 precordial leads.

Precordial Leads – **Left side**

- V1 – 4th intercostal space (ICS), R of sternum

- V2 – 4th ICS, L of sternum

- V4 – 5th ICS, midclavicular

- V3 – between V2/V4

- V6 – 5th ICS, midaxillary

- V5 – 5th ICS between V4/V6

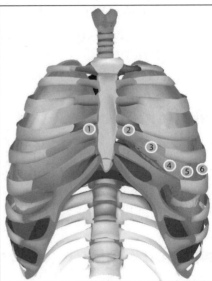

12-Lead EKG *– Lead placement*

Certain conditions, including inferior wall ST segment elevation, myocardial infarction, and patients less than 8 years old, require a right-sided 12-lead EKG. Limb leads are placed in the normal fashion, but the precordial leads are placed as illustrated below.

Precordial Leads – **Right side**

- V1 – 4th ICS, L of sternum

- V2 – 4th ICS, R of sternum

- V4 – 5th ICS, midclavicular (R) (most sensitive and specific to R ventricular infarction)

- V3 – between V2/V4

- V5 – 5th ICS between V4/V6

- V6 – 5th ICS, midaxillary

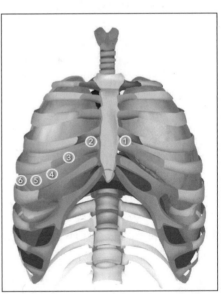

Right-sided 12-Lead EKG *– Lead placement*

Verify the Leads Recorded on an EKG

After acquiring an EKG, the technician should verify that each of the leads is free of artifact and has properly recorded on the EKG paper. Sometimes, the stylus on the machine gets dirty and is unable to print in a certain region of the EKG paper. If certain leads did not print on the EKG paper, first verify that the leads did not accidentally fall off the patient. Also ensure that the EKG electrodes and wires are securely connected, and ensure that the wires are securely plugged into the EKG device. If a certain area still isn't printing, or if the recording is very faint, try changing the cables on the machine. If the problem persists, contact the manufacturer for direction.

Upload a Completed EKG to a Patient's Electronic Medical Record

Become familiar with your institution's policy on uploading EKGs to the patient's electronic medical record. Ensure that patient identifiers have been entered onto the EKG. It is critical to verify that the EKG being attached to the patient's record is that patient's EKG. Follow established policies and guidelines to prevent errors in medical record-keeping.

Mount a Completed EKG for a Patient's Chart

As with uploading a complete EKG to a patient's electronic record, become familiar with your institution's policy on mounting a completed EKG to a patient's chart. Ensure that patient identifiers have been entered onto the EKG. Some facilities require attaching stickers with bar codes to identify the patient and any test results such as an EKG.

Measure a Patient's Heart Rhythm from the EKG Tracing

A number of different methods exist to systematically approach the EKG for interpretation. The underlying rhythm can be interpreted using a simple five-step method (shown below). First, calculate the heart rate, both atrial and ventricular. Next, measure the PR interval, then measure the QRS duration. Determine if the rhythm is regular, irregular, or irregularly irregular. Lastly, use the findings to interpret the underlying rhythm.

The following is a handy template to use while learning how to interpret arrhythmias.

Rate: Atrial _____ Ventricular _____

PR interval: _____

QRS duration: _____

Rhythm: (circle one)   Regular   Irregular   Irregularly irregular

Arrhythmia (interpretation): _____

Inspect the Waveforms of a Cardiac Cycle for Symmetry, Direction, and Amplitude

Identify the direction of the wave deflection.

Positive – A positive deflection is a wave that exists above the isoelectric line. Any part of a wave that exists above the isoelectric line is said to be positive, even if it is moving downward on the EKG paper. Once the wave reaches the isoelectric line and continues to travel downwards, then the wave becomes negatively deflected.

Negative – A negative wave is a wave that exists below the isoelectric line. Any part of a wave that exists below the isoelectric line is said to be negative, even if it is moving upward on the EKG paper. Once the wave reaches the isoelectric line and continues to travel upward, then the wave becomes positively deflected.

Determine T wave symmetry – T wave symmetry is defined as a T wave that is symmetrical with respect to the Y axis. In other words, a T wave whose right and left sides form mirror images on the vertical axis are said to exhibit symmetry.

Determine P wave symmetry – P wave symmetry is defined as a P wave that is symmetrical with respect to the Y axis. In other words, a P wave whose right and left sides form mirror images on the vertical axis are said to exhibit symmetry.

Determine the amplitude of a wave – The amplitude of any wave is measured using the horizontal grid lines on the EKG. Each small square is exactly 1 mm tall. Locate the lowest and highest points of the wave. Count the number of small boxes between the two points. The answer is the number of small boxes in millimeters.

Measure a Patient's Heart Conduction from the EKG Tracing

Interval	Expected reference range
PR	0.12 to 0.2 seconds
QRS	0.04 to 0.10 seconds*

Note – Different cardiology experts list varying ranges for a normal QRS interval, but it is generally understood that "normal" must be less than 0.12 seconds.

P wave – Electrical activity associated with SA node impulse and depolarization of the atria.

PR interval – The PR interval represents the time it takes for the SA node to fire, atria to depolarize, and electricity to travel through the AV node. The PR interval is measured from the beginning of the P wave to the beginning of the QRS complex.

QRS complex – The QRS complex represents the time it takes for the ventricles to depolarize. The QRS complex is measured from the end of the PR interval to the J point.

ST segment – The ST segment represents the early phase of ventricular repolarization. The shape of the ST segment is very important when looking for patterns of ischemia. Refer to the Many Faces of Ischemia section later in the study guide for specifics related to ischemia and ST segment changes.

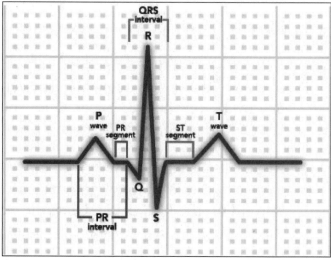

EKG tracing – Parts of a waveform

J point – The J point represents the exact point in time where ventricular depolarization stops and ventricular repolarization starts. The J point occurs at the end of the QRS complex, or where the ST segment begins. During myocardial ischemia the J point can elevate or depress below baseline. Refer to the ischemia section of the study guide for specific changes related to myocardial ischemia.

QT interval – The QT interval represents one complete ventricular cycle; in other words, it represents one complete cycle of ventricular depolarization and repolarization. The QT interval is measured from the beginning of the Q wave to the end of the T wave.

P-P interval – The P-P interval represents the amount of time between atrial depolarization cycles (between P waves). The P-P interval is measured from the beginning of one P wave to the beginning of the next P wave.

R-R interval – The R-R interval represents the amount of time between ventricular depolarization cycles (between R waves). The R-R interval is measured from the beginning of one R wave to the beginning of the next R wave.

Identify the Major Classifications of Arrhythmias from the EKG Tracing

Rhythms that originate in the SINUS node:

- Regular sinus rhythm

- Sinus bradycardia

- Sinus tachycardia

- Sinus arrhythmia

EKG findings common to sinus rhythms:

- P wave present

- P wave is upright and rounded

- P wave amplitude less than 2.5 mm

- P wave duration less than 0.11 seconds

- QRS complex usually narrow

Regular (normal) Sinus Rhythm

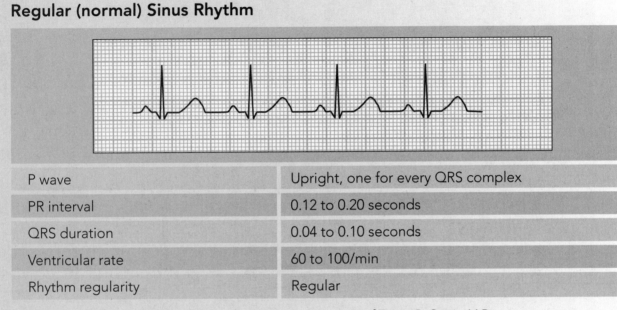

P wave	Upright, one for every QRS complex
PR interval	0.12 to 0.20 seconds
QRS duration	0.04 to 0.10 seconds
Ventricular rate	60 to 100/min
Rhythm regularity	Regular

Rhythm strip from 12-Lead ECG: The Art of Interpretation, courtesy of Tomas B. Garcia, M.D.

Sinus Bradycardia

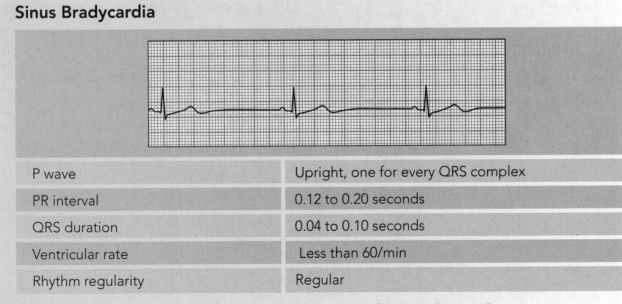

P wave	Upright, one for every QRS complex
PR interval	0.12 to 0.20 seconds
QRS duration	0.04 to 0.10 seconds
Ventricular rate	Less than 60/min
Rhythm regularity	Regular

Rhythm strip from 12-Lead ECG: The Art of Interpretation, courtesy of Tomas B. Garcia, M.D.

Sinus Tachycardia

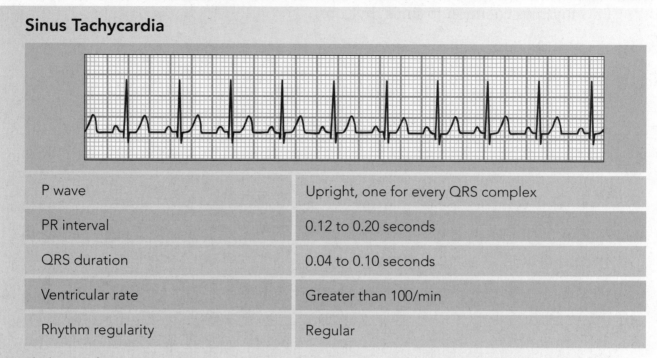

P wave	Upright, one for every QRS complex
PR interval	0.12 to 0.20 seconds
QRS duration	0.04 to 0.10 seconds
Ventricular rate	Greater than 100/min
Rhythm regularity	Regular

Rhythm strip from 12-Lead ECG: The Art of Interpretation, courtesy of Tomas B. Garcia, M.D.

Sinus Arrhythmia

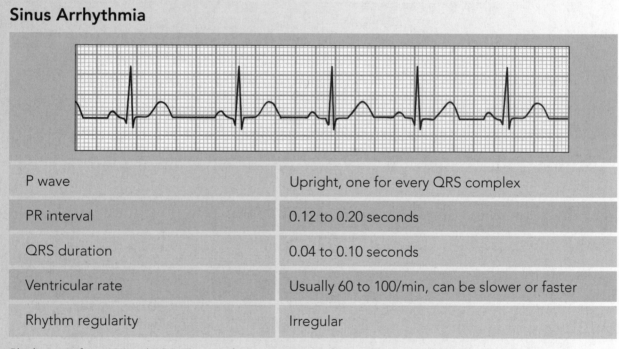

P wave	Upright, one for every QRS complex
PR interval	0.12 to 0.20 seconds
QRS duration	0.04 to 0.10 seconds
Ventricular rate	Usually 60 to 100/min, can be slower or faster
Rhythm regularity	Irregular

Rhythm strip from 12-Lead ECG: The Art of Interpretation, courtesy of Tomas B. Garcia, M.D.

Rhythms that originate in the ATRIA:

- Atrial fibrillation

- Atrial fibrillation with rapid ventricular response

- Atrial flutter

- Premature atrial complex

- Supraventricular tachycardia (SVT)

EKG findings common to atrial rhythms:

- P wave absent or abnormal shape

- Fibrillatory (f) waves present

- Flutter (F) waves present

- QRS complex usually narrow

Atrial Fibrillation

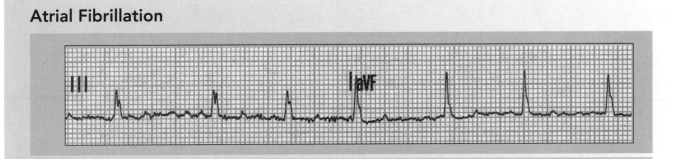

P wave	None, fibrillatory waves (f)
PR interval	None
QRS duration	Less than 0.12 seconds
Ventricular rate	60 to 100/min
Atrial rate (if different than ventricular rate)	300 to 600/min
Rhythm regularity	Irregularly irregular

Atrial Fibrillation with Rapid Ventricular Response (AF-RVR)

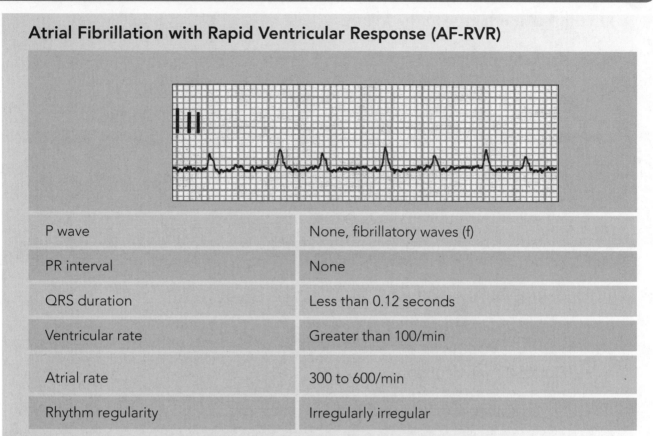

P wave	None, fibrillatory waves (f)
PR interval	None
QRS duration	Less than 0.12 seconds
Ventricular rate	Greater than 100/min
Atrial rate	300 to 600/min
Rhythm regularity	Irregularly irregular

Atrial Flutter

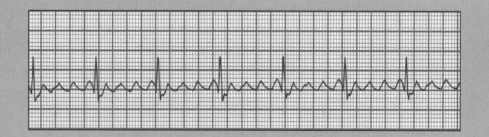

P wave	None, flutter waves (F)
PR interval	None
QRS duration	Less than 0.12 seconds
Ventricular rate	Usually 60 to 100/min, often seen at 130, 150, 160
Atrial rate	240 to 320/min
Rhythm regularity	Regular (irregular with variable conduction)

Supraventricular Tachycardia (SVT)

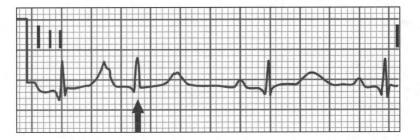

P wave	May be hard to find. If present, one per QRS complex
PR interval	Usually not measurable
QRS duration	0.04 to 0.10 seconds
Ventricular rate	150 to 240/min
Rhythm regularity	Regular

Premature Atrial Complex (PAC)

PACs are atrial depolarizations that occur early in the cardiac cycle. The characteristic findings on an EKG include:

- A P wave (may be buried in the preceding T wave)

- A QRS complex that follows

- A QRS that looks the same as the QRS complexes in the underlying rhythm

PACs are not rhythms! They are complexes that appear in an underlying rhythm. First name the underlying rhythm, and then add PAC. For example, the tracing above reveals a regular sinus rhythm with one PAC. The premature beat is the beat that occurs early in the cycle, followed by a rest period known as a compensatory pause. This pause is a built-in delay mechanism enabling the heart to resume its electrical activity on time following a premature beat.

Rhythms that originate near the A/V JUNCTION:

- Junctional rhythm

- Junctional bradycardia

- Accelerated junctional rhythm

- Junctional tachycardia

- Premature junctional complex

EKG findings common to junctional rhythms:

- P wave absent or inverted

- QRS complex on the long end of normal (can be wide)

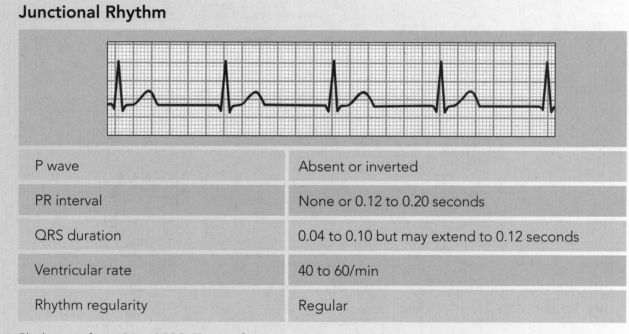

Junctional Rhythm

P wave	Absent or inverted
PR interval	None or 0.12 to 0.20 seconds
QRS duration	0.04 to 0.10 but may extend to 0.12 seconds
Ventricular rate	40 to 60/min
Rhythm regularity	Regular

Rhythm strip from 12-Lead ECG: The Art of Interpretation, courtesy of Tomas B. Garcia, M.D.

Junctional Bradycardia

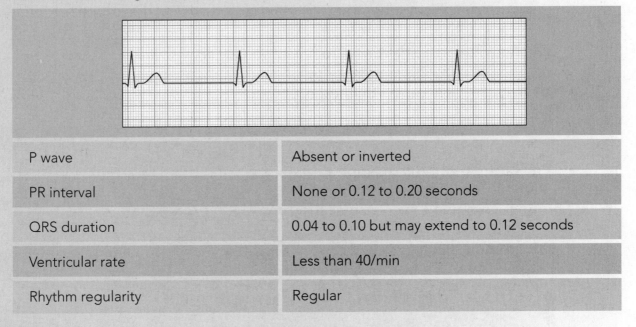

P wave	Absent or inverted
PR interval	None or 0.12 to 0.20 seconds
QRS duration	0.04 to 0.10 but may extend to 0.12 seconds
Ventricular rate	Less than 40/min
Rhythm regularity	Regular

Accelerated Junctional Rhythm

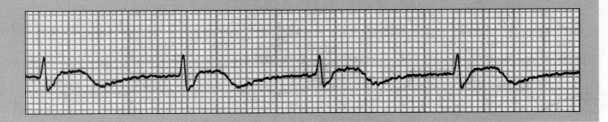

P wave	Absent, inverted, retrograde, or inverted and retrograde
PR Interval	None, or 0.12 to 0.20 seconds
QRS Duration	0.04 to 0.10 but may extend to 0.12 seconds
Ventricular Rate	Greater than 60/min
Rhythm regularity	Regular

Rhythms that originate in the VENTRICLES:

- Idioventricular rhythm

- Polymorphic (Torsades de pointe) ventricular tachycardia

- Ventricular tachycardia (monomorphic)

- Ventricular fibrillation

- Premature ventricular complex

EKG findings common to ventricular rhythms:

- QRS complex wide

Idioventricular Rhythm (Ventricular Escape Rhythm)

P wave	None
PR interval	None
QRS duration	Greater than 0.12 seconds
Ventricular rate	20 to 40/min
Rhythm regularity	Regular

In the following strip for polymorphic ventricular tachycardia (PMVT), notice the varying amplitude of the QRS complexes.

Polymorphic (Torsades de Pointe) Ventricular Tachycardia

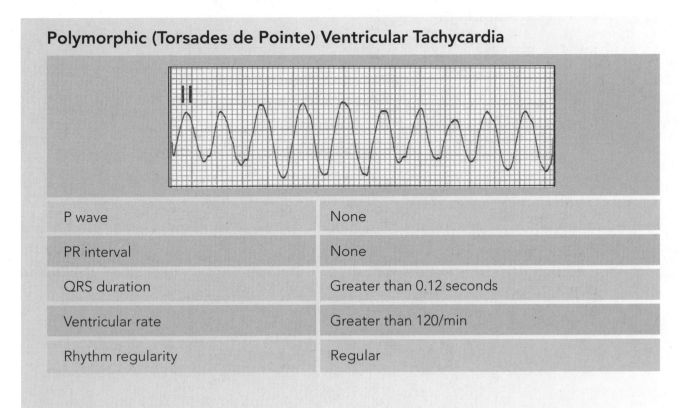

P wave	None
PR interval	None
QRS duration	Greater than 0.12 seconds
Ventricular rate	Greater than 120/min
Rhythm regularity	Regular

In the following ventricular tachycardia strip, notice the identical amplitude of all the QRS complexes.

Ventricular Tachycardia (Monomorphic)

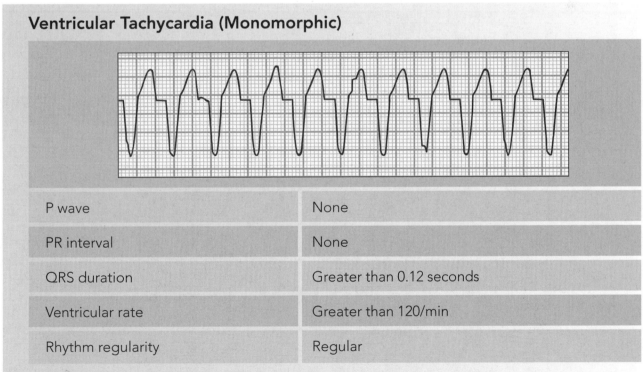

P wave	None
PR interval	None
QRS duration	Greater than 0.12 seconds
Ventricular rate	Greater than 120/min
Rhythm regularity	Regular

Rhythm strip from 12-Lead ECG: The Art of Interpretation, courtesy of Tomas B. Garcia, M.D.

Ventricular fibrillation is an extremely chaotic rhythm with no discernable waves.

Ventricular Fibrillation

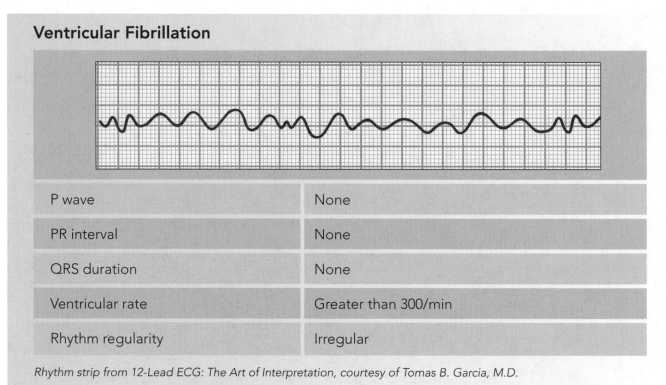

P wave	None
PR interval	None
QRS duration	None
Ventricular rate	Greater than 300/min
Rhythm regularity	Irregular

Rhythm strip from 12-Lead ECG: The Art of Interpretation, courtesy of Tomas B. Garcia, M.D.

Asystole is the absence of electrical activity in the heart.

Asystole

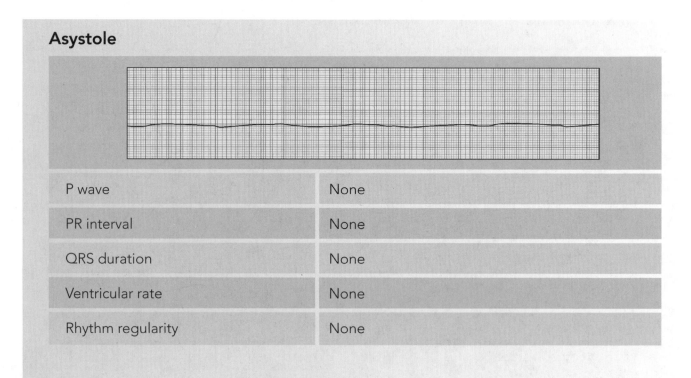

P wave	None
PR interval	None
QRS duration	None
Ventricular rate	None
Rhythm regularity	None

Premature Ventricular Complex (PVC)

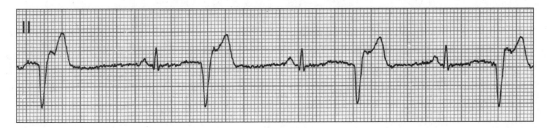

PVCs are ventricular depolarizations that occur early in the cardiac cycle. The characteristic findings on the EKG include:

- Absent P wave preceding the early QRS

- A wide QRS complex

- A QRS that looks different than the QRS complexes in the underlying rhythm

- The direction of the QRS complex and the T wave oppose one another

Like PACs, PVCs are not rhythms. They are complexes that appear in an underlying rhythm. First name the underlying rhythm, then add PVC. For example, the tracing above reveals a regular sinus rhythm with PVCs. PVCs can appear in many different patterns. They can also come in many different shapes. When a single PVC appears, name the underlying rhythm and add "with a PVC." PVCs can be unifocal in nature, in which all of the PVCs look the same because they come from the same area of origin. PVCs also can appear with different shapes; in this case, the term "multifocal PVCs" is used. PVCs can also appear in groups. For example, in the tracing above, PVCs occur as every other complex. This pattern is called ventricular bigeminy.

Heart Blocks

Heart blocks are a special set of arrhythmias that indicate a difficulty in communication or no communication between the atria and ventricles. A heart block is often communicated as being first-degree, second-degree type 1, second-degree type 2, or third-degree heart block. It is important to remember that proper identification of the arrhythmia includes interpretation of the atrial and ventricular rhythm and the degree of block that exists between the two. See the note in the third-degree heart block section on page 31.

First-degree heart block represents a slow or delayed conduction through the AV node, resulting in a prolonged PR interval. Specifically, the PR segment elongates in first-degree heart block.

First-Degree Heart Block

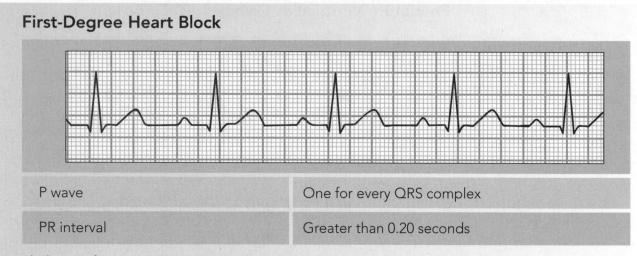

P wave	One for every QRS complex
PR interval	Greater than 0.20 seconds

Rhythm strip from 12-Lead ECG: The Art of Interpretation, courtesy of Tomas B. Garcia, M.D.

Second-Degree Type I (Mobitz I, Wenckebach)

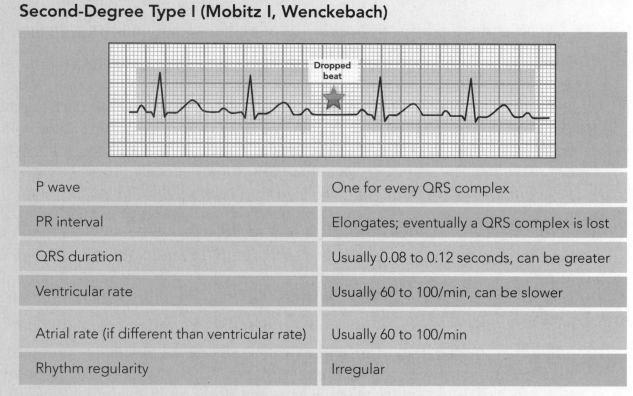

P wave	One for every QRS complex
PR interval	Elongates; eventually a QRS complex is lost
QRS duration	Usually 0.08 to 0.12 seconds, can be greater
Ventricular rate	Usually 60 to 100/min, can be slower
Atrial rate (if different than ventricular rate)	Usually 60 to 100/min
Rhythm regularity	Irregular

Rhythm strip from 12-Lead ECG: The Art of Interpretation, courtesy of Tomas B. Garcia, M.D.

Second-Degree Type 2 (Mobitz II)

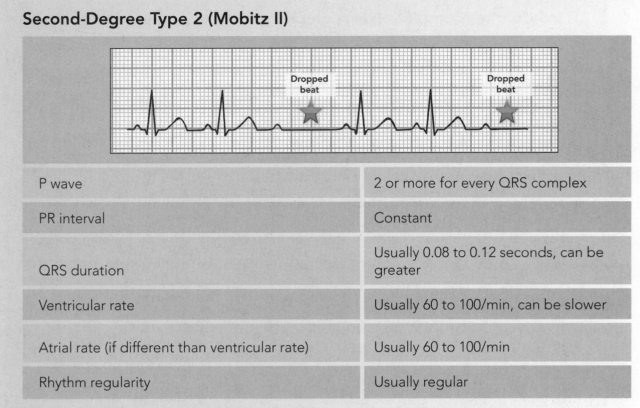

P wave	2 or more for every QRS complex
PR interval	Constant
QRS duration	Usually 0.08 to 0.12 seconds, can be greater
Ventricular rate	Usually 60 to 100/min, can be slower
Atrial rate (if different than ventricular rate)	Usually 60 to 100/min
Rhythm regularity	Usually regular

Rhythm strip from 12-Lead ECG: The Art of Interpretation, courtesy of Tomas B. Garcia, M.D.

Third-Degree Heart Block

Third-degree heart block is characterized by a complete lack of association between atria and ventricles. P waves can be seen marching through the rhythm, and none are responsible for triggering ventricular depolarization. The ventricular activity is completely independent of atrial activity and is often seen as a junctional or ventricular escape rhythm.

Note: Although it is standard practice to simply state "third-degree heart block," it's important to remember that three distinct things are happening in the tracing below:

- Atrial activity – Sinus tachycardia

- Ventricular activity – Junctional rhythm (junctional escape rhythm)

- Communication between the two – Third-degree or complete heart block. The signal from the atria is completely blocked from reaching the ventricles.

Third-Degree (Complete Heart Block)

P wave	One or more for every QRS complex
PR interval	Absent
QRS duration	Usually 0.08 to 0.12 seconds, can be greater
Ventricular rate	Usually 60 to 100/min, can be slower
Atrial rate (if different than ventricular rate)	Usually 60 to 100/min
Rhythm regularity	Regular

Rhythm strip from 12-Lead ECG: The Art of Interpretation, courtesy of Tomas B. Garcia, M.D.

Heart Blocks Made Simple

Perform a normal arrhythmia interpretation on the tracing. If you find more P waves than QRS complexes, evaluate the following:

1. Measure the RR interval

2. Measure the PR interval

If the RR interval is CONSTANT, the block must be second-degree type 2 or third-degree. If the PR interval varies, how does it vary?

- If it elongates, the block must be second-degree type 1.

- If there is no association, the block must be third-degree.

Identify the Major Variances to Waveforms Related to Ischemia, Injury, or Infarction

J point – The J point is the junction point between the QRS complex and the ST segment. It signifies the end of ventricular depolarization and the beginning of ventricular repolarization. For the purposes of this course, think of acute myocardial injury and infarction as a problem of repolarization. This will prompt you to look for anomalies on the right side of the QRS complex.

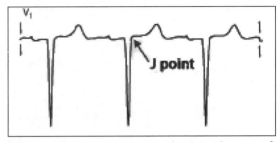

The J point – *From 12-Lead ECG: The Art of Interpretation, courtesy of Tomas B. Garcia, M.D.*

Ischemia – The classic pattern of myocardial ischemia is ST segment depression and/or T wave inversion. Deeply inverted T waves are a frequently encountered presentation of ischemia.

Injury – The classic pattern of myocardial injury is ST segment elevation myocardial infarction (STEMI).

STEMI is diagnosed using the following criteria:

1. ST segment elevation in two or more contiguous leads

    o   Greater than 1 mm in the limb leads

    o   Greater than 2 mm in the precordial leads

2. Reciprocal changes may also be present.

Infarction – Two main electrocardiographic changes can be observed days to weeks after myocardial infarction; complete resolution of and normalization of the tracing, or the development of a pathological Q wave. It is of critical importance to remember that the presence of pathological Q waves does not rule out an acute cardiac event.

Localization of ischemia on the EKG – Localization of ischemia, injury, or infarction is performed using the following criteria:

Leads	Area of Involvement
II, III, aVF	Inferior wall
V1, V2	Septum
V3, V4 or V1 to V4	Anterior wall
Leads I, aVL	Lateral wall – high
Leads V5, V6	Lateral wall – low
Leads V7 to V9	Posterior wall
Lead V4R	Right ventricle

Reciprocal changes – Reciprocal changes are changes that occur as a result of opposing view angles between leads. In other words, if lead A "sees" ST segment elevation, lead B "sees" ST segment depression. Reciprocal changes are highly confirmatory for acute ischemic/injury events.

Reciprocal leads – The most important reciprocal leads are:

- Leads II, III, aVF: reciprocal to leads I, aVL

- Leads V1 to V3: reciprocal to leads II, III, aVF

The Many Faces of Ischemia

(Note: Information and images in this section were previously published in the following text: American Academy of Orthopaedic Surgeons, *Nancy Caroline's Emergency Care in the Streets, Seventh Edition.* 2012: Jones & Bartlett Learning, Burlington, MA. www.jblearning. com. Reprinted with permission.)

The tracings on the following pages represent common electrocardiographic findings suggestive of myocardial ischemia.

The "J" Point

If the J point is depressed or elevated, as shown on the tracings that follow, it can suggest ischemia.

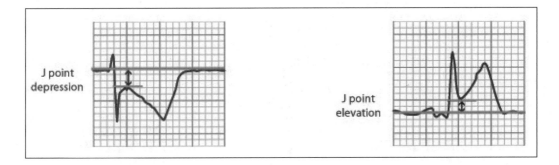

ST Segment Morphology

Convex – A convex ST segment favors ischemia. Test for this by drawing a line from the J point to the peak of the T wave, as shown below. If the line superimposes or if the T wave is above the line, the segment is convex.

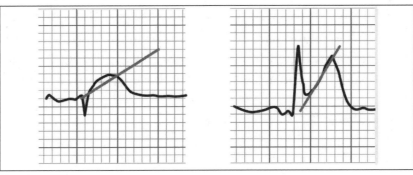

Convex ST segments

Concave – A concave ST segment favors benign conditions, but beware – ischemia can also manifest with this pattern, as seen in this STEMI:

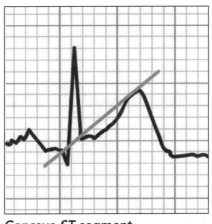

Concave ST segment

All of the examples below illustrate myocardial ischemia. The horizontal and down-sloping ST segments are always pathological findings. A "slow" up-slope is most often a pathological finding. A rapidly up-sloping ST segment is generally a normal electrocardiographic change, as demonstrated during exercise stress testing.

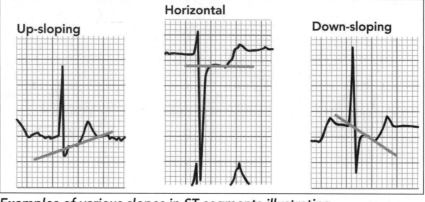

Examples of various slopes in ST segments illustrating myocardial ischemia

T Wave Morphology

The diagram that follows shows when the appearance of the T wave indicates ischemia. The apex of the T wave elevates and forms a peaked appearance, and the height of the T wave exceeds half the overall height of the QRS. During ischemia, the T wave becomes symmetrical with respect to the Y axis, and the base of the T wave broadens.

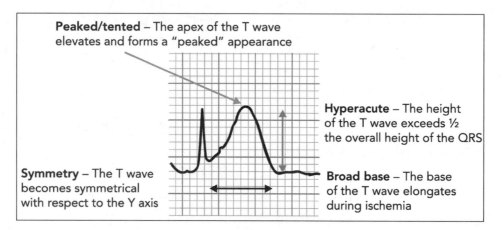

Respond to Potentially Life-Threatening Arrhythmias

According to the American Heart Association's Emergency Cardiac Care Guidelines (2010), two of the most important interventions for cardiac arrest are 1) high-quality cardiopulmonary resuscitation (CPR), and 2) early defibrillation. Technicians should maintain CPR certification and be able to use an automatic external defibrillator (AED). Technicians should become familiar with institutional guidelines or protocols to fully understand their role during resuscitation efforts.

Ventricular fibrillation (VF) – Ventricular fibrillation is a disorganized, chaotic, non-perfusing, and lethal dysrhythmia. The technician plays an important role in the response to VF. First, the technician must recognize the lethal rhythm. Patients often experience symptoms such as dizziness, feeling of impending doom, chest discomfort, and shortness of breath immediately before the arrest or at the time of arrest. The technician should immediately call for help using the established guidelines for the facility. The technician should initiate CPR as quickly as possible, ensure emergency services are notified, and send another person to retrieve the AED, if available. The technician should be prepared to assist with other tasks requested by the physician or other advanced healthcare worker.

Ventricular tachycardia (VT) – Ventricular tachycardia is an organized ventricular rhythm that often results in precipitous drops in blood pressure and level of consciousness. Ventricular tachycardia may continue to produce a pulse but often deteriorates to a pulseless rhythm or into VF. Similar to the response for VF, the technician must first recognize the lethal rhythm. Patients often experience symptoms such as dizziness, feeling of impending doom, chest discomfort, and shortness of breath immediately before the arrest or at the time of arrest. The technician should immediately call for help using the established guidelines for the facility. The technician should initiate CPR as quickly as possible if the patient does not have a pulse or completely loses consciousness, ensure emergency services are notified, and send another person to retrieve the AED, if available. The technician should be prepared to assist with other tasks requested by the physician or other advanced health care worker.

Asystole – Asystole is the complete cessation of electrical activity in the heart. Common causes of asystole include large pulmonary embolism, large myocardial infarction, respiratory arrest (hypoxia) and overdose. Other causes include hypothermia, acidosis, electrolyte abnormalities, tension pneumothorax and trauma. If the technician recognizes asystole on the EKG, another lead should immediately be checked to confirm asystole. Patients may or may not complain of any symptoms prior to arrest. If a patient's rhythm deteriorates to asystole, the technician should immediately call for help using the established guidelines for the facility. The technician should initiate CPR as quickly as possible, ensure emergency services are notified, and send another person to retrieve the AED, if available. The technician should be prepared to assist with other tasks requested by the physician or other advanced healthcare worker.

Bradycardia – Bradycardia is defined as a slow heart rate. The technician is responsible for recognizing when the patient's vital signs, including heart rate, fall outside of expected parameters. The technician should notify the physician if the patient develops bradycardia using established methods of communication in the facility. The technician should continue to monitor the patient until care is transferred to another health care worker. The technician should also be prepared to assist with placing pacing pads on the patient.

Tachycardia – Tachycardia is defined as a fast heart rate. As with bradycardia, the technician should notify the physician if the patient develops tachycardia using established methods of communication in the facility. The technician should continue to monitor the patient until care is transferred to another health care worker and be prepared to assist with placing defibrillation pads on the patient.

Verify EKG Machine Paper Speed

Every EKG tracing prints the paper speed at the top or bottom of the paper. The most common paper speed is 25 mm/second. Another common paper speed is 50 mm/second. The faster paper speed is sometimes used to space out EKG waves when the heart rate is very fast. The faster speed enables certain waves to become visible on the tracing.

Verify EKG Machine Sensitivity

Every EKG tracing starts with a calibration marker before printing any waveforms. The calibration marker looks like an upside-down U shape with 90-degree angles. Another way to describe this is to imagine a rectangle resting on its short edge. The bottom edge of the rectangle is absent. The calibration marker measures 5 mm wide by 10 mm tall. The marker represents a calibration of 10 mm per millivolt (mV), the standard EKG gain. The gain is often also printed near the top or bottom of the tracing and represented with a 1X or 2X or 3X to represent normal, twice the size, or three times the size, respectively.

Maintain EKG Equipment and the Work Environment

Every manufacturer makes specific recommendations on how to perform user tests, clean the machine, change paper, maintain the machine, etc. Refer to the user manual and the institution's policies and guidelines to properly perform these tasks. The CPCT should be familiar with how to perform a daily user test, clean the machine, keypad, wires and other components, properly connect the device to a power source (AC power, DC power, etc.), and how to change the paper.

It is best practice to maintain a clean work environment. This includes keeping machines clean, consumables stocked, and work areas free of clutter. A clean work environment can also reduce the potential for errors. For example, if the work area is kept clean and organized, the chance of accidentally applying the wrong patient information to the EKG is reduced.

Recognize Pacemaker Spikes on an EKG Trace

Electrical "spikes" may also be seen immediately prior to the QRS complex, such as on the following rhythms:

Paced Ventricular Rhythm (Ventricular Pacer)

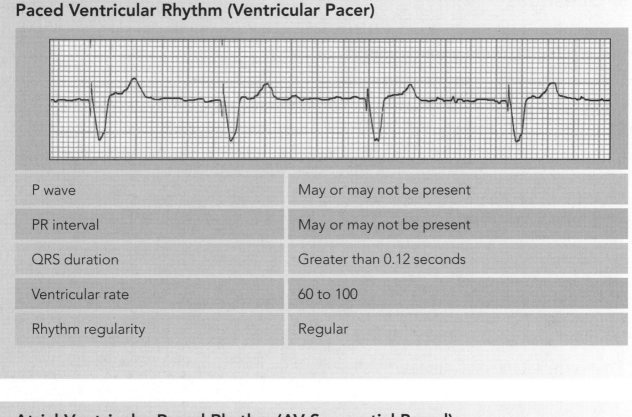

P wave	May or may not be present
PR interval	May or may not be present
QRS duration	Greater than 0.12 seconds
Ventricular rate	60 to 100
Rhythm regularity	Regular

Atrial-Ventricular Paced Rhythm (AV Sequential Paced)

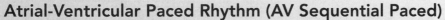
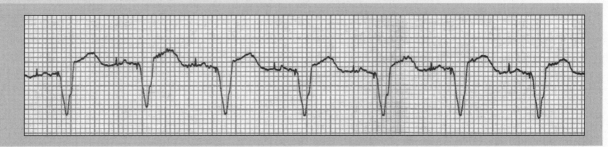

P wave	Present
PR interval	120 to 200
QRS duration	Greater than 0.12 seconds
Ventricular rate	60 to 100
Rhythm regularity	Regular

Summary

This chapter presented the information necessary to systematically approach the EKG and interpret arrhythmias encountered in the clinical setting. In addition, the chapter included pictures and real EKG tracings to promote rhythm recognition.

Drill Questions

Use the tracing below to answer questions 1 to 5.

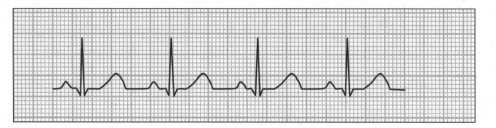

1. What is the patient's heart rate?

    A. 65/min
    B. 85/min
    C. 120/min
    D. 180/min

2. What is the PR interval duration?

    A. 0.10 seconds
    B. 0.30 seconds
    C. 0.16 seconds
    D. 0.25 seconds

3. What is the QRS duration?

    A. 0.02 seconds
    B. 0.09 seconds
    C. 0.12 seconds
    D. 0.20 seconds

4. Which of the following is the approximate QT interval duration?

    A. 0.10 seconds
    B. 0.28 seconds
    C. 0.38 seconds
    D. 0.48 seconds

5. Which of the following types of rhythms is displayed above?

    A. Sinus rhythm
    B. Sinus bradycardia
    C. Junctional rhythm
    D. Ventricular tachycardia

Use the tracing below to answer questions 6 to 8.

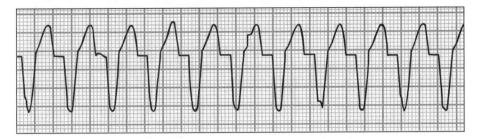

6. Which of the following types of rhythms is displayed above?

    A. Sinus rhythm
    B. Sinus bradycardia
    C. Junctional rhythm
    D. Ventricular tachycardia

7. After viewing this rhythm, what action should the CPCT take first?

    A. Perform rescue breathing.
    B. Call for help and the automated external defibrillator.
    C. Check for a medical alert bracelet.
    D. Administer high-flow oxygen.

8. What is the patient's heart rate?

    A. 60/min
    B. 90/min
    C. 136/min
    D. 170/min

Use the tracing below to answer question 9.

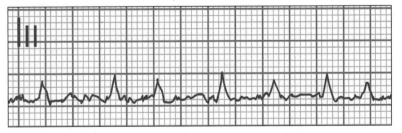

9. Which of the following types of rhythms is displayed above?

    A. Sinus rhythm with PACs
    B. Variable bradycardia
    C. Junctional rhythm
    D. Atrial fibrillation with rapid ventricular response

Use the tracing below to answer question 10.

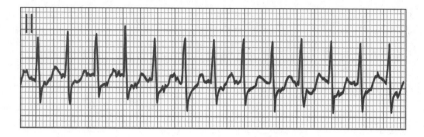

10. Which of the following types of rhythms is displayed above?

    A. Sinus rhythm
    B. Supraventricular tachycardia
    C. Junctional tachycardia
    D. Ventricular tachycardia

Drill Answers

Use the tracing below to answer questions 1 to 5.

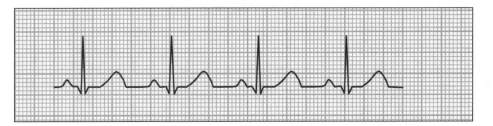

1. What is the patient's heart rate?

   A. 65/min
   B. 85/min
   C. 120/min
   D. 180/min

   The correct heart rate for the above tracing is 65/min.

2. What is the PR interval duration?

   A. 0.10 seconds
   B. 0.30 seconds
   C. 0.16 seconds
   D. 0.25 seconds

   The PR interval is measured from the beginning of the P wave to the beginning of the QRS complex. Each small box represents .04 seconds. The PR interval in this tracing is 4 boxes in duration, or 0.16 seconds.

3. What is the QRS duration?

   A. 0.02 seconds
   B. 0.09 seconds
   C. 0.12 seconds
   D. 0.20 seconds

   The QRS duration is measured from the beginning of the Q wave to the end of the S wave. Each small box represents 0.04 seconds. The QRS in this tracing is 3 boxes in duration, or 0.12 seconds.

4. Which of the following is the approximate QT interval duration?

    A. 0.10 seconds
    B. 0.28 seconds
    C. 0.38 seconds
    D. 0.48 seconds

The QT interval is measured from the beginning of the Q wave to the end of the T wave. Each small box represents 0.04 seconds. The QT interval in this tracing is approximately 12 small boxes in duration, or approximately 0.48 seconds.

5. Which of the following types of rhythms is displayed above?

    A. Sinus rhythm
    B. Sinus bradycardia
    C. Junctional rhythm
    D. Ventricular tachycardia

A sinus rhythm has one P wave per QRS complex, a rate of 60 to 100/min, and a PR interval of less than 0.20 seconds. The rate in this tracing is too fast to be sinus bradycardia, and junctional rhythms do not have upright P waves. Ventricular tachycardia is characterized by a faster rate, wide QRS complex, and the absence of P waves.

Use the tracing below to answer questions 6 to 8.

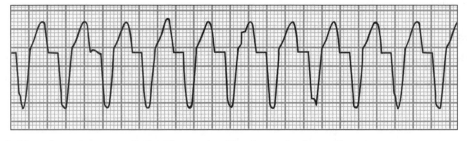

6. Which of the following types of rhythms is displayed above?

    A. Sinus rhythm
    B. Sinus bradycardia
    C. Junctional rhythm
    D. Ventricular tachycardia

This is ventricular tachycardia because it has a wide QRS complex, no P waves, and a heart rate greater than 120/min. The rate is too fast to be a sinus rhythm or sinus bradycardia, and the absence of a P wave further rules out those two rhythms. The rate is too fast for a junctional rhythm, and the QRS complex is too wide.

7. After viewing this rhythm, what action should the CPCT take first?

    A. Perform rescue breathing
    B. Call for help and the automated external defibrillator.
    C. Check for a medical alert bracelet.
    D. Administer high-flow oxygen

The American Heart Association recommends calling for help and the AED. Among the options above, the next step is to perform rescue breathing. Then, the technician should check for a medical alert bracelet. Lastly, the technician should administer high-flow oxygen.

8. What is the patient's heart rate?

    A. 60/min
    B. 90/min
    C. 136/min
    D. 178/min

The most accurate method for determining the heart rate of tachyarrhythmias is the 1500 method. In this case, there are 11 mm between RR complexes. 1,500 / 11 = 136/min.

Use the tracing below to answer question 9.

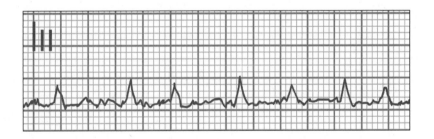

9. Which of the following types of rhythms is displayed above?

    A. Sinus rhythm with PACs
    B. Variable bradycardia
    C. Junctional rhythm
    D. Atrial fibrillation with rapid ventricular response

AF RVR is characterized by an irregularly irregular heart rhythm, a heart rate greater than 100/min, and the absence of P waves. The heart rate is too fast for this rhythm to be a sinus rhythm with PACs, variable bradycardia, or a junctional rhythm, and a sinus rhythm with PACs would have visible P waves.

Use the tracing below to answer question 10.

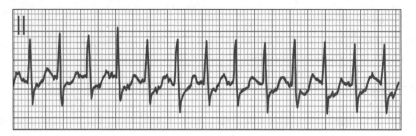

10. Which of the following types of rhythms is displayed above?

    A. Sinus rhythm
    B. Supraventricular tachycardia
    C. Junctional tachycardia
    D. Ventricular tachycardia

    SVT is characterized by absent or retrograde P waves, a heart rate greater than 150/min, and narrow QRS complexes. The heart rate is too fast for this tracing to represent a sinus rhythm or junctional tachycardia, and the QRS complexes are too narrow for it to represent ventricular tachycardia.

Terms and Definitions

Angina pectoris – The sensation of pain or discomfort in the chest. Typically divided into "stable" and "unstable" episodes. Stable angina typically occurs with exercise and is relieved with rest or medication. Attacks usually last less than 20 minutes and occur with an expected pattern or frequency. Unstable angina is characterized by pain that occurs suddenly and without warning. Pain may last in excess of 20 minutes and may not be relieved with the usual measures. It represents a change in frequency and character from the patient's "usual" pain.

Aorta – The largest artery in the human body. The aorta carries oxygenated blood away from the heart.

Aortic valve (aortic semilunar) – The aortic semilunar valve prevents blood in the aorta from returning to the left ventricle during diastole

Apex – The lower pointed end of the heart

Arrhythmia – An abnormal heart rhythm

Arteriosclerosis – A chronic disease characterized by thickening and hardening of the arteries

Artifact – Electrical or magnetic interference that alters the EKG tracing

Asystole – The absence of any electrical activity in the heart

Atherosclerosis – Plaque buildup on the inner lining of blood vessels

Atrioventricular (AV) node – The AV node consists of specialized tissue that is able to regulate the impulses between atria and ventricles.

Atrium – A small muscular pouch-like structure that fills the ventricles with blood

Augmented leads – Leads created by combing two of the three limb leads to create a positive electrode. The third creates the negative electrode

Base – The top of the heart

Baseline – An electrically neutral area on the EKG

Bicuspid valve (mitral) – A valve in the heart that is situated between the left atrium and the left ventricle and prevents the backflow of blood into the right left atrium during diastole. Its flaps consist of two triangular cusps.

Bradycardia – Slow heart rate

Bundle branch – The bundle branches are part of the conduction system responsible for triggering ventricular muscle contraction

Bundle of His – The bundle of His is part of the conduction system responsible for conducting a stimulus to the septum and bundle branches

Cardiac arrest – The absence of cardiac activity

Coronary arteries – The arteries that supply oxygenated blood to the myocardium

Depolarization – A loss of polarization resulting from a sudden influx of sodium ions into the cardiac muscle cells. This results in contraction.

Ectopic – Originating in an area of the heart other than the sinoatrial node

Electrocardiograph (EKG) – A graphic representation of the electrical activity of the heart

Electrode – A specialized interface between the human body and an EKG machine

Endocardium – The innermost layer of the heart

Epicardium – The outermost layer of the heart

Inferior vena cava (IVC) – The largest vein in the human body. The IVC returns de-oxygenated blood to the heart.

Intercostal – Between the ribs

Ischemia – Insufficient oxygenation of tissue

Leads – Flexible or solid insulated conductors connected to or leading out from an electrical device. These conductors are typically placed on the skin surface and designed to measure electrical impulses.

Mediastinum – One of three compartments inside the chest. The mediastinum encapsulates the heart and great vessels.

Midaxillary – An imaginary line through the axillary region that separates the front and back of the human body

Midclavicular – An imaginary line through the middle of the clavicle that extends vertically

Myocardial infarction – Ischemia and death of heart muscle tissue

Myocardium – The middle muscular layer of the heart

Pacemaker – A medical device that provides artificial stimulation to the heart muscle to trigger contraction

Pericardium – A serous sac that encases the heart, is formed from two layers, and is usually filled with a small amount of fluid

PQRST waves – The standard waveforms found on the EKG tracing. Each wave corresponds to a specific event within the heart's electrical cycle.

Precordial leads – Six EKG leads placed on the anterior chest to record electrical activity of the heart, mainly the electrical impulses originating in the ventricles or the heart's anterior wall

Pulmonary artery – The only artery in the body that carries de-oxygenated blood. The pulmonary arteries carry blood to the lungs.

Pulmonic valve (pulmonary semilunar) – The pulmonary semilunar prevents blood in the lungs from returning to the right ventricle during diastole

Pulmonary vein – The only vein in the body that carries oxygenated blood. The pulmonary veins carry blood from the lungs to the heart.

Purkinje fiber – Fibers that serve to conduct electrical impulses through the right and left ventricles.

Repolarization – The process of moving sodium from inside the cell to the outside, and potassium from outside the cell to the inside. Repolarization involves establishing an electrical gradient across a cell membrane.

Septum – A dividing wall or partition, such as the one found between the atria and the ventricles

Sinoatrial (SA) node – A small mass of tissue, located in the right atrium, which serves to originate impulses that stimulate the heartbeat. SA node deplorarization corresponds to the P wave on the electrocardiogram.

Superior vena cava – The second-largest vein in the human body

Tachycardia – Fast heart rate

Tricuspid valve – The tricuspid valve separates the right atrium from the right ventricle

Vasoconstriction – The act of constricting a blood vessel

Vasodilation – The act of opening a blood vessel

Ventricle – The ventricles are responsible for pumping blood to the lungs and entire body

 CASE STUDIES

Patient Triage

Fred Jones, a 62-year-old patient, is admitted to a facility after he fainted at work. Mr. Jones cannot remember if he ate breakfast. His weight is 95.3 kg (210 lb) and his height is 6 feet. His temperature is 37.3° C (99.14° F), and he reports taking baby aspirin, as well as medication used to control his cholesterol and high blood glucose. His blood pressure is 144/89, his pulse is 102, his respiratory rate is 20/min, and his O² saturation is 98%. After determining that his blood glucose level is 45 mg/dL, the nurse administers two glucose tablets.

1. Which of the following vital signs should a CPCT report to a nurse immediately?

   A. Blood pressure 186/82 mm Hg
   B. Temperature 37.3° C (99.14° F)
   C. Oxygen saturation 94%
   D. Respiratory rate 22/min

2. Which of the following sites should a CPCT use to measure the rate of an irregular pulse?

   A. Apical
   B. Carotid
   C. Radial
   D. Ulnar

3. Which of the following blood glucose results should the nurse report immediately?

   A. 45 mg/dL
   B. 98 mg/dL
   C. 100 mg/dL
   D. 122 mg/dL

4. What is the fifth vital sign?

   A. Pain
   B. Temperature
   C. Pulse
   D. Respirations

153

5. When measuring the blood glucose level of an adult, a CPCT should use which of the following sampling methods?

    A. Finger stick
    B. Heel stick
    C. Venous sample
    D. Urine sample

Patient Triage: Answers

1. Which of the following vital signs should a CPCT report to a nurse immediately?

   A. Blood pressure 186/82 mm Hg
   B. Temperature 37.3° C (99.14° F)
   C. Oxygen saturation 94%
   D. Respiratory rate 22/min

   This blood pressure reading is very high and should be reported to a nurse immediately.

2. Which of the following sites should a CPCT use to measure the rate of an irregular pulse?

   A. Apical
   B. Carotid
   C. Radial
   D. Ulnar

   This site should be used to measure an irregular pulse.

3. Which of the following blood glucose results should the nurse report immediately?

   A. 45 mg/dL
   B. 98 mg/dL
   C. 100 mg/dL
   D. 122 mg/dL

   This value is very low and should be reported to the nurse.

4. What is the fifth vital sign?

   A. Pain
   B. Temperature
   C. Pulse
   D. Respirations

   Pain is commonly referred to as the fifth vital sign.

5. When measuring the blood glucose level of an adult, a CPCT should use which of the following sampling methods?

    A. Finger stick
    B. Heel stick
    C. Venous sample
    D. Urine sample

This is the preferred method for measuring blood glucose in an adult patient.

Holter Monitor

Mr. Lopez is a 42-year-old male who has been experiencing palpitations and dizziness. Sarah, a technician, has been instructed to apply a Holter monitor on Mr. Lopez. After reading his medical file, Sarah notes that he is currently not taking any medications, has no cardiac history and has no known drug allergies.

Sarah explains the procedure to Mr. Lopez and tells him what to expect over the next 24 hours. She then prepares his skin and applies the electrodes. After she applies the Holter monitor, Mr. Lopez leaves.

1. Which of the following describes proper lead placement for a 5-lead device?

   A. Two electrodes are placed over the bone at the fourth rib to the right of the sternum and the fifth rib at the left midaxillary line.
   B. Two electrodes are placed over the ninth rib at the right midaxillary line to act as a ground.
   C. Two electrodes are placed over the manubrium.
   D. Five electrodes are placed at the position of V1 to V5.

2. Which of the following describes proper preparation of the patient prior to applying electrodes?

   A. Clean the skin with alcohol, remove any hair with a razor, and abrade the epidermis.
   B. Clean the skin with soap and water and abrade the skin vigorously.
   C. Apply an adhesive to the skin before placing the electrodes over the adhesive.
   D. Provide the patient with instructions to apply the electrodes before exercising.

3. Which of the following is considered to be a positive Holter test?

   A. Sinus rhythm with premature atrial complexes
   B. Sinus rhythm with ST segment elevation
   C. Sinus rhythm with no episodes of tachycardia
   D. Sinus rhythm with a heart rate of 84/min

4. Which of the following statements would indicate Mr. Lopez understands Holter monitor procedures?

   A. "The monitor may be removed when exercising."
   B. "If I feel symptoms such as dizziness or palpitations, I should then attach the monitor."
   C. "I have a pacemaker, so I can't wear the Holter monitor."
   D. "I should wear the monitor continuously, even during work, sleep and exercise."

5. Which of the following statements by Mr. Lopez would indicate a need for additional education?

    A. "If an electrode falls off or the monitor stops working, I should call the office."

    B. "I should press the event button on the monitor when I have symptoms."

    C. "I should not be concerned by any redness or itching that occurs around the electrodes, as this is a normal response to the conductive gel."

    D. "I should continue to take all medications as prescribed, and record when I take them in my journal."

6. When reviewing the Holter test, Sarah notes that there are unusually long pauses in the EKG throughout the 24-hour period. What is a common cause of this artifact?

    A. Movement of the electrodes

    B. Loose connection of the leads

    C. Dead battery

    D. The monitor was placed in water

7. If Sarah releases information about Mr. Lopez's diagnosis to his employer, which patient right has she violated?

    A. Patient consent

    B. Patient confidentiality

    C. Access to treatment

    D. Refusal of care

Holter Monitor: Answers

1. Which of the following describes proper lead placement for a 5-lead device?

   A. Two electrodes are placed over bone at the fourth rib to the right of the sternum and the fifth rib at the left midaxillary line.
   B. Two electrodes are placed over the ninth rib at the right midaxillary line to act as a ground.
   C. Two electrodes are placed over the manubrium.
   D. Five electrodes are placed at the position of V1 to V5.

   For a 5-lead device, two electrodes are placed over bone at the fourth rib to the right of the sternum and the fifth rib at the left midaxillary line.

2. Which of the following describes proper preparation of the patient skin prior to applying electrodes?

   A. Clean the skin with alcohol, remove any hair with a razor, and abrade the epidermis.
   B. Clean the skin with soap and water and abrade the skin vigorously.
   C. Apply an adhesive to the skin before placing the electrodes over the adhesive.
   D. Provide the patient with instructions to apply the electrodes before exercising.

   To prepare the patient's skin for electrode placement, clean the skin with alcohol, remove hair with a razor, and scrape the patient's epidermis. The skin should not be abraded vigorously. The electrodes contain the adhesive, and they should be applied directly to the skin with no additional adhesive. The technician, not the patient, must apply the electrodes.

3. Which of the following is considered to be a positive Holter test?

   A. Sinus rhythm with premature atrial complexes
   B. Sinus rhythm with ST segment elevation
   C. Sinus rhythm with no episodes of tachycardia
   D. Sinus rhythm with a heart rate of 84/min

   ST segment elevation is a medical emergency and is considered a positive Holter test. A test displaying a sinus rhythm with premature atrial complexes, no episodes of tachycardia, or a heart rate of 84/min is considered a normal test.

4. Which of the following statements would indicate the patient understands Holter monitor procedures?

    A. "The monitor may be removed when exercising."
    B. "If I feel symptoms such as dizziness or palpitations, I should then attach the monitor."
    C. "I have a pacemaker, so I can't wear the Holter monitor."
    D. "I should wear the monitor continuously, even during work, sleep and exercise."

The patient should wear the monitor continuously to ensure capture of any arrhythmias. The patient must not remove the monitor, and the presence of a pacemaker does not interfere with the monitor.

5. Which of the following statements by Mr. Lopez would indicate a need for additional education?

    A. "If an electrode falls off or the monitor stops working, I should call the office."
    B. "I should press the event button on the monitor when I have symptoms."
    C. "I should not be concerned by any redness or itching that occurs around the electrodes, as this is a normal response to the conductive gel."
    D. "I should continue to take all medications as prescribed, and record when I take them in my journal."

The patient should report redness or itching, as they may be signs of allergic reaction or hypersensitivity to the electrodes. The other options are correct statements by the patient. The patient should call the office if an electrode falls off or the monitor stops working, should press the event button when he/she experiences symptoms, and should continue to take and record all prescribed medications.

6. When reviewing the Holter test, Sarah notes that there are unusually long pauses in the EKG throughout the 24-hour period. What is a common cause of this artifact?

    A. Movement of the electrodes
    B. Loose connection of the leads
    C. Dead battery
    D. The monitor was placed in water

A loose connection can cause long pauses in the EKG recording. Movement of the electrodes does not cause long pauses. The EKG will not record at all if the battery is dead. Submersion in water will cause damage to the monitor, and no tracing will be recorded.

7. If Sarah releases information about Mr. Lopez's diagnosis to his employer, which patient right has she violated?

    A. Patient consent
    B. Patient confidentiality
    C. Access to treatment
    D. Refusal of care

Mr. Lopez's diagnosis is confidential and may not be shared with his employer, so this is a violation of patient confidentiality. Patient consent involves educating the patient and obtaining permission to perform a procedure. Mr. Lopez was not denied access to treatment in this scenario and did not refuse treatment.

Anatomy and Physiology

The patient, Mrs. Susan Smith, is a 79-year-old woman who is small in stature and very thin. Her physician has ordered two laboratory tests for her: a complete blood count (CBC), a test that measures hemoglobin concentration, hematocrit, the red blood cell count, several specific aspects of the red blood cells (e.g., amount of hemoglobin in an average red blood cell), the white blood cell count and the white blood cell differential, and the platelet count; and an International normalized ratio (INR), a test that measures the ability of the blood to clot.

The patient is sitting down in the laboratory testing area; the time is 9 a.m. The technician enters the room, identifies himself (using his first name only), identifies himself as the technician, and informs the patient that he will be drawing her blood. The technician asks the patient to identify herself by name, asks her to tell him her date of birth and the last four digits of her Social Security number, and checks the patient's wrist band to see if the information she gave was correct. Except for checking the patient's wrist band, the technician did not make eye contact with the patient during this time; he had been reading the laboratory order forms on a computer. Mrs. Smith is visibly anxious; she shifts nervously in the chair, checks her watch several times, and constantly crosses and uncrosses her legs.

The technician gathers a winged infusion set (a.k.a. Butterfly needle), a tourniquet, an isopropyl alcohol swab, a small adhesive bandage, a 1-inch-by-1-inch gauze pad, and a lavender top collection tube and a blue top collection tube.

After gathering the supplies, he washes his hands, puts on latex disposable gloves and then asks the patient which arm she has prefers to be used; she chooses her left arm. He places her arm on the arm of the chair, supporting it with a pad. He visually identifies and palpates the median antecubital vein and then places the tourniquet around her arm; after the tourniquet is in place, he asks her if it is too tight. He cleans the skin over the vein with the isopropyl alcohol swab, informs the patient that she will feel a slight sensation of pain and then performs the venipuncture. A few seconds after inserting the needle, the technician releases the tourniquet. Again, during the procedure the technician did not make eye contact with the patient, he does not speak to her, and while performing the venipuncture he does not a) ask her how she is feeling or, b) look at her to see if she is okay.

Mrs. Smith had been nervous before the procedure, and after the needle was inserted she begins to sweat and feel dizzy, and she becomes very pale. As the technician withdraws the needle and places the gauze pad on the site of the venipuncture, Mrs. Smith suddenly loses conscious and falls forward out of the chair and on to the floor and strikes her head. The technician lifts her up, places her back in the chair, and when she wakes up, he offers her some water.

1. Why was Mrs. Smith at risk for fainting?

    A. She was actively bleeding.
    B. The ambient temperature was very hot.
    C. She had a heart attack.
    D. She is a thin woman of small stature.

2. What other factor directly contributed to this episode of fainting?

    A. Lack of communication.
    B. High level of stress.
    C. Improper venipuncture technique.
    D. The time of day.

3. The average woman typically has a blood pressure that

    A. is lower than the blood pressure of the average man.
    B. is higher than the blood pressure of the average man.
    C. is no different than the blood pressure of the average man.
    D. fluctuates more than the blood pressure of the average man.

4. What part of the patient care process did the technician fail to perform?

    A. Standard precautions
    B. Identifying the patient
    C. Patient assessment
    D. The venipuncture procedure

5. What could the technician have done to predict the risk of fainting?

    A. He could have used verbal and non-verbal communication.
    B. He could have allowed the patient more time before the venipuncture.
    C. He could have told the patient he had many years of experience.
    D. He could have asked her if she had ever had an episode of fainting.

Anatomy and Physiology: Answers

1. Why was Mrs. Smith at risk for fainting?

    A. She was actively bleeding.
    B. The ambient temperature was very hot.
    C. She had a heart attack.
    D. She is a thin woman of small stature.

    Women typically have lower blood pressure then men, and this is especially true for women who are thin and of small stature. It is possible that the patient was actively bleeding (A), but there was no evidence of this, and it is not something that the technician could have discerned by an assessment. High ambient temperatures (B) can cause fainting, but laboratories are air conditioned. A heart attack (C) can cause loss of consciousness, but again there was no evidence the patient was suffering a heart attack, and the technician could not have determined whether a heart attack was occurring by a simple verbal and visual assessment.

2. What other factor directly contributed to this episode of fainting?

    A. Lack of communication.
    B. High level of stress.
    C. Improper venipuncture technique.
    D. The time of day.

    A high level of stress is a common cause of fainting. The technician did not predict the risk of fainting or notice it was possible because of a lack of communication (A), but this was not a direct cause of the loss of consciousness. The venipuncture (C) was performed correctly, and the time of day (D) would not be a direct cause of fainting.

3. The average woman typically has a blood pressure that

    A. is lower than the blood pressure of the average man.
    B. is higher than the blood pressure of the average man.
    C. is no different than the blood pressure of the average man.
    D. fluctuates more than the blood pressure of the average man.

    The average woman typically has a blood pressure that is lower than the blood pressure of the average man. There is no difference between the genders in fluctuations of blood pressure (D).

4. What part of the patient care process did the technician fail to perform?

    A. Standard precautions
    B. Identifying the patient
    C. Patient assessment
    D. The venipuncture procedure

Standards precautions (A), patient identification (B), and the venipuncture procedure (D) were all performed properly. However, the technician never made assessments (C) to see whether the patient could tolerate the venipuncture or whether she was tolerating the venipuncture.

5. What could the technician have done to predict the risk of fainting?

    A. He could have used verbal and non-verbal communication.
    B. He could have allowed the patient more time before the venipuncture.
    C. He could have told the patient he had many years of experience.
    D. He could have asked her if she had ever had an episode of fainting.

The technician did not ask the patient about her condition before and during the venipuncture, and he did not visually check her condition during the procedure; doing so would not have prevented the episode of fainting, but it would have helped the technician be prepared for that possibility and could prevent possible injury from a fall. Allowing the patient more time prior to the procedure (B) and informing the patient of the technician's experience and competence (C) may help a patient's comfort level, but probably not in this case. Asking about previous episodes of fainting (D) is a very good idea, but in this case it was obvious that the patient was at risk for fainting at that time.

SUMMARY

Earning the CPCT certification demonstrates your commitment to excellence in the field and is evidence of your desire to perform your duties in a professional manner. Not only does certification let employers know you've demonstrated the knowledge necessary for competent practice, it also differentiates you from others who lack certification. This enables you to secure a job more easily and to earn higher wages.

The information in this study guide helps you prepare for the CPCT certification exam by breaking out the information you need to know into 9 sections, including an introduction, patient care, safety, professional responsibilities, infection control, EKG monitoring, phlebotomy, three case studies, and this summary.

Chapter 1 explained your main focus as a CPCT, which is patient care. You learned about basic skills such as patient hygiene care, equipment set up, taking vital signs, documenting care, communicating changes in your patient with the physician or nurse, and performing procedures on your patient.

Chapter 2 taught you how to improve patient safety and prevent workplace injuries, as well as how to recognize and respond to abuse. You also learned techniques for safely transferring patients, ensuring a safe environment, preventing workplace injuries, and responding to emergencies.

Chapter 3 taught you about your professional responsibilities as a CPCT. You read about BCLS certification and HIPAA law. You also learned about the use of proper medical terminology, the chain of command, and the use of therapeutic communication.

Chapter 4 taught you infection control techniques. This includes universal, standard, and transmission-based precautions. Next, the chapter presented the methods for disposing of biohazardous materials and performing aseptic and sterile techniques.

As a CPCT, you will need to know about EKGs. Chapter 5 presented the information you need to systematically approach and record an EKG, as well as how to interpret arrhythmias encountered in the clinical setting.

Chapter 6 taught you how to perform basic venipuncture. The chapter also described finger and heel stick blood collection, special collections, and how to process specimens.

Finally, the case studies presented you with three real-world scenarios to test your knowledge as a CPCT. You used critical thinking skills to correctly complete the discussion questions that followed.

You represent the future of health care. Continuously remain committed to keeping up with changes in the health care system. Also, consistently strive for a greater awareness of others and how to best serve as a member of the health care team. Use the skills you acquired from this study guide to help yourself and other CPCTs succeed. You are a valued member of the health care field.

References

2011 Hospital National Patient Safety Goals. (2011). Retrieved from www.jointcommission.org

Acelo, B. (1998). Patient Care, Basic Skills for the Healthcare Provider. Clifton Park, NY: Delmar-Cengage Learning.

Agency for Healthcare Research and Quality. (2011). Retrieved from http://www.ahrq.gov/qual/nurseshdbk/

American Heart Association Guidelines for CPR and Emergency Cardiovascular Care. (2010). Retrieved from http://www.heart.org/HEARTORG/CPRAndECC/CPR_UCM_001118_SubHomePage.jsp

Chain of Command issues in Health Care. (2011). Retrieved from http://www.ehow.com/list_5839414_chain-command-issues-healthcare.html

Diabetic Support Socks and Sequential Compression Devices (2011). Retrieved from http://diabeticsupportsocks.com/sequential-compression-device/

Elder Abuse and Neglect (1998). Retrieved from http://www.webster.edu/~woolflm/abuse.html

Garcia, T. B., & Miller, G. T. (2004). Arrhythmia recognition: The art of interpretation. Sudbury, Mass.: Jones and Bartlett Publishers.

How to Organize or Prioritize Patient Care. (2008). Retrieved from http://www.ultimatenurse.com/how-to-organize-or-prioritize-patient-care/111/

Institute of Medicine. (2000). To Err is Human: Building a Safer Health System. Washington, DC: National Academy Press.

OSHA Fact Sheet. (2011). Retrieved from www.osha.gov

Patient Safety and Quality: An Evidence-Based Handbook for Nurses. (2008). Retreived from http://www.ahrq.gov/qual/nurseshdbk/

Pendergraph, G. E. (1992). Handbook of phlebotomy (3rd ed. --.). Philadelphia: Lea & Febiger.

Rosenstien A, O Daniel M. (2006). Addressing Disruptive Nurse-Physician Behaviors: Developing Programs and Policies to Improve Outcomes Of Care. Cambridge, MA: Harvard Health Policy Review.

Wilkinson, Judith & Treas, Leslie. (2011). Fundamentals of Nursing. Philadelphia, PA: F.A. Davis.